COUNTER JIHAD

COUNTER JIHAD

America's Military Experience in Afghanistan, Iraq, and Syria

BRIAN GLYN WILLIAMS

PENN

UNIVERSITY OF PENNSYLVANIA PRESS

PHILADELPHIA

A volume in the Haney Foundation Series,
established in 1961 with the generous support of Dr. John Louis Haney.

Published by
University of Pennsylvania Press
Philadelphia, Pennsylvania 19104-4112
www.upenn.edu/pennpress

Printed in the United States of America on acid-free paper
1 3 5 7 9 10 8 6 4 2

A catalogue record for this book is available from the Library of Congress.
ISBN 978-0-8122-4867-8

For my parents, Gareth and Donna Williams,
who encouraged me to explore the world instead of being afraid of it

If you are not able to find an IED or a bullet, then single out the disbelieving American, Frenchman, or any of their allies. Smash his head with a rock, or slaughter him with a knife, or run him over with your car, or throw him down from a high place, or choke him, or poison him.

—ISIS spokesman Abu Mohammed al-Adnani

We kill them [ISIS fighters in Syria and Iraq] whenever we find them.

—Air Force Lt. General John W. Hesterman III

CONTENTS

PREFACE

The average college student today was in grade school on 9/11, and few of them remember what it was like to watch the televised images of Americans plummeting to their deaths out of the burning World Trade Center on that crisp September morning back in 2001. When I ask my own students at my university about the wars that have provided a backdrop to their lives since they were children, many have only a vague understanding of them. Student responses to my inquiries about the reasons for the wars, such as "America invaded Iraq because Saddam Hussein was shipping nuclear weapons to the Afghan leader bin Laden" or "the United States invaded Iraq because the Iraqis attacked America first on 9/11," capture the shocking ignorance many from that generation have today about America's wars that have dominated the news all their lives.

While most college students today have heard about the terrorist group ISIS (the Islamic State in Iraq and Syria), which has seized headlines around the globe since the summer of 2014, few know where this terrorist group–jihadi army came from or what the United States is doing to ostensibly "degrade and destroy" it. There is no sense of historical awareness or context to the bold beheadings of Americans by ISIS terrorists or to America's new aerial war on this terrorist group in Syria and Iraq known as Operation Inherent Resolve. For all intents and purposes, ISIS, which is seen as a "critical threat to America" by 84 percent of Americans, seems to have just appeared out of the blue to conquer one-third of Syria and Iraq.[1] The prequel to the sudden rise of ISIS (i.e., America's land wars in Iraq and Afghanistan) remains an unknown quantity for this generation, few of whom have ever heard of Tora Bora, Donald Rumsfeld, Abu Ghraib, Blackwater, Haditha, General David Petraeus, Fallujah, Mullah Omar, General Stanley McChrystal, or Abu Musab Zarqawi.

As for those older generations who lived through these extraordinary times that saw the United States deploy two and half million of its men and women across the globe to fight in the mountains of Afghanistan or deserts of Iraq, most of us have only a series of disconnected images of the events of that time. These images and memories are often based on fleeting twenty-second CNN or Fox newscasts or half-remembered newspaper articles that hardly jell together to provide an easily digested, macro overview. It is difficult to gain a bird's-eye view of jumbled events that are still unfolding and not fully understood at the time.

But that is exactly what I have set out to do here. My aim is to shine a retrospective light on the wars in Afghanistan, Iraq, and Syria in order to "historicize" the disparate events once collectively known as the War on Terror. The objective is to weave all these disjointed stories together into one accessible narrative that tells us how we got to the point where ISIS conquered an area in the Middle East larger than Britain or Israel with eight million people living under its rule. It is only by re-creating this complex story that we can come to see how the United States got dragged back into a war in the sands of the Middle East with an unprecedentedly violent jihadi terrorist army and how it aims to prevent something similar from happening in Afghanistan by deploying thousands of "residual" troops.

This book is an effort to stand back from these seminal events that were followed by millions, but not fully understood at the time, and make them comprehensible with the aim of understanding why U.S. forces are today involved in wars in three Muslim countries. This book can be thought of as an "after action report" of the sort the military issues after engagements (only on a far grander scale), with the aim of explaining the past and uncertain future of our military engagements in Afghanistan, Iraq, and Syria. On one level the aim of this book is to chronicle this constantly unfolding story that takes place on shifting sand and provide specific details or "granularity," as the military calls it. On another level it is a broad, sweeping overview spanning events from the 1948 conquest of Palestine by Israeli troops to the beginning of the collapse of the ISIS state in 2016.

I should, however, state that this history of counterterrorism and warfare in distant lands and tragedy in the United States is not intended for experts alone. It is meant to be a guide for all those who want to learn from the mistakes and the successes of the wars in the Middle East and Central Asia and apply them to the present and future. It is a record of the extraordinary events of 2001–16 that affected the lives of millions in the United States, Europe, Central Asia, South Asia, North Africa, the Middle East, and beyond. It is a journey that those who have become disconnected from the wars should take so that they can pass on its lessons to future generations.

This is certainly a journey that those in both American political parties need to take before they politicize this issue and blame Barack Obama or George W. Bush for creating the preconditions for the rise of ISIS. It is only by taking this background journey that the observer of history can understand the political implications stemming from ISIS's recent conquests of one-third of Iraq and Syria and the true nature of the resurgent Taliban's threat to post–Operation Enduring Freedom Afghanistan.

My own journey to understand America's twenty-first-century wars began in 2003. In the summer of that year I flew to Kabul, Afghanistan, and traveled in a convoy over the mighty Hindu Kush Mountains to the deserts of the north to live with an Afghan warlord named General Abdul Rashid Dostum. Dostum's horse-mounted Uzbek Mongol tribesmen had just helped the Americans defeat the Taliban in 2001, and I was eager to meet this larger-than-life field commander. My aim was to delve into the secrets of Afghanistan and find out how Dostum had helped U.S. Special Forces overthrow the Taliban regime in just two months, with less than a dozen U.S. lives lost.[2]

General Dostum was heartened by my quest for knowledge but gave me a gentle warning before agreeing to our interview. As we sat on the porch of his compound with turban-wearing gunmen around us, he wagged a finger at me and said, "Hoja [professor], you are an American, and you are hungry for quick answers like many of your countrymen. But you must overcome your typical American impatience and do something that few of your countrymen do. You must learn about our past."

"It is only by patiently traveling back in time that you can understand us and our world and why you and your countrymen came here. You see Americans usually don't concern themselves with history. They move fast through their modern lives. They think the past of these recent events began on the day the terrorists attacked your towers of glass and steel. But we have a long history before that sad day. You must learn it first before you can comprehend these more recent events."

Over the next few weeks with Dostum, and during subsequent visits to Afghanistan, where I traveled extensively, I took the Afghan Uzbek commander's words to heart. I began to infuse them with the missing ingredient into the war that was unfolding around me . . . historical context.

Gradually I began to understand the blood vendettas that drove Dostum's Uzbeks to wage war on their enemies, the Taliban who belonged to the Pashtun ethnic group. I began to master the differences between the Sunni Islam of the

Uzbeks and the Shiite Islam of their neighbors the Hazaras. I learned why some Afghans—the Uzbeks, Hazaras, and Tajiks—hated bin Laden, while others—the Pashtun Taliban—were willing to go to war to provide him sanctuary. It was all so much more complex than the simplistic world I had constructed based on shallow CNN or Fox News snippets. The media had posited a black-and-white world of good Americans fighting bad Muslims; I found the real world to be far more complex and containing nearly an infinite number of shades of gray.

As I met with U.S. Special Forces, tribal khans (chieftains), Taliban prisoners of war, village storytellers, Afghan intelligence officials, and newly liberated women, the one-dimensional, American-centric story I had in my mind began to dissolve. Replacing it were history, ethnicity, religion, politics, culture, and foreign terrain that now became familiar. The vast terra incognita of the War on Terror and its peoples ceased to be a brief sound bite on CNN and became three-dimensional.

I had similar experiences in the Middle East where I met Syrian refugees fleeing the ISIS fanatics, interviewed the famed female Kurdish Peshmerga fighters facing ISIS in their frontline positions, and met members of the ancient group of pagans known as the Yazidis who had been massacred and enslaved by ISIS. In Pakistan, I had the chance to interact with Pashtun tribesmen living in the remote tribal regions who feared their Taliban conquerors and praised Obama's drone blitz on their tormentors. These were the first steps in my journey to understanding the history of the War on Terror.

I had a similar experience with my own countrymen as I lectured at Special Operations Command in Tampa, Florida, and to U.S. Marines deploying to fight in Afghanistan at Camp Pendleton, traveled to the notorious Al Qaeda prison at Guantanamo Bay and the Canadian Supreme Court to serve as an expert witness in terrorism cases, advised the U.S. Army's Information Operations team at NATO's International Security and Assistant Force Headquarters, in Kabul, Afghanistan, ranged Afghanistan's countryside working for the CIA's Counterterrorism Center in tracking suicide bombers, met with drone pilots, and taught my students at the university about Iraq and Afghanistan.

On many levels, I was given a unique front-row perspective to the first global war of the twenty-first century. It was at this time that I was introduced to the term "counter jihad" which was used by some members of the team I was working with at the U.S. Army's Joint Information Operations Warfare Command at Lackland Airbase. I felt this was an interesting description for America's military and counterintelligence efforts to rollback and defeat militant Islamists across the globe.

It was while working alongside members of the military and intelligence communities engaged in "counter jihad" that I began to study the war from my own country's perspective. I began to learn how America's history, with its own peculiarities and idiosyncrasies, propelled it to launch two wars against vastly different enemies . . . simultaneously. This journey took me from the beginning of America's special relationship with Israel to the dark days in the summer of 2014 when ISIS surprised the world by launching a bold conquest of northern Iraq.

This story of America and its history was as important to me as the story of the Uzbeks and other Afghan tribes, for it helped me understand the twenty-first-century superpower that invaded two separate *states* in an effort to destroy a *stateless* terrorist entity known as Al Qaeda. It also helped me understand what made Americans, many of whom could not translate Al Qaeda, Baathist, or the Taliban into English, send their sons and daughters to fight and die against these very foes.

The story of America's wars in the Muslim world involves understanding not just the exotic peoples of the Middle East and Central Asia and their pre-9/11 history, it involves understanding ourselves. It also involves understanding what makes Americans act the way they do and why this infuriates those who desperately hate them in places like Iraq, Syria, and Afghanistan.

The question of why the terrorists hate Americans is of utmost concern for me as an educator, government analyst, and field researcher. In my history classes, I often ask my American students why the terrorists attacked the United States on 9/11. Inevitably a student will answer that they hate America for not being Muslim. They hate our unveiled women, Hollywood, our liberal views on clothing, sex, alcohol, cigarettes, homosexuality, and so on. In other words, it is our very way of life that drives them to suicidal/homicidal terrorism.

To this I respond by asking my students why the terrorists do not attack Brazil, Scandinavia, Germany, Thailand, or some other "decadent" (by American standards) secular-liberal society? Surely Mohamad Atta, the 9/11 team commander, did not fly his plane into a civilian-packed World Trade Center simply to express his frustration with the culture that produced Beyoncé's risqué music videos. There has to be something deeper that drove this intelligent man who spoke English, German, and Arabic and had earned an M.A. in architecture from a prestigious German university to incinerate himself and kill thousands in the process.

For far too long we Americans have lazily explained ourselves and the terrorists' hatred for us with such simple statements as "they hate us for our freedom." This sort of flat, unnuanced explanation for the terrorists' suicidal fury is hardly a satisfactory explanation for why Atta carried out the greatest terrorist outrage in history.

To understand what made Mohamad Atta hate America more than he loved his own life, one has to take the Uzbek general Dostum's advice and patiently probe the pre-9/11 history of America's interaction with the Muslim world. One must go back to historic roots of the hatred and America's role in fanning its flames to understand the wars that saw America spend approximately $5 trillion in a time of economic depression and lose approximately seventy-seven hundred lives fighting disparate enemies that are still far from beaten.[3]

This background journey is especially crucial for understanding the latest iteration in what was once called the Global War on Terror, the campaign to defeat ISIS, and the campaign to prevent the return of the Taliban known as Operation Resolute Support. It is only by patiently engaging in this background journey that one can understand the spectacular rise of the ISIS jihadi army and its conquest of northern Syria and Iraq from 2013 to 2016 and the ongoing effort to prevent the collapse of the pro-U.S. Ashraf Ghani government in Afghanistan. As will be demonstrated, the rise of ISIS and its carving out of a "caliphate" in the heart of what had once been two comparatively secular Arab lands did not come out of the blue. It was directly related to America's invasion of Iraq and the destabilization of that former secular Baathist regime.

The same can be said of the Taliban in Afghanistan. The ongoing war against a newly emboldened Afghan foe did not come out of the blue. There is a long history of U.S. involvement in the mountains of Afghanistan going back to the Soviet occupation of that country in the 1980s that explains this fourteen-year conflict, which shows no sign of ending.

It has been said that history is never dead in the realms the United States has invaded. The past is a prologue and guide for what is to come in this tumultuous part of the world littered with the remains of empires and faiths. Unless we learn this history, we will never be able to truly understand the lessons from the unprecedented events that took place from 2001 to 2015. For, as will be demonstrated, 9/11 and the subsequent wars it helped spawn in three countries most certainly did not happen out of the blue because Muslim terrorists woke up one day and decided they hated America's freedoms. There was actually a long prehistory to the events in the Middle East and Central Asia that must be patiently explored if one is to have an understanding of the foundation for America's long wars in these sands.

MAP 1. Pakistan, Afghanistan, and the Federally Administered Tribal Agencies.

MAP 2. The Federally Administered Tribal Agencies.

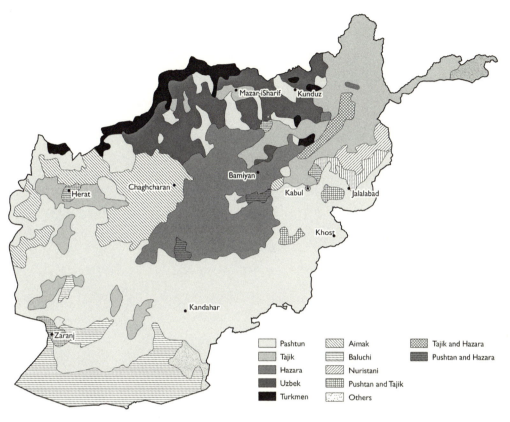

MAP 3. The major ethnic groups of Afghanistan.

Pashtun
Tajik
Hazara
Uzbek
Turkmen

Aimak
Baluchi
Nuristani
Pushtan and Tajik
Others

Tajik and Hazara
Pushtan and Hazara

CHAPTER 1

Planting the Seeds for a Global Conflict

Our attacks against you will continue as long as U.S. support for Israel
continues. It is not fair that Americans should live in peace as long as our
[Palestinian] brothers in Gaza live in the worst conditions.

—Osama bin Laden

Leave the Arabian Peninsula defeated and stop supporting the coward Jews
in Palestine!

—Saudi-born 9/11 terrorist Abdul Aziz al Omari's
videotaped warning to America

The Prehistory of 9/11:
Israel, the Palestinians, and the Americans

Long before there was the "War on Terror" there was terrorism in the Middle
East in the land of Palestine/Israel. The roots of this terrorism go back mil-
lennia and involve the biblical kingdom of Israel. The Jewish kingdom of Israel was established by the legendary King David in roughly the year 1000
B.C. King David's people had migrated perhaps two hundred years earlier
from Egypt and fought a long, brutal war for control of a land known to its
local population as Canaan.

At the time of the Israelites' brutal invasion, Canaan was inhabited by
indigenous Canaanites and a powerful people from the Greek islands known

as the Philistines. The coastal area where the latter people lived was named Philistia or Palestine. After two centuries of warfare, the Israelites defeated the Philistines, conquered Canaanite Jerusalem, and made it the capital of David's small kingdom. His son Solomon then built a temple in Jerusalem to the Israelites' one God, Yahweh.

The kingdom of Israel was seen by the Jews as a holy land given to them, and them exclusively, by God. Unfortunately, neighboring empires were not so concerned with the self-proclaimed links between the Jews and the land bequeathed to them by their God and frequently overran it and added it to their empires. Over the centuries, Israel split into two quarreling substates known as Judea and Samaria, which were then conquered by Assyria and Babylon (two empires based in what is today Iraq). Then came the conquering Persians, Alexander the Great, and finally the Romans.

The Jews, strict monotheists, chaffed under pagan Roman rule and heavy taxation and revolted in roughly A.D. 70. The powerful Romans then launched a genocidal campaign against the Jews and destroyed their sacred temple in Jerusalem and renamed the city Aelia Capitolina. More than half a million Jews were killed at this time. Later, in A.D. 135, the rebellious Jews were driven from their homes and killed in the tens of thousands.

In succeeding years, the vast majority of Jews were exiled from the Roman province of Palestine and scattered across the ancient world. Those Jews who lived beyond the borders of their former homeland lived in a condition known as Diaspora (a Greek word roughly meaning "to be scattered from one's home place"). Under subsequent Roman emperors, Jews were barred from living in Jerusalem, and the land was once again renamed Palestine (i.e., the land of the Philistines).

In the following centuries, the Romans and their successors, the East Romans or Byzantines, converted to the new faith of Christianity. At this time most people living in the region of Palestine also converted to Christianity. These local Christians later adopted Arabic language following the Arabic Muslim conquests and became Christian Arabs. The descendants of these ancient Christians are today known as the Christian Palestinians and live in such towns as Bethlehem. Few Americans are aware that a (declining) portion of the Palestinian Arabs are in fact ancient Christians. There is also an ancient Arab Christian population found in nearby Iraq that was largely destroyed in the aftermath of 2003's Operation Iraqi Freedom and Christian population in Lebanon, Syria, and Egypt.

In the A.D. 600s, Muslim Arabs poured out of the Arabian desert with their new Islamic faith and conquered the East Roman Christian province of Palestine. They later built one of the first great Muslim religious complexes, the Dome of the Rock Mosque or Al Aqsa ("the Farthest" Mosque), directly on the very site of the Jews' former Temple Mount, which they also believed was sacred ground. Muslims believed the Prophet Muhammad made a mystical night journey on the horse Buraq from Arabia to the Temple Mount in Jerusalem. From there he ascended to heaven and was told that Muslims should pray five times a day. Jerusalem thus became, along with Mecca and Medina in Arabia, one of the three holy pilgrim sites of Islam. Muslim Arabs have lived in Jerusalem and Palestine alongside the older population of Christians continuously since this time and are called Palestinians.

While many claim that Jews and Muslims have been enemies since this time, history indicates otherwise. During this period, for example, the new Arab Muslim rulers allowed Jews to immigrate back to Jerusalem, and a community was established there. In 1099, however, much of this Jewish community was slaughtered by invading Christian Crusaders from Europe, who considered Jews (whom they blamed for the death of Jesus Christ) to be no better than Muslim infidels. In fact Jews were horribly oppressed in medieval Europe by Christians, who accused them of all sorts of bizarre acts, such as kidnapping Christian babies and sacrificing them in their synagogues or desecrating Christian communion. Superstitious Christian mobs often slaughtered Jews who had been living peacefully in their midst after accusing them of such acts of blasphemy. Fortunately for the Jews, the Christian Crusaders were expelled from Jerusalem by the great Muslim warrior Saladin, and Jews were subsequently allowed to return in small numbers to Jerusalem.

Most Jews, however, remained scattered in the Diaspora in venues ranging from Iraq to England. On the whole, however, diasporic Jews fared much better under Muslim rule than under Christian rule. For example, when Christian Crusaders reconquered most of Spain from the comparatively tolerant Muslims who had ruled it from 711 to 1492, they persecuted Spanish Jews. Most of Spain's Jewish population fled the Spanish Catholic Inquisition to the greatest Muslim state of the time, the Ottoman Empire. During this period the Ottoman city of Salonika became the greatest Jewish center in the world. This stems in part from the fact that Ottomans, as Muslims, recognized Jews as fellow "Peoples of the Book" (Ahl al Kitab in Arabic, a term that also applied to Christians who followed the Book, the Book being the Torah, the Bible, or the Qur'an). While Jews had to pay a *jizya* tax similar to the one levied on Christians to avoid military service, they were not oppressed by the Muslims as "idol worshippers" like the recently conquered pagan Zoroastrians of Iran (Persia) or polytheistic Hindus of India were.

As the Jews continued to suffer in Christian countries, Europe began to modernize under secular nation-states in the 1700s. At this time the novel concept of "nationalism" (the notion that every ethnic, linguistic, or tribal group on the earth is a "nation" and has the "natural right" to a national homeland, motherland, or fatherland) began to spread in post-Napoleonic Europe. Napoleon did much to destroy the old empires and principalities of Europe, and this led to the creation of such modern nation-states as Germany (previously Germany had been divided into over a dozen smaller principalities and kingdoms that had different dialects and little common political history).

From western Europe, the novel idea of nationalism began to spread to the mighty Muslim Ottoman Empire, which included most of the Arab, Turkish, and Kurdish Middle East as well as southeastern Europe and North Africa. As the Christian peoples of eastern Europe (Greeks, Serbs, Bulgarians, Romanians, etc.) began to revolt against their Ottoman sultans (emperors) and carve out their own exclusive nation-states, the "bug" of nationalism began to spread among diasporic Jews living uncomfortably in late nineteenth-century Christian Europe. Those Jews living in terrible conditions in places like Russia (where the tsar's Cossacks frequently attacked them) or even France (which had a prominent case where a Jewish officer was falsely convicted of treason) began to dream of creating a nation-state of their own for their scattered people living in the Diaspora. This would allow them to reconstruct their largely forgotten language of Hebrew, preserve their culture, and avoid discrimination by Christians.

The obvious location for this motherland or homeland would be in the Ottoman province of Palestine, which had been inhabited by Muslim Arabs for roughly thirteen hundred years. Jews who wanted to recreate the ancient biblical kingdom of David's Israel (a kingdom known in ancient texts as Zion) called themselves Zionists.

In the 1880s, groups of European Zionists approached the Ottoman sultan in Istanbul, Turkey, and requested the right to set up settlements in the province of Palestine. While initially resisting their requests, the sultan ultimately saw in the European Jews an industrious Western people that could use their hard work and capital to modernize this backwater province, so he eventually gave them his blessing to buy land there. Local Ottoman Turkish and Arab landowners then began to sell plots of land to the incoming Jews, particularly on the coast. At this time Christians who supported the emigration of Jews to the Ottoman Empire described Arab Palestine as "a land without a people for a people without a land." But, as will be seen, the indigenous Arab Palestinian population, which had been living in these lands in some cases since the expulsion of the Jews by the Romans in A.D. 135, certainly did not define Palestine as a "land without a people."

From this time period until World War I (which took place from 1914 to 1918) Jews immigrated to Ottoman Palestine and bought up land from local Muslim Palestinian and Turkish landowners. At first this process was peaceful, because the local Arabs considered the Jews to be fellow Peoples of the Book and good neighbors. But as more and more Jews with their foreign ways poured into the land, they began to clash with the local Arab villagers and nomadic Bedouin. As World War I drew to a close there were deep tensions between Palestine's local Arab population and the incoming Jews.

During World War I, the Ottoman Empire fought on the side of the Germans against the British, French, Americans, and Russians and thus ended up on the losing side of the conflict. After the war, the victorious British seized control of the province of Palestine and neighboring Arab lands of Jordan and Iraq from the defeated Ottomans. The British then ruled Palestine from this time period until 1948 and tried desperately to keep the peace between the clashing Jews and Palestinians.

At this time both sides engaged in violence, which led to tit-for-tat killings and acts of terrorism. The Arabs created a terrorist militia known as the Black Hand, while the Jews established two terrorist groups known as the Stern Gang and Irgun. The Black Hand was quickly wiped out by the British, but the Jewish groups went on to blow up the King David Hotel in Jerusalem in 1946 (killing ninety-one people of various nationalities) and carry out the massacre of dozens of Palestinian villagers in 1948 in the village of Deir Yassin.[1]

Prior to this terrorism, however, during World War II the (predominantly Christian) Germans carried the historic European oppression of Jews to the extreme and killed millions of them during the Holocaust. In the aftermath of the war, stunned American soldiers uncovered vast death camps in Germany and Eastern Europe that exposed the hidden horrors of the Holocaust to the world. At this time, pressure mounted for Britain to give up its colonial possessions in the Middle East, including Palestine, which had grown increasingly violent as more Jews fled there to escape the horrors of the Nazi

Holocaust. By this time the population of Jews in Palestine had risen to roughly six hundred thousand while the Palestinian Arabs came to approximately 1.2 million.

In 1947, the British agreed to depart Palestine and allow the newly created United Nations to partition the land evenly between the Jews and the much larger Palestinian Arab population. The eastern half would go to the Palestinian Arabs, while much of the west around the new Jewish coastal city of Tel Aviv would go to the Jews. Unsatisfied with this equal division, the Arabs fatefully rejected the plan. Both sides then prepared for an inevitable war once the British pulled out.

On May 14, 1948, 1,878 years after the destruction of Jerusalem by the ancient Romans, the Jews in Palestine declared the existence of a new state once again to be known as Israel. In response, the neighboring Arab states of Egypt, Jordan, Syria, Iraq, Saudi Arabia, and Lebanon invaded Palestine to drive out the Jews. With their backs once again to the wall, the Jews, who often had better training, morale, and equipment, fought back ferociously and won the Arab-Israeli War of 1948. In the process, they expanded their portion of territory by 40 percent and forced out more than seven hundred thousand defeated Palestinian Arabs from their homes (it should be stated that some of these Palestinians also voluntarily fled the Jews because their leaders told them to). While the new Jewish state did not have an overall policy of ethnic cleansing, its leaders took advantage of ad hoc expulsions of Palestinians and the voluntary flight of others to enlarge the Jewish state's territory.

The defeated Palestinians were compressed into a small strip of remaining Palestinian territory on the Mediterranean Sea next to Egypt known as the Gaza Strip (an area, named after the ancient Philistine town of Gaza, that is only thirty-four miles long by seven miles wide and is inhabited by two million people) and lands on the western bank of the Jordan River around Jerusalem (the so-called West Bank). Tens of thousands of Palestinian refugees also fled to southern Lebanon, where they lived in grim refugee camps, and to the kingdom of Jordan, where they eventually became citizens. Arabs across the Middle East bemoaned the fate of their fellow Arabs in Palestine and called these tragic events Al Naqba (the Disaster).

While most Westerners are familiar with the term Holocaust or Shoah, few know the term Al Naqba. For their part, the Palestinians have the bitter memory of their lost ancestral graveyards, villages, fields, orchards, places of worship, and homes forever burned in their collective memory. They bemoan the loss of most of their ancestral homeland, Palestine, and for decades fought to regain it. The neighboring Arab states swore to avenge their Palestinian Arab brothers and planned on destroying the new state of Israel, while the exiled Palestinians dreamed of returning to their lost lands.

In 1967, the Israelis fought another war to repel attacking Syrians, Egyptians, and Jordanians and were astoundingly successful. During the war they went on to occupy the Gaza Strip and West Bank (as well as territory from Syria and Egypt) and thus gained direct control of the entire land of Palestine, including the holy city of Jerusalem, which they directly annexed to Israel. Tens of thousands of Palestinians again fled at this time to Jordan and elsewhere. This war was known as the Six-Day War, but Palestinians have a saying, "Israel may have won the war in six days, but they have been fighting the seventh day ever since."

For Arabs and Muslims across the world the loss of holy Jerusalem, site of the Dome of the Rock, was a tremendous blow, and millions seethed with anger. For the Palestinians it meant much more: it meant the direct occupation of their only remaining free territories in the West Bank and Gaza by their mortal enemies. For the Israelis, it meant gaining control of the capital of their ancient state and site of the Wailing Wall, the last remnant of their great temple to their God, Yahweh.

As their last holdouts were conquered by the new state of Israel, the defeated Palestinians resolved to continue the fight via terrorism to make the Jews' conquest of their lands costly. In the 1970s the Palestinian terrorist group known as the Palestinian Liberation Organization (PLO) hijacked airplanes and launched terrorist attacks on Jews in Israel proper and those who began to settle in the newly occupied lands of the West Bank and Gaza Strip in large numbers. It became obvious to the Palestinians that the Jewish settlers were trying to create permanent "facts on the ground" by squeezing them out of their last remaining lands in the West Bank and Gaza. In response, the Palestinians fought back with terrorism to make this land grab costly. Perhaps the Palestinians' most notorious terrorist attack in this period was the killing of eleven Israeli athletes at the 1972 Munich Olympics.

It should be stated that this early terrorism was not modern-style jihadi suicide terrorism, nor was it based on Islamic extremism. The PLO was a Leftist, secular organization that received its weapons and funds from socialist Arab countries such as Iraq, Syria, and Egypt and support from the Soviet Union. As their name indicated, the PLO's main goal was to "liberate" their lost lands, not wage jihad for the sake of Allah (God).

Despite this terror campaign, Israel poured tens of thousands of Jews into the newly conquered West Bank and created settlements on land confiscated from local Palestinians. This process of confiscating land and building settlements goes on to this very day. As recently as the summer of 2016, Israel allocated $20 million for the expansion of settlements in the Palestinian West Bank.

As the conditions for the impoverished Palestinians worsened, their youth rose up in popular revolts known as the Intifadas (the "Uprisings" of 1987–93 and 2000–2005), and a new, distinctly Islamic form of terrorism rose among the Palestinians. After 1987 the terrorist group known as Hamas (the Arabic acronym for the Islamic Resistance Movement) began to send waves of suicide bombers into Israel to kill Jews, even as the PLO chose another course and made peace with Israel in 1993. Hamas's campaign of suicide bombing attacks, often against cafés or buses carrying Israeli civilians, began in 1993 and represented the first suicide terror campaign by a Sunni Muslim group (this terror campaign was against Israel of course; neither Hamas nor the PLO had a policy of carrying out terrorism against the United States of America or Western countries).

Today the relatively moderate PLO, or PA (Palestinian Authority) as it is now known, governs the West Bank and is officially at peace with the occupying force of Israel, while Hamas's extreme fundamentalist rule is limited to the Gaza Strip. Interestingly, in 2005 Israel pulled out of the Gaza Strip and turned over its Jewish settlements to the Palestinians. This was part of the "land for peace" policy of the Israeli government. But far from bringing peace, the Gaza-based Hamas continued to wage jihad against Israel by launching missiles into southern Israel and on one occasion capturing one of its soldiers. Such terroristic provocations resulted in a massive Israeli retaliatory invasion of Gaza in 2009, which led to the death of over one thousand Palestinians, many of them civilians. Tensions flared up again in 2012 when Hamas began firing rockets into Israel in an effort to force an end to an Israeli-imposed blockade on their territory. These rockets killed civilians and for the first time made it as far as Jerusalem and Tel Aviv (Israel responded by bombing Gaza and killing the military head of Hamas with a drone strike). Hamas' charter still calls for the destruction of Israel.

The Gaza-based Hamas and Israel went to war again for fifty days in the summer of 2014 after Hamas began raining rockets down on southern Israel in an attempt to end the blockade of the Gaza Strip and after the tit-for-tat killing of three Israeli boys and one Palestinian boy. Israel ended up invading

Gaza to destroy dozens of tunnels built by the Palestinians to sneak into Israel and Egypt. Israel also bombarded Gaza for several weeks straight, killing roughly two thousand Palestinians, the majority of them civilian (by contrast just sixty-seven Israelis died, and most of them were soldiers).

Tensions flared up again in the fall of 2015 and winter of 2016 when twenty eight Israelis were killed by Palestinian youth, most in stabbings. In March 2016 a visiting American student was stabbed to death in the Jaffa neighborhood of Tel Aviv by a twenty two year old Palestinian tied to Hamas (he was the second American killed in the stabbing spree).

As many as one hundred and eighty Palestinians, most of them assailants, were killed in the same period. Most of the knife attacks on Israeli civilians were carried out by young lone wolves who had been radicalized by the Internet and galvanized by false rumors that Israel was restricting access to the Al Aqsa mosque. At this time Palestinian arsonists also set fire to the tomb of the biblical patriarch Joseph, which is revered by Jews in the West Bank. But the underlying reason for the upswing in terrorism, which led to fears of a third Intifada, was the Palestinians' realization that their people's dreams for an independent state were fading.

Israel also exacerbated problems with the moderate Palestinian Authority government on the West Bank in 2012. It did so by declaring that it would confiscate even more Palestinian territory on the West Bank to build thousands of new Israeli houses, thus preventing the eventual creation of a contiguous future Palestinian state on these Palestinian lands.[2] This was despite the fact that every member of the UN Security Council, except the United States, issued statements condemning the Israelis for once again annexing land the Palestinians wanted for their future capital.[3]

This is the history of (secular Palestinian) PLO and (religious) Hamas terrorism against Israel in a nutshell. The question the reader may ask is what does all this tragic history of mass expulsion from land and terrorism have to do with the distant United States of America?

The history of ties between the United States and this region is complicated and goes back to World War II, when President Franklin Roosevelt opposed the creation of a Jewish state. Roosevelt's opposition was based on his belief that American support for Israel would antagonize allied Arab states that were supplying oil to the U.S. In 1948, however, President Harry Truman recognized the new state of Israel, among the world's first states to do so. But this did not necessarily mean close ties to Israel. In fact, in 1956, when the Israelis (along with Britain and France) invaded Egypt, the U.S. helped force them out of Egyptian territory in the Sinai Desert. Initially then the U.S. did not "have a dog in the fight" between Israel and the Arabs and remained a neutral arbitrator. The main supplier of weapons to Israel at this time was France, which sold the weapons not out of any deep emotional support for Zionism, but for profit.

This changed in the 1960s during the presidency of Lyndon Johnson. After the 1967 Six-Day War between the Arabs and Israel, the United States began to sell F-4 Phantom fighter jets and other military hardware to Israel. This was, in part, because several socialist Arab countries that supported the Palestinians, such as Egypt, Syria, and Iraq, had allied themselves to the Soviet Union. Supporting Israel was seen not so much as pro-Zionist as anti-Soviet.

At this time, the United States tried using its newfound leverage with Israel to get it to pull out of the occupied Palestinian territories of Gaza and the West Bank via a UN resolution. The Israeli parliament, however, firmly rejected America's proposal and voted to maintain the occupation and continued Jewish settlement of these recently conquered Palestinian territories. Such continued occupation of the West Bank has been strongly supported by Israel's fundamentalist Jews, who claim that the West Bank is part of the biblical patrimony bequeathed to their people by their God, Yahweh.

During the 1973 Yom Kippur Arab-Israeli War, U.S. support for Israel included an airlift of supplies to its Jewish allies. Then, in 1978–79, the United States pushed Egypt, the largest and most powerful Arab nation, to recognize the state of Israel, thus infuriating many in the Arab Middle East. Many Egyptians never forgave their leader, Anwar Sadat, for signing peace with Israel, and he was subsequently killed by Egyptian extremists who considered him a traitor.

As for Israel, to this very day the United States supports its Jewish ally by providing it with $3 billion per year (the Obama administration began negotiations to raise it to $3.7 in March 2016) and supplying it with weapons, such as the Apache Longbow attack helicopter and F-15 and F-16 fighter jets. While the U.S. did help broker the 1993 Oslo peace accords between the Israelis and the PLO, which led to the creation of the Palestinian Authority (PA) in the West Bank, America is not seen by most Arabs as an even-handed broker in the Palestinian-Arab conflict. America is seen as Israel's protector.

This fact is best demonstrated for Arabs in America's use of its veto in the United Nations Security Council to defeat votes that criticize Israel for such actions as the expulsion of Palestinians and the never-ending process of confiscating more Palestinian land and building of more Jewish settlements in the occupied West Bank. Many Arabs, and Muslims in general, see U.S. support for Israel, a key democratic ally of the United States in the Mideast, as a "knee-jerk" or "reflexive" response.

The Arabs also realize that vocal, outward support for Israel is seen as a litmus test for American politicians of all stripes, regardless of their political affiliation (the only exception to this being Republican presidential candidate Ron Paul, who has repeatedly stated that America's support for Israel hurts its ties to the Arab world). U.S. Christian congregations and charities, such as the International Fellowship of Christians and Jews, similarly support Israel against the Palestinians (often without realizing that some Palestinian Arabs are Christians). Many American Christian fundamentalists, such as those belonging to the group Christians United for Israel (CUFI), believe that by strongly supporting Israel against the Arabs they are helping to bring about the "the Rapture" (involving Armageddon and the return of Christ to take Christian believers to heaven).

The Arabs are also aware that one of the most powerful political lobbies in the United States is the American Israeli Political Affairs Committee (AIPAC). U.S. politicians of all backgrounds fight to get this influential group's endorsement by competing to demonstrate their pro-Israeli credentials. Any American politician who demonstrates weak support for Israel, even on issues strictly related to continuing Israeli confiscation of Palestinian lands in the occupied West Bank, runs the risk of being labeled "anti-Israeli." Being labeled anti-Israeli is of course the death sentence for any U.S. politician's campaign.

Terrorists such as the insurgent groups in Iraq, the Lebanese Shiite group Hezbollah, Hamas, Pakistani jihadists, ISIS (Islamic State in Iraq and Syria), and Al Qaeda all consider America's strong support for Israel versus the Arabs to be the basic starting point for their jihads. *America's pro-Israel stance is the cornerstone and foundation of the Muslim terrorists' deep hatred of the United States, and no understanding of anti-American terrorism can be made without understanding this crucial background.* It is this aspect of America's foreign policy—more than America's non-Muslim culture, Hollywood, alcohol use, liberal clothing, and relaxed sexual mores, and the like—that drove Mohamad Atta and his Al Qaeda terrorists to turn a civilian-packed jetliner into a guided missile on 9/11.

But the perception that America (the "Great Satan" in the language of the terrorists) is not even-handed in its dealings with Israel (the "Little Satan") and the Palestinians is not the only foundation for the modern jihad that led to the birth of Al Qaeda and other Muslim terrorist groups. The next set of seeds were planted not in the deserts of Palestine/Israel but in the Spin Ghar Mountains of Afghanistan's border with Pakistan. It was this region that proved to be the incubator for both the Afghan Taliban (the Students) and the Arabic group Al Qaeda al Jihad (the Base of Holy War).

Jihad in the Mountains of Afghanistan

By the 1980s much of the Muslim world's attention had been diverted from the Israeli conquest of Muslim lands in Palestine to the atheist Soviets' invasion of the backward Central Asian country of Afghanistan. It was this genocidal war that saw as many as 1.5 million Afghan tribesmen killed by the Soviets' modern, mechanized army that galvanized the second wave of modern jihadism. This war actually began in April 1978 when a group of Afghan Communists overthrew their own country's president and inaugurated a campaign to forcefully liberate women, redistribute land to the poor, destroy the old village elites, and weaken the conservative influence of mullahs (religious officials). In response, conservative villagers across the land declared jihad on the "infidel" Afghan Communist government and began to burn the newly built schools, women's and children's health clinics, and other visible signs of the secular Communist authorities.

As the Islamic rebels or *mujahideen* (literally "those who wage jihad") began to spread their influence throughout the Afghan countryside, the Soviets saw them as a threat to their "little brother" Communist allies in Afghanistan. With conditions in Afghanistan deteriorating because of popular revulsion against harsh Communist policies, the Soviets decided to intervene directly. Their goal was to protect Communism in neighboring Afghanistan and bolster the besieged Afghan Communist government army in its fight against the mujahideen Islamist rebels.

On December 25, 1979, the Soviet Union invaded the undeveloped land of Afghanistan with a massive army that ultimately rose to eighty thousand troops. While their initial goal was to strengthen the Afghan Communist army so it could wage war in the countryside against the rebels, the Soviets quickly got sucked into direct combat against the Afghan mujahideen guerillas. In this respect the their "mission creep" transition from supporting an unpopular regime against local rebels, to actually fighting the rebels on behalf of their embattled local allies, resembled that of the Americans' "mission creep" in Vietnam. But the Soviets never committed enough troops to win the war, and their numbers never came close to the U.S. troop commitment of five hundred thousand in Vietnam.[4]

The anti-Soviet mujahideen rebels' greatest leader was to be the legendary Ahmad Shah Massoud, the Lion of Panjsher. Massoud was a French-speaking ethnic Tajik (i.e., member of Afghanistan's second-largest ethnic group, which speaks the Persian language of Dari). His base was found in the northeastern Hindu Kush Mountain valley of the Panjsher (Five Lions). From this natural fortress he and his skilled guerillas sallied out to attack Soviet convoys bringing supplies down from the Soviet Union to the main Soviet bases near Kabul. The majority of the Soviets' losses came at the hands of this charismatic guerilla leader, whose fighters were known by the Russians as *dukhi* (ghosts).[5]

In response to Massoud's bold raids, the Soviets invaded his base in the Panjsher Valley nine times but were unable to capture or kill the elusive rebel commander. His fighters simply retreated up side valleys and ambushed Soviet columns that came in search of them before melting away again.

But not all of Afghanistan's ethnic groups supported the Islamic rebels. While the dominant Pashtuns (an Aryan ethnic group in the south and east who also live across the border in the tribal regions of neighboring Pakistan) and the Tajiks did most of the fighting, the Hazaras (a Shiite Mongol group in the central mountains) largely sat the war out and remained neutral. One ethnic group, the Uzbeks (Turko-Mongols descended from Genghis Khan's Golden Horde), however, decided to fight for the Soviets against the mujahideen rebels. They were driven largely by the fact that the Soviets had modernized the Soviet republic of Uzbekistan (an ethnic-based republic located to the north of Afghanistan located in the USSR), and this served as a beacon for oppressed Afghan Uzbeks. The Afghan Uzbeks also fought to gain autonomy from their traditional oppressors, the Aryan Pashtuns, who created Afghanistan by conquering their lands in the 1880s. The leader of the pro-Communist Uzbeks was a burly commander named General Abdul Rashid Dostum.

As this was the period of the Cold War, the CIA also took an interest in the Soviet invasion of Afghanistan and decided to arm the anti-Soviet mujahideen rebels, who were described in grandiose terms as "freedom fighters." The CIA, which had been caught unawares by Moscow's invasion, feared that the Soviets were moving closer to the Persian Gulf and its oil reserves. At this time, America launched its greatest covert operation ever, Operation Cyclone, a vast effort to channel millions of dollars in funds, arms, and supplies to the Afghan rebels. The Americans' goal was to "bleed" the Soviets much as they themselves had been bled in the jungles of Vietnam in the 1960s and

1970s. U.S. national security advisor Zbigniew Brzezinski famously traveled
to Pakistan's border with Afghanistan and promised the mujahideen that the
United States would help them get their mosques back. Far from being opposed to jihad, American tax dollars went to pay for Muslim holy war in this
bipolar Cold War period.

By 1986 the CIA was also sending Stinger ground-to-air missiles to the
rebels to shoot down Soviet Hind and Hip attack helicopters and MiG and
Sukhoi fighter bombers. Prior to this, the heavily armored Soviet Hind gunships in particular had proven to be deadly in hunting rebels and destroying
convoys smuggling weapons over the border of Pakistan for the mujahideen.
The Stingers and billions of U.S. and Saudi dollars helped level the playing
field and gave the Afghan rebels, whose numbers soared to over 150,000, a
fighting chance against the powerful Soviets.

By the mid-1980s as many as two thousand Soviet soldiers were dying per
year in the killing mountains of Afghanistan, and the Americans were thrilled
(by contrast the Americans lost roughly twenty-two hundred soldiers in fifteen years in Afghanistan). The Soviet war in Afghanistan gave the United
States a chance to pay back the Russians for their covert efforts to support the
North Vietnamese Communists and Viet Cong during the Vietnam War.

It was at this time (mid- to late 1980s) that small numbers of Arab volunteers from such countries as Saudi Arabia, Algeria, Egypt, Sudan, Yemen, and
elsewhere (but very few from socialist Iraq, which was a Soviet client state)
began to travel to Afghanistan to help their Muslim brethren in the jihad
against the Soviet "infidels." Their chief leader was a Palestinian from Jordan
named Abdullah Azzam.

Azzam quickly became the pied piper of jihad as he traveled from the
Middle East to the United States recruiting volunteers and funds for the pan-
Muslim jihad in Afghanistan. One of Azzam's most important recruits was a
devout Saudi millionaire named Osama bin Laden. Bin Laden's father, Mohammad, was a self-made billionaire who had taught his son to hate the Jews
for expelling the Palestinians and conquering the Dome of the Rock in Jerusalem. When bin Laden heard the stories of Muslims once again being killed,
this time in the remote Central Asian land of Afghanistan, he was moved to
travel there to assist them in their struggle.

The young bin Laden subsequently traveled to Peshawar, Pakistan, a frontier city near the Afghan border that served as a rear area staging ground for
Afghan mujahideen. There the mujahideen received financial support from
the Pakistani ISI (Inter Services Intelligence, i.e. the Pakistani equivalent to

the CIA), which chose which Afghan mujahideen groups received U.S., Saudi, and Pakistani funds. Interestingly, the Pakistani Islamist president, Zia ul Haq, chose to send most of the funds to support extremist mujahideen leaders such as Gulbuddin Hekmatyar, a Pashtun whom bin Laden supported, as opposed to moderates like Massoud the Tajik. In the process of supporting radical jihad in neighboring Afghanistan, President Zia also helped spread militant Islam through his own country, which had originally been established on secular principles. At this time Pakistani officers were so involved in the Afghan jihad that they even crossed into Afghanistan to direct operations.

While living in Peshawar, bin Laden used his wealth to help Abdullah Azzam establish the Services Office, which served as a guesthouse for Arab volunteers traveling to the region to help fight in Afghanistan. The U.S. government would later call the Services Office a "precursor for Al Qaeda."[6] But it should be stressed that the United States never sponsored bin Laden or the other Arab volunteers in Afghanistan as many people (often with a certain amount of glee) erroneously claim. On the contrary, bin Laden saw the pro-Israeli Americans (who made a far greater contribution to the Afghan rebels than the few thousand Arab volunteers) as trespassers in his "holy war" against Soviet atheism and secularism. On those few occasions when he encountered American or Western war correspondents in Afghanistan, bin Laden threatened to kill them.

American funds were, however, used to support several fundamentalist Afghan mujahideen commanders who would later go on to become their enemies. Among them was the aforementioned Gulbuddin Hekmatyar, the Pashtun fanatic whose followers had previously thrown acid in unveiled women's faces to force them to give up their liberal ways, and Jalaluddin Haqqani, who would later go on to join a new group known as the Taliban (i.e., the "Students," a Pashtun militant group that conquered most of Afghanistan by the late 1990s, which should not be confused with the anti-Soviet mujahideen rebels of the 1980s). During the 1980s anti-Soviet jihad, U.S. congressman Charlie Wilson, a strong supporter of the Afghan rebels, described Haqqani as "goodness personified."

It should also be stated that bin Laden did not, as many claim, "defeat the Soviets." In fact bin Laden fought only in one mountain skirmish against the Soviets in 1987 at a place called Jaji. It was the experience of surviving direct combat with the Soviet special forces that galvanized bin Laden and served as a personal epiphany. Convinced that God had protected him and his small unit of roughly twenty-five Arab volunteer fighters, bin Laden was inspired to wake up the long dormant spirit of jihad across the secularizing Middle East, which was dominated by pro-American dictators and kings (in Egypt, Jordan, Saudi Arabia, Bahrain, Kuwait, Qatar, and United Arab Emirates) or socialist dictators (in Iraq, South Yemen, and Syria). To fulfill his Islamist agenda, bin Laden and Azzam created a group known as Al Qaeda al Jihad (the Base for Holy War) in Peshawar, Pakistan, in 1988–89.

Unfortunately for bin Laden the fundamentalist dreamer, his hopes that he could use newly liberated, post-Soviet Afghanistan as a base to spread his new brand of global jihadism were thwarted. This was because when the Soviets finally withdrew in defeat from Afghanistan in February 1989, they left behind a surprisingly strong Afghan Communist government and army. With continued Soviet support, this local Afghan Communist government would actually go on to outlast its "big brother" the Soviet Union by several months. The mujahideen rebels failed in their only attempt to take an Afghan city, Jalalabad in the east, and failed to transition from guerilla warfare to siege warfare. The Afghan Communist government lasted for three long years and did not fall until the spring of 1992, when its greatest general, the powerful Uzbek commander Dostum, defected and joined with the Tajik mujahideen leader Massoud the Lion of Panjsher, to overthrow it.

This then inaugurated a period known as the Afghan Civil War of 1992 to 1996. At this time the Pashtun mujahideen commander Gulbuddin Hekmatyar, the "Acid Thrower"; Massoud, the Lion of Panjsher; and Dostum, the secular Uzbek warlord; and other warlords fought one another in a civil war. Hekmatyar destroyed much of Kabul during the war by indiscriminately shelling civilian-packed neighborhoods. Meanwhile, Dostum was defeated in Kabul and created a comparatively liberal realm in the north of Afghanistan based on the holy city of Mazar i Sharif. This was in an area that had been dominated by moderate Sufi Uzbeks for centuries. In essence, during the Afghan Civil War, the country that the ruling Pashtuns had brutally forged in the nineteenth century fractured along ethnic lines.

At this time, Massoud, the relatively moderate Tajik commander, controlled the capital, Kabul, and Tajik lands in the northeast. In the center of the country the Shiite Mongol Hazaras also had a period of peace and autonomy without the dominant Sunni Pashtun repressing them. It is a common misconception that anarchy prevailed in the *entire* country during this period. In fact the northern tribes, the Uzbeks, Hazaras, and Tajiks, ruled themselves quite successfully during this period (with the notable exception of Kabul, which all four Afghan ethnic groups fought for).

In the southern land of the Aryan Pashtuns, however, chaos prevailed. The Pashtun mujahideen used their weapons to prey on the common people. This southern Pashtun area became known as Yaghestan (roughly "chaos-istan"). While the lands of the northern tribes, the Uzbeks, Tajiks, and Hazaras, were ruled by moderate warlords such as Dostum and Massoud, the lands of the conservative Pashtuns, Afghanistan's traditional rulers, descended into darkness. For several years the Pashtuns suffered under the misrule of mujahideen-turned-predators, who raped women and boys, robbed travelers, grew opium, and plundered villages. In the Pashtun lands of the south, the once-glorious name of the mujahideen became synonymous with brutal violence.

As the noble jihad against the Soviets devolved into a bloody struggle for power in the Pashtun south, bin Laden and the other Arab volunteers in Afghanistan left the country in disgust. This was in part because their candidate to rule Afghanistan, the extremist Pashtun leader Gulbuddin Hekmatyar, was unable to defeat the Massoud-Dostum alliance and gain control over the capital. Massoud strongly opposed the presence of fanatical Arab fighters in Afghanistan once the anti-Soviet jihad was over.

Thousands of these so-called Afghan Arab war veterans then returned to their home countries in the Arab world and tried spreading the jihad revolution. This led to a bloody civil war in Algeria that killed tens of thousands in the 1990s, and to a vicious terrorist campaign in Egypt. It was only by carrying out a policy of mass arrests that President Hosni Mubarak, the pro-U.S. secular ruler of Egypt who took power after the assassination of President Anwar Sadat, was able to put down this fundamentalist threat to his country.

By this time some of the Afghan Arabs had joined with bin Laden to create a terrorist group in Peshawar, Pakistan, known as Qa'idat al-Jihad (the Base for Holy War) or Al Qaeda. Their aim would later be to overthrow the "Near Enemy," that is Mubarak, the secular dictator of Egypt, as well as the socialist leaders of Iraq (Saddam Hussein) and Syria (Hafez Assad), and others, and create a transnational Islamic caliphate.

Bin Laden, the group's emir, or leader, would subsequently leave Pakistan and return to his native Saudi Arabia. In Saudi Arabia bin Laden was treated as a hero and admired by many fundamentalist Saudis for leaving his wealth behind and traveling to Afghanistan to fight jihad for the faith. He was seen as a man of conviction who put his money where his mouth was. At this time bin Laden took advantage of his newfound fame to give talks throughout

Saudi Arabia urging Saudis to boycott U.S. goods to punish America for its strong support of Israel. This earned bin Laden support among many Saudi Wahhabis (a strict fundamentalist version of Islam that has been enforced in the Arabian Peninsula since the nineteenth century). Bin Laden also warned his audiences about the threat of the socialist secular ruler of Iraq, Saddam Hussein. Bin Laden would later claim, "I said many times in my speeches at the mosques, warning that Saddam will enter the [Persian] Gulf. No one believed me."[7] It is important to note that bin Laden vocally attacked Hussein at this time and in no way saw this secular ruler as an ally.

Bin Laden's rare period of peace came to an end when his prediction that Hussein posed a threat to the Arab Gulf states came true. On August 2, 1990, the powerful army of Iraq invaded the neighboring country of Kuwait. The small state of Kuwait had been involved in several disputes with its larger Iraqi neighbor over loans Kuwait had made to Iraq and over oil drilling in a disputed frontier region. All these events led to the fateful decision by Hussein to invade tiny Kuwait, a U.S. ally, in August 1990.

While Hussein did not seem to foresee it at the time, this event would make him the enemy of the Americans. This fateful action would have ripple effects that would ultimately lead to the U.S. invasions of Iraq in 1991 during the so-called First Gulf War and again in 2003 during Operation Iraqi Freedom.

The Seminal Importance of the First Gulf War of 1990–91

Before going into the history of America's first war in Iraq, a brief introduction to this country's history is in order. It is only by patiently unraveling this complex history that one can understand the nuances concerning the George Bush Jr. administration's controversial justification for invading Iraq in the spring of 2003. As will be shown, the secular government in Iraq (at least until it began to allow some token signs of Islam after 1991) has had a completely different historical trajectory than the conservative religious theocracy that was bin Laden's homeland, Saudi Arabia.

Iraq was originally a province of the very same Ottoman Empire that ruled over Arab Palestine for five hundred years. During their long rule over the province of Iraq, the Sunni Ottoman Turks placed Sunni Iraqi Arabs in positions of power in the province to the detriment of Shiite Arabs. This stemmed in part from the fact that the Ottoman Sunni (majority) Muslims were engaged in a centuries-long battle with the Shiite (minority) Muslims who ruled neighboring Iran. The deep hatred between the predominant Sunnis (as much as 90 percent of the world's Muslims are Sunnis) and Shiites resembled the hatred between Catholic Christians and Protestant Christians in Northern Ireland and in other areas in Europe throughout the centuries. Nonetheless, despite the discrimination against them, the repressed Shiites grew to become the majority in Ottoman Iraq, in part because this land housed some of their most sacred holy spots in the towns of Najaf and Karbala.[8] The Shiite Arabs of Ottoman Iraq also had strong ties with the neighboring Shiite country of Iran, the world's premiere Shiite state.

The takeaway point from this history is that for hundreds of years Ottoman Iraq was dominated by a Sunni Arab minority (20 percent of the province's population), which repressed and discriminated against the devout Shiite Arab majority (60 percent of the population). In fact, it can argued that Iraq had been ruled by Sunnis ever since the advent of Islam in the region. It would be the invading Americans who in 2003 overthrew this ancient tradition of Sunni dominance of Iraq and, in the process, stirred the Sunni beehive. Once stirred, the newly disenfranchised Sunnis would turn the central Iraq region known as the Sunni Triangle into a bloody killing ground for the American invaders from 2003 to 2008. Many Sunnis came to hate the Americans for removing them from power and came to see the American invaders as their enemy.

In addition to the Sunni and Shiite Arabs, there was a third group in Iraq that was of interest. This group was known as the Kurds. The Kurds were an Aryan group, distantly related to the Iranians, who emerged in the Middle East in the mists of time. The Kurds, who form the fourth-largest ethnic group in the Middle East, were never allowed to form an ethnic empire of their own the way the neighboring Arabs, Turks, and Iranians did. The Kurds, who number approximately thirty million today, were in fact ruled by all these peoples over the course of time. As predominantly moderate Sunnis, however, the Kurds tended to side with the Ottoman Turks against the Shiite Iranians.

Sadly, the Kurds' Sunni affiliation did not gain them any sense of equality with the Sunni Turks. When the Ottoman Empire fell apart during World War I, the ruling Turks included the major portion of the Kurdish homeland in their new country called Turkey. The Turks then repressed Kurdish culture and identity in their new state. In the 1980s a Kurdish Communist rebellion was launched in the undeveloped Kurdish lands in southeastern Turkey led by the Kurdistan Worker's Party (the PKK). The PKK fighters fought the

Turkish army and launched raids from the Kandil region in Kurdish northern Iraq. An offshoot of the PKK known as the YPG (People's Protection Units) also fought for the repressed Kurdish minority in northern Syria starting in 2011.

The divided Kurds of Turkey, Iran, Iraq, and northern Syria became the world's largest ethnic group to be deprived of a nation-state. The stateless Kurds have a famous saying that captures their sense of isolation, "we have no friends but the mountains."

In the newly created state of post-Ottoman Iraq, the Kurds, who live in the northeastern mountains, fought ferociously for decades against the ruling Sunni Arab government of Baghdad for freedom. Iraq's Sunni Arab rulers responded by launching invasions of the Kurdish mountains and carrying out a policy of ethnic cleansing designed to "Arabize" Kurdish lands in the plains around the strategic oil town of Kirkuk. During the genocidal Al Anfal campaign in the 1980s, Hussein's troops led away over 180,000 Kurds and systematically killed them in the deserts of the south. The untamed Kurdish fighting force of 115,000 Peshmergas (Those Who Confront Death), however, managed to carve out an autonomous zone in the mountainous north after 1991. This de facto "Kurdistan" was the closest thing the scattered Kurds of Turkey, Syria, Iraq, and Iran could call a free homeland.

Iraq was thus a country made up of three ethnic-sectarian groups who often interacted on a personal level on the streets, but had diametrically opposed political aspirations. The Sunnis' aspiration was to keep the reins of power firmly in their hands. This was seen by the Sunni Arabs of Iraq as the natural order of things. The Kurds wished for autonomy or outright independence from their Arab oppressors. And the Shiite Arab majority longed for an end to the repression and discrimination against them by the dominant Sunni Arab minority.

Another key aspect of Iraqi history should be mentioned, the importance of tribes. It is difficult for postmodern Americans or other industrialized Westerners to understand the salience of tribal affiliation for most Iraqi Arabs who live in the countryside. There are vast tribal confederations that are ruled by chieftains (sheikhs) that demand the loyalty of millions of Iraqi Arabs who have not been urbanized. This was to be a key fact that the Americans would overlook during their 2003 invasion.

It should also be noted that Iraq had a relatively secular tradition of rule that went all the way back to the late Ottoman period. This tradition compared drastically to the neighboring Saudi Arabian theocracy, where harsh, medieval-style Islamic law was enforced by a religious police force known as the *mutaween*. In Saudi Arabia, alcohol was forbidden, females could not drive or vote, and religious councils promulgated strict religious laws for society. In contrast to the puritanical Saudi Wahhabi state that spawned the likes of bin Laden, various Iraqi officials joined the Iraqi Communist Party and worked to arrest or repress popular religious leaders, especially among the underprivileged but devout Shiites.

In light of this, it is not surprising that in 1959 Iraq established close ties with the Soviet Union during the rule of General Abd al Karim Qasim.[9] Iraq also supported a Marxist-Communist regime in the Arab Gulf state of Yemen. The Soviets reciprocated by helping develop Iraq's military, sending them infantry weapons, Scud short-range missiles, tanks, and MiG jet fighters. Iraq thus became a Soviet client state at this time, while Saudi Arabia's ruling family (but not necessarily its deeply religious people) became closely allied to the Americans.

But it was not the Iraqi Communist Party that was to ultimately govern Iraq, but another Left-leaning secular party known as the Baathist (Renaissance) Party. This socialist-Arab nationalist party was founded in the 1940s by a Syrian Arab Christian named Michael Aflaq. It called for the construction of a modern, secular-socialist society in the Arab world. The Baathists seized power in Iraq in the 1960s and began to build a centralized, socialist state. Under the Baathist regime anyone who wanted to rise up in Iraqi society and be successful had to join the Baathist Party. This meant that everyone in a position of authority, from parliament members to school principals to plant managers, were card-carrying members of the ruling Baathist Party. This was in many ways similar to the Communist system in the Soviet Union. Interestingly enough, the Baathist Party included many women who rose to high positions in the Iraqi government at a time when women were forced to wear *niqabs* (full body veils) and be driven to locations by male drivers in Saudi Arabia (women could not and still cannot drive in Saudi Arabia).

In Iraq, an ancient community of Christians also prospered under Baathist rule, and one of them, Tariq Aziz, even went on to become the foreign minister under Saddam Hussein. In Iraq it was not uncommon to find unveiled, secular women and men mixing in public and even drinking alcohol, something that would have gotten them arrested and sentenced by the religious police in the Wahhabi-dominated theocracy of Saudi Arabia.

Under Baathist rule, Iraq prospered and was heavily developed during the 1970s. This development was aided by the fact that Iraq sat on the world's second-largest reserve of oil. Oil exports helped fund highways, universities (where men and women studied together), the purchase of Soviet weaponry, hospitals, government buildings, and sports arenas, among other things. By the late 1970s Iraq was one of the most developed countries in the Middle East. While there were slums in Baghdad, where repressed Shiites lived in poverty, and there was the perennial issue of the Kurdish rebellions in the semi-autonomous north, Iraq's blend of socialism, oil money, and Soviet support seemed to promise a bright future for her people.

But this future was to be destroyed by the new president of Iraq's Revolutionary Supreme Council, Saddam Hussein. President Hussein was to lead Iraq into a bloody war against its neighbor, Shiite Iran, and to antagonize the powerful Americans by invading their client state of Kuwait. These two events would lead to the loss of hundreds of thousands of Iraqis' lives and see the human and financial potential of this modernizing socialist state squandered in pointless wars.

An exposition on Hussein, the Butcher of Baghdad, the man who created these wars, will show how detrimental he was to his country. While George W. Bush's invasion of Iraq in 2003 is indisputably the most contentious and hotly debated U.S. foreign policy endeavor since the Vietnam War, there should be no debate about the nefarious nature of Saddam Hussein's rule in Iraq.

Hussein came to power in 1979, and among his first moves was to have dozens of members of the government whom he believed to be real or potential enemies unceremoniously dragged out of a parliament session and summarily executed on the spot as their names were called out. This set the tone for his subsequent rule, and the *New York Times* was to later write:

> Hussein was one of the world's indisputably evil men: he murdered
> as many as a million of his people, many with poison gas. He
> tortured, maimed and imprisoned countless more. His unprovoked
> invasion of Iran is estimated to have left another million people
> dead. His seizure of Kuwait threw the Middle East into crisis. More
> insidious, arguably, was the psychological damage he inflicted on his
> own land. Hussein created a nation of informants—friends on
> friends, circles within circles—making an entire population com-
> plicit in his rule.[10]

The most dreaded prison in the gulag system run by Hussein was the Abu Ghraib prison near Baghdad, which held thousands of mainly political prisoners (this is the same prison that would become infamous later on when the United States took it over and used it as a center for the detainment, and ultimately, torture of suspected Iraqi insurgents in 2003). At Abu Ghraib, Hussein's men filmed themselves throwing people off buildings, torturing prisoners, and amputating the limbs of their victims.[11] Tens of thousands of Iraqis were buried in mass graves throughout the country while many more fled Hussein's brutality.

Hussein used the dreaded Mukhabaret secret police to establish himself as dictator and to empower his Sunni Arab clan from the northern town of Tikrit. He also created a cult of personality in Iraq and had statues, photos, and billboards of himself erected throughout the country. Hussein was usually photographed wearing a tailored, Western-style suit and fedora hat, often with a Cuban cigar in his mouth. His favorite movie was said to be the American mafia classic *The Godfather*, and his favorite drink Johnnie Walker whiskey (a habit that would have gotten him arrested in dry Saudi Arabia), and he had a penchant for beautiful women and writing his own novels.[12]

In other words, Hussein was everything that Osama bin Laden, the deeply devout, turban-wearing Saudi jihadi zealot was not. Whereas the bearded bin Laden based his life on the holy Koran and emulated the Prophet Muhammad, Hussein was said to emulate the Soviet dictator Joseph Stalin and was more influenced by Hollywood than Islam. Bin Laden lived the simple life of an ascetic, despite his wealth, while Hussein built extravagant palaces for himself throughout Iraq.

But Iraq's greatest problems were not to be with the Saudi Wahhabi theocracy of bin Laden's Saudi homeland, but with neighboring Shiite Iran. Up until 1979 Iran was ruled by a pro-U.S. ruler known as the Shah of Iran. But in that year the unpopular shah was overthrown by a popular rebellion. A fundamentalist firebrand-cleric named Ayatollah (Ayatollah is a Shiite religious title) Khomeini then took power and transformed secular Iran into a harsh Shiite theocracy. Khomeini then began to spread his Shiite revolution to repressed Shiites in other countries, such as Lebanon (where the Iranians ultimately sponsored the Shiite terrorist group Hezbollah) and Iraq.

Hussein, the Sunni leader of Iraq, felt that the Iranian Shiite revolution threatened his secular rule over millions of devout Iraqi Shiites and decided to act to prevent the religious fervor from Iran unifying the Shiite majority of his own country against his rule. But no one was prepared for the scale of his "containment" efforts. In 1980 Hussein launched a full-scale invasion of the Islamic Republic of Iran designed to take advantage of the revolutionary turmoil in that neighboring country. While many Americans simplistically lump all Muslims together, it is important to note that the subsequent Iran versus Iraq war was to be the longest and most deadly conventional war on the planet since World War II. Hundreds of thousands on both sides would die in the carnage as the Sunni-dominated Iraqis fought in a meat grinder against the Shiite Iranians.

Things quickly went wrong for the Iraqis, and the Iranians rallied to defend their nation using mass human wave attacks to repulse the invaders. Many of those involved in the Iranian counterassaults were Iranian high school–aged children, who were used as cannon fodder to surge across the battlefields absorbing Iraqi munitions and mines. These Iranian youth ran into combat with little training, but confident that the plastic keys around their necks given to them by their commanders would open the doors to paradise should they be "martyred" in combat.

To counter the fanatical Iranian swarm attacks, the desperate Iraqis began to use various weapons that had been banned by the international treaty known as the Geneva Conventions after World War I. During the First World War the various combatant countries used horrible weapons like mustard gas (a chemical weapon delivered by artillery shell that burns and blisters the eyes, skin, and lungs of those exposed to it) to kill or maim hundreds of thousands of soldiers. After the war, these weapons were banned from warfare by international law. Iraq, however, began to deploy these banned World War I–style weapons against the Iranians during the war.

The Iranians of course reported this illegal activity to the United Nations, but one of that body's Security Council members, the United States, did not appear to be overly concerned about the Iraqi deployment of banned WMDs (weapons of mass destruction) such as mustard and tabun gases. This stemmed from the fact that new revolutionary Iranian regime of Ayatollah Khomeini had become an enemy of America after overthrowing the pro-U.S. Shah of Iran in 1979. The Iranian Shiite revolutionaries began to declare the United States the "Great Satan" and even went so far as to flaunt all diplomatic conventions and capture the U.S. embassy in the Iranian capital, Tehran, and take its American personnel hostage for over a year.

Following the old Middle Eastern maxim that the "enemy of my enemy is my friend," the Americans therefore began to offer support to Baathist Iraq *at a time when it was actually deploying banned WMDs* (the irony of this being that the United States would later invade Iraq in 2003 under president George W. Bush and use the supposed existence of Iraqi WMDs as a prime rationale for the invasion). This covert U.S. aid to Iraq during the Iran-Iraq War included dual-use technology (i.e., technology that could be used for civilian or military purposes), millions of dollars in aid, satellite intelligence data on Iranian troop movements, training, and weapons.[13]

During the war, Iraq's restless Kurds in the northern mountains rebelled against Hussein and fought against his forces with Iranian assistance. Hussein brutally responded in 1988 by carrying out one the largest massacres of civilians via chemical weapons in history. As many as five thousand Kurds were gassed to death by WMDs dropped by Iraqi MiG fighter bombers and helicopters on the rebellious eastern Kurdish town of Halabja. It was a scene out of a horror movie as desperate Kurdish parents died holding their children and gas clouds billowed through the town burning the skin of screaming civilians. This atrocity was to be the source of President George W. Bush's subsequent 2002 claim that Hussein "Saddam Hussein is a man who is willing to gas his own people, willing to use weapons of mass destruction against Iraq citizens."[14]

Bush's White House spokesman would also state on the eve of the 2003 U.S. invasion of Iraq that "any person that would gas his own people is a threat to the world."[15] It should, however, be noted that the Kurds, who were fighting with Iranian support against Hussein at the time of the attack, were hardly "his own people," although they were (in theory at least) Iraqi citizens as Bush claimed fourteen years after the incident took place.

Tragically, the American president Ronald Reagan of course did not move to protect the Kurds from Hussein's WMDs at this time. It was only fifteen years later that the younger President Bush would belatedly utilize this atrocity as a rationale for launching a full-scale invasion of Iraq in 2003. He did so by stating, "I'm telling you I made the right decision for America because Saddam Hussein used weapons of mass destruction and invaded Kuwait."[16] Many people in the region felt it was disingenuous of George W. Bush to bring up the 1988 Halabja massacre of Kurds (which happened when the United States was tacitly supporting Hussein against Iran) as a subsequent rationale for overthrowing Hussein after so much time had passed.

Regardless of America's tacit support for Hussein during the war against Iran, the conflict came to an end in 1988. After the war, Iraq was in a state of ruin, and its economy was tattered. During the conflict, the Iraqi government had borrowed considerable money from the neighboring Sunni Arab country of Kuwait to keep the war going against Shiite Iran. After the war, Kuwait refused to forgive Iraq its debt and began drilling for oil in territory claimed by both countries. This incautious move infuriated Saddam Hussein, who had the fifth-largest army in the world. By 1990 Hussein had begun to threateningly move troops toward the border of the "Thirteenth Province" (Hussein's name for Kuwait, which he claimed had been an Iraqi province before being created as an independent state by the nineteenth-century British). At this time, the U.S. ambassador to Iraq, April Glaspie, had a fateful meeting with Hussein wherein she declared, "We [the Americans] have no opinion on your Arab-Arab conflicts, such as your dispute with Kuwait."

Hussein seemed to have inferred from this conversation that the Americans, who had overlooked his previous WMD war crimes against the Iranians and Kurds during the Ronald Reagan administration, would overlook his invasion of Kuwait. So, on August 2, 1990, Hussein's troops rolled across the border into Kuwait and easily defeated its small army of just sixteen thousand soldiers.[17] In Kuwait, Iraqi soldiers engaged in a looting spree and summary executions of resisters. Hussein gambled that the West did not have the stomach to repulse him from Iraq. With this one bold move, he had acquired control of Kuwait which sat on ten percent of the world's oil.

At the time, Iraq was not an enemy of the United States, but this act put Hussein squarely in the sights of new president George H. W. Bush (president 1989–93, often known as George Bush Sr. to delineate him from his son George W. Bush, "Bush Jr."). Bush Sr. called on Hussein to withdraw his troops from Kuwait. In this he was simply backing up the United Nations and the Arab League, both of which called on Iraq to withdraw from Kuwait. When Hussein refused to withdraw, the Americans began to work with the UN and allied Arab states to expel him from Kuwait.

Bush Sr. realized that if U.S. troops were to push Iraq out of Kuwait, they would have to do so from the territory of neighboring Saudi Arabia. This meant convincing the Saudis that Hussein was also a threat to their country. U.S. satellite photos were subsequently presented to the Saudis showing Iraqi troops massed on their borders, potentially for an invasion. Although Saudi frontier scouts saw no sign of the Iraqi troops and Hussein told the top U.S. diplomat in Baghdad, Joe Wilson (who would later make himself famous for debunking Bush Jr.'s claims that Iraq had purchased uranium "yellow cake" from the country of Niger), that he had no intentions of attacking the Saudi Kingdom, the Saudis decided to trust the photos instead.[18]

Many Saudi citizens who distrusted the Americans felt that the Saudi dynasty had been duped into letting American soldiers into their homeland. That is certainly what many conservative Saudi Wahhabis who distrusted pro-Israeli Americans thought when word spread that American "infidels" of both sexes would be arriving in their hundreds of thousands into the holy land of Saudi Arabia. The idea of American Christians and Jews arriving on the holiest soil in the world for Muslims was blasphemy for many fundamentalist Wahhabi Saudis because the Islamic tradition clearly states, "Let there be no two religions in Arabia" (i.e., only Islam is allowed in the holy land). Conspiracy-minded Saudis saw the arrival of U.S. troops in their land as a sign that the all-powerful Americans were secretly pulling the strings of the Saudi dynasty, and they feared a behind-the-scenes takeover of their country.

Among those paranoid Saudis who felt this way was the former mujahideen volunteer from Afghanistan Osama bin Laden. Far from relying on "infidel" Americans to defend Saudi Arabia from a possible Iraqi invasion (which many Saudis were skeptical about), bin Laden offered the Saudis the use of his thousands of "Afghan Arab" jihadi volunteers from Afghanistan. Bin Laden, who had made his reputation by inflating the story of his exploits at the battle of Jaji in 1987, clearly had delusions about the fighting capacity of his irregular fighters from the Soviet jihad. As stated earlier, these Arab Afghan volunteers most certainly did not defeat the Soviet invaders (that was done by Tajik and Pashtun mujahideen like Massoud and Haqqani), and many of the Arabs were actually derided by the Afghan mujahideen as "Gucci jihadis" for being so spoiled and ineffectual in combat. It is not surprising that the Saudi government politely refused bin Laden's bizarre offer to defend their kingdom from the massive battle-hardened, mechanized Iraqi army (the world's fifth largest) and instead turned to the American superpower to defend them.

Thus the die was cast that would lead to the U.S. military presence in the very land where the Prophet Muhammad himself had lived and forged a faith centuries earlier. This "silent occupation" of the core land of the Dar al Islam (Realm of Islam) would become, along with U.S. support for Israel, one of the primary catalysts for bin Laden's subsequent decision to declare a terrorist jihad on the United States of America in 1996.

But bin Laden's terror campaign was many years away, and at this time it was not fundamentalist jihadism that was the threat to the United States, but the secular government of Iraq. To defeat the Iraqis, President George H. W. Bush, who knew many Arab leaders personally, wisely decided to muster an international coalition instead of going it alone. This meant that Americans would not be acting unilaterally in their own self-serving interests, but would be acting as a deputy of the UN and the Arab League to enforce their multilateral resolutions calling for the Iraqis to evacuate Kuwait. America essentially had the mandate of the world community to act in expelling Hussein from Iraq. President Bush's global legitimization was crucial and compares drastically to his son's subsequent decision to invade Iraq in 2003 without the support of the UN, the Arab League, or even several key members of the NATO alliance who opposed the invasion (most notably Germany, France, and Turkey).

The allied coalition mustered by Bush Sr. to expel Iraq from Kuwait in 1990 consisted of thirty-four countries, including Afghanistan, Argentina, Australia, Bahrain, Bangladesh, Canada, Czechoslovakia, Denmark, Egypt, France, Germany, Greece, Hungary, Honduras, Italy, Kuwait, Morocco, The Netherlands, Niger, Norway, Oman, Pakistan, Poland, Portugal, Qatar, Saudi Arabia, Senegal, South Korea, Spain, Syria, Turkey, the United Arab Emirates, the United Kingdom, and the United States.[19] All told more than half a million coalition troops would be mustered by the Americans and their allies to enforce what became known as the "Powell Doctrine." This doctrine, named for the head of U.S. forces in the Iraq operation, General Colin Powell, called for an overwhelming use of force against the enemy to achieve total dominance on the battlefield. It also called for a strong support from the general public back home to overcome the divisiveness of the sort found in the Vietnam era.

The Iraq war was certainly popular in the United States and also had the support of the Arab states of the region and the UN. Most important, the Saudis and Egyptians would play a major role in the war, thus giving it legitimacy in the eyes of the Arab and Muslim worlds. Strategically, a key role was also played by NATO member Turkey (the very country that did not support Bush's son's subsequent 2003 invasion of Iraq) when a force of one hundred thousand Turkish soldiers mustered on the Iraqi border, thus forcing the Iraqis to divert forces to face their northern frontier. Germany, which did not actually send troops (another NATO member that would later oppose the 2003 invasion of Iraq), paid $10 billion to support Bush's 1991 war against Saddam Hussein to expel him from Kuwait.

But for all this global support, the heavy lifting in the January to February 1991 First Gulf War would be carried out by the Americans. While many feared another Vietnam, this battle was not to be fought in the jungles against guerillas, but in frontal combat in the open deserts of Saudi Arabia, Kuwait, and Iraq. The outcome was never in doubt.

The war, code-named "Operation Desert Storm" by the Americans and the "Mother of all Battles" by Hussein, lasted just one hundred days and ended in a total defeat of the Iraqis. The United States and its allies achieved a remarkable victory by gaining total air supremacy after shooting down dozens of Iraqi MiG fighter jets and then by beating the enemy's Soviet- or Chinese-built T-59, 69, and 72 battle tanks in the strategic Battle of Khafji (a border town in Saudi Arabia) and other battles. In final analysis, the vaunted million-man Iraqi army proved to be a paper tiger and could not stand up to a state-of-the-art U.S. military that had everything from F-117 Stealth Fighters, which could not be seen on Iraqi radars, to cruise missiles that could be fired from offshore ships to destroy targets across Iraq with remarkable precision.

The greatest strategic blow came when the allied force of French (who would later oppose Bush Jr.'s 2003 war), British, and Americans invaded southern Iraq and knocked out the elite Republican Guard (a crack Sunni unit), taking out hundreds of Iraqi tanks in the process. By February 25, 1991, the disheartened Iraqis were in full retreat with thousands surrendering to the French, British, and American forces.

As the Iraqis fled, the coalition forces followed them and eventually made it to within 150 miles of the capital of Baghdad before a ceasefire was declared. The conventional war had gone surprisingly well for America and its European and Muslim allies thus far. The Americans, for example, had suffered just 148 combat deaths, compared to as many as one hundred thousand Iraqi killed in action.[20] Many of the Iraqis had been killed when their trenches, tanks, or retreating columns were destroyed by superior American technology (much of this technological advancement came from a defense spending spree launched under President Ronald Reagan).

The big question now was what was the United States to do now that it had achieved its stated, UN-backed strategic objective, namely the liberation of Kuwait? At the time the Bush Sr. administration decided not to continue with the invasion and break into Baghdad with the aim of uprooting the Sunni-dominated Saddam Hussein regime.

There were several reasons for this decision. First, the CIA and neighboring Sunni Arab countries feared that if the United States and its allies toppled Saddam's secular Sunni regime, devout Iraqi Shiites with ties to America's enemy Shiite Iran would come to power and create an Islamic theocracy in Iraq along the lines of Ayatollah Khomeini's regime in Iran. In other words, Operation Desert Storm would become Operation Shiite Empowerment.

Second, President Bush had done a masterful job of forging a coalition backed by the UN and the Arab League, which included the Turks, Germans, French, Saudis, and Egyptians. If he was to exceed his UN mandate and try to forcefully occupy Baghdad and overthrow the entrenched, Sunni-dominated Baathist Party, this would lead to continued war and an open-ended occupation of a hostile land and shatter the temporary UN/Arab League–backed alliance. The Arab states and the UN did not support such ambitious plans as occupying Iraq and waging a total war to forcefully overthrow Hussein's fellow Sunni regime.

The Sunni Arab states in particular feared unleashing the Shiite Arabs in Iraq should Hussein be removed from power. There was also the question of how much stomach the American people had for a total occupation of Iraq that could devolve into a bloody insurgency quagmire, especially as Iraq had not actually attacked the United States, it had only invaded a neighboring Arab country. The general in charge of U.S. operations in Iraq, General "Stormin'" Norman Schwarzkopf, summed up the fears of American military might being caught in a Vietnam-style imbroglio in the deserts of Iraq as follows: "I am certain that had we taken all of Iraq, we would have been like a dinosaur in a tar pit—we would still be there, and we, not the United Nations, would be bearing the costs of the occupation."[21]

Ironically, no one better summed up the U.S. rationale for *not* turning the war to expel Hussein from Kuwait into a full-blown overthrow and occupation than the secretary of defense at the time of the 1991 invasion, Dick Cheney. To confront retroactive criticism of Bush Sr.'s decision not to invade and occupy Baghdad in 1991, Cheney (who as vice president would later go on to gain fame as the greatest proponent of Bush Jr.'s 2003 total invasion and occupation of Iraq) expressed his concerns about being "bogged down in the problems of trying to take over and govern Iraq" as follows:

> All of a sudden you've got a battle you're fighting in a major built-up city, a lot of civilians are around, significant limitations on our ability to use our most effective technologies and techniques. Once we had rounded him [Hussein] up and gotten rid of his government, then the question is what do you put in its place? You know, you then have accepted the responsibility for governing Iraq.
>
> I would guess if we had gone in there, we would still have forces in Baghdad today. We'd be running the country. We would not have been able to get everybody out and bring everybody home. And the

final point that I think needs to be made is this question of casualties. I don't think you could have done all of that without significant additional U.S. casualties, and while everybody was tremendously impressed with the low cost of the [1991] conflict, for the 146 Americans who were killed in action and for their families, it wasn't a cheap war. And the question in my mind is, how many additional American casualties is Saddam [Hussein] worth? And the answer is, not that damned many. So, I think we got it right, both when we decided to expel him from Kuwait, but also when the President made the decision that we'd achieved our objectives and we were not going to go get bogged down in the problems of trying to take over and govern Iraq.[22]

For his part, George Bush Sr. explained his decision not to occupy Iraq and overthrow its government in 1991 as follows:

Trying to eliminate Saddam, extending the ground war into an occupation of Iraq, would have violated our guideline about not changing objectives in midstream, engaging in "mission creep," and would have incurred incalculable human and political costs. . . . We would have been forced to occupy Baghdad and, in effect, rule Iraq. The coalition would instantly have collapsed, the Arabs deserting it in anger and other allies pulling out as well. Under those circumstances, furthermore, we had been self-consciously trying to set a pattern for handling aggression in the post–cold war world. Going in and occupying Iraq, thus unilaterally exceeding the U.N.'s mandate, would have destroyed the precedent of international response to aggression we hoped to establish. Had we gone the invasion route, the U.S. could conceivably still be an occupying power in a bitterly hostile land. It would have been a dramatically different—and perhaps barren—outcome.

Part of the reason the United States did not choose to override its UN mandate and transform the war from one of expulsion from Kuwait to one of occupying and overthrowing the government of Iraq might have lain in Bush Sr.'s moderating, balanced personality. Thomas Friedman has written of Bush, "On foreign policy, the elder Bush maintained a healthy balance between realism and idealism, unilateralism and multilateralism, American strength and American diplomacy. He believed that international institutions like the U.N. could be force multipliers of U.S. power."[23]

But it was exactly this balanced perspective toward the use of U.S. military strength in a multilateral way, through the auspices of the UN and Arab League, that was to disappoint some Americans who wanted to unilaterally go all the way to Baghdad and continue the war without the support of the coalition allies. There was to be a sense of "unfinished business" about the First Gulf War of 1991 that was to percolate among certain hawkish Republican thinkers in the subsequent years. This dissatisfaction would manifest itself in the theories of a small clique of Republican intellectuals who would call themselves the "Neo-Cons" (i.e., New Conservatives). While the Neo-Cons would not be given access to the halls of power under George Bush Sr. or his successor, Bill Clinton, they would come to have a tremendous influence on George Bush Jr. when he assumed the presidency in 2001.

But at the end of the 1991 Gulf War, the Neo-Cons were not in power, and President H. W. Bush, the UN, the Arab League, and the overwhelming majority of the American people were all satisfied with seeing Hussein humiliated and weakened militarily. Bush Sr.'s approval rating soared to 90 percent, in the days after the war's astoundingly successful conclusion, the highest thus far for a president in American history.[24]

America's victory had been unprecedented and exorcized the demons of Vietnam. One cannot underestimate the damage done to Hussein's fighting force in the brief war. Hussein's estimated losses included the destruction of 104 airplanes; 3,700 out of 4,280 battle tanks; 2,400 of 2,870 assorted other armored vehicles; 2,600 of 3,110 assorted artillery pieces; 19 naval ships sunk (6 damaged); and most important, 42 divisions made combat ineffective.[25]

To compound matters the UN passed Resolution 687, which was to have tremendous impact on Iraq over the succeeding years. Surprisingly, few Americans have ever heard of this major UN resolution, despite its tremendous importance. Resolution 687 essentially forced the defeated Iraqis to allow UN arms inspectors into their country to systematically dismantle all of Hussein's WMD programs. Resolution 687 was to pave the way for the subsequent destruction of the very weapons of mass destruction programs that George Bush Jr. would subsequently use as a rationale for invading Iraq in 2003.

The stipulations of Resolution 687 are extremely important in light of the charges leveled by the Bush Jr. administration that Iraq needed to be invaded in 2003 in order to protect America from Iraqi chemical, biological, and nuclear WMDs. Some of Resolution 687's most important clauses included the following:

> 8. [The UN] Decides that Iraq shall unconditionally accept the destruction, removal, or rendering harmless, under international supervision, of:
> (a) All chemical and biological weapons and all stocks of agents and all related subsystems and components and all research, development, support and manufacturing facilities;
> (b) All ballistic missiles with a range greater than 150 kilometers and related major parts, and repair and production facilities;
> 9. Decides, for the implementation of paragraph 8 above, the following:
> (a) Iraq shall submit to the Secretary-General, within fifteen days of the adoption of the present resolution, a declaration of the locations, amounts and types of all items specified in paragraph 8 and agree to urgent, on-site inspection as specified below;
> 10. Decides that Iraq shall unconditionally undertake not to use, develop, construct or acquire any of the items specified in paragraphs 8 and 9 above.[26]

In other words, Iraq's *chemical* and *biological* WMDs were to be destroyed, and all its short- or medium-range ballistic missiles (mainly Scuds or variants thereof) with an ability to damage such neighbors as America's ally Israel were to be destroyed. In addition, further production of these banned weapons was prohibited by the UN. If this were not punishing enough, Resolution 687 also had the following clause:

> 12. [The UN] Decides that Iraq shall unconditionally agree not to acquire or develop nuclear weapons or nuclear-weapons-usable material or any subsystems or components or any research, development, support or manufacturing facilities related to the above; to submit to the Secretary-General and the Director-General of the International Atomic Energy Agency within fifteen days of the adoption of the present resolution a declaration of the locations, amounts, and types of all items specified above; to place all of its nuclear-weapons-usable materials under the exclusive control, for custody and removal, of the International Atomic Energy Agency,

with the assistance and cooperation of the Special Commission as
provided for in the plan of the Secretary-General discussed in
paragraph.[27]

This meant that anything related to *nuclear weapons* production was also to
be destroyed by the UN as well. While Iraq did not have a nuclear power
plant (its first and last attempt to build one had been thwarted in 1981 when
Israel launched a daring air raid on the Iraqi nuclear plant at Osirak and destroyed it), there were legitimate fears that Iraq would once again try to build
a nuclear power program. This clause in Resolution 687 meant that Iraq
could not build a nuclear weapons program in the future. It also meant that
anything related to nuclear weapons was to be destroyed (it should, however,
be emphatically stated that Iraq had *never* developed a nuclear weapon; only
one Muslim country has developed nukes, and that is Pakistan).

To enforce these resolutions, the UN established UNSCOM (the UN Special Commission). This multinational organization's mandate was to:

> Carry out immediate on-site inspections of Iraq's biological, chemi-
> cal and missile capabilities; to take possession for destruction,
> removal or rendering harmless of all chemical and biological
> weapons and all stocks of agents and all related sub-systems and
> components and all research, development, support and manufac-
> turing facilities. . . . The Commission was also requested to assist the
> Director General of the IAEA [International Atomic Energy
> Agency], which, under resolution 687, was requested to undertake
> activities similar to those of the Commission but specifically in the
> nuclear field.[28]

In other words, the UN Special Commission (which included many Americans, including some members who were either CIA agents or inspectors reporting to the CIA) was to be given a carte blanche to move freely around
Iraq investigating and carrying out surprise inspections of all nuclear, chemical, and biological WMD facilities.[29] With American U-2 spy planes flying
overhead to monitor events on the ground, NSA satellites monitoring radio
communications, and inspectors from throughout the world raiding anything that looked suspicious (at one time even ice cream trucks were raided),
UNSCOM set out to systematically destroy Iraq's WMD program.[30]

That is exactly what the UNSCOM proceeded to do in subsequent years during the course of 550 inspections covering some 160 facilities.[31] The UN inspectors destroyed vast quantities of Iraqi WMDs, from 155 mm artillery shells designed to carry mustard gas and R 400 chemical bombs, to labs designed to create biological weapons. With the ever-present threat of the U.S. Air Force backing them up (and U.S. aerial and satellite surveillance helping them find weapons sites), the UNSCOM agents systematically swept over Iraq overseeing the destruction of missiles and chemical and biological weapons. According to the UNSCOM it destroyed:

- 38,537 filled and empty chemical munitions
- 690 tons of chemical weapons agent
- more than 3,000 tons of precursors chemicals
- 426 pieces of chemical weapons production equipment
- 91 pieces of related analytical instruments
- the entire Al-Hakam facility, Iraq's main biological weapons production facility
- a variety of biological weapons production equipment and materials
- 30 missile chemical warheads[32]

UNSCOM also destroyed nuclear-related equipment known as calutrons in 1991.[33] Considerable work was done on destroying Iraq's primitive ballistic missile program as well, although it should be stated that these missiles were mainly Soviet-built Scud missiles or variants called al Samouds that had a short range (they could hit neighboring Saudi Arabia or Israel but were not ICBMs (intercontinental ballistic missiles) of the sort the Soviets used to target cities in North America).

The vast majority of Iraqi WMD material that was destroyed by UNSCOM in the 1990s consisted of chemical and biological weapons of the sort used against Iran in the 1980s and what was found at the Al Hakam lab, Iraq's main center for the development of biological warfare agents. It must emphatically be stated that there were no nuclear plants to be destroyed in Iraq (as mentioned earlier, the Israelis had already bombed Iraq's only (and non-functioning) nuclear power plant at Osirak back in 1981).[34] Besides the previously mentioned calutrons (a mass spectrometer used for separating the isotopes of uranium), there was little to be destroyed in the way of a nuclear weapons program. Of course nuclear power plants are large things and could not be hidden from U-2 spy planes, American NSA satellites, or arms inspectors who were blanketing the country.

In addition, the UN and NATO implemented an arms embargo on Iraq, which meant that Iraq could not import materials to rebuild its destroyed chemical and biological weapons program or inaugurate the building of another nuclear power plant like the one destroyed by the Israelis in 1981. To circumvent this embargo and try to gain battlefield parity with Shiite Iran, Hussein once tried smuggling in parts to build a "Super Gun" (i.e., a massive cannon that could send artillery shells great distances), but the UN and NATO arms inspectors discovered the gun parts before they could be delivered.

Thus Saddam Hussein had his deadly "toys" systematically dismantled and destroyed from 1991 to 1998 by the UN arms inspectors and was prevented by arms sanctions and embargos from reconstituting them. During this period, National Public Radio would report that in 1994 the UN completed "the destruction of Iraq's known chemical weapons and production equipment. IAEA teams largely completed their mandate to neutralize Iraq's nuclear program, including the destruction of facilities Iraq had not even declared to inspectors."[35]

Corroboration for this sort of reporting came from none other than Hussein Kamel, the brother-in-law of Saddam Hussein and the very man who had been in charge of Iraq's WMD program. In 1995 he had a feud with Saddam Hussein and escaped to Jordan to save his life. There he carried out an interview with CNN's Brent Sadler, which is insightful. Here is the most important section in that interview:

> *Sadler:* Can you state here and now—does Iraq still to this day hold
>   weapons of mass destruction?
> *Kamel:* No. Iraq does not possess any weapons of mass destruction. I
>   am being completely honest about this.[36]

Hussein Kamel would also state emphatically, before being subsequently killed by Hussein for revealing state secrets, that "all chemical weapons were destroyed. I ordered the destruction of all chemical weapons. All weapons—biological, chemical, missile, nuclear—were destroyed."[37]

Support for this eyewitness defector's claim came from one U.S. member of the UNSCOM inspection team, Scott Ritter, who would later sum up the results of the UNSCOM WMD inspections in a 1999 interview with the Federation of American Scientists: "When you ask the question, 'Does Iraq possess militarily viable biological or chemical weapons?' the answer is no! It is a resounding NO. Can Iraq produce today chemical weapons on a meaningful scale? No! Can Iraq produce biological weapons on a meaningful scale? No! Ballistic missiles? No! It is 'no' across the board. So from a qualitative standpoint, Iraq has been disarmed. Iraq today possesses no meaningful weapons of mass destruction capability."[38]

But just before Ritter made his emphatic statement, UNSCOM, however, ran into some problems with the Iraqis, who were continuing what had been a cat-and-mouse game with the inspectors. In response, the United States and British warned the UN inspectors to leave the country as they would begin a bombing campaign to destroy any possible remaining chemical or biological facilities. For four days in December 1998, in a campaign known as Operation Desert Fox, President Clinton ordered the systematic bombing of any remaining WMD sites that had not already been destroyed during the seven-year inspection process. Operation Desert Fox aimed to destroy the remaining WMD facilities according to General Shelton, who said, "We're going after everything involved with weapons of mass destruction from transport to manufacturing to delivery."[39]

During the operation, the United States fired more cruise missiles (415) than during the entire 1991 Gulf War (317).[40] The U.S. military subsequently claimed it had destroyed "19 sites housing security details for Hussein's weapons of mass destruction program and 11 weapons of mass destruction industrial and production facilities."[41] In the words of General Anthony Zinni, the intense nationwide bombing campaign "accomplished everything militarily that we wanted it to" and left the Iraqis "so dazed and rattled they were virtually headless."[42] Charles Ferguson of the Council on Foreign Relations would claim, "Militarily, Desert Fox appeared to be a smashing success. It hit 85 percent of its targets and 74 percent of all strikes were highly effective, according to Pentagon analysts."[43]

Operation Desert Fox was essentially the end of the Iraq's WMD program. In the words of Thomas Ricks, *Washington Post* journalist and author of the best seller about the war in Iraq *Fiasco*, the Iraqis had "given up" because their remaining weapons facilities had been destroyed and could not be rebuilt without being detected by the Americans.[44] David Kay was subsequently appointed by President Bush Jr. to be head of the Iraq Survey Group, which was put in charge of finding Iraq's nuclear, chemical, and biological weapons after the 2003 U.S. invasion of Iraq. He would later state that after 1998's Desert Fox, Iraq's WMD program "withered away and never got momentum again."[45] So paranoid was Hussein of being attacked again on such a scale that, when an Iraqi scientist later returned from Russia and claimed he might be able to get a nuclear warhead, Hussein had him executed on the spot for fear that the Americans might hear about it.[46]

Bush Sr.'s and Clinton's policies of containing Hussein and destroying his remaining stockpiles were a resounding success by all accounts. Hussein was essentially defanged by 1998. U.S. Marine general Anthony Zinni, former head of Central Command, would later state, "Containment worked. Look at Saddam—what did he have? He didn't threaten anyone in the region. He was contained. It was a pain in the ass, but he was contained. He had a deteriorated military. He wasn't a threat to anyone in the region."[47]

Clearly Hussein had been neutralized by the UN-backed containment sanctions and traumatized by Clinton's attack in 1998. Many observers felt that the withering destruction caused by the Operation Desert Fox bombing campaign to Iraq's remaining WMD facilities and infrastructure might actually lead to the overthrow of Hussein. Bill Clinton clearly saw regime change in Iraq as a desired outcome. To achieve this objective, Clinton signed into law the Iraq Liberation Act. This act called for "regime change" in Iraq, years before Bush Jr. called for the same thing (although Clinton most certainly never envisioned a full-scale, preemptive invasion and complete occupation of Baghdad and the Republic of Iraq by U.S. forces to achieve this purpose).

But for all the effectiveness of 1998's Operation Desert Fox in wiping out the last remnants of Hussein's WMD program, it did not lead to the overthrow of Hussein's regime. And it should be restated that in preparation for Desert Fox the UN weapons inspectors had all been pulled out of Iraq for their own safety. Extraordinarily, there was thus no way for the United States to determine from 1998 until the eve of the 2003 invasion of Iraq the status of Iraq's obliterated WMD program. While the UN embargo meant that Hussein could not possibly import the equipment needed to rebuild his destroyed WMD programs, the lack of certainty caused by the UNSCOM departure led to considerable speculation about Hussein's subsequent activities (especially among Neo-Cons). This was in part because of Hussein's own propensity to be evasive on the issue.

All evidence in the succeeding years, however, seemed to indicate that Hussein had not begun to rebuild his WMD program from the rubble. A document in the National Security Archives, for example, has the following to say on this vexing issue: "Following Saddam Hussein's 1998 final expulsion of UN weapons inspectors from Iraq, very little new information fell into the hands of U.S. intelligence. Notable exceptions include data from Iraqi Foreign Minister Naji Sabri, recruited as a CIA source, and from Iraqi scientists clandestinely approached by the CIA under a covert program. Both these streams of information denied the existence of Iraqi WMD."[48] In retrospect, the world knows that Hussein did not of course covertly rebuild his shattered *chemical* and *biological* weapons programs (few if any nuclear weapons experts believed he could actually reconstruct a *nuclear* weapons program considering the scale of such a project and the fact the U.S. satellites and planes were constantly flying over Iraq). But at the time (1998–2002) Hussein was deliberately evasive about the matter. At times he seemed to almost be bluffing and pretending he had a good hand of WMD "cards" to play, when his chemical and biological program had in actuality been totally dismantled by UNSCOM, the arms embargo, and 1998's Operation Desert Fox.

The main question then is why did Hussein play such a dangerous bluffing game when both Clinton and his successor Bush Jr. saw Iraq's WMD program as a threat? We now know why. Israeli scholar Amaztia Bara summed up Hussein's rationale in the journal *Foreign Affairs* as follows: "As the millennium approached Saddam played a double game. We know that he eventually gave up his WMD capabilities. But he refused to come clean about this, trying to convince others that he secretly retained a WMD arsenal. On some level he believed it was essential to keep Iran fearful, but his domestic opponents were even more of an audience. He thought it was vital for him to keep the fear of unconventional weapons hanging, like the sword of Damocles, over the heads of Iraq's rebellious Shiite population."[49] The Bush Jr. administration ultimately concurred with the above finding, and the Iraq Survey Group, which was appointed by George W. Bush to look for Iraq's WMDs after the 2003 invasion, declared "Iraq's fears of Iran's growing military strength and Baghdad's concern that inspections would expose its weaknesses to Iran led Baghdad to obfuscate the inspection process."[50]

Thus, in the fateful years and months leading up to 9/11, Hussein miscalculated badly in an effort to intimidate his country's main enemy, Shiite Iran, and his own country's rebellious Shiite population by pretending he still had WMDs to be used against them. With no ability to grasp the drastic nature of the changing climate in the United States in the aftermath of bin Laden's unprecedented mass casualty terrorist attack on September 11, 2001, Hussein continued to stall the return of UN inspections right up until the eve of the March 2003 U.S. invasion (the UN inspectors were not allowed back in until November 2002). According to Charles Duelfer, who led the U.S. WMD hunt in Iraq, Hussein "thought the US intelligence was good enough to figure out the real story."[51]

But by the time the UN weapons inspectors returned to his country in late 2002, it was too late; President Bush Jr., a hawk who was strongly influenced by the Neo-Cons who considered his father's decision to avoid occupying Iraq in 1991 a mistake, was now president. Even as the UN inspectors began to scour Iraq in 2002 in an ultimately unsuccessful search to find any reconstituted chemical or biological WMDs, Bush Jr. fatefully declared, "The United States of America will not permit the world's most dangerous regimes to threaten us with the world's most destructive weapons." Thus Hussein's anti-Shiite weapons of mass destruction bluff backfired. It ultimately led to the unimaginable, a full-scale 2003 U.S. invasion designed to complete what the Neo-Cons called the "unfinished business" of the 1991 Gulf War and save the United States from a WMD threat that no longer existed. Bush and his Neo-Con backers also had grand visions of planting the seeds of transformative democracy in Iraq and believed it would spread to surrounding countries.

But it was not only the seeds of the 2003 U.S. invasion of Iraq that were planted in the First Gulf War of 1991. The seeds of the 2001 invasion of Afghanistan known as Operation Enduring Freedom were also inadvertently planted in the First Gulf War. As improbable as this may seem, the roots of the 2001 U.S. invasion of Taliban-controlled Afghanistan were actually laid in the aftermath of Bush Sr.'s 1991 defeat of Saddam Hussein in Operation Desert Storm. To understand this linkage these two campaigns one must once again turn to the Saudi Wahhabi fundamentalist Osama bin Laden.

Bin Laden watched the war between the American "infidels" and Hussein, the secular-Baathist *munafiq* (hypocrite), with much the same glee that the Americans watched the Soviets and the Nazis fight it out in the beginning of World War II. But bin Laden's joy at watching the United States defeat of Hussein turned to outrage in the wake of the war when President Bush Sr. made the fateful decision to keep American troops in Saudi Arabia after the war. A force of thirty-seven thousand U.S. soldiers was kept in the holy land of Saudi Arabia, mainly in a massive, twenty-five-by-forty-mile air base they had constructed known as Al Sultan.[52] There was also a U.S. military presence at Dahran, four hundred miles from the second holiest city of Medina. Bin Laden and many fundamentalist Saudis saw these developments as both a "stealth occupation" of their homeland and an act of blasphemy in a land where there could be only one religion. One Saudi cleric was to state, "What is happening in the Gulf is part of a larger Western design to dominate the whole Arab and Muslim world."[53] Another would state, "America has occupied Saudi Arabia."[54]

For bin Laden, who saw the world through the lenses of fundamentalist Wahhabi Islam, the U.S. "silent invasion" of his homeland was no different than that of the Jews in Palestine or the Soviets in Afghanistan. Once again the "Zionist Crusaders" were seeking to control the lands of the Muslim believers. At this time bin Laden came to hate the Saudi dynasty for allowing the American "infidels" into his country. When he began to castigate the Saudi leaders for their deal with the American "devil," his Saudi citizenship was revoked.

These events were to begin bin Laden's fateful journey from being a mujahideen hero from the Afghan jihad against the Soviets in the 1980s to an outlaw who declared a terror war on the Americans with the aim of forcing them out of the Dar al Islam. It was this terroristic jihad that would, in the ultimate of ironies, awaken the sleeping American giant and send it across the globe to occupy not one, but two Muslim states in Central Asia and the Middle East . . . all in the name of trying to destroy the threat of bin Laden's *stateless* terrorist organization.

Al Qaeda 101:
The Beginning of bin Laden's Jihadi Terror Campaign

While bin Laden was rightly defined by Americans as a terrorist who called for the killing of their country's civilians, he was seen by many Saudi Wahhabis as pious believer in God who put his money where his mouth was. Bin Laden both funded and fought in the jihad against the Soviets in Afghanistan. But his close relationship with the Saudi royal family began to fray when he became too outspoken in his criticism of their alliance with the Americans. Bin Laden's father had once offered his construction company's bulldozers to help in the Arab war against the Israelis, and bin Laden similarly hated the Americans for their strong support of Israel over the Palestinians. Now these same Americans (including Jewish Americans) were in his own country, and bin Laden could not contain his fury. The image of godless Americans fornicating, drinking alcohol, and profaning Friday, the holy day for Muslims, on Saudi soil was disseminated by many firebrand preachers, and bin Laden seemed to subscribe to it.

As bin Laden's opposition to the Saudi dynasty increased, the Saudis put him under de facto house arrest. But in 1991 he escaped and ultimately made his way to the fundamentalist-dominated African country of Sudan. There he united with hundreds of Afghan Arab jihad volunteers from the 1980s, including the number two in Al Qaeda, Ayman al Zawahiri. Zawahiri, an

Egyptian, was, like bin Laden, an exile from his own homeland who had turned on his country's leaders. Zawahiri dreamed of overthrowing the "Pharaoh" of Egypt, the pro-American secular president, Hosni Mubarak. On one occasion gunmen linked to Zawahiri even tried assassinating Mubarak during a state visit to Ethiopia. This act brought Al Qaeda to the attention of the Egyptians at a time when bin Laden was still not recognized by the Americans as a major threat.

While bin Laden was not on the Americans' radar at this time, another Muslim named Ramzi Yousef caught their attention when he and his followers set off a car bomb in 1993 in the World Trade Center in New York. This bombing, which killed six people, was not carried out by Al Qaeda but by the "Liberation Army, Fifth Battalion." Yousef, a Pakistani, claimed to be attacking the United States for its support of Israel in its wars with the Palestinians. He demanded "an end to all US aid to Israel and an end to diplomatic relations with Israel."[55]

Yousef and his accomplices were subsequently captured when one of them returned to the Ryder company to get his deposit back on the rental truck used to carry the bomb to the World Trade Center (by this time the FBI had found the VIN number on the truck's axel and traced it to a Ryder store in Jersey City). Following his subsequent arrest in Pakistan, Yousef was flown in a helicopter past the World Trade Center by the FBI. One agent told him, "Look down there, they're still standing," to which Yousef replied (in reference to the weakness of his bomb) "They wouldn't be if I had enough money and explosives."[56]

But it was not just U.S. support for Israel that infuriated the terrorists; it was the continuing American presence in the holy land of Saudi Arabia. Two years later (in 1995) this hatred of U.S. troops in the land of Mecca and Medina manifested itself in a bombing in Riyadh, Saudi Arabia. of a U.S.-operated Saudi National Guard building. Five Americans and two Indians were killed in the bombing, which was carried out by Saudis who had fought in Afghanistan (but not Al Qaeda members). In 1996 an even larger bomb was set off outside the Khobar Towers in Khobar, Saudi Arabia, which killed nineteen U.S. servicemen living in this building, which had been built to house U.S. troops. The Saudis blamed the Saudi Shiite group Hizbullah al Hijaz for the blast, but it may have been carried out by local Saudi Wahhabi fundamentalists who resented the U.S. presence in Saudi Arabia.

It should be stated that Saudi fundamentalist extremists were not the only ones engaging in terrorism in the region in the early to mid-1990s. There was also the case of the failed attempt to kill former president Bush Sr. and his family when they visited Kuwait in 1993 to celebrate the liberation of the country from Saddam Hussein's forces. Kuwaiti security services foiled a clumsy attempt by the Iraqi Intelligence Service to set off a remote-control car bomb to kill the former U.S. president and his entourage. Subsequent interrogations of the arrested bombers revealed that they were Iraqi agents.[57]

In retaliation for the attempt on the former president's life, President Clinton bombed the Iraqi Intelligence Headquarters with cruise missiles. Bush Jr. never forgave Hussein for this attempt to kill his father, and in 2002 he described Hussein as "the man who tried to kill my dad."[58]

This brings up a natural question. Because Hussein, the secular ruler of Iraq, hated Bush Sr. and the Americans for repelling him from Kuwait in 1991, and bin Laden, the exiled Saudi jihadi veteran, hated the Americans for their "silent occupation" of the holy land of Saudi Arabia, might not these two vastly different figures have found common cause in carrying out a terror campaign against the Americans?

As it transpires, the 9/11 Commission, a bipartisan Republican/Democrat group that was appointed by President Bush Jr. to analyze the background history of the September 11th attacks, found no evidence of a "collaborative operational relationship" between the socialist ruler of Iraq and the exiled Saudi religious dissident. Far from being allies, during his time in Sudan and later in Afghanistan, bin Laden funded anti–Saddam Hussein Kurdish groups that operated in the autonomous Kurdish areas in the mountains of northern Iraq. While it is true that bin Laden's emissaries once requested that Saddam Hussein allow him to set up their headquarters in his country, the Iraqis did not respond to the request.

The following excerpt from the bipartisan (five Republicans and five Democrats) "9/11 Commission Report" sheds some much-needed light on this vitally important issue of the lack of operational ties between bin Laden and Saddam Hussein. It states:

> Bin Ladin was also willing to explore possibilities for cooperation with Iraq, even though Iraq's dictator, Saddam Hussein, had never had an Islamist agenda—save for his opportunistic pose as a defender of the faithful against "Crusaders" during the Gulf War of 1991. Moreover, *Bin Ladin had in fact been sponsoring anti–Saddam Islamists in Iraqi Kurdistan, and sought to attract them into his Islamic army* [emphasis mine].

To protect his own ties with Iraq, [the Sudanese leader] Turabi reportedly brokered an agreement that Bin Ladin would stop supporting activities against Saddam. Bin Ladin apparently honored this pledge, at least for a time, although he continued to aid a group of Islamist extremists operating in part of Iraq [Kurdistan] outside of Baghdad's control. In the late 1990s, these extremist groups suffered major defeats by Kurdish forces. In 2001, with Bin Ladin's help they re-formed into an organization called Ansar al Islam. There are indications that by then the Iraqi regime tolerated and may even have helped Ansar al Islam against the common Kurdish enemy.

With the Sudanese regime acting as intermediary, Bin Ladin himself met with a senior Iraqi intelligence officer in Khartoum [the capital of Sudan] in late 1994 or early 1995. Bin Ladin is said to have asked for space to establish training camps, as well as assistance in procuring weapons, but there is no evidence that Iraq responded to this request. As described below, the ensuing years saw additional efforts to establish connections.

There is also evidence that around this time Bin Ladin sent out a number of feelers to the Iraqi regime, offering some cooperation. None are reported to have received a significant response. *According to one report, Saddam Hussein's efforts at this time to rebuild relations with the Saudis and other Middle Eastern regimes led him to stay clear of Bin Ladin* [emphasis mine].

In mid-1998, the situation reversed; it was Iraq that reportedly took the initiative. In March 1998, after Bin Ladin's public fatwa [decree] against the United States, two al Qaeda members reportedly went to Iraq to meet with Iraqi intelligence. In July, an Iraqi delegation traveled to Afghanistan to meet first with the Taliban and then with Bin Ladin. Sources reported that one, or perhaps both, of these meetings was apparently arranged through Bin Ladin's Egyptian deputy, Zawahiri, who had ties of his own to the Iraqis.

In 1998, Iraq was under intensifying U.S. pressure, which culminated in a series of large air attacks in December [i.e., Bill Clinton's Operation Desert Fox]. Similar meetings between Iraqi officials and Bin Ladin or his aides may have occurred in 1999 during a period of some reported strains with the Taliban. According to the reporting, Iraqi officials offered Bin Ladin a safe haven in Iraq. Bin Ladin declined, apparently judging that his circumstances in

Afghanistan remained more favorable than the Iraqi alternative. The reports describe friendly contacts and indicate some common themes in both sides' hatred of the United States. *But to date we have seen no evidence that these or the earlier contacts ever developed into a collaborative operational relationship. Nor have we seen evidence indicating that Iraq cooperated with al Qaeda in developing or carrying out any attacks against the United States.* [emphasis mine][59]

CIA head George Tenet firmly agreed with these findings that put daylight between bin Laden and Hussein and stated, "We could never verify that there was any Iraqi authority, direction and control, complicity with al-Qaeda for 9/11 or any operational act against America, period."[60] The 9/11 Commission also found that "Saddam assessed Usama bin Ladin and al-Qaida as a threat rather than a potential partner to be exploited to attack the United States."[61] Support for the bipartisan 9/11 Commission's findings that bin Laden was not in cahoots with Hussein came from a most unusual source, Al Qaeda. One of bin Laden's former Al Qaeda operatives who testified against other Al Qaeda operatives, for example, adamantly stated, "Saddam Hussein he don't believe in Islam. He got something called the Ba'ath (Arab socialist political party). I remember even bin Laden himself in '88 he make lecture against Saddam. He say Saddam is Ba'athist and Saddam one day he going to take over all of Gulf area. I remember that in '88 he make that lecture in Pakistan and everybody listen to that lecture."[62] Another Al Qaeda agent reported of bin Laden, "He doesn't believe [Saddam] is a Muslim. So he never liked or trusted him."[63] Prince Turki, a Saudi leader who knew bin Laden personally, stated, "Iraq does not come very high in the estimations of bin Laden. He thinks of Saddam Hussein as an apostate, an infidel or someone who is not worthy of being a fellow Muslim."[64] Jamal al Fadl, an Al Qaeda defector, told U.S. authorities that bin Laden criticized Saddam "sometimes for attacking Muslims and killing women and children, but most importantly for not believing in most of Islam and for setting up his own political party, the Baath [Socialist Party]."[65] Bin Laden said of Hussein's Socialist-Baathist party, "Socialists are infidels wherever they are."[66]

Peter Bergen, a terrorism analyst for CNN who actually interviewed bin Laden in Afghanistan, agreed and emphatically declared, "Al Qaeda's leader had long been an opponent of the Iraqi dictator."[67] Hamid Mir, a Pakistani journalist who interviewed bin Laden, said of the Al Qaeda leader: "He condemned Saddam Hussein in my interview. He gave such kind of abuses that

it was very difficult for me to write, [calling Hussein a] socialist motherfucker. [He said], 'The land of the Arab world, the land is like a mother, and
Saddam Hussein is fucking his mother.' He also explained that Saddam Hussein is against us [i.e., against Al Qaeda], and he discourages Iraqi boys to
come to Afghanistan."[68] A Palestinian journalist who interviewed bin Laden
similarly found that the Al Qaeda leader despised Saddam Hussein. This
source stated, "He [bin Laden] didn't like him [Hussein], and he told me he
wanted to kick him out of Iraq, as he considered the Ba'th regime to be an
atheist regime. He considered Saddam Hussein an atheist, and he hates an
atheist."[69]

Daniel Benjamin of the *New York Times* reported in an article entitled
"Saddam Hussein and Al Qaeda Are Not Allies": "Iraq and Al Qaeda are not
obvious allies. In fact, they are natural enemies. A central tenet of Al Qaeda's
jihadist ideology is that secular Muslim rulers and their regimes have oppressed the believers and plunged Islam into a historic crisis. Hence, a para-
mount goal of Islamist revolutionaries for almost half a century has been the
destruction of the regimes of such leaders."[70] Saddam Hussein seemed to feel
the same way about bin Laden. Hussein, who proudly supported Palestinian
terrorists in their war with Israel, would declare, "If we had a relationship
with Al Qaida and we believed in that relationship, we wouldn't be ashamed
to admit it. Therefore I would like to tell you directly that we have no relationship with Al Qaida."[71] Daniel Benjamin has written:

> Like other Middle Eastern rulers, Saddam Hussein has long recog-
> nized that Al Qaeda and like-minded Islamists represent a threat to
> his regime. Consequently, he has shown no interest in working with
> them against their common enemy, the United States. This was the
> understanding of American intelligence in the 1990's. In 1998, the
> National Security Council assigned staff to determine whether that
> conclusion was justified. After reviewing all the available intelligence
> that could have pointed to a connection between Al Qaeda and Iraq,
> the group found no evidence of a noteworthy relationship.[72]

Prior to the Bush Jr. administration's 2002 propaganda efforts to convince the
American people that Al Qaeda and Hussein were one and the same, the CIA
declared, "Saddam has viewed Islamic extremists operating inside Iraq as a
threat."[73] After the 2003 invasion of Iraq under Bush Jr., the CIA and FBI interviewed a captured Saddam Hussein and his top leaders. The U.S. intelli-

gence community collected a wealth of evidence from these Iraqi prisoners that clearly demonstrated the lack of linkage between Saddam Hussein and bin Laden.

All this discussion about the considerable daylight between President Hussein and bin Laden the Wahhabi exile might seem academic, but for the fact that in 2002–3 the Bush Jr. administration began to speak of a "sinister nexus" that bound Osama bin Laden, the stateless Saudi fundamentalist terrorist, with Saddam Hussein, the head of the Iraqi socialist state. This was an effort to create what some critics have called the myth of "Osama bin Hussein."

Before this counterintuitive claim was disseminated as a rationale for invading Iraq in 2003, however, no serious scholar or analyst of the region found any evidence of a merging of these two disparate groups (i.e., between Iraq, a socialist state with many targets that could be destroyed in retaliation for a terrorist strike, and Al Qaeda, a stateless terrorist organization dedicated to holy war hiding out in Sudan, Pakistan, and Afghanistan). The analogy in American terms might be the improbability of the Ku Klux Klan, a group of white supremacist racists in the American south, making an alliance with the Crips or the Bloods, two African American street gangs from Los Angeles.

Perhaps the most important evidence that bin Laden was *not* working with the Iraqis came in 1996 when he and his followers were finally expelled from their sanctuary in Sudan under Saudi, Egyptian, and U.S. pressure. Commonsense would dictate that if Hussein and bin Laden were indeed allies, as the Bush Jr. administration later claimed in 2003, then bin Laden would have then fled from Sudan to Iraq to set up his terror camps there. Instead, Bin Laden flew to eastern Afghanistan on his private jet and there found a base in the eastern Pashtun belt. His timing was most propitious for, even as bin Laden the fanatical fundamentalist settled in Afghanistan in search of a new home, a fanatical army of black-turbaned Pashtun fundamentalists was conquering the southeastern parts of the country. History would call these ethnic Pashtun militants the Taliban (i.e., the Students, not to be confused with the mujahideen "freedom fighters" who fought the Soviets in the 1980s), and they would offer bin Laden's followers sanctuary.

Many Americans have a hard time distinguishing between Iraqi Socialist-Baathists, Afghan Taliban, and fundamentalist Al Qaeda (a difficulty compounded by the Bush Jr. administration's tendency to deliberately blur the differences between the secular Iraqi government and Al Qaeda religious zealots), but the distinctions are of vital importance. Some background on the Taliban movement will demonstrate why.

The origins of the Taliban lay in the chaos surrounding the Soviet withdrawal from Afghanistan in 1989 and the final collapse of the local Afghan Communist government to the mujahideen rebels in 1992. In the aftermath of the disintegration of the Communist government in Afghanistan, the various ethnic-based Afghan mujahideen parties carved the country up into separate ministates. In the north, the plains around the shrine town of Mazar i Sharif were dominated by General Dostum and his comparatively secular Turko-Mongol Uzbeks. The central Hindu Kush mountain section of the country was dominated by the Shiite Mongol Hazaras. The northeast and the capital were dominated by Massoud, the Lion of Panjsher, and his Persian Dari Tajiks. In all these areas (except Kabul, which was fought over) stability prevailed as the country's various ethnic groups took advantage of the collapse of the Pashtun-dominated Afghan central state to rule themselves for the first time in a century. It is a myth that all warlords in Afghanistan were vicious killers. The war leaders of all the above-mentioned northern ethnic groups ruled their own peoples successfully and were popular with their own ethnic constituencies.

But in the south, in the territory of Afghanistan's ruling race, the ultra-conservative Aryan Pashtuns, chaos prevailed. There, the ex-mujahideen turned their guns on the villagers that had previously supported them in their jihad against the Soviets and began to prey on them. Mujahideen-turned-bandits raped local women, robbed or murdered the common people, and fought for control over territory and the increasingly important opium trade. In a typical case of the Pashtun mujahideen violence against civilians, in 1994 a warlord in the town of Sangesar captured an extended family traveling through his district. He and his men then brutally killed all the males and turned the women into sex slaves.

Fortunately for the women and girls from the captured group, a local mullah named Omar who was teaching a group of young Talibs (Religious Students) at a nearby madrassa (religious seminary) heard about the situation and decided to intervene. As it transpired, the mullah was himself an ex-mujahideen who had given up jihad and devoted his life to teaching Islam. He armed his students and attacked the offending mujahideen warlord's compound. Against all odds, the Talibs overran the warlord's base, freed the captured women and girls, and hung the warlord rapist from the barrel of a tank as a warning to others. Thus was born the militant Pashtun brotherhood known as the Taliban (plural for Talib).

When word of the obscure mullah's success spread, other Taliban joined his movement and they began to spread throughout the southern province of Kandahar, the heartland of the Pashtuns. As the snowballing Taliban movement spread in the Pashtun lands they were welcomed by the local people who were tired of the violence of the mujahideen *topakayan* (gunmen).

But freedom from the rapaciousness of the mujahideen warlords came at a steep price, for the Taliban were similar to the fanatical Wahhabis who had conquered Saudi Arabia in the nineteenth century. When they entered a district they began to brutally enforce a harsh brand of Islam known as Deobandism that was even stricter than the already conservative brand of Islam found among the Pashtuns. Television sets were destroyed as "satanic devices," girls were forced out of schools to protect their morality, women were forced out of jobs, those who were accused of theft had their hands cut off, young eloping couples who wanted to choose their own spouses were stoned to death in public, music was banned, and any form of "un-Islamic" entertainment, from dog fighting to dancing to the Afghan pastime of kite flying, was strictly forbidden by the grim Taliban puritans.

By 1995, the Taliban had begun to pour out of the Pashtun belt and attack the other ethnic groups that had carved out mini–ethnic states in the north and center of the country. The Taliban were trying to forcefully reconstitute the centralized state of their Pashtun forefathers with themselves once again in charge, thus they were both religious fanatics and Pashtun ethnic warriors.

The Taliban military offensives were aided by the fact that thousands of Pashtuns from the neighboring country of Pakistan poured across the artificial border separating their lands and supported their Pashtun Taliban brothers in their conquests. The Pakistani Pashtuns lived in two frontier provinces in Pakistan known as the FATA (Federally Administered Tribal Agencies) and the North West Frontier Province. These wild Pashtun lands had been sliced off from nineteenth-century Afghanistan by the British colonial conquerors of India and had been included in the country that would later (in 1947) come to be known as Pakistan.

It should also be mentioned that the Pakistani ISI (Inter Services Intelligence) supported the Taliban conquest of Afghanistan as well. The Pakistanis felt that it would benefit them to have a unified, Islamic Afghanistan next door to assist them should they ever commence a major war with their archenemy, India. It did not bother the Pakistanis that in supporting the fanatical Taliban with fuel, funds, noncommissioned officers, and weapons, they were cynically helping to convert Afghanistan into a harsh, religious prison camp.

It is also a common misconception that the United States of America sponsored the Taliban fanatics in the 1990s. Many people take a certain satisfaction in the notion that the Americans inadvertently created a fundamentalist Taliban Frankenstein in Afghanistan that it later had to confront after 9/11. This comes from a misguided notion that the Taliban "Students" of the mid to late 1990s (who waged war against the mujahideen warlords) were actually the mujahideen "freedom fighter" rebels whom the CIA supported during the 1980s anti-Soviet jihad. In reality, the Clinton administration's views toward Mullah Omar's regime at the time of its conquests went from neutral to overtly hostile in light of the Taliban's almost medieval-style treatment of women. Clinton ultimately enacted sanctions against the Taliban regime for its basing of Al Qaeda terrorists on its territory and brought up its abuses of women in the UN. *At this time the United States never sponsored or aided the Taliban in their brutal conquest of Afghanistan.*

Never was the fact that Afghanistan was being brutally transformed into a medieval-style theocracy more vividly demonstrated than when the Taliban conquered the relatively liberal, cosmopolitan city of Kabul in 1996. When they conquered the Afghan capital, the Taliban were horrified to find women working with men and going out in public without burqas (full body veils). The Taliban social conservatives immediately fired all women from their jobs, even teachers, gynecologists and other doctors, and closed down the city's girls' schools. The Taliban's Orwellian morality enforcers from the Ministry for the Promotion of Virtue and Prevention of Vice then began to publicly execute "sinners" in Kabul's soccer stadium and to strictly enforce shariah Islamic law in this Tajik-dominated city of relatively urbane moderates.

Fortunately for the majority of Tajiks, their defender, Massoud, the "Lion of Panjsher," was able to build defensive lines to the north of Kabul that protected their ethnic enclave in the mountainous northeast. As the Taliban swarmed onto the northern plains conquering Dostum's secular Uzbek realm based on Mazar i Sharif in 1998 and subjugating the land of the Shiite Hazara "heretics" (the Taliban were strict Sunnis) in the same year, Massoud was able to defend his people and keep the Taliban fanatics out of the last free section of Afghanistan. Massoud was thus the last man standing in the moderate opposition to the Taliban known as the Northern Alliance. But it should be stated that his fragile Tajik enclave in the northeast represented no more than 10 percent of Afghanistan; in the rest of the country Taliban darkness prevailed.

It was around the time of the Taliban's conquest of Kabul that Osama bin

Laden and his exiled Al Qaeda followers arrived in eastern, Pashtun-dominated Afghanistan following their expulsion from Sudan in 1996. At first the Taliban did not know what to make of the mysterious Arabs who settled into preexisting jihadi training camps in the Pashtun east. But the Taliban's messianic leader, Mullah Omar, fatefully came to see in the Arab exiles' leader, bin Laden, a kindred spirit. Both men were deeply devout, and bin Laden approved of Mullah Omar's forceful creation of a "pure" Islamic state in Afghanistan. Bin Laden even followed the Taliban in recognizing Mullah Omar as the "Commander of the Faithful." To aid his Taliban hosts, bin Laden recruited thousands of Arabs and Uzbekistanis from the Islamic Movement of Uzbekistan to come and fight in their army in the fanatical 055 International Jihad Brigade. While most Westerners think of Al Qaeda as sleeper-cell terrorists, most members of the organization were actually jihadi fighters who had served on the front line against Massoud's Tajik moderate rebels in the northeast.

In return for this military assistance, Mullah Omar offered bin Laden and his Arab followers the ancient Pashtun tribal protection known as *melmastiia* (the duty to protect an honored guest with one's life). While it has been demonstrated that Al Qaeda *did not* develop an alliance with the secular Saddam Hussein, history tells us that bin Laden's terrorist group indisputably established a close, symbiotic relationship with its fundamentalist Taliban hosts. Al Qaeda in effect became a state-within-a-state in Afghanistan, and bin Laden played an increasingly important role in the country and its government.

The relationship was not, however, always smooth. In 1998, for example, Bin Laden annoyed his Taliban hosts by issuing a fatwa, or religious pronouncement, that stated: "For over seven years the United States has been occupying the lands of Islam in the holiest of places, the Arabian Peninsula, plundering its riches, dictating to its rulers, humiliating its people, terrorizing its neighbors, and turning its bases in the Peninsula into a spearhead through which to fight the neighboring Muslim peoples. . . . All these crimes and sins committed by the Americans are a clear declaration of war on Allah, his messenger, and Muslims." The fatwa went even further and proclaimed "to kill the Americans and their allies—civilians and military—is an individual duty for every Muslim who can do it in any country in which it is possible to do it." This fatwa was signed by the World Islamic Front, a group of Al Qaeda–allied jihadi groups that included Ayman al Zawahiri's Egyptian Islamic Jihad organization, which merged with Al Qaeda; the Jamiat Ulema

Pakistan; the Harakat ul-Jihad-i-Islami/Bangladesh; and the Gama'a al-Islamiyya in Egypt. Needless to say, Saddam Hussein most certainly did not sign the joint fatwa creating the World Islamic Front.

At the time, Mullah Omar warned bin Laden about needlessly antagonizing the powerful Americans, but the Al Qaeda chief seemed to be unconcerned about the danger he was putting his Pashtun hosts in. It should be stated that there were also moderates in the Taliban government who disliked Mullah Omar's close relationship with bin Laden and felt that the Arab millionaire (who actually lost access to much of his money when his family cut him off under Saudi pressure) put their Islamic regime at risk. This point was about to be reinforced by bin Laden's next action, which took his movement from the organizational stage to the operational stage in terrorism.

While bin Laden's fatwas went largely unnoticed in the United States, he soon gained the Americans' attention when terrorists from his group bombed two U.S. embassies in the east African countries of Kenya and Tanzania. In August 1998, Al Qaeda detonated near-simultaneous bombs outside U.S. embassies in the Kenyan capital of Nairobi and in the Tanzanian capital of Dar es Salaam. The massive Kenyan blast killed 201 Kenyans and twelve Americans, while the smaller Tanzanian blast killed eleven Tanzanians. The vast majority of those killed in the bombings were thus Africans, several of whom were Muslims.

In response to the unprecedented slaughter of hundreds of Africans and a dozen Americans, President Clinton launched the highly unsuccessful Operation Infinite Reach. This operation involved shooting long-distance Tomahawk cruise missiles from offshore naval vessels at targets in Sudan and Afghanistan. The first and most obvious targets were bin Laden's terror camps located in eastern Afghanistan in the Khost region. Unfortunately, bin Laden was not there at the time of the barrage of eighty cruise missiles, which killed a few locals and low-level militants.

Had the strike been successful, Clinton would have probably decapitated Al Qaeda before it attacked the U.S. mainland on 9/11. As it was, Clinton was later derided by Bush Jr. for "firing a 2 million dollar missile at a tent to hit a camel in the butt."[74] Most important, the cruise missile attack was seen by Mullah Omar as a violation of Afghanistan's sovereignty, and it actually drove him closer to his Saudi guest, bin Laden. The American failure to kill bin Laden also made him a superstar among many young, disenfranchised Arab men in the Middle East who longed for a role model who could stand up to the powerful, pro-Israeli Americans and their own dictatorial, pro-American leaders. After the attack, Pashtuns in neighboring Pakistan began to name their children Osama, and many Arab fanatics traveled to his camps in eastern Afghanistan to train for jihadi terrorism. Thus the attacks backfired and acted as a recruitment drive for bin Laden's Al Qaeda.

While the Afghan targets—bin Laden's terror camps in the Pashtun belt known as Farouq, Muawai, and Zhawar—made perfect sense, the subsequent cruise missile targeting of a factory that produced half of the country's pharmaceuticals, in the Sudanese capital of Khartoum, was based on flawed intelligence. This bad intelligence stated that the Sudanese factory was somehow producing weapons of mass destruction for the Afghan-based bin Laden. U.S. officials subsequently admitted that there was "no proof that the plant had been manufacturing or storing nerve gas," but by then the plant had been totally destroyed by a barrage of twelve cruise missiles, and one innocent Sudanese civilian had been killed.[75] A Boston University professor of chemistry who subsequently analyzed the debris at the site of the attack found no evidence of any chemicals used in WMDs, only traces of ibuprofen.[76] Thus the first U.S. administration to erroneously link bin Laden to nonexistent WMDs was not the Bush Jr. administration in 2002–3, but the Clinton administration in 1998.

Not surprisingly, after 9/11 some Republicans tried to retroactively paint Clinton as being weak on terrorism as a result of his failure to kill bin Laden. But that is post facto armchair quarterbacking, and it should be stated that in 1998 the American people would not have stomached a military invasion of Afghanistan, the "Graveyard of Empires," to eradicate a handful of terrorists who had killed only twelve Americans in east Africa. At the time, Clinton's use of Tomahawk cruise missiles to surgically take out bin Laden's camps was the most effective means of killing the terrorists in this remote, landlocked Central Asian country (there were no armed Predator drones at this time). When Clinton and his national security advisor, Richard Clarke, later asked the Pentagon to launch a helicopter raid on bin Laden's compounds with Special Operations Command operators (like the one that eventually killed bin Laden under Obama in May 2011), the chairman of the military's Joint Chiefs of Staff, Hugh Shelton, rejected such proposals as "dumb-ass ideas, not militarily feasible," and "something in a Tom Clancy novel" that ignored "the time-distance factors."[77]

So Clinton was forced to rely on cruise missiles and to enact sanctions against the Taliban regime to force them to hand over bin Laden. In 1999, Clinton signed an executive order imposing sanctions on the Taliban, which began: "I, WILLIAM J. CLINTON, President of the United States of America, find that the actions and policies of the Taliban in Afghanistan, in allowing territory under its control in Afghanistan to be used as a safe haven and base of operations for Usama bin Ladin and the Al-Qaida organization who have committed and threaten to continue to commit acts of violence against the United States and its nationals, constitute an unusual and extraordinary threat to the national security and foreign policy of the United States." Clinton (and his successor Bush Jr.), however, failed to send weapons, supplies, ammunition, trainers, communication equipment, special forces, and funds to support Massoud and his outgunned anti-Taliban rebel forces in the northeast of Afghanistan. This despite the Lion of Panjsher's well-known opposition to bin Laden and his pleas for help to fight the common enemy. Had Clinton or Bush Jr. assisted Massoud, they would have been able to wage a proxy war against Al Qaeda's Taliban hosts and destabilize bin Laden's sanctuary even as the Saudi terrorist used his Afghan haven to plan the 9/11 attacks. But at the time (1998–2001), the local Afghan Taliban were not themselves seen as the actual enemy, so neither president was willing to take the aggressive step of waging a proxy war against them.

Only one farsighted U.S. official envisioned such an eventuality, the above-mentioned chief national security advisor, Richard Clarke. It was Clarke who called for arming Massoud's troops so they could take the fight to the Taliban and their Al Qaeda 055 International Brigade allies. Clarke's now declassified Blue Sky Memo called for "massive support to anti-Taliban groups such as the Northern Alliance led by Ahmad Shah Massoud," as well as winning over Pakistani support and the targeted killings of Al Qaeda leaders using newly developed Predator aerial drones.[78] It should, however, be stated that at this time Predator unmanned spy drones were still unarmed and could be used only to scout out bin Laden's location for Tomahawk strikes.

In the meantime, the increasingly infamous bin Laden was planning yet another attack on the United States, which he called the "Far Enemy." His plan was to sink a U.S. fighting vessel docked in his ancestral homeland of Yemen. On January 3, 2000, Al Qaeda operatives loaded a boat full of explosives to drive into the side of the USS *The Sullivans*, a guided missile destroyer, docked in the Yemeni port of Aden. But the terrorists' boat was too overloaded with explosives and promptly sank.

Undeterred, Al Qaeda launched a second attack, on the USS *Cole*, in October 2000. This attack on the destroyer was successful and blasted a forty-by-forty-foot hole in the side of the frigate and killed seventeen sailors. Al Qaeda subsequently released a video montage of the attack claiming responsibility for it. Of the strike, a triumphant bin Laden declared, "The destroyer is the capital of the West and the small boat represented Mohammad."[79] There were few conspiracy theorists in the West and or the Middle East at the time who claimed the Jews or the U.S. president actually carried out the bold strike as was to subsequently be the case after the 9/11 attack.

This was the setting at the time of the end of Bill Clinton's presidency in late 2000 and early 2001. As the new president, George Bush Jr., prepared to take control of the White House, the departing president feared that the incoming Bush Jr. administration did not have a grasp on the seriousness of the Al Qaeda threat. Richard Clarke, who stayed on as chief counterterrorism advisor under Bush, wrote in his memoir *Against All Enemies*:

> When Clinton left office many people, including the incoming Bush administration leadership, thought that he [Clinton] and his administration were obsessed with al Qaeda. After all al Qaeda had only killed a few Americans. . . .
> Why was Clinton so worked up about al Qaeda and why did he talk to president-elect Bush about it and have Sandy Berger raise it with his successor National Security Advisor, Condi Rice? In January 2001, the new [Bush Jr.] administration really thought Clinton's recommendation that eliminating al Qaeda be one of their highest priorities, well, rather odd.[80]

When Bush Jr. assumed the presidency in January 2001, Richard Clarke spent months pressuring the new administration to meet with him to take steps against what he felt was an imminent threat to the United States. He warned, "Something really spectacular is going to happen here, and it's going to happen soon."

But when Clarke was finally given the chance to brief Bush's national security advisor, Condoleezza Rice, about the Al Qaeda threat, he reported, "her facial expression gave me the impression that she had never heard of them before."[81] Five months after Bush Jr. came to office, in April 2001, Clarke was finally able to get his meeting with the Deputies Committee in the Situation Room to discuss the looming Al Qaeda danger. But there he found that the focus was not on the Al Qaeda terror threat to the United States that had clearly manifested itself in the African embassy bombings, the USS *Cole* bombing, and a failed Al Qaeda plot at Los Angeles Airport, but on "Iraqi terrorism." In his memoir Clarke recalled his shocking discussion with Bush Jr.'s deputy secretary of defense, Paul Wolfowitz (of whom we will hear much later):

> Rice's deputy, Steve Hadley, began the meeting by asking me to brief the group. I turned immediately to the pending decisions needed to deal with al Qaeda. "We need to put pressure on both the Taliban and al Qaeda by arming the Northern Alliance [rebels] and other groups in Afghanistan. Simultaneously, we need to target bin Laden and his leadership by reinitiating flights of the Predator."
>
> Paul Wolfowitz, Donald Rumsfeld's deputy at Defense, fidgeted and scowled. Hadley asked him if he was all right. "Well, I just don't understand why we are beginning by talking about this one man bin Laden," Wolfowitz responded.
>
> I answered as clearly and forcefully as I could: "We are talking about a network of terrorist organizations called al Qaeda, that happens to be [led] by bin Laden, and we are talking about that network because it, and it alone, poses an immediate threat to the United States."
>
> "Well, there are other groups that do as well, at least as much. Iraqi terrorism for example" [Wolfowitz replied].
>
> "I am unaware of any Iraqi-sponsored terrorism directed at the United States, Paul, since 1993 [the attempt on Bush Sr.'s life], and I think FBI and CIA concur in that judgment, right, John?" I pointed at CIA Deputy Director John Mclaughlin, who was obviously not eager to get in the middle of a debate between the White House and the Pentagon but nonetheless replied, "Yes, that is right Dick. We have no evidence of any Iraqi terrorist threat against the U.S." Finally Wolfowitz turned to me and said "You give bin Laden too much credit."[82]

Clarke was not the only one who found it difficult to get the "principals" of the Bush administration, including Condoleezza Rice, to act on the increasing "chatter" coming from intelligence sources on impending Al Qaeda plots. The intelligence intercepts on the eve of 9/11 seemed to indicate that Al Qaeda was planning a major attack on the U.S. mainland, and Clarke was clearly worried. CIA head George Tenet and CIA Counterterrorism Center chief Cofer Black also tried, but failed, to alert Rice and Defense Secretary Donald Rumsfeld to the threat. An article in the *Washington Post* details this failed intervention:

> On July 10, 2001, two months before the attacks on the World Trade Center and the Pentagon, then-CIA Director George J. Tenet met with his counterterrorism chief, J. Cofer Black, at CIA headquarters to review the latest on Osama bin Laden and his al-Qaeda terrorist organization. Black laid out the case, consisting of communications intercepts and other top-secret intelligence showing the increasing likelihood that al-Qaeda would soon attack the United States. It was a mass of fragments and dots that nonetheless made a compelling case, so compelling to Tenet that he decided he and Black should go to the White House immediately. Tenet called Condoleezza Rice, then national security adviser, from the car and said he needed to see her right away. There was no practical way she could refuse such a request from the CIA director. But Tenet had been having difficulty getting traction on an immediate bin Laden action plan, in part because Defense Secretary Donald H. Rumsfeld had questioned all the National Security Agency intercepts and other intelligence. Could all this be a grand deception? Rumsfeld had asked. Perhaps it was a plan to measure U.S. reactions and defenses.
>
> Tenet had the NSA review all the intercepts, and the agency concluded they were of genuine al-Qaeda communications. On June 30, a top-secret senior executive intelligence brief contained an article headlined "Bin Laden Threats Are Real." Tenet hoped his abrupt request for an immediate meeting would shake Rice. He and Black, a veteran covert operator, had two main points when they met with her. First, al-Qaeda was going to attack American interests, possibly in the United States itself. Black emphasized that this amounted to a strategic warning, meaning the problem was so serious that it required an overall plan and strategy. Second, this was a major foreign policy problem that needed to be addressed immediately. They needed to take action that moment—covert, military, whatever—to thwart bin Laden. . . . Tenet and Black felt they were not getting through to Rice. She was polite, but they felt the brush-off. President Bush had said he didn't want to swat at flies. . . . Besides, Rice seemed focused on other administration priorities,

especially the ballistic missile defense system that Bush had cam-
paigned on. She was in a different place. . . .

Black later said, "The only thing we didn't do was pull the trigger
to the gun we were holding to her head."[83]

As the "threat indicators" rose to a fever pitch on August 6, 2001, approximately a month prior to the 9/11 attacks, Bush received a PDB (President's
Daily Brief) compiled by the CIA entitled "Bin Ladin Determined to Strike in
the US." This document, which has some redactions, clearly demonstrates
that George Tenet's CIA was urgently trying to warn the president of an impending Al Qaeda attack on the U.S. mainland. It read:

> Clandestine, foreign government, and media reports indicate bin
> Laden since 1997 has wanted to conduct terrorist attacks *in the US*
> [emphasis mine]. Bin Laden implied in U.S. television interviews in
> 1997 and 1998 that his followers would follow the example of World
> Trade Center bomber Ramzi Yousef and "bring the fighting *to
> America*" [emphasis mine].
>
> After U.S. missile strikes on his base in Afghanistan in 1998, bin
> Laden told followers he wanted to retaliate *in Washington* [emphasis
> mine], according to a——service. An Egyptian Islamic Jihad (EIJ)
> operative told—service at the same time that bin Laden was plan-
> ning to exploit the operative's access to the U.S. to mount a terrorist
> strike. . . .
>
> Nevertheless, FBI information since that time indicates patterns
> of suspicious activity in this country consistent with preparations for
> hijackings or other types of attacks, including recent surveillance of
> federal buildings in New York.
>
> The FBI is conducting approximately 70 full-field investigations
> throughout the U.S. that it considers bin Laden–related. CIA and the
> FBI are investigating a call to our embassy in the UAE in May saying
> that a group of bin Laden supporters *was in the U.S.* [emphasis mine]
> planning attacks with explosives.[84]

The *New York Times* would later write of the document, "In a single 17-
sentence document, the intelligence briefing delivered to President Bush in
August 2001 spells out the who, hints at the what, and points towards the

where of the terrorist attacks on New York and Washington that followed 36 days later."[85]

The bipartisan 9/11 Commission would later state that "the system was blinking red" about an imminent Al Qaeda attack, but Bush would later state that the "Bin Ladin Determined to Strike in the US" PDB document contained "nothing about an attack on America." He further stated, "I'm satisfied that I never saw any intelligence that indicated there was going to be an attack on America."[86] For her part, National Security Advisor Condoleezza Rice stated that there was "nothing about the threat of attack in the U.S." in the Presidential Daily Briefing the president received on August 6. She also stated before the 9/11 Commission, "there was nothing demonstrating, or showing that, something was coming in the United States. If there had been something, we would have acted on it."[87]

Retroactive denials of advance warnings by the CIA of a terror strike aside, history clearly shows that the Bush White House was not focused on or aware of the magnitude of the impending Al Qaeda threat to the United States in the days, weeks, and months before 9/11. This despite warnings of an impending attack on the U.S. from Richard Clarke, the CIA, the FBI, and former president Clinton. There were no cruise missile attacks on bin Laden's bases where the 9/11 terrorists trained, there were no stepped-up security measures or alerts at home, there was no armed support for Massoud's struggling anti-Taliban forces in northeastern Afghanistan, and so on. Ron Gutman has written of bin Laden that, on the eve of the largest terror attack in world history, the U.S. government was "seemingly determined to play down his role as U.S. enemy number one."[88]

As the tragedy of 9/11 loomed on the horizon, bin Laden himself, however, warned the Americans that he was coming for them. In spring 2001, he issued a video commemorating his attack on the USS *Cole* in Yemen wherein he stated, "We give you the good news that the forces of Islam are coming." In June 2001 he also gave an interview to a Saudi journalist in which he warned, "In the next few weeks we will carry out a big surprise, and we will attack American and Israeli interests."[89] The British also intercepted a conversation between bin Laden and an associate in Pakistan wherein bin Laden "refers to an incident that will take place in the U.S., on, or around 9/11, and discusses possible repercussions."[90]

In August 2001, U.S. intelligence services also intercepted a conversation between two Al Qaeda operatives (one of whom claimed to be "studying

airplanes"), which predicted, "This will be one of those strikes that will never
be forgotten. It will wreak such a great havoc that they will never know how
to put things in order. This is a terrifying thing."[91] Another Afghan-based Al
Qaeda operative stated, "This information [about the impending attacks on
America] being so commonly known amongst everybody in the training
camps, what was stopping them [the Americans] from assassinating bin
Laden?"[92] A British journalist for the *New York Times* reported that Arab
fighters in Afghanistan were bragging about a "huge forthcoming attack on
America" prior to 9/11.[93]

In August 2001 the CIA developed information that bin Laden was "increasingly determined to strike on US soil."[94] Cofer Black, the head of the
CIA's Counterterrorism Center, boldly predicted in August 2001, "We are
going to be struck very soon, many Americans are going to die, and it could
be in the US." Black later complained that top leaders in Washington proved
to be unwilling to act on his warnings unless they are given "such things as
the attack is coming in the next few days and here is what they are going to
hit."[95] Just prior to Black's warning, the British government also warned Bush
about the possibility of multiple hijackings.[96]

If all this was not enough to set off alarm bells in the Bush White House,
moderates among bin Laden's Taliban hosts appear to have learned of his
plans to attack the United States and decided to warn America in the summer
of 2001, according to the BBC. The BBC reported that

> An aide to the former Taleban foreign minister, Wakil Ahmad
> Muttawakil, has revealed that he was sent to warn American diplomats
> and the United Nations that Osama bin Laden was due to launch a
> huge attack on American soil. Neither organization heeded the
> warning, which was given just weeks before the 11 September attacks.
>
> The aide said he had urged the Americans to launch a military
> campaign against al-Qaeda but was told that this was politically
> impossible.
>
> Mr Muttawakil, who was known to be deeply unhappy with the
> Arab and other foreign militants in Afghanistan, learned of Osama
> bin Laden's plan in July. The attack was imminent, he discovered, and
> it would be huge. Bin Laden hoped to kill thousands of US citizens.[97]

Warnings also came from Massoud, the last man standing in the Northern
Alliance opposition to the Taliban and Al Qaeda. As the Taliban/Al Qaeda

armies swarmed his defensive trenches in waves in the summer of 2001, this moderate Muslim leader, who had been an American ally in the war against the Soviets, pleaded with the Bush administration for support. Speaking of the terrorist threat manifesting itself in the Al Qaeda training camps in Afghanistan, he darkly predicted, "If President Bush doesn't help us, then these terrorists will damage the United States and Europe very soon and it will be too late."[98] He also hinted that Al Qaeda's "objectives are not limited to Afghanistan." In a secret memo to the CIA, Massoud warned that Al Qaeda was planning, "to perform a terrorist act against the US on a scale larger than the 1998 bombing of the US embassies in Kenya and Tanzania."[99]

But Massoud's desperate entreaties also fell on deaf ears. The Bush administration was disinclined to offend the Taliban regime by openly training and equipping its Northern Alliance opponents. While several key U.S. officials, including counterterrorism chief Richard Clarke and CIA Counterterrorism Center chief Cofer Black, favored sending covert aid and weapons to Massoud's Northern Alliance opposition, such discussions were never translated into direct action. As Al Qaeda plotted to overwhelm Massoud's fragile opposition sanctuary in the northeast of Afghanistan and kill thousands of Americans in the distant United States, the CIA "showed no sense of urgency in supporting the Northern Alliance."[100]

Fortunately, one man responded to Massoud's pleas for help in the battle against the fanatics, the previously exiled Afghan Uzbek opposition leader General Dostum. Dostum, it will be recalled, had run an independent, secular ministate in the Uzbek-dominated plains of northern Afghanistan around Mazar i Sharif. In 1998, however, this powerful warlord's state had been overrun by the Taliban, who then brutally enforced harsh shariah law on his moderate Uzbek people. Dostum then fled to exile in Turkey to save his life.

But in the spring of 2001 Dostum heeded Massoud's call for assistance and flew back to Afghanistan to join the desperate fight against the Taliban in one last battle. There he linked up with Massoud in his northeastern mountain enclave, then flew via helicopter into the high peaks of the inaccessible Hindu Kush Mountains of central Afghanistan. In the mountain heights he raised a small fighting force of two thousand tough Uzbek horsemen (the Uzbeks are the descendants of Genghis Khan's nomadic Mongol armies). From the mountain peaks, Dostum's horse-mounted Uzbek guerillas raided the Taliban occupation forces in the plains around Mazar i Sharif and forced them to divert forces from their summer campaign against Massoud's embattled lines.[101]

This diversion helped Massoud survive the Taliban's much heralded 2001 summer offensive. Thus Dostum and Massoud's lonely battle against a much larger Taliban army went on into the late summer months of 2001 with no support from the Bush administration, which was focused on Iraq.

Meanwhile, in distant North America, the hot topic in Washington in the final days of August and early September 2001 was Democratic congressman Gary Condit's alleged affair with his murdered intern Chandra Levy. Few Americans knew or cared about the desperate struggle of moderate Muslims in the mountains of Afghanistan against a theocratic regime known as the Taliban, or an exiled Saudi Arab's threats against their nation.

On September 9, 2001, it barely made news in America when word came that Massoud, the legendary guerilla commander who had defeated the Soviets in Afghanistan and fought for six years to defend his moderate enclave from the Taliban, had been killed by Al Qaeda suicide bombers. As it transpired, on that day two Arab suicide bombers posing as television reporters blew up their bomb-camera during a recorded interview with Massoud, killing the leader and inspiration of the Northern Alliance opposition to the Taliban.

In so doing, the terrorists killed the one man capable of keeping the fanatics out of the last remaining free portion of Afghanistan. His death was a signal for the Taliban to storm his defensive trenches and try to overwhelm his resistance pocket. As thousands of Taliban and Al Qaeda fanatics blitzed his defenses, the surviving Tajik Northern Alliance subcommanders, however, kept word of Massoud's death from their men on the front lines. They told them only that the Taliban had tried to kill their beloved leader. Against all odds, the outgunned Tajik fighters held off the Taliban and survived the two-day offensive on September 9 and September 10, 2001.

But the Tajik component of the Northern Alliance was clearly in disarray, and word of Massoud's death could not be kept hidden from the men desperately guarding the defensive lines indefinitely. Sooner or later they would learn that the Lion of Panjsher, their beloved Amir Sahib (Lord Commander), had been killed by bin Laden's assassins—as a gift to the Taliban—and their morale would fall.

The Tajiks were not the only ones disheartened by the death of the charismatic Massoud. It should not be forgotten that Dostum and his small band of two thousand horse-mounted Uzbek riders were waging an increasingly desperate diversionary campaign against the Taliban from the barren heights of the Hindu Kush Mountains. The Taliban were gradually closing in on their positions with a force of five thousand.

When Dostum heard of Massoud's death, he realized he had been "promoted" to the most visible face of the Northern Alliance opposition. He quickly held a war *shura* (council) with his turbaned mountain riders and asked them if they wanted to continue the fight, despite the death of their ally Massoud. History tells us that Dostum's loyal *cheriks* (raiders) all agreed to follow their pasha (commander) and fight to the death against their people's oppressors. But without external support from the Americans, they all realized that they would sooner or later be tracked down and defeated by their more powerful Taliban foes. Time was clearly not on their side. With the death of Massoud and their small force's impending defeat, it was only a matter of time before the Taliban destroyed the last free sanctuaries in Afghanistan and fanaticism prevailed throughout the land.

This then was the long prehistory to Al Qaeda's attack on the United States and the more recent setting in the remote country of Afghanistan and in the U.S. as the sun rose over the eastern seaboard on the fateful day of September 11th, 2001. That morning NSA analysts went through their intercepts from the night before but did not get to two intercepted messages from Afghanistan to Saudi Arabia that read, "the match is about to begin," and "tomorrow is zero hour."[102] Other electronic intercepts from the day before said, "Watch the news," and "Tomorrow will be a great day for us."[103] Even if the U.S. intelligence services had found these messages on the morning of 9/11 (they did not find them until September 12), the ominous predictions were too vague to have prevented the attacks of 9/11.

The extraordinary events of September 11, 2001, would link Afghanistan and the United States together in what would become America's longest war and would inaugurate a period known to history as "the War on Terror." And, while few could have foreseen it at the time, the events of 9/11 would also galvanize America to go even further than initially intended and invade not only Taliban Afghanistan, but Saddam Hussein's Iraq, to finish the "unfinished business" of Bush Sr.'s presidency. Thus bin Laden's attack, designed to drive the U.S. out of the Muslim world, would, ironically enough, lead to the American occupation of not one but two Muslim countries, including one that had gladly offered him and his Al Qaeda followers sanctuary, Afghanistan, and one, distant Iraq, that he saw as being led by a secular Baathist infidel.

CHAPTER 2

America Goes to War in Afghanistan

America has been hit by Allah at its most vulnerable point, destroying, thank God, its most prestigious buildings.

—Osama bin Laden

9/11: Al Qaeda Attacks the U.S. Mainland

We now know that in the months before 9/11, nineteen Arab hijackers infiltrated America without the knowledge of the CIA or FBI, who were often at odds with one another, and began training to fly passenger jets or to serve as "muscle" on hijacked planes. Among the hijackers were fifteen Saudis, two Arabs from the United Arab Emirates, one Lebanese, and the team commander, Mohamad Atta, an Egyptian. It should be clearly stated that there were *no Iraqis* among the Al Qaeda sleeper-cell team that attacked America on 9/11 and that the terrorists trained in Taliban-controlled Afghanistan, not Saddam Hussein's Iraq. A Presidential Daily Brief given to President George W. Bush ten days after the attack based on the views of the intelligence community also stated that there was "scant credible evidence that Iraq had any significant collaborative ties with Al Qaeda."[1]

As perennial American-haters in the Middle East and fringe conspiracy theorists subsequently leaped to blame Israel and America itself for the 9/11 attacks (which actually followed a pattern of previous Al Qaeda attacks against U.S. targets in Tanzania, Kenya, and Yemen), bin Laden repeatedly took credit for them. He did so in official statements, in pre-9/11 video footage of himself with the actual hijackers, and in several interviews with reporters wherein he revealed previously undisclosed details of the attacks.[2] In one scene on a tape released by the Arabic network Al Jazeera, bin Laden called on his followers to support the hijackers *before* they went on their suicide mission, saying, "I ask you to pray for them and to ask God to make them successful, aim their shots well, set their feet strong and strengthen their hearts."[3]

The actual Al Qaeda "hands-on" planner of the 9/11 attack, a Yemeni named Ramzi bin al Shibh, described the euphoria that swept bin Laden's inner circle when they watched the televised images of the attack in their Afghan training camp as follows:

> The day of the attack all camps and residential compounds in Afghanistan were put on high alert. Brothers were dispersed. The message [of the attack] was great news for Sheikh Abu Abdallah [bin Laden], may God protect him.
>
> When they found out the brothers cried "Allah-u-Akbar! Thanks to God!" And cried. Everyone thought that this was the only operation [the first attack on the World Trade Center tower]. We said to them "Wait, wait." Suddenly another brother, Marwan [the hijacker who was a friend of Ramzi bin al Shibh], was violently ramming the [second] plane into the Trade Center in an unbelievable manner! We were watching live and praying "God . . . aim . . . aim . . . aim . . . aim."[4]

For his part, Osama bin Laden gleefully listened to the news report. According to his driver Salim Hamdan, "after each strike, bin Laden held up another finger for his joyful, incredulous followers, promising yet another one."[5]

We now know that the Al Qaeda terrorists hijacked planes being flown from the East Coast to California for the simple fact that they carried full tanks filled with flammable jet fuel for the long trip. The first two planes hit World Trade Center (WTC) 1 and 2 and barely caused the buildings to shudder, so well built were they. But the WTC architects had not envisioned hijacked planes being flown into them (prior to this, hijacking did not mean suicidal attacks turning planes into human guided missiles; it meant capturing planes and making demands). The Federal Emergency Management Agency subsequently found that the buildings' joists (similar to beams) were weakened by the unexpectedly intense jet-fuel fires. This later caused a progressive "pancake" collapse once the joists melted.

Just prior to the WTC's collapse, millions of Americans watched their televisions live as people in the burning buildings were forced to leap to their deaths from the massive structures onto the streets below. Several news commentators reporting live on the unfolding tragedy broke into tears, so horrific were the real-time images of Americans plummeting to their deaths on the sidewalks below. When the buildings finally collapsed in massive clouds of dust and debris, they trapped and killed thousands more inside who were burnt or crushed to death in a horrible instant.

In total, 2,752 people died in the World Trade Centers, including 157 passengers on the hijacked planes. Another 125 people died in the Pentagon and fifty-eight in a hijacked plane that hit it later in the morning. More would have died, but for the fact that the Pentagon was so well built that the section that was hit did not collapse until half an hour after the attack. Another forty-three people also died when United Airlines Flight 93 was hijacked and its passengers, alerted to the fact that hijacked planes were being flown into buildings, fought back against the hijackers. This caused the hijacked aircraft to crash into an open field in Shanksville, Pennsylvania. Its ultimate target was most likely the White House or the Capitol Building, thus potentially allowing the terrorists to strike at America's financial might (the WTC), military control (the Pentagon), and political power (the Capitol).

It was the greatest terrorist attack in world history and greatest foreign attack on the U.S. mainland. In all there were 2,996 victims, not including the nineteen hijackers. The closest American experience had been the December 7, 1941, Japanese attack on the U.S. military base at Pearl Harbor in the Pacific territory of Hawaii (which was not yet a state at the time), which killed 2,402 primarily military personnel. But the 9/11 destruction had largely taken place in the heart of America's greatest city, not on a distant military base, and involved the televised death of thousands of civilians. It would ultimately cost the United States $178 billion in economic loses and property damage.[6]

After the attack, President Bush gave a televised speech that was to comfort millions of grieving Americans who did not understand the historic roots of the horrible act and to display a steely resolve to deal with those who carried it out. Below is the text of Bush's powerful speech to his grieving nation:

Good evening.

Today, our fellow citizens, our way of life, our very freedom came under attack in a series of deliberate and deadly terrorist acts. The victims were in airplanes or in their offices—secretaries, business-men and women, military and federal workers. Moms and dads. Friends and neighbors.

Thousands of lives were suddenly ended by evil, despicable acts of terror. The pictures of airplanes flying into buildings, fires burn-ing, huge structures collapsing, have filled us with disbelief, terrible sadness and a quiet, unyielding anger.

These acts of mass murder were intended to frighten our nation into chaos and retreat. But they have failed. Our country is strong. A great people has been moved to defend a great nation.

Terrorist attacks can shake the foundations of our biggest buildings, but they cannot touch the foundation of America. These acts shatter steel, but they cannot dent the steel of American resolve. America was targeted for attack because we're the brightest beacon for freedom and opportunity in the world. And no one will keep that light from shining.

Today, our nation saw evil, the very worst of human nature, and we responded with the best of America, with the daring of our rescue workers, with the caring for strangers and neighbors who came to give blood and help in any way they could.

Immediately following the first attack, I implemented our government's emergency response plans. Our military is powerful, and it's prepared. Our emergency teams are working in New York City and Washington, D.C., to help with local rescue efforts.

Our first priority is to get help to those who have been injured and to take every precaution to protect our citizens at home and around the world from further attacks.

The functions of our government continue without interruption. Federal agencies in Washington which had to be evacuated today are reopening for essential personnel tonight and will be open for business tomorrow. Our financial institutions remain strong, and the American economy will be open for business as well.

The search is underway for those who are behind these evil acts. I've directed the full resources for our intelligence and law enforce-ment communities to find those responsible and bring them to justice. *We will make no distinction between the terrorists who committed these acts and those who harbor them* [emphasis mine].[7]

President Bush then went on to visit the smoldering ruins of the World Trade Centers with several firemen. There he seized the imagination of his grieving people when he spontaneously grabbed a bullhorn from a fireman and told the crowd, which was clamoring for him to speak louder, "I can hear you! The rest of the world hears you! And the people who knocked these buildings down will hear all of us soon!"[8]

Bush's from-the-hip style determination to deal with the terrorists seemed to resonate with the mood of grieving Americans, who discovered a new-found determination to punish those who had carried out the 9/11 massacre. In the days after 9/11, George Bush's approval rating soared to an unprece-dented 92 percent, surpassing the 90 percent approval rating of his father in the aftermath of the successful conclusion of the First Gulf War.[9]

But Bush had a softer side as well and also visited a Washington, D.C., mosque, six days after the attack to head off Islamophobia in America. There he called the mosque congregants his "friends" and said of 9/11, "These acts of violence against innocents violate the fundamental tenets of the Islamic faith. And it's important for my fellow Americans to understand that."[10]

Bush and America's search to find out who had "knocked these buildings down" did not take long. The evidence that Al Qaeda had perpetrated the attack came in quickly and actually began even as the flights were being hi-jacked. Members of one hijacked plane's flight crew called their employers from the aircraft to give the seat numbers of the men who had hijacked the plane. The FBI quickly tracked down their identities (the hijackers used their real names). Within minutes the names began to appear on a list the FBI had of known Al Qaeda operatives. The FBI then called chief counterterrorism advisor Richard Clarke and announced "We got the passenger manifests from the airlines. We recognize some names, Dick. They're al Qaeda."[11]

While one television commentator was to erroneously theorize that the attack was the work of Palestinian terrorists (who had never actually attacked America), one did not have to be a CIA analyst to see Al Qaeda's hand in the attacks. Those in the CIA's Counterterrorism Center, the FBI, and of course chief counterterrorism advisor Richard Clarke, who had reported that the system was "blinking red" prior to 9/11, had no doubt who had perpetrated the destruction. Many strands of evidence accumulated over time to prove that Al Qaeda had carried out the 9/11 outrage.

The most damning evidence came from the National Security Agency, which intercepted a phone call from an Al Qaeda operative in Afghanistan to a phone number in the former Soviet republic of Georgia at 9:53 A.M. on the morning of 9/11 (i.e., fifteen minutes after Flight 77, the third hijacked plane, hit the Pentagon). The caller from Afghanistan said he "had heard the good news" and that a fourth target was yet to be hit (i.e., by Flight 93, which was flying at that time toward Washington, D.C.).[12] A video later emerged of bin Laden gloating about the 9/11 attacks with a visitor and stating:

> We calculated in advance the number of casualties from the enemy, who would be killed based on the position of the tower. We calculated that the floors that would be hit would be three or four floors. I was the most optimistic of them all. . . . We had notification since the previous Thursday that the event would take place that day. We had finished our work that day and had the radio on. . . . Muhammad [Atta] from the Egyptian family [meaning the Al Qaeda Egyptian group], was in charge of the group. . . .
>
> The brothers, who conducted the operation, all they knew was that they have a martyrdom operation and we asked each of them to go to America but they didn't know anything about the operation, not even one letter. But they were trained and we did not reveal the operation to them until they are there and just before they boarded the planes.[13]

In 2006, bin Laden, who was perhaps frustrated by the fact that most Arabs or Muslims did not believe his followers carried out 9/11, subsequently proclaimed, "I was responsible for entrusting the 19 brothers with those raids."[14] An unnamed country's intelligence service (probably France) also intercepted a phone call bin Laden made to his stepmother on September 9, 2001, wherein he stated, "In two days, you're going to hear big news and you're not going to hear from me for a while."[15] It later transpired that the thirteen "muscle" members of the 9/11 hijacking team recorded farewell videos of themselves in Kandahar, Afghanistan, before departing to America to take part in the "Planes Operation." Two 9/11 hijack pilots, Ziad Jarra and Mohamad Atta, also filmed themselves training in Afghanistan.[16] Other video footage was also aired on Al Jazeera (the Fox News/CNN of the Middle East), which showed images of Osama bin Laden meeting with the hijackers and 9/11 planners, including Ramzi bin al Shibh, and two martyrdom farewell messages from hijackers who were on the 9/11 flights.[17] One of the hijackers who purchased a seat on the 9/11 planes also filmed a last testament, which Al Qaeda later posted online, wherein he is praised by bin Laden and states, "We shall come at you from your front and back, your right and left."[18] Another 9/11 hijacker earlier warned a librarian in Hamburg, Germany (where the plotters met), "There will be thousands of dead. You will think of me. . . . You will see. In America something is going to happen. Many people will be killed."[19]

Yet another 9/11 hijacker filmed a testament that was shown on Al Jazeera wherein he warned the Americans, "Leave the Arabian Peninsula defeated and stop supporting the coward Jews in Palestine."[20] In addition, the FBI found the luggage of Mohamad Atta (the 9/11 team leader) that did not make it on the flight and discovered stolen American Airlines uniforms in it. Captured Al Qaeda planner Ramzi bin al Shibh later told his interrogators that Mohamad Atta conveyed the actual date of the hijacking to him. Key details of the hijacking were made known when bin al Shibh and the actual planner behind 9/11, Khaled Sheikh Muhammad, were arrested in Pakistan and later interrogated by American officials.

There is other evidence as well, including wire transfers of money to the "martyred" hijackers from known Al Qaeda members. Also the FBI later accessed the hijackers' e-mail accounts and found messages wherein they talked about the upcoming 9/11 attack in advance. If this were not enough, one of the Al Qaeda hijackers, Zacarias Massaoui, was arrested before 9/11 when he drew the attention of his trainer by asking "how much fuel is on board a 747 and how much damage could it cause if it hit anything?"[21]

Further evidence came from the skeptical Pakistani journalist Hamid Mir, who interviewed bin Laden and his followers in the weeks after 9/11. Mir wrote of his experience: "I was not ready to say that bin Laden is involved in the attacks. You see, I was questioning the accusation that he is involved. When I visited Afghanistan I spent some days there. I was totally changed because I saw the pictures of Atta [the lead hijacker] hanging in the [Al Qaeda] hideouts. Privately they admitted everything. They said they [the ones who attacked on 9/11] are our brothers."[22]

Despite the fact that the 9/11 attacks were carried out by Arabs whose names are known because they appeared on FBI lists as known Al Qaeda operatives and despite the fact that they left martyrdom videos in Afghanistan, fringe elements lost no time in blaming *anyone* but Al Qaeda for the attacks. This process began in the Arab world, where Egyptian 9/11 team leader Mohamed Atta's father refused to believe that his dead son could have carried out such sickening slaughter and destruction. An Associated Press reporter interviewed Atta's father and left the following account:

> Mohammed al-Amir Atta no longer practices law, but when it comes to his son, he can still put up a spirited defense—loud, long arguments that allow few interruptions and carefully evade the key questions: Was his son really the lead hijacker in the Sept. 11 attacks? How does he live with the knowledge? Does he still believe his son is alive? The answers given by the snowy-haired, 68-year-old Egyptian in his apartment near the Pyramids tend to echo the anguish, defiance and inherent contradictions that have typified many Arab responses in the three years since the planes crashed into the twin trade towers and the Pentagon.
>
> First, the denial: The attacks weren't the work of Muslim fanatics. "Look to Mossad," Israeli intelligence. Next, the rationalization: "No nation has done as much evil in the world as America did, and you do not expect God to punish it?" And then the defiance: "If a Palestinian flies a plane and strikes the White House and kills Bush, his wife and his daughters he will go to heaven. So will any Muslim who defends his faith."[23]

Across the Arab and Muslim world, millions followed in the footsteps of Atta's father and instinctively constructed an alternative universe where the 9/11 hijackers were not actually Arab Al Qaeda Muslim fanatics, but someone else entirely. Theories ranged from it being the work of America's closest ally in the Middle East, Israel (the most popular myth, which was believed by 40 percent of Egyptians), to it having been the work of the Americans themselves.[24] The most popular myth in the region was and is that the Israeli Mossad intelligence agency carried out the attack and that "4,000" Jews did not report to work in the World Trade Center on the day of the attack (in fact approximately 450 Jews died on 9/11, i.e. 15 percent of those killed in the attack).[25]

Below are some of the typical bizarre conspiracy theories touted by Arabs or Muslims in the aftermath of 9/11 collected by the *National Review*:

- "I have a sneaking suspicion that George W. Bush was involved in the operations of September 11, as was [Secretary of State] Colin Powell."

Samir Atallah quoted in the *Al-Sharq Al-Awsat* ("Voice of the East," London), September 13, 2001.

- In November 2002, the Saudi royal-family website, Ain Al-Yaqeen, quoted the powerful Saudi interior minister, Prince Nayef, as saying: "It is impossible that 19 youths carried out the operation of September 11, or that bin Laden or Al Qaeda did that alone. . . . I think (the Zionists) are behind these events."

- An American Muslim scholar, Salah Sultan, gave an interview to Saudi Al-Resala TV on May 17, 2006: "September 11 could not have been carried out entirely from outside (America)—by Muslims or others. . . . The entire thing was of a large scale and was planned within America in order to enable America to control and terrorize the entire world."

- Throughout September 2005, Al-Jazeera aired a special titled *The Truth Behind 9/11*. Part IV, which aired September 30, was devoted to the Mossad's involvement, including a segment about their "agents . . . dancing and cheering in front of the World Trade Center."[26]

- A journalist in Pakistan found the locals believed: "The Jews did it. That's exactly what they are saying: the mayor, the businessman, the journalist, the baby doctor . . . everyone. And, as one of them said, 'Osama is totally innocent!' "[27]

When one asks such conspiracy-minded Muslims why Bush or "the Jews" carried out the massive 9/11 operation in an open democracy where President Bill Clinton could not even keep his illicit relationship with his intern Monica Lewinsky secret, the answer usually comes down to Iraq and oil. The mass terrorist attacks on America's trade, military, and political leadership (including the failed one in Pennsylvania), it is knowingly theorized, were "secretly" carried out so that the United States could conquer Iraq and seize its oil (of course independent post-U.S. Iraq controls its oil today, not the U.S., which departed the country in 2011).

But such self-obvious explanations as to why Jews/Bush slaughtered almost three thousand people on 9/11 fail the commonsense test. For, as the world knows, in the days and weeks after 9/11 the United States did *not* accuse oil-rich Iraq of carrying out the attacks; instead it accused the Afghanistan-based Al Qaeda network. Bush famously stated, "The evidence we have gathered points to a person named Osama bin Laden." The U.S. subsequently invaded Afghanistan, an inhospitable, mountainous country with virtually no natural resources aside from opium (let alone an oil supply), to destroy bin Laden's terrorist network.

If Bush/Jews really had a nefarious plan to kill U.S. military personnel in the Pentagon, American civilians in the World Trade Center, and U.S. politicians in the White House or Capitol, then why not simply blame it on Saddam Hussein in the first place and directly invade Iraq? Why launch America's longest war, at a cost of $100 billion per year, against the Taliban in the inhospitable, resourceless mountains of the Afghan "Graveyard of Empires"? Contrary to popular myths, there is no oil in Afghanistan or sufficient natural resources that would warrant an invasion.

When asked such commonsensical questions, the Muslim conspiracy theorists inevitably fail to respond in a coherent fashion and usually end up accusing their questioner of being "brainwashed by the Jewish-controlled American media."

To compound matters, fringe conspiracy theorist "truthers" in America and the West have also constructed alternative narratives to explain 9/11. These alternative-universe theories speak of the World Trade Center being destroyed not by the planes that clearly flew into them before the eyes of millions, but by "secret controlled explosions." These conspiracy theorists also speak of the Pentagon being hit by a missile, not a plane; of Flight 93 being shot down over Shanksville, Pennsylvania, by a missile, and so on. While there are reams of evidence supporting the U.S. government's position, from airplane wreckage at the Pentagon that was easily noticeable to thousands of drivers passing on the nearby highway, to flight manifests on the planes with the names of the 9/11 hijackers, whose martyrdom videos were found in Afghanistan, there is not a shred of evidence to support the "anyone-but-Al-Qaeda-did-it" conspiracy theorists in the West or the Muslim world.

But such conspiracy-based realities can be expected in a world where many people believe aliens built the pyramids, that the moon landings were faked, that Obama is a crypto-Muslim working for Al Qaeda, and that there was no Holocaust. What is far more alarming, however, is that there have been American politicians who have succumbed to the allure of subscribing to lunatic fringe conspiracy theories about 9/11. For example, a Missouri Democrat Caucus chairman with Bangladeshi origins named Rabbi Alam asked in 2012 "why 9/11 was an official holiday for all Jewish people [who] worked in the WTC." He also asked, "What's the reason not a single Jew was killed on that day?"[28]

But perhaps the most dangerous example of this trend to seek alternative answers as to who was responsible for 9/11 actually took place with a high-ranking member of the Bush administration. Mere days after 9/11 happened, even as the World Trade Center smoldered and burnt bodies were being collected, President Bush called a meeting of the "Principals" in his cabinet to discuss America's next move. During the meeting, Deputy Secretary of Defense Paul Wolfowitz (who earlier accused Richard Clarke of "giving too much credit" to bin Laden when he tried warning him of the impending Al Qaeda threat) tried diverting blame for the attack from bin Laden *to Iraq.* Reading accounts of his comments one cannot help but feel that Wolfowitz was trying to take advantage of the 9/11 tragedy to divert a grieving American public into a full scale war against Baathist Iraq.

Below is a CIA operative's eyewitness account of an extraordinary meeting wherein Paul Wolfowitz, the second most powerful civilian in charge of the U.S. military, called for attacking not the Al Qaeda perpetrators of the 9/11 mayhem, but Saddam Hussein, who had nothing to do with it:

> It was making sense. All of the people here were sticking to their roles as I had imagined them. They were all calm and polite. They were rational.
>
> Then it got weird.
>
> With no prelude, prompt or reference point that I could fathom, Wolfowitz launched into a monologue.
>
> "Iraq. We must focus on Iraq—9/11 had to be state-sponsored. Iraq is central to our counterterrorism strategy." He spoke with great emphasis. There was a short pause, with no response. So he lectured in this vein for another couple of minutes. Then he stopped as abruptly as he had started.
>
> There was a heavy silence round the table. I looked around the room. Still nobody said anything.
>
> *What is he smoking?* I wondered.
>
> There was nothing in our intelligence collection or analysis that implicated Iraq in 9/11. On the contrary, Saddam Hussein was a secular ally with no affinity for AQ [Al Qaeda] ideology or for AQ as an ally of convenience. While Saddam was a terrorist and supported terrorist groups, especially those in the radical Palestinian networks, he saw AQ as more of a threat than an ally. Moreover, AQ had organized and trained, and plotted the 9/11 attack from Afghanistan, not Iraq.

I sat mum. It seemed too strange to warrant a response, particularly from me, the new guy, policy rookie, field spook. But neither did anybody else challenge Wolfowitz. I dismissed the commentary as temporary contorted logic, an aberration of an otherwise intelligent and responsible political leader. I had no idea what would unfold in the next couple of years [i.e., the Bush Jr. administration's subsequent massive effort to convince the American people that Iraq was linked to Al Qaeda].[29]

Chief counterterrorism advisor Richard Clarke expressed his own shock at the efforts by Wolfowitz and Wolfowtiz's boss, the secretary of defense, Donald Rumsfeld, to divert efforts from Al Qaeda terrorists in Afghanistan to the Republic of Iraq. Clarke recalls walking into the meeting with these two top Pentagon officials that he thought would focus on the perpetrators of 9/11, Al Qaeda. Instead he found Rumsfeld focused on "getting Iraq." According to Clarke, "Then I realized with almost a sharp physical pain that Rumsfeld and Wolfowitz were going to try to take advantage of this national tragedy to promote their agenda about Iraq. Since the beginning of the administration, indeed well before, they had been pressing for a war with Iraq."[30] Clarke would also recall:

> Rumsfeld was saying that we needed to bomb Iraq. And we all said . . . no, no. Al-Qaeda is in Afghanistan. We need to bomb Afghanistan. And Rumsfeld said there aren't any good targets in Afghanistan. And there are lots of good targets in Iraq. I said, "Well, there are lots of good targets in lots of places, but Iraq had nothing to do with it."
>
> Initially, I thought when he said, "There aren't enough targets in—in Afghanistan," I thought he was joking. I think they wanted to believe that there was a connection, but the CIA was sitting there, the FBI was sitting there, I was sitting there saying we've looked at this issue for years. For years we've looked and there's just no connection.[31]

Clarke would later vent, "Having been attacked by Al Qaeda, for us to now go bombing Iraq in response would be like our invading Mexico after the Japanese attacked us at Pearl Harbor."

Investigative journalist Bob Woodward provided additional details of

Wolfowitz's bizarre attempt to divert the war from Al Qaeda to Iraq in his best seller based on his time spent in the Bush White House entitled *Bush at War*:

> Wolfowitz seized the opportunity. Attacking Afghanistan would be uncertain. He worried about 100,000 American troops bogged down in the mountains fighting in Afghanistan six months from then. In contrast, Iraq was a brittle, oppressive regime that might break easily. It was doable. He estimated there was a 10 to 50 percent chance Saddam was involved in the September 11 terrorist attacks. The U.S. would have to go after Saddam at some time if the war on terrorism was to be taken seriously. . . .
>
>   [Secretary of State Colin] Powell objected. You're going to hear from your coalition partners, he told the president. They're all with you, every one, but they will go away if you hit Iraq.[32]

Donald Rumsfeld's notes from September 11, 2001, had the following notations he asked himself: "Judge whether good enough hit Saddam Hussein at same time. Not only Osama bin Laden." The notes also stated: "Go massive" and "Sweep it all up. Things related and not."[33] In a similar vein, Wolfowitz glibly (and incorrectly!) stated, "Making war on Iraq might be easier than against Afghanistan."[34]

President Bush would ultimately end the debate and make the decision to attack Afghanistan, not Iraq (initially at least). Bush would state, "No, we've had no evidence that Saddam Hussein was involved with September the 11th."[35] Woodward claimed of Bush, "he didn't want to use the war on terror as an excuse to settle an old score [with Iraq]."[36] But ominously Bush would later tell National Security Advisor Condoleezza Rice, "We won't do Iraq now. But it is a question we're gonna have to return to."[37]

Having decided not to divert America's war efforts from Al Qaeda in Afghanistan to finish the "unfinished business" of the 1991 Gulf War in Iraq, it was decided that the United States would give the Taliban an ultimatum: Turn over bin Laden and the other Arab terrorist "guests" or "share their fate."

In Afghanistan, Taliban mullahs reacted to stunning news from America by panicking and denying their Arab guests' guilt. When U.S. secretary of state Colin Powell called on them to "either help us rip them up" or suffer "the full wrath of the United States and other countries," the Taliban appeared at a loss.[38] While some Taliban moderates were in favor of publicly trying bin Laden's Arab Al Qaeda terrorists, Mullah Omar and the extremist wing of the Taliban vehemently overrode them. Far from turning bin Laden over, Mullah Omar proclaimed, "Osama Bin Laden will be the last person to leave Afghanistan," and he warned his people not to be "cowards."[39]

Mullah Omar seemed to have bought into the conspiracy theories that America, or the Jews, carried out 9/11 in order to create a pretext to invade his country. In so doing he avoided facing the reality of the fact that bin Laden had betrayed him by attacking the United States, even though he had been warned by Mullah Omar not to antagonize the powerful Americans. An October 2001 interview sheds some light on the Taliban leader's state of mind on the eve of America's invasion:

Mullah Omar: Neither Osama nor the Taliban has the resources to implement the recent incidents against the United States. I believe the perpetrators were from inside the United States itself.

Ismail: How?

Omar: For example, the investigation has not taken into account the absence on the same day of the incident of 4,000 Jews who worked in the World Trade Centers in New York.[40]

Mullah Omar later told a Pakistani journalist, "I will never deliver bin Laden. I believe God will help us."[41] The Taliban's messianic leader, it seemed, was incapable of grasping the true nature of the dangerous position bin Laden had put him and his theocratic regime in on 9/11. The unparalleled destruction on September 11th would not be met with another wave of cruise missiles as had been the case following the killing of twelve Americans in the embassy bombings east Africa in 1998. The Americans had come to see the September 11th attack as an act of "war" and would respond by bringing war to Afghanistan.

When confronted with the news of the Taliban's defiance, the Bush administration had no recourse but to move against the clear and present danger emanating from Afghanistan. As the Taliban miscalculated and drew a line in the sand, Richard Armitage, the deputy secretary of state, summed up America's position as follows: "we told the Taliban in no uncertain terms that if this happened, [it's] their ass. No difference between the Taliban and Al Qaeda now. They both go down."[42] President Bush would later declare, "Every nation has a choice to make. In this conflict, there is no neutral ground. If any government sponsors the outlaws and killers of innocence, they have become outlaws and murderers themselves. And they will take that lonely path at their own peril."[43] This policy of dealing forcefully not just with the terrorists, but with states that harbored them, would become known as the Bush Doctrine.

Infuriated by Mullah Omar's decision to stand by Al Qaeda, President Bush ordered his top general to "rain holy hell" on them.[44] As for bin Laden, the head of the CIA's Counterterrorism Center, Cofer Black, was more blunt. Black ordered his Special Activities operatives to "capture Bin Laden, kill him, and bring me his head back in a box on dry ice."[45]

By late September the die was cast, and the Taliban's fate was sealed; the United States and its powerful NATO allies were ready to go to war with Afghanistan's fundamentalist Pashtun Taliban "host" as well as the Al Qaeda "parasite."[46]

In light of the overwhelming military power arrayed against them, the Taliban's almost suicidal obstinacy has baffled many to this day. Far from acquiescing to the American demands, as U.S. carrier fleets steamed toward the Indian Ocean and tens of thousands of U.S. troops prepared to be deployed to the remote region, Taliban spokesman Sohail Shaheen boldly declared, "The Soviets also invaded and occupied Afghanistan, but defeat became their destiny. *Insha'Allah* [God willing], the Americans will meet the same fate. This is the beginning of the *Jihad*."[47] Mullah Omar confidently predicted, "They will receive a tougher lesson than their Russian predecessors."[48]

Bizarrely, it also appeared that those who would certainly be the main target of the U.S.-led coalition, bin Laden's Arab 055 Ansar (Supporters) Brigade fighters, similarly relished the chance to fight the American "infidels." For young Arab fighters who had grown up hearing the story of bin Laden's heroic victory over the Soviets in the 1987 battle of Jaji, this was their chance to gain glory. Many Arab Ansars assumed that the "cowardly" Americans—whom they felt had cut and run from Somalia following the infamous 1993 "Black Hawk Down" incident—did not have the stomach to wage a full-scale war in the mountains of Central Asia.

Referring to the televised mutilation of downed U.S. airmen's bodies in the streets of Mogadishu by Somali crowds in 1993, Al Qaeda's military head, Muhammad Atef, crowed, "America will not realize its miscalculations until its soldiers are dragged in Afghanistan like they were in Somalia."[49] One of bin Laden's Arab comrades expressed similar hubristic optimism in less flowery terms when he predicted, "We fucked the Soviets, now we are going to fuck the Americans."[50] Al Qaeda's leaders clearly felt that an American invasion would be playing into their hands, for their long-term strategic goal was to "embroil the United States in a war of attrition outside its borders."[51] Clearly bin Laden wanted America to get sucked into a quagmire fighting dedicated jihadis in an unforgiving environment.

Such belligerence on the part of the Taliban and Al Qaeda naturally infuriated Americans, many of whom came to confuse the long suffering Afghan people with their Taliban oppressors or bin Laden's Arab terrorist network. In a knee-jerk response that displayed precisely the sort of arrogance that drove many Muslim extremists to hate the United States in the first place, some Americans even called for the punitive "nuking of Afghanistan back to the stone ages."[52] This, despite the fact that *no Afghans*, not even the local Taliban, had been involved in the planning or execution of Al Qaeda's 9/11 attack.

Fortunately, cooler heads prevailed in formulating the U.S. response to the stupendous destruction caused by Al Qaeda in New York; Washington, D.C.; and Shanksville, Pennsylvania. Far from reacting precipitously, the White House responded by calmly marshaling its intelligence, military, and political resources to understand the nature of the enemy. In so doing, the American diplomatic, military, and intelligence communities began to put the pieces into place for one of the greatest victories in modern military history.

Operation Enduring Freedom:
The 2001 Destruction of Al Qaeda's Afghan Sanctuary

By resisting the urge to act rashly, the United States ultimately formulated a sound strategy for "eviscerating" the Taliban regime that was more thought out and nuanced than bin Laden could have foreseen. The multifaceted response crafted by America's military, diplomatic, and intelligence services would ultimately see the Taliban regime overthrown and Al Qaeda deprived of its sanctuary before Christmas 2001. All this at the cost of fewer than a dozen American lives. It was to be a success on a scale, and with a rapidity, that bin Laden, who was eagerly expecting a full-scale military invasion and resulting quagmire, could not have foreseen.

The dynamics behind this victory are still not fully understood to this day, and this has led some to post facto underestimate the very real problems that the U.S. military faced at the time. But the speed with which America's response to 9/11 achieved its goals should not lead to a retroactive discounting of the real obstacles that it faced at the time. British admiral Sir Michael Boyce described the impending Afghan conflict as "the most difficult operation ever under-taken by this country post-Korea."[53]

But, as it transpired, one farsighted U.S. official had already drawn up an outline for an intelligence-driven war against the Taliban. Eight months prior to 9/11, counterterrorism chief Richard Clarke had provided the CIA with a plan known as the Blue Sky Memo, which called for arming the Northern Alliance and using its fighters to attack Al Qaeda.[54] This memo, which was shelved until 9/11, called for "massive support to anti-Taliban groups such as the Northern Alliance led by Ahmad Shah Massoud," as well as winning over Pakistani support and the targeted killings of Al Qaeda leaders using remote control Predator aerial drones.[55] As this secret memo makes clear, it was the CIA that suggested the linking up of U.S. Special Forces with the Northern Alliance opposition, not the military, which had no contingency plans for invading landlocked Afghanistan.[56]

Of even greater importance was Pakistan. It was an open secret that Pakistan, the world's second most populous Muslim country, was also the primary cross border sponsor of the Taliban. An intelligence brief by Richard Clarke from January 2001 had stated, "The Pakistani Army has provided the Taliban with advisors, intelligence, training, equipment, and placed personnel in Taliban units."[57] Another report was more specific and claimed "munitions convoys depart Pakistan late in the evening hours and are concealed to reveal their true contents."[58]

If Pakistan could be won over to the anti-Taliban coalition, the United States could bring a halt to this logistic support for the Taliban and request the help of Pakistani Frontier Corps in cutting off Al Qaeda's escape routes. Everyone understood that Pakistan's assistance would be crucial in providing the "anvil" to the U.S. "hammer" in the conflict ahead.

Proffering the "stick" as a motivator, U.S. deputy secretary of state Richard Armitage threatened that Pakistan would be "bombed back to the Stone Ages" if it did not join the U.S.-led effort.[59] If, on the other hand, it chose to join the coalition, the "carrot" would come in the form of billons of U.S. dollars in strategic aid and global acceptance.

Pakistan's leader, Pervez Musharraf, felt that his country's Taliban protégés had become "both unpredictable and ungrateful" and decided to join the U.S.-led coalition.[60] But he did so with one caveat, that he would not be undermined among his own people by clumsy U.S. actions. Specifically, America was to avoid a bloodbath in Afghanistan that would be seen by the fierce Pashtun tribes of Pakistan's neighboring Northwest Frontier Province (or Khyber Pakhtunkhwa as it is now known) and the Federally Administered Tribal Agencies (FATA) as a reprise of the ham-fisted Soviet invasion of the 1980s. Fleeing Al Qaeda Arabs would be fair game for arrest if they crossed into Pakistan, but the local Pashtun Taliban were not going to be hunted if they fled to Pakistan seeking sanctuary. Pakistan could not afford to antagonize the fierce Pashtun tribesmen, who made up 15 percent of their country.

Musharraf further impressed on the Americans the need to take all measures necessary to avoid falling into the trap of being portrayed on Al Jazeera as an infidel Goliath at war with the Muslim Davids. Images of U.S. troops occupying Afghan villages, inflicting collateral damage on innocent Afghan civilians, and marching into Kabul flying U.S. flags would only play into bin Laden's hands. To the extent that it was possible, the U.S. invasion of Afghanistan would have to be more subtle than that of the twentieth-century Soviets and nineteenth-century British.

While America's airpower could be used to destroy troop concentrations and communication facilities, Afghanistan was, however, clearly not a "target-rich environment," in air force jargon. As Secretary of Defense Donald Rumsfeld eloquently put it, "B-52s are powerful and can do certain things within reasonable degrees of accuracy, but they can't crawl around on the ground and find people."[61]

For the U.S. planners, Richard Clarke's Blue Sky Memo was the obvious solution to the problem that had bedeviled them as it became apparent that the United States would be launching an invasion of Afghanistan. Namely, how do you deploy "boots on the ground" in Afghanistan, without "leaving a heavy footprint"?[62]

It was at this time that the CIA received a satellite phone call from a relatively unknown Afghan Uzbek opposition figure calling himself General Dostum. Dostum, it will be recalled, had just returned to Afghanistan six months earlier to fight a lonely battle against the Taliban alongside Massoud. He clearly saw 9/11 as a godsend, for it would enable him to link up with the powerful Americans to fight his Taliban foes. Dostum sent his condolences to the Americans for their loses on 9/11 and told them that he had a force of roughly two thousand rebel horsemen located high in the central Hindu Kush Mountains. He explained that the Taliban were his people's blood enemies and had conquered their secular northern Afghan realm in 1998.

Dostum's riders were chomping at the bit to fight alongside the Americans against the common Taliban/Al Qaeda enemy to free their people and punish those who had terrorized both the Uzbeks and the Americans.

But that was not all. Dostum was a man of action, and he had a plan. His goal was to unite with the Americans and break out of the mountains and seize the holy shrine town of Mazar i Sharif, northern Afghanistan's most sacred spot. Dostum was convinced that this strategic move would both offer the Americans an airbase in Afghanistan to insert ground troops and weaken the morale of the superstitious Taliban. He and his men were raring to go and had already gone on the offensive against a Taliban-controlled mountain district known as Zari.[63]

Dostum's stunning message was welcome news to Cofer Black at CIA headquarters and Henry Crumpton, the CIA leader who was charged with executing operations in Afghanistan. Here was an indigenous Afghan Muslim leader with boots on the ground in this inaccessible country who knew the lay of the land and had a bold plan. The CIA could not have asked for more and quickly dispatched a six-man Special Activities Division team from the neighboring country of Uzbekistan to liaise with Dostum in his mountain hideout. By late September the CIA officers, led by two experienced operatives with many years in the region, R. J. and Dave Tyson, and been inserted by Black Hawk helicopter into Dostum's remote mountain base. These Uzbek- and Tajik-speaking special operators quickly began to lay the groundwork for the subsequent insertion of a twelve-man Special Force A-Team.[64]

As this was happening, CIA teams were also being inserted into the Northern Alliance enclave of the recently murdered Tajik leader Massoud. There CIA operatives Gary Bernsten and Gary Schroen met with the slain Massoud's successor, Fahim Khan. But they found that the disheartened Tajiks were less willing to go on the offensive than Dostum's scrappy Uzbeks. Regardless, the CIA operatives laid the groundwork for the subsequent insertion of Green Beret A-Teams into the Tajik opposition enclave in the northeastern mountains as well.

As these CIA Special Activities Division operators were being covertly inserted into Northern Alliance opposition enclaves, the United States officially declared the commencement of Operation Enduring Freedom on October 7, 2001. On that day the U.S. bombed Taliban targets in Kabul, Kandahar (the spiritual headquarters of the Taliban in southern Afghanistan), and the eastern city of Jalalabad. Over the next few days B-52s and B-1s flying from the British-controlled Indian Ocean island of Diego Garcia and F-14s and F-18s flying from the carriers USS *Carl Vinson* and USS *Enterprise* bombed the Taliban's limited air defenses, command and control centers, and training grounds. The American aircraft also bombed Mullah Omar's compound in Kandahar and any compound or facility thought to be inhabited by Al Qaeda or Arab fighters. The British Royal Navy also fired as many as fifty cruise missiles at targets throughout the country.

But the Americans largely avoided bombing the Taliban's front lines facing the Tajiks in the northeast. As a result Fahim Khan and his Tajiks complained about the lack of bombing on the front lines and the United States responded by using F-18 Hornets to attack the Taliban's field positions to the north of Kabul on the Shomali Plain.

The precision of the bombing was aided by the fact the U.S. had, by late October, inserted a Green Beret A-Team made up of twelve Special Force operators known as Triple Nickel (ODA 555, Operational Detachment Alpha) into the Tajik enclave to help direct bomb strikes. Beginning on October 21, Green Berets from Triple Nickel used a hideout (an abandoned air control tower at the former Soviet airfield of Bagram) to call in precision strikes on nearby Taliban lines. Taliban convoys bringing in supplies from Kabul were also spotted and targeted by the Green Berets. As the precision bombs went off on the enemy's static lines, the Tajik rebels cheered with jubilation and patted their American comrades on the back. They all realized that they now had the support of the world's most powerful air armada.

But for all the precision the new class of bombs known as JDAMS (Joint Direct Attack Munitions, i.e. bombs that had been retrofitted or specially produced to be GPS guided) exhibited on the Shomali Plain, the Taliban held their lines, and Fahim Khan's Tajik fighters did not appear to be prepared to storm the enemy's entrenched positions. Across Afghanistan the Taliban were coming to feel that they could ride out the bombing campaign. Many were eager to confront the Americans on the ground and scorned them as "cowards" for fighting from afar with airplanes.

But the American response was not to be limited to aerial bombardments, for it was a well-known rule of modern combat that wars cannot be won from the air alone. The Americans also had another Northern Alliance warlord to work with, and he was more than eager to go on the offensive. On October 19, the United States infiltrated a heliborne A-Team known as Tiger 02 (ODA 595) from Karshi, Uzbekistan, into the mountains of the Hindu Kush to liaise with the other major component of the Northern Alliance opposition, General Dostum. On that night the Green Berets were flown into the opposition enclave near the Darya Suf Valley, high in the rebel-controlled Hindu Kush Mountains, and met by Dostum and his turbaned Uzbek Mongol horsemen. The A-Team led by Captain Mark Nutsch, a Kansan who had rodeo experience, then mounted on the local Uzbeks' horses and split up to maximize their numbers. After riding for up to two days through the rugged mountains, each Green Beret subteam began fighting with the local Taliban by calling in precision bomb strikes.[65]

Nutsch's team was also joined by U.S. Air Force forward air controllers from Operational Detachment Command 53, who called in laser-guided bombs on the Taliban positions in the Darya Suf Valley. These Taliban tank and artillery emplacements were preventing Dostum and his raiders from breaking out of the mountains. Dostum took advantage of the bomb strikes to launch cavalry charges on the Taliban positions. At times Dostum timed his charges to come moments after the Taliban's positions had been bombed by JDAMs. Using this remarkable combination of medieval-style cavalry charges and state-of-the-art satellite-guided bombs delivered by carrier-borne aircraft, Dostum finally began to gather momentum against the larger Taliban force by late October 2001.[66] In my extensive interviews with Captain Nutsch, he recalled that his A-Team was galvanized by Dostum's sheer determination to break out of the mountains and seize Mazar i Sharif.

At this time a picture of one of the air force air controllers, Master Sergeant Bart Decker, riding on a horse with Uzbek horsemen in the mountains was sent to Centcom (Central Command, the U.S. command in charge of Operation Enduring Freedom based in MacDill Airbase, Tampa) and declassified for the media by Secretary of Defense Donald Rumsfeld. Rumsfeld used the picture and an "after action report" written by Green Beret leader Mark Nutsch, which described the joint U.S.-Uzbek cavalry campaign, to show his critics that the United States was making headway on the ground in Afghanistan.

But these covert operations did not appease the critics, who began to speak of a Vietnam-style quagmire and endless war. By the beginning of November, the Americans and their British and Australian allies had been at war for almost a month with no visible signs of movement on the ground, and many were questioning the pace of the war.

But unbeknownst to the American public, by November 8 Dostum and his local allies, Ustad Atta, a Tajik commander who now had his own A-Team, and Mohammad Moheqeq, a Hazara commander, had broken out of the

Darya Suf Valley and were surging northward down the nearby Balkh Valley toward the shrine town of Mazar i Sharif, located down on the plains to the north. As the Dostum-led Northern Alliance rebel force snowballed and gathered riders and momentum, the Taliban understood all too clearly the magnitude of the threat. If the rebels broke out of the mountains and took Mazar i Sharif, the Taliban (who were seen as occupiers in the Uzbek and Tajik dominated plains of the north) could be routed in this key strategic area.

In desperation, the Taliban sent additional troops to keep the Uzbek, Tajik, and Hazara horsemen bottled up in the Balkh Valley. But the Taliban's reinforcement column was spotted by an American air force combat controller, who called in U.S. aircraft known in the local dialect as *beeping joe doos* (B-52s) and *avcis* (literally "hunters" smaller F-18s), and these planes obliterated the Taliban's support convoys.

At that time, Dostum took to mocking and threatening the Taliban on their radios, declaring that he had a "death ray," which he was using to kill their men. Dostum also claimed to have *malaks* (angels) sent by Azrail the Angel of Death on his side. Many superstitious Taliban believed him and lost heart and defected to his mounting force.[67]

Having destroyed the Taliban's support columns, the joint Uzbek-Tajik-Hazara-American cavalry force then fought its way past a heavily defended Taliban bottleneck at the Tangi Gap and broke out of the mountains on November 8. The victorious allies, with horse-mounted CIA, Green Beret, and U.S. Air Force soldiers riding alongside them, then charged north and on November 9 rode into Mazar i Sharif, the crucible of the north.

While the U.S. Special Forces were "locked and loaded" upon arrival in the city, there were no Taliban to be seen; they had all fled to the east to the town of Kunduz, where there was a sympathetic Pashtun population. As the weary American soldiers, who had been fighting in harsh conditions in the mountains for weeks, rode alongside Dostum through cheering crowds to the Shrine of Ali in the center of town, they compared it to the liberation of Paris during World War II. Once at the ancient shrine in Mazar i Sharif, Dostum and his jubilant men said prayers of thanks while the Americans fulfilled a previous vow and buried burnt pieces of the World Trade Center near the mosque.[68]

As Dostum had predicted, the fall of Mazar i Sharif weakened the Taliban, who dug in at Kunduz in the east and prepared to fight to the finish. With thousands of locals coming out to greet him, Dostum led his men east alongside those of Ustad Atta to confront the Taliban holdouts in Kunduz. As the victorious Northern Alliance allies closed in on the town from the west, a

Tajik force led by commander Daoud Daoud moved toward Kunduz from the east. The Taliban army of the north, which included hundreds of fanatical 055 Arab fighters and thousands of Pakistani Pashtun volunteers who had crossed the border to join in the jihad against the Americans, was trapped.

But before the allies could destroy the entrapped Taliban army, the Tajik forces of Fahim Khan finally went on the offensive. With U.S. precision-guided bombs clearing their path, they finally broke out of their lines and raced southward across the Shomali Plain toward Kabul on November 12. By now the Taliban's fighting spirit had been broken, and they began to flee southward from the capital, a largely Tajik city, toward their tribal lands in the south. Fahim Khan and his Green Berets subsequently entered Kabul to be greeted by cheering crowds who killed any Arab they found on the streets unlucky enough not to have fled to the south or east.

As Kabul fell on November 13, the Hazaras in the middle of the country in the Hindu Kush Mountains sensed momentum had switched to their side and rose up against the disheartened Taliban who were occupying their villages. With another team of Green Berets calling down bombs on the Taliban to break their spirit, the Hazaras forced the Taliban garrisons of the mountains to flee. As they fled, the Taliban burnt scores of Hazara hamlets and killed numerous Hazara civilians.

Meanwhile, to the west, another anti-Taliban commander named Ismail Khan, a legendary anti-Soviet Tajik mujahideen leader, led his men out of the mountains of Ghor Province with a Green Beret team by his side and attacked the western city of Herat. By now the Taliban were unwilling to fight to occupy non-Pashtun lands and fled this great northern city as well. Dostum's bold seizure of Mazar i Sharif had, as he promised, broken the fighting spirit of the Taliban in the north. The dam had seemingly broken, and half of the country had been liberated. With the exception of the Taliban army trapped in Kunduz, the northern half of the country was miraculously free of the Taliban. All this with zero American deaths and only three hundred U.S. troops on the ground. Events on the ground had far outpaced Centcom's most optimistic expectations for a long winter campaign with a full-scale invasion by fifty thousand troops in the spring.

But the southern lands of the conservative Pashtuns, who made up the Taliban and 40 percent of the country's population, still remained firmly in Taliban hands. It was at this time that Centcom began working with an exiled Pashtun dissident head of the Popalzai subtribe to raise a rebellion in the south. The Pashtun chieftain, who spoke polished English, a rarity among

Afghanistan's leaders, went by the name of Hamid Karzai. Karzai blamed the Taliban for killing his father and was willing to sneak into the Pashtun south from neighboring Pakistan to raise a rebellion. In late November he did just that and was given a Special Force A-Team of his own, known as ODA 574, led by Captain Jason Amerine.

Karzai, some of his followers, and ODA 574 were infiltrated from Pakistan into Uruzgan Province, and there they began to go from village to village gathering disaffected Pashtun tribesmen to join his rebel force. Alarmed by the news, the Taliban rushed a convoy of some fifty trucks filled with hundreds of fighters to crush his incipient rebellion before it could spread throughout the Pashtun heartlands. But Amerine and his team, forewarned of the Taliban's advance, called in precision airstrikes from F-18s on the enemy convoy and wiped it out, killing hundreds.

Impressed by the firepower that Karzai and his American friends could call on, the Pashtun tribes, sensing victory, joined him en masse. The snowballing rebel force then joined up with a local anti-Taliban warlord named Gul Agha Sherzai, who had eight hundred men, and an ex-Taliban tribal leader named Naqibullah, who led a powerful tribe, and marched on Kandahar, the capital of the Pashtun south. With the United States pounding their positions and the rebels pouring in from the north, the Taliban decided to retreat in early December.

At roughly this time, a U.S.-sponsored summit of exiled Afghan leaders met in Bonn, Germany, and chose the tribal leader Hamid Karzai as the interim leader of Afghanistan. As for Mullah Omar, the "Commander of the Faithful" and messianic head of the disintegrating Taliban movement, he was last seen fleeing into the countryside on the back of a motorbike.

Mullah Omar and thousands of hardcore Taliban fighters fled across the border into the Pashtun tribal lands known as the FATA (Federally Administered Tribal Agencies) in neighboring Pakistan. There, and in the neighboring province of Baluchistan, the local Pashtun tribes offered them the hospitality of melmastiia. These die-hards would bide their time in their off-limits sanctuary, an autonomous region established by the nineteenth-century colonial British that had never been entered by the Pakistani army. They knew the Americans could not chase them into the sovereign nation of Pakistan, nor could the Pakistanis invade this rugged, off-limits tribal zone that was part of their country in name only.

Back in Afghanistan, other so-called village Taliban simply melted back into their villages and hid their weapons to fight another day. These local

Taliban had been stunned by their defeat and waited to see what the Americans would do.

But the U.S.–NATO–Northern Alliance victory in Afghanistan was far from complete, for the actual target of Operation Enduring Freedom, Osama bin Laden, had not been killed or captured. While there had been some notable successes, such as the killing of the number three in Al Qaeda, its military leader, Muhammad Atef, by a remote-controlled aerial drone in mid-November, and the killing of scores of Arab 055 fighters, bin Laden had escaped Kandahar before it fell. From Kandahar, he and hundreds of his Arab followers fled eastward toward the Afghan border city of Jalalabad. At Jalalabad, bin Laden spoke to a large crowd of local Pashtun tribesmen and Arab followers and handed out wads of cash before heading south to a frontier mountain base built in the Spin Ghar Mountains in the 1980s at a place called Tora Bora (Black Dust). There he and approximately three hundred of his men dug into a cave complex built by the anti-Soviet mujahideen and prepared to resist the Americans.

The Americans were not far behind, and soon Gary Bernsten and his CIA team and a team of Green Berets and Delta Forces arrived in a nearby valley. From there they could hear bin Laden talking on the radio and began to call in bombing strikes on the Tora Bora cave complex by December. As the air force pummeled his positions with everything from deep penetrating bunker buster bombs to Daisy Cutters (the largest bomb in the U.S. arsenal at the time), bin Laden and his men suffered terribly. Bin Laden himself barely survived the bombing, and scores of his men were killed. To compound matters, the United States had deputized local Pashtun and Pashai tribesmen to attack his complex.

But Centcom did not mine the escape routes into nearby Pakistan nor send in a large contingent of U.S. troops to overrun the base. Much to the fury of Bernsten, who felt the U.S. was a "whisker away" from bin Laden, the terrorist who had the blood of thousands of Americans on his hands was subsequently able to bribe some of the U.S.-backed Pashai tribesmen attacking him into letting him escape. On or around December 16 bin Laden and hundreds of his followers were able to slip into wild FATA region of neighboring Pakistan, leaving scores of dead comrades behind at Tora Bora. According to one Delta Force commander who was there at the time, bin Laden's last radio message to his followers was "I'm sorry for getting you involved in this battle, if you can no longer resist, you may surrender with my blessing."[69]

While America's tribal mercenaries turned a blind eye, bin Laden and his followers fled over the mountains into the Tirah Valley in the Pakistani tribal agency of Kurram. They were said to have been guided by the torches of sympathetic pro-Taliban Pashtun tribesmen. There they took advantage of their deep connections among the local FATA tribesmen going back to the 1980s anti-Soviet jihad and the Pashtun tradition of melmastiia to request sanctuary. Bin Laden and hundreds of his followers had thus succeeded in escaping to one of the most inaccessible places in the world among the fierce Orakzai and Afridi Pashtun tribes of Kurram Agency. Bin Laden's escape into the FATA was America's greatest blunder in the War on Terror, for this was sovereign Pakistani territory. Pakistani president Musharraf could never allow U.S. troops to directly invade his nation in pursuit of their Muslim enemies for fear of backlash among his own people, who distrusted the Americans.

Bin Laden's escape proved to be a fiasco, and for years pundits blamed Centcom head General Tommy Franks for letting the object of the world's largest manhunt escape into one of the most inaccessible tribal zones in the world. Bin Laden was subsequently able to avoid detection by scattering his family and followers and fleeing first to the Pashtun frontier town of Peshawar, then to the scenic Swat Valley in the North West Frontier Province of Pakistan. From there he fled with two Pashtun helpers to the town of Haripur near the capital of Islamabad, and finally to the Pakistani military town of Abbottabad.

All the towns bin Laden hid in were located in the North West Frontier Province, a rugged tribal zone next to the FATA, which was also inhabited by Pashtun tribes. Far from living in a cave, as many in the west suspected, bin Laden ended up reuniting with his four wives and sons and living in a million-dollar concrete compound in Abbottabad, just a few miles from Pakistan's version of the West Point military academy. During this time, bin Laden even sired four more children with his wives.

From 2005 to 2011, bin Laden lived in complete isolation on the top floor of his spartan compound as a virtual prisoner in the resort town of Abbottabad. While he did make the occasional video broadcast to galvanize his followers and let the Americans know he was still alive, his days of personally running Al Qaeda were over. Bin Laden was simply too high value a target to risk running the day-to-day operations of his atomized organization. Many in Al Qaeda and the larger jihadist movement also turned on him for his decision to attack the powerful Americans, thus leading to the overthrow of the allied Taliban government and the scattering of Al Qaeda from its sanctuary (he would later be forgiven by these fanatics when ISIS arose from the ashes of post-U.S.-invasion Iraq).

But bin Laden was one of the lucky ones; many of his followers met a worse fate. True to their word, the Pakistanis ultimately arrested hundreds of Arabs linked to Al Qaeda, who fled into their country from Afghanistan, and turned them over to the Americans. Most of these were then transported to the U.S. naval base in Guantanamo Bay, Cuba, a legal limbo where U.S. mainland laws and the Geneva Conventions on the handling of prisoners of war seemingly did not apply. There the suspected terrorists would be held for years in captivity without being put on trial, a situation that many human rights activists both at home and abroad felt was a stain on America's reputation. Supporters of the Gitmo (Guantanamo Bay) detention facility on the other hand claimed that the captured terrorists were, in Secretary of Defense Donald Rumsfeld's words, the "worst of the worst." They were officially declared "unlawful combatants." The prisoners were not defined as American criminals who deserved their Miranda rights and the rights accorded to American citizens by the U.S. judicial system, nor were they defined as captured enemy soldiers deserving of the protection of the Geneva Convention. They were defined as terrorists.

Among the highest-ranked Al Qaeda operatives to be arrested by the Pakistanis was Khaled Sheikh Muhammed (KSM), the actual originator of the 9/11 attack, who had convinced bin Laden to support his "planes operation," and Ramzi bin al Shibh, the hands-on planner of the attack. KSM was arrested in a safe house run by one of Pakistan's many pro-Taliban religious parties in the military town of Rwalpindi, near the Pakistani capital, while bin al Shibh was arrested by Pakistani security forces after a gunfight in the southern city of Karachi. Another prominent Al Qaeda operative arrested by the Pakistanis was the Al Qaeda–linked base commander Abu Zubaydah, who was also apprehended after being seriously wounded in a gunfight, this time in the Pakistani town of Faisalabad.

Another large group of thousands of Taliban and hundreds of Arabs was also captured when the northern Afghan town of Kunduz, destination of the Taliban's northern army following the capture of Mazar i Sharif, was finally captured by Northern Alliance commanders Dostum, Atta, and Daoud on November 26. The final fall of the city came after U.S. forces bombarded the Taliban and Arab 055 Brigade holdouts in Kunduz with everything from B-52s to AC-130 Specter gunships. Having lost hundreds of their comrades to the merciless bombardment, thousands of Taliban and hundreds of Pakistani and Arab volunteers surrendered to General Dostum. More Pakistanis would have been captured had it not been for the fact that the Pakistani air force flew out hundreds of their countrymen during the so-called Airlift of Evil.[70] The airlift was permitted by the Americans as a means of letting the Pakistani leader Pervez Musharraf save face with his generals after his about-face in abandoning the Taliban and joining the Americans.

Thousands of Pakistanis were nonetheless captured in Kunduz. Dostum then had the survivors transported across the desert to the nineteenth-century castle of Qala i Jengi and to a prison complex in his home base of Sheberghan. The prisoners in Qala i Jengi (the Fortress of War), however, rose up and rebelled when they were being interrogated by two CIA agents, Dave Tyson and Micheal Spann. Having brutally killed Spann (the first U.S. casualty in the War on Terror), the Taliban and Al Qaeda prisoners then seized an ammunition depot in the castle/prison and tried breaking out. This would have been disastrous for the Northern Alliance because the Taliban could have then scattered into nearby Mazar i Sharif and waged guerilla war.

U.S. and British Special forces were called to the scene and began firing on the revolting prisoners from the castle walls and calling in airstrikes from U.S. aircraft. The revolt was finally suppressed on December 1 after several days of intense fighting and the strafing of the prisoners by AC-130 Specter gunships and several JDAM bombing runs. When the smoke cleared only eighty-six of the estimated three hundred to five hundred foreign prisoners were alive. Among them was an oddity, a young American from California named John Walker Lindh, who had joined the Taliban and renamed himself Abdul Hamid. Lindh was subsequently transported to America and sentenced to twenty years in prison for his role in fighting alongside the Taliban.

It was subsequently discovered that an additional eight hundred Pakistani Taliban volunteers were also holed up in the Sultan Razia school in Mazar i Sharif. When a local mullah visited them to ask them to surrender, the Pakistanis gunned him down in cold blood. In response, U.S. Special Forces called in four airstrikes on the building. The survivors then fled the burning school only to be gunned down by vengeful Northern Alliance troops. Few if any of the Pakistanis survived the battle.

The loss of hundreds of Pakistani tribesmen in Afghanistan proved to be an embarrassment for the Pakistani government, which had been unable to stop a local firebrand named Mullah Sufi Muhammad from recruiting young Pakistani Pashtuns in the FATA to fight in Afghanistan. Sufi Muhammad was later arrested by the Pakistani authorities and charged with misleading the country's youth.

In addition to the deaths of hundreds of Arab and other foreign Ansars killed in the battle of Qala i Jengi and Pakistanis in the Sultan Razia school, there have been accusations made that hundreds of Taliban prisoners of war died of asphyxiation during their transportation from Kunduz to Dostum's prison at Sheberghan. Thus far, however, there has been no evidence to prove these charges, and there certainly was no systematic effort by Dostum to kill his prisoners à la the infamous massacre of Shiites by Sunni members of ISIS in 2014. In fact thousands of the Pakistani and Afghan Taliban were safely transported to Sheberghan, where they remained Dostum's prisoners until the Afghan government forced him to release them in waves in subsequent years.[71] There I extensively interviewed dozens of them and found that the Taliban prisoners of war had no knowledge of a massacre of thousands of their comrades in transport containers, as had been reported.

Considering Afghanistan's bloody history, what was remarkable about the overthrow of the Taliban regime, which weeks before had seemed entrenched and prepared to resist a full-scale Soviet-style invasion, was how smoothly it went. There were less than a dozen U.S. deaths (several of these came from an errant bomb strike), although thousands of Taliban died in the conflict. In addition, there was no systematic plundering and very little ethnic conflict and retribution of the sort that would totally devastate post-U.S.-invasion Iraq from 2003 to 2008 and cost the lives of tens of thousands. Across the country there just seemed to be collective sense of relief that the brutal Taliban regime had been overthrown so easily. As more U.S. troops were flown into the country to establish large bases in Kandahar, Bagram (an ex-Soviet base an hour north of Kabul), Kabul, Rhino (in the south), and smaller bases elsewhere, there seemed to be a sense of hope in this long-suffering country.

But the Taliban and their fanatical Arab friends still had one last battle in them. Following the fall of Kabul and Kandahar, Taliban and Arab fighters fought back in one major battle in the eastern province of Paktia in February and March 2002. During "Operation Anaconda" U.S. heliborne troops were inserted into a Taliban/Al Qaeda–controlled valley known as the Shah-i Kot near the Pakistani border. There they were engaged by as many as two hundred tough jihadi fighters, who shot down one of the large U.S. Chinook transport helicopters and killed eight Americans before retreating over the Pakistani border with their forces largely intact.

This was to be the last major resistance of the Taliban during the opening stages of Operation Enduring Freedom. In approximately five months, the United States and its allies had done the unexpected and overthrown the Taliban regime with a minimum of U.S. and coalition deaths. They had then put in place a new pro-U.S. government that would go on to hold democratic elections in 2004 and elect Karzai as president. All this with no more than 350 initial U.S. boots on the ground. It was a miracle compared to the Soviet debacle, which led to fourteen thousand deaths in just over eight years of fighting. Tragically, however this success was also to inspire Secretary of Defense Donald Rumsfeld to carry out the subsequent "light" invasion of Iraq using far fewer troops than his generals wanted.

In the following months and years, millions of Afghans poured back into the country to take advantage of the new sense of hope, improved security conditions, and influx of foreign rebuilding funds. Millions of children, including girls for the first time in years, began to attend school. New buildings went up in Kabul to replace those that had been bombed out in the civil war, several of them steel-and-glass skyscrapers. Women began to play a role in parliament; Karzai was overwhelming elected president in the country's first election in 2004; and cell phone stores, video shops, and hairdressers began to appear in the once grim streets of Kabul and elsewhere. Women who had been forced out of work by the Taliban gradually began to appear in the workplace without burqas (at least in Kabul and the Hazara lands). The UN also sent in teams to de-mine fields that had been planted with landmines during the years of war. On many levels the fanaticism of the Taliban, who had horribly oppressed the population and pushed the country into the Dark Ages, was rolled back.

NATO would also get involved in bringing security to the long-suffering Afghans through the auspices of ISAF (the International Security and Assistance Force), which was made up of members from Britain, France, The Netherlands, Canada, and Australia, whose governments allowed them to fight. There were also ISAF members from Germany, Bulgaria, the Czech Republic, Poland, Albania, Italy, Spain, Greece, Iceland, Portugal, Romania, Slovakia, and Turkey, whose casualty-phobic parliaments insisted they could fight only when fired on.

In the provinces, PRTs (Provincial Reconstruction Teams, i.e., U.S. military construction units) set themselves to the task of rebuilding the countryside's shattered infrastructure and enforcing DDR (Disarmament, Demobilization, and Rehabilitation of armed mujahideen militias that had dominated the land since the fall of the Communists). The PRTs engaged in building everything from schools, dams, and wells to roads and government buildings.

While there was some rumbling of discontent among many sullen villagers in the conservative Pashtun south, the homeland of the Taliban, in the lands of the Uzbeks, Hazaras, and Tajiks, and even in many Pashtun villages, coalition troops were most welcome. As newly laid tarmac roads replaced the pitted-out gravel roads from Kabul to such cities as Kandahar in the south and Kunduz and Mazar i Sharif in the north, Afghanistan seemed to be on the way to development and progress. While there were one or two suicide bombings by what Secretary of Defense Rumsfeld called "dead-enders," there was a newfound sense of optimism in the land.[72] As the Afghan government flag replaced the white flag of the Taliban with the old tricolored flag and newly recruited Afghan National Army and Afghan National Police began to appear in the provinces, the grounds for the optimism did not appear to be unfounded.

But even as the groundwork for democracy was laid in the seemingly fertile soil of post-Taliban Afghanistan, there were unsettling rumors from the Pashtun tribal lands in neighboring Pakistan. It was whispered that the Taliban's exiled leader, Mullah Omar, was regrouping the Taliban's inner Shura (Council) in the Pakistani city of Quetta in Baluchistan province. Travelers from the FATA region of South Waziristan also told stories of thousands of Taliban who had openly regrouped there under the leadership of a local Pakistani Pashtun Taliban leader named Nek Muhmmad. It was said they were biding their time and waiting to see what the Americans and their Western allies would do. These sources also claimed that a powerful pro-Taliban warlord from eastern Afghanistan named Jalaludin Haqqani had begun to gather Pashtun fighters to reenter Afghanistan to wage a guerilla jihad from the Pakistani FATA province of North Waziristan. Most ominously, Haqqani threatened the Americans, stating, "We will retreat to the mountains and begin a long guerrilla war to reclaim our pure land from infidels and free our country like we did against the Soviets. . . . The Americans are creatures of comfort."[73]

But such threats did not faze the Americans, who by 2002 seemed to have developed a supreme sense of confidence in their abilities. After all, the seemingly entrenched Taliban regime had been overthrown with roughly a dozen U.S. deaths. The Taliban's will to fight had seemingly been broken by America's twenty-first-century airpower (the Pentagon did not focus on the fact that Afghan leaders like Dostum had supplied them with a proxy army to defeat the Taliban on the ground). So confident was the Bush administration and Pentagon that the war in Afghanistan had been won they limited the number of U.S. troops in the Texas-sized mountainous country to a mere six thousand soldiers in 2002 (this number rose to ten thousand by 2003).[74]

By 2003 the low-level war in Afghanistan had increasingly become known as the "Forgotten War," as the Bush White House began to refocus on another country, Iraq. Even as the Taliban and its allies regrouped in the FATA and prepared to wage a guerilla jihad, the United States' attention began to be diverted toward the Iraqi ruler Saddam Hussein. As early as February 2002 the U.S. began preparations for a massive invasion of Socialist-Baathist Iraq, which was accused of having dangerous weapons of mass destruction that it might hand over to the scattered remnants of bin Laden's Al Qaeda hiding out in Pakistan's tribal zones. The head of Central Command, General Tommy Franks, summed up this redirection of NSA satellites, Special Forces, and Predator drones from Afghanistan to Iraq as follows: "we have stopped fighting the war on terror in Afghanistan. We are moving military and intelligence personnel and resources out of Afghanistan to get ready for a future war in Iraq." Tommy Franks described the downgraded mission in Afghanistan as a mere "manhunt."[75]

Eventually 75 percent of U.S. military's new unmanned Predator spy drones would be transferred from Afghanistan to the new theater of action in Iraq.[76] Elite Special Forces that had developed close working relationships with the local Afghan tribes would also be replaced by regular army units as the Green Berets were withdrawn from the "Other War" in Afghanistan for a looming war against Iraq.

Claiming that it had "decisively eviscerated" its enemies in Afghanistan, Bush showed the American people (and the down-but-far-from-out Taliban) where America would be heading during his famous January 29, 2002, State of the Union speech. In this speech, Bush essentially claimed that the UN sanctions and embargo against Iraq had failed catastrophically since the UN inspectors had been voluntarily withdrawn for their own protection in 1998 (on the eve of President Clinton's Operation Desert Fox). He also suggested that the Iraqi Baathist regime was interested in providing weapons of mass destruction to bin Laden's shattered Al Qaeda organization, which was hiding out in the FATA region of Pakistan. Bush began the massive redirection of the American power from the "Forgotten War" in Afghanistan to the new war against Hussein's Iraq by stating:

Iraq continues to flaunt its hostility toward America and to support terror. The Iraqi regime has plotted to develop anthrax and nerve gas and nuclear weapons for over a decade. This is a regime that has already used poison gas to murder thousands of its own citizens, leaving the bodies of mothers huddled over their dead children. This is a regime that agreed to international inspections then kicked out the inspectors [*sic* the inspectors were not kicked out by Hussein, they were withdrawn by the U.N.]. This is a regime that has something to hide from the civilized world.

States like these, and their terrorist allies, constitute an axis of evil, arming to threaten the peace of the world. By seeking weapons of mass destruction, these regimes pose a grave and growing danger. They could provide these arms to terrorists, giving them the means to match their hatred. They could attack our allies or attempt to blackmail the United States. In any of these cases, the price of indifference would be catastrophic.[77]

As for bin Laden, the perpetrator of the slaughter of thousands of Americans on 9/11, in March 2002 Bush stated, "Deep in my heart I know the man is on the run, if he's alive at all. Who knows if he's hiding in some cave or not; we haven't heard from him in a long time. And the idea of focusing on one person is—really indicates to me people don't understand the scope of the mission. Terror is bigger than one person. And he's just—he's a person who's now been marginalized. . . . So I don't know where he is. You know, I just don't spend that much time on him to be honest with you."[78] The signal to the Taliban and Al Qaeda by all these developments was that the White House and the Pentagon were moving on from the "completed" mission in Af/Pak (Afghanistan and Pakistan), which had been downgraded to a "manhunt," to the more important "unfinished business" of the 1991 Gulf War. The Neo-Cons had finally come to have their day in the sun. While Iraq was clearly in their War on Terror sites (an irony that must not have been lost on bin Laden, who had earlier called Hussein a "socialist motherfucker"), the regrouping Taliban would quickly come to let the distracted Americans know that they at least had not forgotten the original war in Afghanistan.[79]

CHAPTER 3

Hype:
Selling the War on Iraq
to the American People

Simply stated, there is no doubt that Saddam Hussein now has weapons of mass destruction. There is no doubt that he is massing them to use against our friends, against our allies, and against us. . . . Many of us are convinced that [Saddam Hussein] will acquire nuclear weapons fairly soon.

—Vice President Dick Cheney, 2002

We destroyed them. We told you. By God, if I had such weapons, I would have used them in the [2003] fight against the U.S.

—Iraqi President Saddam Hussein when asked in 2003
by his U.S. captors about his nonexistent WMDs

Weapons of Mass Destruction:
Diverting the War from Al Qaeda to Baathist Iraq

In spite of the fact that the Bush administration had shifted its focus from bin Laden's stateless terrorist organization to the state of Iraq by early 2002, Al Qaeda and its affiliates were far from beaten. While Al Qaeda Central had been shattered, what can best be described as "franchise groups" or affiliates that were not directly controlled by bin Laden popped up in places like Turkey, Indonesia, and North Africa. It was almost like the fun fair game "Whack a Mole."

This phenomenon was best demonstrated in the October 12, 2002, bombing in Bali, Indonesia. In this atrocity, a suicide bomber from the Al Qaeda–affiliated Indonesian terrorist group Jemaah Islamiyah set off a bomb in a packed tourist bar while another bomber detonated a powerful truck bomb outside. In total 202 people, mainly Australian tourists, were killed in the bombings, which totally destroyed two night clubs frequented by foreigners. Yet bin Laden had not planned this operation; it was homegrown "self starter."

In his seminal works *Understanding Terror Networks* and *Leaderless Jihad,* former CIA field operative and forensic psychiatrist Dr. Marc Sageman argued that Al Qaeda Central had lost much of its command and control structure when it was decimated and forced into hiding during Operation Enduring Freedom.[1] Increasingly, terrorist attacks in places like Bali, Indonesia (2002), Djberba, Tunisia (2002), Istanbul, Turkey (2003), Khobar, Saudi Arabia (2004), Madrid, Spain (2004), London, England (2005), and elsewhere would be carried out by start-up jihadi cells that shared Al Qaeda's philosophy, but were not directly controlled by bin Laden himself. The hydra-like terrorist threat to the United States and its allies was in many ways metastasizing and spreading following the destruction of Al Qaeda Central in 2001.

For this reason the CIA realized that the intelligence war on Al Qaeda and its affiliates would continue despite the White House's total focus on Iraq by 2002–3. The Agency's hunt was still on for bin Laden; his number two, Zawahiri; and countless other Al Qaeda operatives or members of newly emerging splinter groups like Indonesia's Jemaah Islamiyah, Turkey's El Kaida Turka (Turkish Al Qaeda), Al Qaeda in the Islamic Maghreb (North Africa), Abu Sayyaf (a Philippine jihadist group), or Al Qaeda in the Arabian Peninsula.[2] The pressure to prevent another 9/11 was clearly on the CIA, which had failed to penetrate Al Qaeda before that tragic day.

Domestically, the FBI and NSA stepped up their surveillance operations (including using controversial wireless taping of phones), and the newly created Homeland Security Department, led by Tom Ridge, began to coordinate antiterrorism operations in the United States. Internationally, the CIA began a process known as "extraordinary rendition," wherein it had suspected terrorists apprehended abroad then taken to so-called black sites, where they were interrogated.[3] These black sites were found in countries like Poland, Bulgaria, Romania, the Czech Republic, Hungary, Azerbaijan, Egypt, Morocco, Libya, Algeria, and Diego Garcia, where critics have argued that prisoners could be tortured by CIA agents without fear of later being prosecuted at home.

It was in the midst of this desperate hunt for Al Qaeda and its affiliates who had stepped up operations against the United States that the CIA began to come under a new and different kind of pressure from Vice President Dick Cheney's office and the Neo-Cons in the White House. Cheney wanted "actionable intelligence" not on the continuing Al Qaeda threat, but on Saddam Hussein's Iraq. The Republic of Iraq, not Al Qaeda, was to be new focus of the CIA as the Bush White House sought to link this socialist nation not only to the Pakistan-based bin Laden, but to weapons of mass destruction, *including nukes*. The CIA's deputy director Michael Morell was to say of this unprecedented intrusion by politicians in the CIA's business of intelligence analysis: "Not only had the vice president's staffers written their own analytic papers to get their view's into the secretary's [Powell's] speech [to the UN in February 2003 on Iraqi WMDs], they also parachuted into CIA headquarters to lobby for their point of view. . . . The degree of [intelligence] analysis being done by political appointees was unprecedented in my career. Officials in the vice president's office were trying to be both the analysts and the policy makers."[4] Michael Morell would also say "[Vice President Cheney's chief of staff Scooter] Libby's attempts to intimidate [CIA terrorism analysis chief Jami] Miscik was the most blatant attempt to politicize intelligence I ever saw in thirty-three years in the business."[5]

But Vice President Cheney's task of convincing the CIA that Iraq was a WMD threat was difficult because, as of late 2001, the intelligence community had concluded that "Iraq did not appear to have reconstituted its nuclear weapons program," while the International Atomic Energy Agency (IAEA) had declared back in 1998 that "there are no indications that there remains in Iraq any physical capability for the production of weapons-usable nuclear material of any practical significance."[6] The IAEA report's main author, a British nuclear safety engineer, was confident in his findings and stated that it was "highly unlikely" that Iraq could have secretly recreated a nuclear program without it being detected. In his words, "This is not kitchen chemistry. You're talking factory scale, and in any operation there are leaks."[7] Michael Gordon and General Bernard Trainor in their best seller *Cobra II* similarly stated, "Because Iraq had not been an immediate flashpoint, did not have nuclear weapons, and, in the view of the intelligence agencies, lacked the means to launch a direct attack on the United States, Iraq had long been considered by the CIA as a 'Tier 2' country—a secondary priority for the overstretched U.S. intelligence network."[8]

Back before 9/11 drastically changed the Bush administration's way of thinking, key members of the White House team agreed with these assessments. For example, Secretary of Defense Donald Rumsfeld stated in February 2001, "Iraq is probably not a nuclear threat at the present time."[9] In that same month, Secretary of State Colin Powell similarly stated that Iraq "has not developed any significant capability with respect to weapons of mass destruction."[10]

Far from wanting to overthrow Iraq's leadership, there were fears at this time that any effort to overthrow Hussein could destabilize the country and the wider region. The CIA's deputy director Michael Muller would state, "Many at the Agency were concerned that bringing down Saddam would open Pandora's box."[11]

This would all change by 2002. The above-quoted findings of the U.S. intelligence community and IAEA on the lack of Iraqi WMDs and CIA fears of destabilizing the region would not deter the Bush White House. The White House would subsequently cherry-pick evidence of nuclear and other types of WMDs to convince the American people of the dire Iraqi nuclear threat to their country. In the process, they would also conflate Osama bin Laden, the exiled Wahhabi fundamentalist terrorist hiding out in the remote tribal regions of Pakistan, with Saddam Hussein, the socialist tyrant, to create the myth of "Osama bin Hussein."

The story of how the Bush White House successfully convinced the American people that Hussein was a nuclear, chemical, and biological weapons terrorist threat to them and then succeeded in diverting the war from metastasizing Al Qaeda/regrouping Taliban to the Republic of Iraq is one of intelligence that was deliberately manipulated by politicians. It is also the story of how CIA head George Tenet allowed his organization to be used by the Bush administration as a propaganda tool to legitimize and help sell a war against Hussein, all in the name of fighting another group known as Al Qaeda.

The story actually begins in 1996 with creation by a group of political thinkers known as Neo-Cons, who were not in the Clinton government, of a U.S. plan to embolden Israeli military policy vis-à-vis its Arab enemies. The Neo-Con plan, which was crafted by, among others, Richard Perle, Douglas Feith, and David Wurmser, three Jewish American Neo-Cons who would go on to become senior advisors to President Bush Jr., called for an end to Israel's policy of giving land back to Palestinians in return for peace. The Neo-Con plan, known as "A Clean Break: A New Strategy for Securing the Realm," also called for the replacement of Saddam Hussein by a "puppet leader friendly to Israel."[12] According to James Bamford, author of *A Pretext for War*, the report's authors recommended that Israel launch "a major unprovoked regional war in the Middle East, attacking Lebanon and Syria and ousting Iraq's Saddam Hussein. Then, to gain the support of the American government and people, a phony pretext would be used as a reason for the original invasion."[13] That pretext, in the words of the document's authors, would consist of "drawing attention to its [Syria's] weapons of mass destruction program."[14]

When the Israeli government received the Neo-Cons' Clean Break plan for launching preemptive wars against both Iraq and Syria under the guise of a search for weapons of mass destruction, they promptly disregarded it as too unrealistic and dangerous to be sold to the Israeli people. At the time (1996), the Clinton administration, like its predecessor the Bush Sr. administration, also kept the Neo-Cons and their dangerous plan for wars of aggression at arm's length. But five years later, with the election of Bush Jr. to the presidency, several Neo-Cons were appointed as senior advisors to the White House, including Douglas Feith (undersecretary of defense), Richard Perle (chairman of the Defense Policy Board at the Pentagon), and David Wurmser (Middle East advisor to Vice President Dick Cheney).

It was at this time the Clean Break project was dusted off and brought to the attention of the White House, only with the United States playing the role that had been proposed for Israel. Writing in 2002 for Britain's the *Guardian*, Brian Whitaker was to presciently warn, "With several of the *Clean Break* paper's authors now holding key positions in Washington, the plan for Israel to *transcend* its foes by reshaping the Middle East looks a good deal more achievable today than it did in 1996. Americans may even be persuaded to give up their lives to achieve it."[15]

Right-wing conservative Patrick Buchanan was to similarly write a scathing critique of the plan in the *Conservative American*, which was provocatively titled "Whose War?" with a subheading that stated, "A neoconservative clique seeks to ensnare our country in a series of wars that are not in America's interest." Buchanan was to warn, "Their [the Neo-Cons'] plan, which urged Israel to re-establish 'the principle of preemption,' has now been imposed by Perle, Feith, Wurmser & Co. on the United States."[16] Buchanan would also claim in his book *Where the Right Went Wrong: How the Neoconservatives Subverted the Reagan Revolution and Hijacked the Bush Presidency* that Bush Jr. had been warned by the Neo-Cons that he must "exploit the horror of that atrocity [9/11] and channel America's rage into a series of wars on nations [Iraq, Syria, and Iran], none of which had attacked us, but all of which were hostile to Israel, or he, President Bush, would face political retribution."[17]

Disinclined to provoke the powerful Neo-Cons, who formed the intellectual underpinning of his administration, Bush went along with their Clean Break strategy. Among Bush's first steps in fulfillment of the Neo-Cons' Clean Break plan was the termination of America's decades-long effort to push Israel and the Palestinians to reaching a compromise for peace. In essence, the Bush administration disengaged itself entirely from the peace process as the Clean Break authors had suggested.[18] This gave Israel a carte blanche to deal with the Palestinians as forcefully as it saw fit without any moderating U.S. influence. As Ron Suskind put it, "After more than thirty years of intense engagement—from Kissinger and Nixon to Clinton's last stand—America was washing its hands of the conflict in Israel. Now, we'd focus on Iraq."[19]

Having fulfilled the first half of the Neo-Cons' Clean Break strategy and abandoned the idea of pushing Israel to make peace with the Palestinians, the Bush administration then turned to Iraq. CIA director George Tenet was asked in 2002 during a National Security Council meeting if he had any proof of Iraqi weapons of mass destruction, which could be used as a means to justify a war against Iraq as called for in Clean Break. Tenet showed Bush a grainy overhead photo of an average factory in Iraq that he said "might" be a weapons of mass destruction (WMD) plant, but he had to admit "there was no confirming intelligence."[20]

But the CIA's initial lack of evidence of Iraqi WMDs did not faze the Neo-Cons. By this time one of the White House Neo-Cons, David Wurmser, had been charged with creating a secret intelligence unit known as the Office of Special Plans. This unit has been described as a "pro-war propaganda cell" and was tasked with gathering damning WMD evidence of the sort needed to justify an invasion of the Republic of Iraq.[21] A document in the National Security Archives referred to this as "advocacy" and "threat manipulation."[22] In his book a *Pretext for War*, James Bamford writes that Wurmser's intelligence unit "would pluck selective bits and pieces of thread from a giant ball of yarn and weave them together into a frightening tapestry."[23] The group's ultimate goal was not to analyze a potential terrorist/WMD threat but, in Bamford's words, to "frighten and deceive the rest of the country."[24]

The professional spies and analysts at the CIA were deeply concerned by Wurmser's propaganda cell. One CIA officer described the OSP (Office of Special Plans) as "dangerous for US national security and a threat to world peace. [The OSP] lied and manipulated intelligence to further its agenda of removing Saddam It's a group of ideologues with pre-determined notions of truth and reality. They take bits of intelligence to support their agenda and ignore anything contrary. They should be eliminated."[25]

While the CIA professionals were initially attempting to assess the veracity of the bold claims subsequently being made by the White House's Office of Special Plans that Iraq possessed chemical, biological, and even *nuclear* weapons, the British government complained that "intelligence and facts were being fixed around the policy" of justifying a war with Iraq.[26] One U.S. Air Force officer who was familiar with Wurmser's intelligence/propaganda cell's work said, "It wasn't intelligence,—it was propaganda. They'd take a little bit of intelligence, cherry-pick it, make it sound much more exciting, usually by taking it out of context, often by juxtaposition of two pieces of information that don't belong together."[27] U.S. State Department weapons proliferation expert Greg Thielman was to similarly state of Wurmser's cell, "They were cherry-picking the information that we provided to use whatever pieces fit their overall interpretation. Worse than that, they were dropping qualifiers and distorting some of the information that we provided them to make it more alarmist and dangerous than the information we were giving them."[28] Paul Pillar, the national intelligence officer for the Near East and South Asia similarly stated, "After 9/11 the [Bush] administration was trying to hitch Iraq to the wagon of terror."[29] Critics claimed the White House was in essence, "bundling" Iraq with the preexisting war on bin Laden's terror network.

Even as Wurmser's unit worked to cherry-pick WMD intelligence that would build the case for convincing the American people about the necessity of invading Iraq, Vice President Dick Cheney began making regular visits to CIA headquarters at Langley to pressure the agency into producing intelligence to support an invasion of Iraq. Cheney's eight to fifteen visits to CIA headquarters were unprecedented for a vice president and in one case led to him firing a briefer whose findings did not support the theory that Iraq had WMDs. The chilling message to the CIA was clear. The White House was planning an invasion of Iraq, and those who uncovered dissenting evidence that did not bolster their preexisting war plans did so at their own risk. And so the chastised CIA and Wurmser's intelligence/propaganda unit began to build the case to sell the war on Iraq to the American people.

The evidence that Iraq possessed deadly WMDs that was ultimately gathered by Wurmser's group and the intelligence community (after dismissing all evidence to the contrary) consisted of several strands. These strands of evidence are not known by most Americans, who simply have a vague awareness that some WMD claims were made. These strands are, however, worth knowing considering the fact that almost forty-five hundred Americans made the ultimate sacrifice in implementing the Iraqi invasion that stemmed from this cooked-up evidence.

This deep dive into the murky world of tampered evidence is not, however, for the casual reader. It is a demolition of the false intelligence that led the United States into an invasion of another country and an attempt to shed an expository light on what is one of the biggest lies in American history. Those readers who are more interested in following the narrative of combat operations in the War on Terror may wish to skip to the following chapter on the 2003 invasion of Iraq that was premised on false intelligence and the statements to be critically assessed below.

For those who wish to probe this tremendously important issue, whose specificities are understood by very few Americans (despite the widespread controversy and acrimony stemming from it to this very day), the evidence that was boldly manufactured by the Neo-Cons and the intelligence community included the following items.

Yellowcake Uranium from Niger

This strand of supporting evidence was based on a forged document from Italy, which was made to resemble an official Nigerien government document referencing the transfer of "five hundred tons" of yellowcake (a uranium oxide powder that is a step in the process of enriching uranium) by sea from the yellowcake-producing African nation of Niger to Iraq in 2000. The Italian document was such an amateurish forgery that it listed Nigerien state organizations that no longer existed, had the signature of Nigerien officials that had been out of office for over a decade, and even had an inaccurate version of the Nigerian national emblem.[30]

The Italians, who knew the document came from a known con man, felt it was a fake and stated their "strong objections" to its authenticity. The French DGSE intelligence service found that the report's information was "not reliable at all and probably based on fake intelligence."[31] The CIA's WIN-PAC (Weapons, Intelligence, Nonproliferation, and Arms Control Center) declared, "it appears that the results from this source will be suspect at best, and not believable under most scenarios." The International Atomic Energy

Agency concurred and found the document to be an "obvious" fake.[32] The State Department's Bureau of Intelligence and Research felt the "uranium purchase agreement probably is a hoax."[33]

The CIA station chief in Rome considered the yellowcake document to be "far fetched" and, after sending it on to CIA Headquarters, they determined that Iraq had "no known facilities for processing or enriching the [yellowcake] material."[34] The Department of Energy agreed and stated that "the amount of uranium specified far exceeds what Iraq would need even for a robust program."[35] For all these reasons, the CIA strongly warned Bush not to use the African uranium charges in a subsequent speech to the UN because it was "not solid enough."[36] The CIA would also call the fears of Nigerien yellowcake being sent to Iraq "overblown" and state "the evidence is weak."[37]

A U.S. State Department official similarly pointed out that there was no way that five hundred tons of yellowcake (one sixth of Niger's yearly total output) could be secretly diverted across Africa and the Middle East to Iraq without it becoming public knowledge.[38] The State Department even created a report entitled "Niger: Sale of Uranium to Iraq is Unlikely."[39] The State Department's intelligence agency also found that "the French appear to have control over the uranium mining, milling and transport process and would seem to have little interest in selling uranium to the Iraqis."[40] French intelligence services, which were pressured by the CIA to investigate the matter in their former colony of Niger, also stated that the sale of such a massive quantity of banned material had not taken place.[41]

If all this were not enough, the French-led international consortium that ran the yellowcake-producing mine in Niger assured the U.S. ambassador to Niger that there was "no possibility" that Niger had diverted the uranium to Iraq.[42] The Nigeriens themselves said it would be "difficult, if not impossible, to arrange a special shipment of uranium to a pariah state given these controls."[43] Chief UN weapons inspector Hans Blix subsequently queried, "With their [nuclear] facilities destroyed, why should Iraq have sought to buy yellowcake? ... The yellowcake story did not seem to stand up to common sense."[44]

But despite all the above statements by multiple and diverse sources confirming that the Niger yellowcake documents were fake and that the transfer of yellowcake from Niger to Iraq could not possibly have happened, when Wurmser's intelligence/propaganda unit the OSP heard of the discounted yellowcake uranium document it felt it was just the sort of WMD "evidence" they were looking for to justify an invasion. Wurmser's unit felt the totally discredited yellowcake story was the "smoking gun" needed to prove that Hussein was restarting his nuclear weapons program and it was promptly passed on to Vice President Cheney. Ignoring all the previous dissent and warnings that yellowcake story was fake, Cheney then passed the bogus yellowcake evidence on to Secretary of State Colin Powell. Not knowing the story was full of holes, Powell then went before Congress and confidently stated, "With respect to the nuclear program, there is no doubt that the Iraqis are pursuing it."[45]

Cheney demanded that the CIA look further into the yellowcake claims that were described in the false Italian documents, so the CIA turned to Ambassador Joe Wilson, the husband of Valerie Plame, a CIA operative in charge of dealing with Iraq's WMD program. Wilson, a former State Department employee, had worked for years in Africa, including Niger, and knew the region well. In February 2002, he traveled to Niger to explore the yellowcake issue and met with numerous Nigerien officials at the behest of the CIA. The Nigeriens not surprisingly told him that no such sale had taken place and that the mine that produced the yellowcake was controlled by a French-controlled international consortium that would never allow Iraq to obtain the banned uranium material. Wilson noted that a five-hundred-ton shipment of yellowcake, like the one that the fake Italian document suggested had been shipped to Iraq, would be "impossible to hide." He subsequently reported his findings that there was "nothing to the story" to the CIA and thought the matter was over.

But on January 28, 2003, President Bush gave a State of the Union Address that stated as fact that Iraq had acquired uranium from Africa. After warning that "the gravest danger facing America and the world . . . is outlaw regimes that seek and possess nuclear, chemical and biological weapons," he said what became known as the famous 16 words: "The British government has learned that Saddam Hussein recently sought significant quantities of uranium from Africa." Bush's claim was based on a British document known as the September Dossier, which the U.S. government subsequently found to be false (CIA director George Tenet concurred and called many of its assertions "shit").[46]

Regardless of the actual source of Bush's unsubstantiated Africa uranium claim, Ambassador Joe Wilson was shocked by the president's assertion that Iraq had acquired uranium from Africa. Wilson felt he had already disproved the notion of uranium yellowcake being shipped to Iraq from the African country of Niger.

In March of 2003 the United States invaded Iraq and in subsequent
months proved unable to find any of the Iraqi chemical, biological, or nuclear
weapons it had claimed were in the country. By July of that year, an increasingly frustrated Wilson had come to the conclusion that the Bush administration had painted the worst-case scenario as the *only* scenario when it came
to the Iraqi WMD program. He subsequently made the bold decision to go
public with his story. On July 6, 2003, Wilson published an opinion piece in
the *New York Times* provocatively titled "What I Didn't Find in Africa." He
began: "Did the Bush administration manipulate intelligence about Saddam
Hussein's weapons programs to justify an invasion of Iraq? Based on my experience with the administration in the months leading up to the war, I have
little choice but to conclude that some of the intelligence related to Iraq's nuclear weapons program was twisted to exaggerate the Iraqi threat." He would
then go on to tell his own experience:

> I spent the next eight days drinking sweet mint tea and meeting with
> dozens of people [in Niger]: current government officials, former
> government officials, people associated with the country's uranium
> business. It did not take long to conclude that it was highly doubtful
> that any such transaction had ever taken place. . . . In short, there's
> simply too much oversight over too small an industry for a sale to
> have transpired. . . .
>
> Before I left Niger, I briefed the ambassador on my findings,
> which were consistent with her own. I also shared my conclusions
> with members of her staff. In early March, I arrived in Washington
> and promptly provided a detailed briefing to the C.I.A. I later shared
> my conclusions with the State Department African Affairs Bureau. . . .
> I thought the Niger matter was settled and went back to my life. . . .
>
> Then, in January, President Bush, citing the British dossier,
> repeated the charges about Iraqi efforts to buy uranium from
> Africa. . . .
>
> The question now is how that answer [Wilson's negative assess-
> ment] was or was not used by our political leadership. If my infor-
> mation was deemed inaccurate, I understand (though I would be
> very interested to know why). If, however, the information was
> ignored because it did not fit certain preconceptions about Iraq, then
> a legitimate argument can be made that we went to war under false
> pretenses.

Wilson's bold assertions that America went to war "under false pretenses" so early into the Iraq campaign began a public debate about whether or not the intelligence leading to the invasion of Iraq had been deliberately manipulated by the Bush White House. As the office that had pressured the CIA to investigate the Niger yellowcake charges, the vice president and his staff were especially sensitive to the mounting criticism. In the subsequent debate on the validity of the WMD intelligence, which was played out on the cable news shows and press, conservative *Wall Street Journal* reporter Robert Novak subsequently "outed" Wilson's wife, Valerie Plame, as a CIA "operative" on his show. This effectively ended Plame's career as an undercover agent running covert WMD operations in the Middle East. Many observers wondered how the classified information on her had been leaked to Novak. Her husband, Ambassador Joe Wilson, felt it had to be someone at the White House who had deliberately leaked the information as retribution for his explosive column in the *New York Times*.

The story took an interesting turn when the FBI got into the act, as it was a federal offense to reveal the identity of a covert CIA operative like Plame. The CIA's investigation ultimately took them to Vice President Dick Cheney's office. During the investigation Cheney's chief of staff, Scooter Libby, was subsequently found to have lied to investigators and was convicted on four accounts related to obstruction of justice, false statements, and perjury. He was then sentenced to thirty months in prison and a fine of $250,000 (President Bush subsequently commuted the sentence). A Hollywood movie of the so-called Plamegate affair titled *Fair Game* was subsequently made, which presented a sensationalized account of a vindictive Bush White House out to punish Wilson and Plame for their role in undermining the president's case for invading Iraq.

Meanwhile, in post-occupation Iraq, U.S. weapons investigators led by David Kay, the White House–appointed head of the Iraq Survey Group, which was commissioned to find evidence of WMDs in Iraq, continued their search for evidence of a nuclear weapons program that might have used yellowcake. Their primary target was the Taiwatha nuclear facility outside of Baghdad. There they found a "decayed infrastructure, aging machine tools, and other equipment that had not been used for years."[47] They also examined the Iraqi records looking for evidence of an order for a shipment for yellowcake and found nothing. In other words, Iraq did not have an active nuclear program that would have required tons of yellowcake and had never requested the massive shipment of Nigerien uranium. Thus the yellowcake story was ultimately debunked by the Bush administration's own WMD inspectors.

When it was all over, Elisabetta Burba, an investigative reporter for the Italian newsweekly *Panorama* who first purchased the fake Nigerian documents from the con man and provided them to the U.S. embassy in Rome, said, "You know I feel bad. . . . With the documents I brought to them, they justified the war."[48] When the yellowcake claim was subsequently disproved, CIA director George Tenet said of Bush's famous State of the Union declaration that uranium had been shipped from Africa to Iraq: "These 16 words should never have been included in the text written for the president."[49]

Aluminum Tubes

The story of this second strand of bogus WMD evidence begins in 2001, when the Iraqis ordered a shipment of aluminum tubes openly from the Internet. They were to be shipped from Hong Kong via an Australian company to make conventional 81 mm rockets (eighty-one millimeters is roughly three inches). As was typically the case during the embargo years, the aluminum tubes were, however, confiscated (in Jordan in this case) before they could reach Iraq, in order to prevent them from being used for weapons. The story might have ended there but for the fact that the Bush White House pounced on the aluminum tubes as evidence that Hussein was trying to use them to build rotors for a gas centrifuge (a machine used to enrich uranium, which could then be used for a nuclear weapon).

In September 2002, Vice President Cheney went on the Sunday morning talk shows and unequivocally declared that Saddam Hussein was "trying, through his illicit procurement network, to acquire the equipment he needs to be able to enrich uranium—specifically, aluminum tubes." He then claimed, "Increasingly, we believe that the United States may well become the target of those activities."[50]

National Security Advisor Condoleezza Rice similarly declared that the aluminum tubes "are only really suited for nuclear weapons programs, centrifuge programs." Rice then issued an ominous warning that would later become famous when she said, "We don't want the smoking gun to be a mushroom cloud."[51]

Secretary of State Colin Powell similarly stated, "he [Hussein] is still trying to acquire, for example, some of the specialized aluminum tubing one needs to develop centrifuges that would give you an enrichment capability.

So there's no question that he has these weapons, but even more importantly, he is striving to do even more, to get even more."[52]

President Bush also declared in September 2002, "Iraq has made several attempts to buy high-strength aluminum tubes used to enrich uranium for a nuclear weapon. Should Iraq acquire fissile material, it would be able to build a nuclear weapon within a year."[53] Then in October of that same year, he claimed: "The evidence indicates that Iraq is reconstituting its nuclear weapons program. Saddam Hussein has held numerous meetings with Iraqi nuclear scientists, a group he calls his 'nuclear mujahideen'—his nuclear holy warriors. Satellite photographs reveal that Iraq is rebuilding facilities at sites that have been part of its nuclear program in the past. Iraq has attempted to purchase high-strength aluminum tubes and other equipment needed for gas centrifuges, which are used to enrich uranium for nuclear weapons."[54] But the bold claims by the White House that the confiscated aluminum tubes were designed to be used as rotors for a nuclear gas centrifuge was soon questioned by experts in the field. The Department of Energy (DoE), whose experts have been described as having "virtually the only expertise on gas centrifuges and nuclear weapons programs in the United States government,"[55] for example, stated its opposition to the theory that the aluminum tubes were intended for a gas centrifuge as follows:

> Based on the reported specifications, the tubes could be used to manufacture gas centrifuge rotor cylinders for uranium enrichment. However, our analysis indicates that the specified tube diameter, which is half that of the centrifuge machine Iraq successfully tested in 1990, is only marginally large enough for practical centrifuge applications, and other specifications are not consistent with a gas centrifuge end use. Moreover, the quantity being sought suggests preparations for large-scale production of centrifuge machines, for which we have not seen related procurement efforts—and the tubes' specifications suggest a centrifuge design quite different from any Iraq is known to have. . . .
>
> While the gas centrifuge application cannot be ruled out, we assess that the procurement activity more likely supports a different application, such as conventional [i.e., nonnuclear] ordnance production. For example, the tube specifications and quantity appear to be generally consistent with their use as launch tubes for man-held anti-armor rockets or as tactical rocket casings.

Also, the manner in which the procurement is being handled (multiple procurement agents, quotes obtained from multiple suppliers in diverse locations, and price haggling) seems to better match our expectations for a conventional Iraqi military buy than a major purchase for a clandestine weapons-of-mass destruction program.[56]

The IAEA (International Atomic Energy Agency) agreed with the Department of Energy's assessment and, after an extensive investigation, stated: "The IAEA's analysis to date indicates that the specifications of the aluminum tubes sought by Iraq in 2001 and 2002 appear to be consistent with reverse engineering of rockets. While it would be possible to modify such tubes for the manufacture of centrifuges, they are not directly suitable for it."[57] The head of the IAEA, Mohammad El Baradei, would subsequently state:

I think it's difficult for Iraq to hide a complete nuclear-weapons program. They might be hiding some computer studies or R. and D. [research and development] on one single centrifuge. These are not enough to make weapons. There were reports from different member states [the United States and the UK] that Iraq was importing aluminum tubes for enrichment, that they were importing uranium from Africa. Our provisional conclusion is that these tubes were for rockets and not for centrifuges. They [the Iraqis] deny they have imported any uranium since 1991.[58]

El Baradei would also state, "we have to date found no evidence that Iraq has revived its nuclear weapons programme since the elimination of the programme in the 1990s."[59]

But such dissenting testimony was once again overridden (or deliberately ignored) by the White House, which issued directives to the intelligence community to prove its theory that aluminum tubes were for the construction of a nuclear centrifuge. Under intense pressure from the Bush administration, the American intelligence community produced what was subsequently roundly criticized as a flawed document, the October 2002 NIE (National Intelligence Estimate, a yearly roundup by the nation's fifteen intelligence services). This rushed document from the intelligence community stated: "Most agencies believe that Saddam's personal interest in and Iraq's aggressive attempts to obtain high-strength aluminum tubes for centrifuge rotors—as well as Iraq's attempts to acquire magnets, high-speed balancing machines, and machine tools—provide compelling evidence that Saddam is reconstituting a uranium enrichment effort for Baghdad's nuclear weapons program. (DOE agrees that reconstitution of the nuclear program is underway but assesses that the tubes probably are not part of the program.)"[60]

But the NIE's rushed assessments on aluminum tubes would later be described as "stunningly wrong."[61] The Republican chair of the Senate Intelligence Committee, Pat Roberts, would subsequently say of the flawed October 2002 NIE, "Today we know these assessments were wrong. And, as our inquiry will show, they were also unreasonable and largely unsupported by the available evidence."[62] Thomas Ricks, a Pulitzer Prize–winning journalist for the *Washington Post* and *Wall Street Journal*, would write of the flawed 2002 NIE, which was used by the Bush administration to scare skeptics, "As a professional intelligence product it was shameful."[63]

But in the fall of 2002, the NIE was used by the Bush administration to convince skeptics in Congress that Iraq was indeed ordering aluminum tubes to reconstitute its shattered nuclear weapons program. With the confiscated aluminum tubes in hand (the only physical evidence the White House would ever roll out to prove its theory that Iraq was developing banned WMDs), the Bush administration continued to make its case that the tubes were meant solely for uranium enrichment. On January 28, 2003, in his annual State of the Union address, Bush asserted, "Our intelligence sources tell us that he [Hussein] has attempted to purchase high-strength aluminum tubes suitable for nuclear weapons production." But the real coup de grâce in the campaign to convince the American people that the aluminum tubes were for nuclear programs came when the widely respected secretary of state, Colin Powell, lent his significant stature to the claim during his famous speech to the UN on February 5, 2003. There Powell, who had the respect of Democrats and many world leaders who were highly skeptical of the rest of the Bush administration's rationale for launching an invasion of Iraq, emphatically stated:

> Saddam Hussein is determined to get his hands on a nuclear bomb. He is so determined that he has made repeated covert attempts to acquire high-specification aluminum tubes from 11 different countries, even after inspections resumed. These tubes are controlled by the Nuclear Suppliers Group precisely because they can be used as centrifuges for enriching uranium.
>
> By now, just about everyone has heard of these tubes, and we all

know that there are differences of opinion. There is controversy about what these tubes are for. *Most U.S. experts think they are intended to serve as rotors in centrifuges used to enrich uranium* [emphasis mine]. Other experts, and the Iraqis themselves, argue that they are really to produce the rocket bodies for a conventional weapon, a multiple rocket launcher.

Let me tell you what is not controversial about these tubes. First, all the experts who have analyzed the tubes in our possession agree that they can be adapted for centrifuge use. Second, Iraq had no business buying them for any purpose. They are banned for Iraq.

But despite Powell's claim that "most U.S. experts think they are intended to serve as rotors in centrifuges used to enrich uranium," there were many dissenting voices among the experts. David Albright, a physicist and former weapons inspector who directed the Institute for Science and International Security, observed, "The vast majority of gas centrifuge experts in this country and abroad who are knowledgeable about this case reject the CIA's case [made in the NIE]."[64] Albright called the Bush administration's claims "misleading" and said administration officials "were selectively picking information to bolster a case that the Iraqi nuclear threat was more imminent than it is, and, in essence, scare people."[65]

Retired nuclear scientist Dr. Houston Wood, one of the top experts in the world on centrifuges, concurred and stated, "it would have been extremely difficult to make these tubes into centrifuges. It stretches the imagination to come up with a way. I do not know any real centrifuge experts that feel differently."[66] Peter Zimmerman, the Senate Foreign Relations Committee's scientific advisor, who had a Ph.D. in physics, was so alarmed by the seemingly deliberate misread by the Bush administration on the aluminum tubes and other issues that he said, "They're going to war and there is not a damn piece of evidence to support it."[67]

These were not the only dissenting voices. The intelligence agency in Colin Powell's own State Department stated of the aluminum tubes, "In fact, the most comparable US system is a tactical rocket—the US Mark 66 air-launched 70 mm rocket—that uses the same, high-grade (7075-T6) aluminum, and that has specifications with similar tolerances."[68] Such dissent did not of course make it in Powell's famous February 2003 speech at the UN, and the aluminum tubes went on to become one of the main selling points for the invasion of Iraq.

But the theory that the tubes were intended to be used for gas centrifuge rotors was one of the first pieces of evidence to collapse in 2003 once the United States occupied the Iraqi sites that the White House claimed were intended for nuclear weapons production. After David Kay, the head of the White House–appointed Iraq Survey Group, searched the sites he shocked the Bush administration by claiming, "The tubes issue was an absolute fraud."[69] After investigating the tubes and the targeted facilities in post-occupation Iraq the IAEA agreed and stated: "Extensive field investigation and document analysis have failed to uncover any evidence that Iraq intended to use these 81mm tubes for any project other than the reverse engineering of rockets. . . . Based on available evidence, the IAEA team has concluded that Iraq's efforts to import these aluminum tubes were not likely to have been related to the manufacture of centrifuges and, moreover, that it was highly unlikely that Iraq could have achieved the considerable re-design needed to use them in a revived centrifuge programme."[70] When the IAEA investigated the Nasr munitions factory in Iraq, where the Iraqis manufactured 81 mm rockets, they found endless rows of the suspect tubes, which indicated that they were for rocket production, not gas centrifuges to enrich uranium for a nonexistent nuclear weapons program.[71]

In the ultimate rebuke to the Bush administration on the aluminum tubes issue, on July 9, 2004, a Senate committee on prewar intelligence published a report with a subsection boldly titled "Iraq Was Not Reconstituting Its Nuclear Program." This report concluded that "the judgment in the National Intelligence Estimate (NIE), that Iraq was reconstituting its nuclear program, was not supported by the intelligence." It further stated that "the information available to the Intelligence Community indicated that these tubes were intended to be used for an Iraqi conventional rocket program and not a nuclear program."[72] The report then reached several conclusions that were highly critical of the NIE report and the CIA's intelligence that the tubes being designed for centrifuge rotors.[73]

In response to all these findings that strongly disproved the Bush administration's claims about the nefarious uses for the aluminum tubes, the CIA belatedly acknowledged that "Iraqi interest in aluminum tubes appears to have come from efforts to produce 81-mm rockets, rather than a nuclear end use."[74] Thus the aluminum tubes, the White House's only tangible evidence in hand of WMDs in Iraq, was definitively debunked by the nation's intelligence services, the Senate Intelligence Committee, the Iraqi Survey Group, which the Bush administration had appointed, many of the country's top nuclear scientists, and the scientists at the IAEA. Like the yellowcake strand before it, the aluminum tube issue was definitively proven to be a false rationale for invading the Republic of Iraq.

Iraqi WMD Drones

One of the more frightening Iraqi WMD claims made by the Bush administration in order to justify the invasion of Iraq concerned Hussein's development of remote controlled UAVs (unmanned aerial vehicles, also known as drones) to attack the U.S. mainland. In October 2002, for example, President Bush declared: "We've also discovered through intelligence that Iraq has a growing fleet of manned and unmanned aerial vehicles that could be used to disperse chemical and biological weapons across broad areas. We're concerned that Iraq is exploring ways of using these UAVs for missions targeting the United States."[75] Bush would also paint a chilling picture of Iraqi drones (that were apparently far more advanced than anything the U.S. Air Force or CIA had) flying over the American mainland spraying chemical and biological weapons when he stated: "Iraq has developed spray devices that could be used on unmanned aerial vehicles with ranges far beyond what is permitted by the UN Security Council. A UAV launched from a vessel off the American coast could reach hundreds of miles inland."[76] Secretary of State Colin Powell subsequently showed a picture of a small drone during his momentous presentation to the UN Security Council in February 2003. On this occasion he stated: "UAVs outfitted with spray tanks constitute an ideal method for launching a terrorist attack using biological weapons. Iraq could use these small UAVs, which have a wingspan of only a few meters, to deliver biological agents to its neighbors or, if transported, to other countries, including the United States." Powell said there is "ample evidence that Iraq has dedicated much time and effort to developing and testing spray devices that could be adapted for UAVs." The flawed 2002 NIE report similarly reported that the Iraqis had UAVs "probably intended to deliver biological warfare agents." Most alarmingly, it also stated, "Baghdad's UAVs could threaten Iraq's neighbors, US forces in the Persian Gulf, and if brought to, or into, the United States, the US Homeland."

Such claims were unquestioningly picked up by the media, even though the U.S. Air Force's far more advanced program had only just completed the decade-long process of finally arming its own Predator drones in the fall of 2001. News networks uncritically parroted the alarmist drone reports from the NIE and the White House. A typical example of this was a *Fox News* report titled "Iraqi Drones May Target US Cities," which chillingly stated: "Iraq could be planning a chemical or biological attack on American cities through the use of remote-controlled 'drone' planes equipped with GPS tracking maps, according to U.S. intelligence. The information about Iraq's unmanned aerial vehicle (UAV) program has caused a 'real concern' among defense personnel, senior U.S. officials tell Fox News. They're worried that these vehicles have already been, or could be, transported inside the United States to be used in an attack, although there is no proof that this has happened." "This isn't brain surgery," Air National Guard chief Paul Weaver told Fox News in reference to how easy it would be to assemble a UAV. "The key is getting it into the country. . . . If they could organize something like Sept. 11," Weaver said, "this would be very doable."[77]

But the U.S. Air Force officially disagreed with the glib notion of ultra-advanced Iraqi UAVs/drones somehow being infiltrated into America and then spraying deadly chemical and biological gases over U.S. cities. In fact the air force, the primary organization in the United States that had developed America's own drone program, was deeply skeptical of this bizarre accusation being made by the Bush White House. The air force registered its dissent of the flawed 2002 NIE statement on drones as follows: "Iraq is developing UAVs primarily for reconnaissance rather than delivery platforms for CBW [chemical, biological weapon] agents. The capabilities and missions of Iraq's new UAV remains undetermined, but in this view its small size suggests a role of reconnaissance. CBW delivery is an inherent capability of UAVs probably but is not the impetus of Iraq's recent UAV programs."[78] The air force felt the primitive Iraqi drones were far too small to deliver chemical weapons and rejected all notions of links between Iraqi UAVs and biological weapons delivery missions. The proposed chemical weapons dispersal potential of the Iraqi drones was a WMD delivery capacity that even the CIA and U.S. Air Force's own advanced drones had not yet developed at this time.

The air force's doubts were confirmed in March 2003 on the eve of the U.S. invasion of Iraq when Western journalists were allowed by the Iraqi government to see the notorious Iraqi drones for themselves. A reporter from the Associated Press reported his findings in an article titled "Iraqi Drone Looks More Like Model Airplane":

AL-TAJI, Iraq—A remotely piloted aircraft that the United States has warned could spread chemical weapons appears to be made of balsa wood and duct tape, with two small propellers attached to what look like the engines of a weed whacker. Iraqi officials took journalists to the Ibn Firnas State Company just north of Baghdad on Wednesday, where the drone's project director accused Secretary of State Colin Powell of misleading the U.N. Security Council and the public. "He's making a big mistake," said Brig. Imad Abdul Latif. "He knows very well that this aircraft is not used for what he said."

In Washington's search for a "smoking gun" that would prove Iraq is not disarming, Powell has insisted the drone, which has a wingspan of 24.5 feet, could be fitted to dispense chemical and biological weapons. He has said it "should be of concern to everybody."

The drone's white fuselage was emblazoned Wednesday with the words "God is great" and the code "Quds-10." Its balsa wood wings were held together with duct tape. Officials said they referred to the remotely piloted vehicle as the RPV-30A.

Latif said the plane is controlled by the naked eye from the ground. Asked whether its range is above the 93-mile limit imposed by the United Nations, he said it couldn't be controlled from more than five miles. . . . "This RPV is to be used for reconnaissance, jamming and aerial photography. We have never thought of any other use. . . ."

Iraq seized on the issue of the drone—along with early reports from Washington that Iraqi fighter jets threatened a U.N.-sponsored U-2 reconnaissance plane on Tuesday—as proof that Washington is trying to mislead the world about Iraq's weapons programs in its push for war.[79]

Later in that month (March 2003), the United States invaded Iraq in search of WMDs and subsequently seized the suspected Iraqi WMD drones in the initial days of Operation Iraqi Freedom. An Associated Press journalist reported the underwhelming results of the subsequent analysis of the captured Iraqi "WMD drones":

Huddled over a fleet of abandoned Iraqi drones, U.S. weapons experts in Baghdad came to one conclusion: Despite the Bush administration's public assertions, these unmanned aerial vehicles weren't designed to dispense biological or chemical weapons. The evidence gathered this summer matched the dissenting views of Air Force intelligence analysts who argued in a national intelligence assessment of Iraq before the war that the remotely piloted planes were unarmed reconnaissance drones. In building its case for war, senior Bush administration officials had said Iraq's drones were intended to deliver unconventional weapons. Secretary of State Colin Powell even raised the alarming prospect that the pilotless aircraft could sneak into the United States to carry out poisonous attacks on American cities.[80]

But the U.S. Air Force, which controls most of the American military's UAV fleet, did not agree with that assessment from the beginning. And analysts at the Pentagon's Missile Defense Agency said the air force view was widely accepted within their ranks as well. Instead, these analysts believed the drones posed no threat to Iraq's neighbors or the United States, officials in Washington and scientists involved in the weapons hunt in Iraq told the Associated Press:

> "We didn't see there was a very large chance they (UAVs) would be used to attack the continental United States," Bob Boyd, director of the Air Force Intelligence Analysis Agency, said in an AP interview. "We didn't see them as a big threat to the homeland." Boyd also said there was little evidence to associate Iraq's UAVs with the country's suspected biological weapons program. . . .
>
> The lack of success in uncovering unconventional weapons, after warnings that Iraq posed an immediate danger, has led critics and some former government analysts to suggest the administration exaggerated the threat posed by Saddam.[81]

After the invasion, the UN was also given a chance to analyze Iraq's unsophisticated drones and found "no clear indication to show that Iraq had planned to develop the L-29 RPV [remotely piloted vehicle] to deliver a CBW [chemical and biological weapons] agent." Rather they were designed for "conventional military purposes such as air defense training, data collection and surveillance."[82] Thus Iraq's notorious "WMD drones" also went the way of the yellowcake and aluminum tubes before them and were proven to be a false threat by both the UN and America's own specialists.

In the aftermath of the Iraqi UAV fiasco, Ben Nelson, a U.S. senator who had been convinced to vote in support of the Iraq invasion based on the false drone evidence, furiously stated:

> I, along with nearly every Senator in this Chamber, in that secure room of this Capitol complex, was not only told there were weapons of mass destruction—specifically chemical and biological—but I was looked at straight in the face and told that Saddam Hussein had the means of delivering those biological and chemical weapons of mass destruction by unmanned drones, called UAVs, unmanned aerial vehicles. Further, I was looked at straight in the face and told that UAVs could be launched from ships off the Atlantic coast to attack eastern seaboard cities of the United States. Is it any wonder that I concluded there was an imminent peril to the United States?
>
> We now know, after the fact and on the basis of Dr. Kay's testimony today in the Senate Armed Services Committee, that the information was false; and not only that there were not weapons of mass destruction—chemical and biological—but there was no fleet of UAVs, unmanned aerial vehicles, nor was there any capability of putting UAVs on ships and transporting them to the Atlantic coast and launching them at U.S. cities on the eastern seaboard.[83]

"Curveball" and Mobile Weapons Labs

One of the more alarming pieces of evidence cited by the Bush White House as a rationale for preemptively launching a full-scale invasion of Iraq to protect American citizens was the purported existence of Iraqi mobile weapons labs said to be built in trailers or train cars. The prospect of elusive WMD labs covertly moving around Iraq while mixing up deadly anthrax or botulinum toxins was frightening because they could not be located and destroyed by American bombers. By now Americans knew about the deadly effects of anthrax following the 2001 anthrax attacks wherein five people were killed and several others infected when they opened letters sent with anthrax spores in them by a disgruntled American bio-weapons expert.

The primary source for the information on the notorious Iraqi mobile anthrax-botulinum labs was a defecting Iraqi chemical engineer who had appealed for asylum in Germany in 1999. This Iraqi engineer was given the code name "Curveball" to protect his identity. When the BND (German intelligence) interviewed him, he told them he had worked as a technician on the Iraqi mobile labs. The Germans then shared the information with the American Defense Intelligence Agency and the CIA but expressed their strong doubts about its veracity. This strand then became the cornerstone for one of the most important pieces of evidence used by the Bush administration and intelligence community to justify the invasion in Iraq. In his January 28, 2003, State of the Union Address, Bush declared: "From three Iraqi defectors we know that Iraq, in the late 1990s, had several mobile biological weapons labs. These are designed to produce germ warfare agents and can be moved from place to a place to evade inspectors. Saddam Hussein has not disclosed these facilities. He has given no evidence that he has destroyed them."[84] Bush provided even more alarming concrete details in February of that year when he emphatically stated: "The Iraqi regime has actively and secretly attempted to obtain equipment needed to produce chemical, biological and nuclear weapons. First-hand witnesses have informed us that Iraq has at least seven mobile factories for the production of biological agents, equipment mounted on trucks and rails to evade discovery. Using these factories, Iraq has produced within just months hundreds of pounds of biological poisons."[85] In his powerful February 5, 2003, speech before the UN, which convinced many of the skeptics, Secretary of State Powell was to go even further and eloquently rehearse an alarming scenario using paintings of what the Iraqi "mobile weapons labs" were supposed to look like; no actual photos of the labs were actually available, so artistic sketches were created instead. Powell stated:

> One of the most worrisome things that emerges from the thick intelligence file we have on Iraq's biological weapons is the existence of mobile production facilities used to make biological agents. Let me take you inside that intelligence file and share with you what we know from eyewitness accounts. We have first-hand descriptions of biological weapons factories on wheels and on rails. The trucks and train cars are easily moved and are designed to evade detection by inspectors. In a matter of months, they can produce a quantity of biological poison equal to the entire amount that Iraq claimed to have produced in the years prior to the Gulf War.
>
> Although Iraq's mobile production program began in the mid-1990s, UN inspectors at the time only had vague hints of such programs. Confirmation came later, in the year 2000. The source was an eyewitness, an Iraqi chemical engineer who supervised one of

these facilities. He actually was present during biological agent production runs. He was also at the site when an accident occurred in 1998. 12 technicians died from exposure to biological agents. . . . This defector is currently hiding in another country with the certain knowledge that Saddam Hussein will kill him if he finds him. His eyewitness account of these mobile production facilities has been corroborated by other sources.[86]

When the German BND intelligence agents saw Powell's emphatic speech on the mobile labs, which they realized was probably based on the Curveball defector in their custody whom they did not trust, they were stunned. So were several members of the CIA who had been involved in the case. The *Los Angeles Times* reported their subsequent reaction as follows:

> The senior BND officer who supervised Curveball's case said he was aghast when he watched Powell misstate Curveball's claims as a justification for war. "We were shocked," the official said. "Mein Gott! [My God!] We had always told them it was not proven. . . . It was not hard intelligence." . . .
>
> The German officer warned that Curveball had suffered a mental breakdown and was "crazy," the now-retired CIA veteran recalled. . . . "Second, there are a lot of problems. Principally, we think he's probably a fabricator."
>
> "The fact is, there was a lot of yelling and screaming about this guy," said James Pavitt, then chief of clandestine services, who retired from the CIA in August 2004. "My people were saying, 'We think he's a stinker.'" . . . [But] the analysts refused to back down. In one meeting, the chief analyst fiercely defended Curveball's account, saying she had confirmed on the Internet many of the details he cited. "Exactly, it's on the Internet!" the operations group chief for Germany, now a CIA station chief in Europe, exploded in response. "That's where he got it too," according to a participant at the meeting.[87]

There were solid reasons for the CIA station chief's concerns about the veracity of Curveball's story of mobile weapons labs. As it turned out, the Americans had never actually been allowed to interview Curveball. For this reason, his claims of the existence of mobile labs could not be verified, and the CIA station chief in Berlin sent a message to a superior stating, "The source is problematical. . . . To use information from another liaison's service's source whose information cannot be verified on such an important, key topic should take the most serious consideration."[88] MI6, the British foreign intelligence service, cabled the CIA and informed the Agency that British intelligence "is not convinced that Curveball is a wholly reliable source" and that "elements of [his] behavior strike us as typical of fabricators."[89]

The German intelligence officers dealing with Curveball agreed and said, "This was not substantial evidence. We made clear we could not verify the things he said."[90] The Germans would also describe Curveball as "crazy" and a "fabricator."[91] To compound matters, other Iraqi defectors claimed that the Iraqi WMD trailers being described by Curveball were actually being used to make hydrogen.[92] In response to all these doubts and skepticism, a CIA analyst, Tyler Drumheller, actually removed the Curveball section from Powell's speech. Drumheller would later recall, "We thought we had taken care of the problem, but I turn on the television [for Powell's speech] and there it was, again."[93] Drumheller would go on to state, "My mouth hung open when I saw Colin Powell use information from Curveball. It was like cognitive dissonance."[94] Drumheller kept his job, but other dissenting voices at the CIA were fired to keep them quiet. George Packer was to write in his book *The Assassins' Gate: America in Iraq*, "The cost of dissent was humiliation and professional suicide. After seeing Wolfowtiz chew down a four star general I don't think anyone was going to raise their head and make a stink about it."[95] While Powell removed much of the unsubstantiated claims that had been inserted into his speech by Wurmser's OSP intelligence/propaganda unit because he felt they were bogus (at one point he said, "I'm not going to read this, this is bullshit"), he kept the mobile weapons lab assertions in.[96] Many skeptical Democratic leaders were convinced by Powell (who had their respect for his relative moderation) and subsequently voted in favor of the war after his convincing February 5, 2003, speech to the UN on WMDs. Among those Democrats who voted for the war were Senators Hillary Clinton and John Kerry, both of whom would later be haunted by their votes when they ran for president.

Kerry and Clinton were not the only ones who fell for Powell's speech. Ironically, the Iraqis themselves were so convinced by Powell that they "scoured the country for trailers" according to a former CIA official. "They were in real panic mode. They were terrified that this was real, and they couldn't explain it."[97] Of course they could not find the "WMD trailers" because they did not exist. Neither could the UN, which was allowed into Iraq to begin inspections in November 2002, on the eve of the U.S. invasion. Carrying out as many as six inspections a day, UN inspectors actually inspected the sites that Curveball had claimed were producing the WMD trailers, and they found that these sites could not have produced the mobile labs. In fact the UN investigated all the other sites confidently presented as WMD sites by the Bush administration and found no evidence of WMDs there either. The man in charge of the UN investigation, Hans Blix, would later state: "We went to a great many sites that were given to us by [U.S.] intelligence, and only in three cases did we find anything—and they did not relate to weapons of mass destruction. That shook me a bit, I must say. I thought 'My God, if this is the best intelligence they had and we find nothing, what about the rest?' "[98]

In desperation, the fearful Iraqis announced, "Since the US does not believe us, let the CIA agents accompany the UN inspectors and go where they want to go; we will allow that. . . . Let the CIA agents guide the inspectors to the suspect sites."[99] In other words, the Iraqis gave the CIA a carte blanche to investigate any purported WMD sites before the 2003 U.S. invasion in a last bid effort to try fending off the American attack. Dedicated to going to war regardless of the Iraqi offers and UN's negative findings on the WMD trailers, Secretary Rumsfeld called the Iraqi offer a "stunt," and Bush dismissed the UN investigation as a "ploy."[100] Then, on March 19, 2003, the U.S.-British invasion began. Approximately fifteen hundred U.S. troops and analysts were designated to search for WMDs following the March 2003 invasion and subsequent toppling of the Hussein regime. It did not take them long to find what they felt might be the suspect WMD trailers near the northern town of Mosul. When President Bush heard about the discovery he triumphantly proclaimed: "We found the weapons of mass destruction. We found biological laboratories. You remember when Colin Powell stood up in front of the world, and he said, Iraq has got laboratories, mobile labs to build biological weapons. They're illegal. They're against the United Nations resolutions, and we've so far discovered two. And we'll find more weapons as time goes on. But for those who say we haven't found the banned manufacturing devices or banned weapons, they're wrong, we found them."[101]

National Security Advisor Condoleezza Rice similarly stated on June 3, 2003: "But let's remember what we've already found. Secretary Powell on February 5th talked about a mobile, biological weapons capability. That has now been found and this is a weapons laboratory trailer capable of making a lot of agent that—dry agent, dry biological agent that can kill a lot of people. So we are finding these pieces that were described."[102] But, as with the aluminum tubes (which were subsequently proven to be casted to make artillery shells not gas centrifuges) and Iraqi drones (which were harmless), the evidence that the discovered trailers were "mobile weapons labs" quickly collapsed as well. The WMD claims began to unravel when the British investigated the suspect trailers and found that they were clearly used to produce hydrogen for weather balloons, not WMDs. In fact they were trailers that had been sold to the Iraqis by the British themselves in the 1980s.[103] One British expert stated, "They are not mobile germ warfare laboratories. You could not use them for making biological weapons. They do not even look like them. They are exactly what the Iraqis said they were—facilities for the production of hydrogen gas to fill balloons."[104] Another analyst concurred and said, "The equipment was singularly inappropriate [for biological weapons production]. We were in hysterics over this. You'd have better luck putting a couple of dust bins on the back of the truck and brewing it in there."[105]

The Iraq Survey Group, which had been appointed by the Bush White House to investigate this and other claims, agreed with the British refutation of the WMD trailer claims. After launching an "exhaustive investigation" of the two trailers they found that they could not be "be part of any BW [biological weapons] program."[106] David Kay, the head of the Bush-appointed Iraq Survey Group, would further state, "the consensus opinion is that their actual intended use was not for the production of biological weapons."[107]

The DIA (Defense Intelligence Agency) carried out its own investigation of the suspect trailers and was similarly "unequivocal in its conclusion that the trailers were not intended to manufacture biological weapons."[108] One expert who studied the trailers said, "There was no connection to anything biological," while another shared an epithet that came to be associated with the trailers "the biggest sand toilets in the world."[109]

As the WMD trailer evidence collapsed like the yellowcake, aluminum tubes, and drone claims before it, U.S. analysts investigated the Iraqi defector Curveball, who had made the bogus claims in the first place. When they visited the Iraqi plant where Curveball claimed to have previously been a site manager, they found that he had only been a low-level trainee there. Furthermore, he had actually been fired long before he claimed to have worked there building mobile WMD biolabs. From there he had gone on to become a taxi driver. The *Los Angeles Times* reported an investigation into Curveball in Iraq by a CIA agent known only as "Jerry":

Jerry and his team interviewed 60 of Curveball's family, friends and co-workers. They all denied working on germ weapons trucks. Curveball's former bosses at the engineering center said the CIA had fallen for "water cooler gossip" and "corridor conversations." "The Iraqis were all laughing," recalled a former member of the survey group. "They were saying, 'This guy? You've got to be kidding.'" Childhood friends called him a "great liar" and a "con artist." Another called him "a real operator." The team reported that "people kept saying what a rat Curveball was."[110]

Curveball, whose real name was subsequently revealed as Rafid Ahmed Alwan al-Janabi, later confessed to British reporters that he had made up the whole WMD mobile labs claim. The British newspaper the *Independent* reported the confession in an article titled "Man Whose WMD Lies Led to 100,000 Deaths Confesses All":

Curveball, the Iraqi defector who fabricated claims about Iraq's weapons of mass destruction, smiles as he confirms how he made the whole thing up. It was a confidence trick that changed the course of history, with Rafid Ahmed Alwan al-Janabi's lies used to justify the Iraq war.

He tries to defend his actions: "My main purpose was to topple the tyrant in Iraq because the longer this dictator remains in power, the more the Iraqi people will suffer from this regime's oppression." The chemical engineer claimed to have overseen the building of a mobile biological laboratory when he sought political asylum in Germany in 1999. His lies were presented as "facts and conclusions based on solid intelligence" by Colin Powell, US Secretary of State, when making the case for war at the UN Security Council in February 2003. But Mr Janabi, speaking in a two-part series, Modern Spies, starting tomorrow on BBC2, says none of it was true. When it is put to him "we went to war in Iraq on a lie. And that lie was your lie," he simply replies: "Yes."[111]

Britain's *Guardian* similarly reported an interview with Curveball wherein he revealed his lie as follows: "With the US now leaving Iraq, Janabi said he was comfortable with what he did, despite the chaos of the past eight years and the civilian death toll in Iraq, which stands at more than 100,000. 'I tell you something when I hear anybody—not just in Iraq but in any war—[is] killed, I am very sad. But give me another solution. Can you give me another solution? . . . They gave me this chance. I had the chance to fabricate something to topple the regime.' "[112] In 2004, the CIA would respond to the debunking of Curveball by sending a message out to its field offices stating, "Discrepancies surfaced regarding the information provided by Curveball in this stream of reporting, which indicate that he lost his claimed access in 1995. Our assessment, therefore, is that Curveball appears to be fabricating in this stream of reporting."[113]

Thus the WMD trailers, the Bush White House's final piece of evidence, went the way of the WMD drones, aluminum tubes, and yellowcake shipments from Niger and was definitively debunked. The *Washington Post* reported CIA head George Tenet and Colin Powell's gradual realization that the weapons labs were false too as follows: "They had hung on for a long time, but finally Tenet called Powell to say, 'We don't have that one, either.' "[114]

As it became obvious to Powell that the information he had been given on the labs by the intelligence community had "blown up in his face," he directly criticized the intelligence community, which had given him the flawed evidence. He would go on to state, "It was presented to me in the preparation of that [portfolio of evidence] as the best information and intelligence that we had. They certainly indicated to me that it was solid. Now it appears not to be the case that it was solid."[115]

When asked if he felt the collapse of all the WMD evidence he confidently presented to the world at the UN in February 2003 to bolster the war case had tarnished his reputation, Powell said, "Of course it will. It's a blot. I'm the one who presented it on behalf of the United States to the world, and [it] will always be a part of my record. It was painful. It's painful now."[116] Powell, who essentially became the fall guy for the Bush administration and Neo-Cons after initially speaking out to prevent Paul Wolfowitz from diverting the war to Iraq back in 2001, would also say, "the intelligence system did not work well. . . . There were some people in the intelligence community who knew at the time that some of those sources were not good, and shouldn't be relied upon, and they didn't speak up. . . . That devastated me."[117] The CIA's deputy director, Michael Morell, would later make a remarkably brave apology to Powell stating: "I am absolutely confident that no one at CIA intentionally misled him, politicized analysis, or tried to provide anything but the best information—but CIA and the broader intelligence community clearly failed him and the American public. So, as someone in the chain of command at the time the Iraq WMD analysis was provided, I would like to use this opportunity to publicly apologize to Secretary Powell."[118] The Silberman Robb Commission on Intelligence Capabilities of the United States Regarding Weapons of Mass Destruction, a panel created by President Bush, would similarly castigate the intelligence community for its failures on Curveball and other false WMD threats. After stating that the Defense Intelligence Agency "did not even attempt to determine Curveball's veracity," it stated, "Worse than having no human sources is being seduced by a human source who is telling lies." The commission would also state, "That the NIE (and other reporting) didn't make clear to policymakers how heavily it relied on a single source that no American intelligence officer had ever met, and about whose reliability several intelligence professionals had expressed serious concern, is a damning comment on the Intelligence Community's practices."[119]

Claims of "Stockpiles" of Chemical-Biological Weapons and the Lingering Myth that the U.S. Found Iraqi WMDs

One of the most alarming claims made by Powell in his famous February 5, 2003, speech to the UN was that "Iraq has stockpiled chemical and biological weapons and is rebuilding the facilities to make more of those weapons."[120] He also stated, "Our conservative estimate is that Iraq today has a stockpile of between 100 and 500 tons of chemical weapons agent. That is enough agent to fill 16,000 battlefield rockets."[121] Secretary of Defense Rumsfeld stated that Saddam "has amassed large clandestine stocks of biological weapons, including anthrax and botulism toxin and possibly smallpox. His regime has amassed large clandestine stockpiles of chemical weapons, including VX and sarin and mustard gas."[122] Bush similarly claimed, "Our intelligence officials estimate that Saddam Hussein had the materials to produce as much as 500 tons of sarin, mustard and VX nerve agent."[123]

These and other frightening accusations made by members of the Bush administration suggested Iraq was producing and "stockpiling" hundreds of "tons" of WMDs on an industrial scale. A sampling of Powell's speech to UN on February 5, 2003, sheds insight into the sheer magnitude of WMDs the Bush White House claimed Hussein had at his disposal:

> When Iraq finally admitted having these weapons in 1995, the quantities were vast. . . . Iraq declared 8,500 liters of anthrax, but UNSCOM estimates that Saddam Hussein could have produced

25,000 liters. If concentrated into this dry form, this amount would be enough to fill tens upon tens upon tens of thousands of teaspoons. And Saddam Hussein has not verifiably accounted for even one teaspoon-full of this deadly material. . . .

And they have not accounted for many of the weapons filled with these agents such as there are 400 bombs. This is evidence, not conjecture. This is true. This is all well-documented. . . .

Second, as with biological weapons, Saddam Hussein has never accounted for vast amounts of chemical weaponry: 550 artillery shells with mustard, 30,000 empty munitions and enough precursors to increase his stockpile to as much as 500 tons of chemical agents. If we consider just one category of missing weaponry—6,500 bombs from the Iran-Iraq war—UNMOVIC says the amount of chemical agent in them would be in the order of 1,000 tons. These quantities of chemical weapons are now unaccounted for.

To make his case in his February 5, 2003, speech to the UN, Powell showed slides of WMD warehouses and facilities taken by satellites that indicated that these were no small buildings that could simply be hidden or secretly dismantled and transferred piece by piece to Syria (as many who refused to accept that they had been duped on the issue subsequently claimed). Surprisingly, Saddam Hussein concurred and stated, almost in desperation: "These weapons do not come in small pills that you can hide in your pocket. These are weapons of mass destruction, and it is easy to work out if Iraq has them or not. . . . I tell you Iraq has no weapons of mass destruction whatsoever. We challenge anyone who claims we have them to bring forward evidence and present it to world opinion."[124] The Iraqis also defended themselves using commonsense, saying, "Building such WMD weapons costs billions of dollars and huge [electric] power sources. The idea that such projects could be moved around in trucks or stashed away in presidential palaces stretches the imagination."[125]

Considering the massive scale and size of the WMD programs and stockpiles and production lines the Bush administration claimed Hussein was hiding, they should have been easy to find and display to the world. But when the UN investigated the targeted sites described as WMD locations by the United States from November 2002 to February 2003, they could not find the "stockpiles" of banned substances the Bush administration claimed were there.

Undeterred by the failure of the UN, which was distrusted by the Bush administration for seemingly undermining its rationale for invading Iraq, the search was relaunched after the United States invaded. In spring of 2003, the Seventy-Fifth Exploitation Task Force, whose motto was "find, exploit, eliminate," was tasked with finding the WMD stockpiles (a failed search that was vividly portrayed in the Hollywood blockbuster *Green Zone*, starring Matt Damon).

When this U.S. task force also failed to find WMDs, David Kay's White House–appointed Iraq Survey Group took over the search. While they did raid several laboratories and scientists' homes and find simple equipment and plans for carrying out *future* chemical and biological weapons research, there were no "vast" quantities of WMDs or "stockpiles" like the ones described by Powell in his speech. Kay, who had been a true believer in the existence of WMDs prior to the invasion, would later admit, "Let me begin by saying, we were almost all wrong, and I certainly include myself here."[126] Kay would also say, "My summary view, based on what I've seen, is that we are very unlikely to find large stockpiles of weapons. I don't think they exist."[127] Kay would also state, "Information found to date suggests that Iraq's large scale capability to develop, produce and fill new CW [chemical weapon] munitions was reduced if not entirely destroyed during Operation Desert Storm and Desert Fox, 13 years of UN sanctions and UN inspections. To date we have not uncovered evidence that Iraq undertook significant post-1998 steps to actually build nuclear weapons or produce fissile material."[128] And he would further state, "We have to date been unable to locate any such [WMD] munitions."

Having told the world that Iraq had vast stockpiles of WMDs, Colin Powell would later recant his previous claim and state, "I was mightily disappointed when the sourcing of it all became suspect and everything started to fall apart. The problem was the stockpiles. None have been found. I don't think they ever will be. I will forever be known as the man who made the case."[129] Yet despite the fact that there were no iconic photographs of U.S. troops triumphantly uncovering vast hidden stockpiles of WMDs or production facilities for chemical, biological, or nuclear weapons (not to mention mobile bio labs, WMD drones, gas centrifuges, or other nuclear facilities) or photographs available on Google images, many Americans continue to stubbornly believe that WMDs were in fact found in Iraq. A poll conducted in 2012 by Dartmouth University government professor Benjamin Valentino for YouGov found that fully 63 percent of Republican respondents still believed that Iraq had WMDs when the United States invaded back in 2003. By contrast, 27 percent of independents and just fifteen percent of Democrats shared that view.[130]

This despite the fact that Bush, like Powell before him, ultimately acknowledged that the search for WMDs had ended in failure as reported in his own memoir *Decision Points*. Bush wrote, "No one was more shocked and angry than I was when we didn't find the weapons. I had a sickening feeling every time I thought about it. I still do."[131] When discussing the lack of WMDs, Bush would later state, "It is true that much of the intelligence turned out to be wrong."[132] In an interview with ABC's Martha Raddatz, Bush would once again confirm the lack of WMDs in Iraq:

> *Raddatz:* Just let me go back because you brought this up. You said Saddam Hussein posed a threat in the post-9/11 world. They didn't find weapons of mass destruction.
> *Bush:* That's true. Everybody thought they had them.[133]

During the 2004 annual Radio and Television Correspondents Dinner, Bush even presented a photo of himself looking under Oval Office furniture and jokingly said, "Those weapons of mass destruction have got to be somewhere. Nope, no weapons over there . . . maybe under here?" (to which the chairman of the Democratic National Committee said, "This is a very serious issue. We've lost hundreds of troops, as you know, over there. Let's not be laughing about not being able to find weapons of mass destruction").[134] On yet another occasion Bush said "Now, look, I didn't—part of the reason we went into Iraq was—the main reason we went into Iraq at the time was we thought he had weapons of mass destruction. It turns out he didn't, but he had the capacity to make weapons of mass destruction."[135]

Secretary of Defense Rumsfeld also acknowledged making at least one "misstatement" about WMDs in Iraq.[136] He stated, "It appears that there were not weapons of mass destruction there."[137] When asked by the BBC about the lack of WMDs in Iraq, Rumsfeld would later say, "Why the intelligence proved wrong, I'm not in a position to say."[138]

National Security Advisor Condoleezza Rice acknowledged, "What we have is evidence that there are differences between what we knew going in and what we found on the ground."[139] Secretary of State Colin Powell would also state, "Of course I regret that a lot of it turned out be wrong."

To compound matters, the Iraq Survey Group (ISG) created by President

Bush to scour post-invasion Iraq and find hidden WMDs ultimately reported the following definitive findings to the U.S. government once their search was complete:

- "Saddam Hussein ended the nuclear program in 1991 following the Gulf war. ISG found no evidence to suggest concerted efforts to restart the program."
- "In practical terms, with the destruction of the Al Hakam facility, Iraq abandoned its ambition to obtain advanced BW [biological warfare] weapons quickly. ISG found no direct evidence that Iraq, after 1996, had plans for a new BW program or was conducting BW-specific work for military purposes."
- "While a small number of old, abandoned chemical munitions have been discovered, ISG judges that Iraq unilaterally destroyed its undeclared chemical weapons stockpile in 1991. There are no credible indications that Baghdad resumed production of chemical munitions thereafter."[140]

It is the last point that was seized on by many die-hard WMD supporters as "evidence" that Iraq actually had stockpiles of WMDs that were a threat to the United States. The ISG reported further details on the "old, abandoned chemical munitions" stating, "A total of 53 munitions have been recovered, all of which appear to have been part of pre-1991 Gulf war stocks based on their physical condition and residual components."[141]

Fox News triumphantly reported the findings of the rusted shells to its audience as proof that the war in Iraq had been warranted after all. Republican senator Rick Santorum went so far as to proclaim, "we now have found stockpiles" when he heard about the decaying "pre-1991" Iraqi munitions.[142] Many true believers who refused to accept the fact that their leaders had misled them tenaciously clung to the discovery of corroded shells as proof that the full-scale invasion of the Republic of Iraq (which cost America the lives of almost forty-five hundred servicemen and women, tens of thousands wounded, and cost $800 billion) was worth it.

Unfortunately, the head of the Iraq Survey Group, David Kay, dismissed even this last-ditch attempt to produce evidence of a WMD "stockpile" threat in Iraq, stating that the U.S. experts on Iraq's chemical weapons were in "almost 100 percent agreement" that nerve agents produced in the 1980s for the shells had degraded to the point where it was no longer harmful. Kay also noted that the abandoned chemical munitions found were "less toxic than most things that Americans have under their kitchen sink at this point."[143]

In his memoir, *Known and Unknown*, Rumsfeld agreed on the lack of stockpiles and said, "Saddam Hussein didn't have ready stockpiles of WMD our intelligence community believed we would uncover. The shift in emphasis suggested that Iraq's intentions and capability for building WMD had somehow not been threatening. Many Americans and others around the world accordingly came to believe the war was unnecessary."[144]

Other intelligence officials concluded the old munitions were "so degraded that they couldn't now be used as designed."[145] The *Washington Post* reported: "Intelligence officials said the munitions were found in ones, twos and maybe slightly larger collections over the past couple of years. One official conceded that these pre–Gulf War weapons did not pose a threat to the U.S. military before the 2003 invasion of Iraq. They were not maintained or part of any organized program run by Iraqi leader Saddam Hussein."[146] The *New York Times* was to describe the leftover weapons as "corroded and degraded" and "previously demilitarized."[147]

These findings were a far cry from Bush's bold stockpile claim that "Saddam Hussein had upwards of 30,000 munitions capable of delivering chemical agents" or Powell's claim that Iraq had up to "500 tons" of chemical weapons agents.[148] Needless to say, these were not the "stockpiles" Senator Rick Santorum spoke of as proof a WMD threat to America.

The final nail in the coffin for the desperate theory that the abandoned chemical weapons shells posed a serious threat to America and her people came from Charles Duelfer, who took over as head of the Iraq Survey Group after David Kay left. Duelfer stated the findings in an NPR interview with Neal Conan:

> *Mr. Duelfer:* We found, when we were investigating, some residual
> chemical munitions. And we said in the report that such
> chemical munitions would probably still be found. But the ones
> which have been found are leftover from the [1980s] Iran-Iraq
> war. They are almost 20 years old and they are in a decayed
> fashion. It is very interesting that there are so many that were
> unaccounted for, but they do not constitute a weapon of mass
> destruction, although they could be a local hazard.
>
> *Conan:* Mm-hmm. So these—were these the weapons of mass
> destruction that the Bush administration said that it was going
> into Iraq to find before the war?

Mr. Duelfer: No, these do not indicate an ongoing weapons of mass
destruction program as had been thought to exist before the
war. These are leftover rounds, which Iraq probably did not
even know that it had. Certainly, the leadership was unaware of
their existence, because they made very clear that they had
gotten rid of their programs as a prelude to getting out of
sanctions.[149]

Having frightened the American people with images of "tons" of nerve gas
and "stockpiles" of mustard gas and anthrax, it was nothing less than an in-
dictment of the main premise for the war when Duelfer's report concluded by
stating, "Iraq had not possessed military-scale stockpiles of illicit weapons
for a dozen years and was not actively seeking to produce them."[150] The report
also stated, "Iraq's WMD capability was essentially destroyed in 1991."

In other words, the First Gulf War, the subsequent sanctions of UN Resolution 687, and the bombing campaign of Clinton's 1998 Desert Fox had done
their job. Baathist Iraq was effectively contained, its chemical-biological-
nuclear weapons program had been destroyed by 1998, and it was *not* a
WMD threat to the United States. This was something that Hussein, who was
subsequently captured and interrogated by U.S. troops in 2003, had been saying all along. When asked whether he had WMDs, Hussein replied, "No, of
course not, the U.S. dreamed them up itself to have a reason to go to war with
us."[151] Hussein would also famously state, "We destroyed them. We told you.
By God, if I had such weapons, I would have used them in the [2003] fight
against the U.S."[152]

Nicholas Kristof of the *New York Times* was to write the epitaph for the
WMD search in May 2003 when he wrote:

Let's fervently hope that tomorrow we find an Iraqi superdome filled
with 500 tons of mustard gas and nerve gas, 25,000 liters of anthrax,
38,000 liters of botulinum toxin, 29,984 prohibited munitions
capable of delivering chemical agents, several dozen Scud missiles,
gas centrifuges to enrich uranium, 18 mobile biological warfare
factories, long-range unmanned aerial vehicles to dispense anthrax,
and proof of close ties with Al Qaeda. Those are the things that
President Bush or his aides suggested Iraq might have, and I don't
want to believe that top administration officials tried to win support
for the war with a campaign of wholesale deceit.[153]

But in the minds of millions of Americans who refused to accept that they had been deceived by their own leaders, conspiracy theories continued that the Iraqis had somehow evaded high-resolution U.S. spy satellites, U-2 spy planes, and on-the-ground inspectors and had secretly transported tons of WMD material and even whole factories, nuclear reactors, and stockpiles to its enemy, Shiite-Alawite-dominated Syria. But even here, "based on the evidence available at present, ISG [Iraq Survey Group] judged that it was unlikely that an official transfer of WMD material from Iraq to Syria took place."[154] Commonsensically the question many skeptics of the conspiracy theorists asked was why the hostile Shiite-Alawite regime in Syria, which actually had a bona fide WMD program of its own, would want to risk antagonizing the powerful Americans—who were clearly intent on invading their neighborhood—by hiding WMDs for the Sunni-dominated regime in neighboring Iraq. Shiite-dominated Syria, it should be recalled, was an enemy of Sunni-dominated Iraq, and such things matter.

The fact that so many people continued to believe in the existence of Iraqi WMDs—even after the very leaders in the Bush administration who led them to originally believe in them publicly recanted their previous statements as demonstrated above—was based, in part, on the pure certitude of the Bush administration's previous accusations. In retrospect, the absolute certainty expressed by many members of the Bush administration about the existence of WMDs seems outright duplicitous in light of the fact that they knew there were many dissenting or contradictory reports and opinions on the subject matter from various experts and analysts. What is shocking in retrospect was the utter lack of acknowledgement of the widespread dissent by Bush officials when they made their bold, emphatic claims about the existence of Iraqi WMDs. The detailed specifics given about Iraqi WMDs by members of the Bush administration on the eve of the invasion are also shocking considering the fact that most of the evidence was based on conjecture. Members of the Bush administration unequivocally used phrases such as "we know" and "there is no doubt," we have "irrefutable evidence," and "absolute certainty" in reference to Iraq's supposed WMDs.

An analysis of such definitive declarations on Iraqi WMDs made by the Bush administration helps explain why so many Americans still refuse to accept that the primary premise for the 2003 invasion of Iraq, the existence of WMDs, was false. Simply put, many cannot believe that their own leaders spoke with such absolute certainty about the WMDs' existence and that they were subsequently proven to be dead wrong.

Below are a few of many declarative statements by the Bush administration on the existence of Iraqi WMDs that capture the absolute sense of certainty that prevailed in the Bush White House's statements on the eve of the U.S. invasion of Iraq:

> *"We now have irrefutable evidence that* [Saddam] has once again reconstituted his program to take uranium, to enrich it to sufficiently high grade, so that it will function as the base material as a nuclear weapon. . . . *There's no doubt* what he's attempting. *And there's no doubt about the fact* that the level of effort has escalated in recent months."
> —Vice President Dick Cheney

> *"We know* where [Iraq's WMD] are. They're in the area around Tikrit and Baghdad and east, west, south, and north somewhat."
> —Secretary of Defense Donald Rumsfeld

> *"We do know, with absolute certainty*, that he [Hussein] is using his procurement system to acquire the equipment he needs in order to enrich uranium to build a nuclear weapon."
> —Vice President Dick Cheney

> *"We now know* that Saddam has resumed his efforts to acquire nuclear weapons."
> —Vice President Dick Cheney

> *"We know* that the regime has produced thousands of tons of chemical agents, including mustard gas, sarin nerve gas, VX nerve gas."
> —President George Bush

> "This is evidence, not conjecture. *This is true.* This is all well-documented."
> —Colin Powell

> *"Every statement I make today is backed up by sources, solid sources. These are not assertions. What we are giving you are facts and conclusions based on solid evidence."*
> —Colin Powell

"*There can be no doubt* that Saddam Hussein has biological weapons and the capability to rapidly produce more, many more. And he has the ability to dispense these lethal poisons and diseases in ways that can cause massive death and destruction."
—Colin Powell

"*We know* from sources that a missile brigade outside Baghdad was disbursing rocket launchers and warheads containing biological warfare agents to various locations, distributing them to various locations in western Iraq. Most of the launchers and warheads have been hidden in large groves of palm trees and were to be moved every one to four weeks to escape detection."
—Colin Powell

"*What we now know*, from various sources, is that he has continued to improve the, if you can put it in those terms, the capabilities of his nuclear . . . and he continues to pursue a nuclear weapon."
—Vice President Dick Cheney

"*We know* that he [Hussein] has the infrastructure, nuclear scientists to make a nuclear weapon . . . we don't want the smoking gun to be a mushroom cloud."
—Deputy Secretary of Defense Paul Wolfowitz

"They have weaponized chemical weapons, *we know that*. They've had an active program to develop nuclear weapons."
—Secretary of Defense Donald Rumsfeld

"*We know* they have weapons of mass destruction. We know they have active programs."
—Secretary of Defense Donald Rumsfeld

"Intelligence gathered by this and other governments *leaves no doubt* that the Iraq regime continues to possess and conceal some of the most lethal weapons ever devised."
—President George Bush

"Simply stated, *there is no doubt* that Saddam Hussein now has
weapons of mass destruction."
    —Vice President Dick Cheney

When it was subsequently proven that all the above-quoted definitive statements using the phrase "we know" and "there is no doubt" were proven to be
definitively false, there was considerable consternation among many members of Congress who had voted for the war based on the Bush administration's bold assertions. Senator Bill Nelson was to sum up the sense of betrayal
by saying, "The degree of specificity I was given a year and half ago, prior to
my vote, was not only inaccurate; it was patently false."[155]

In 2004, Charles Duelfer, the new head of the Iraq Survey Group that was
looking for Iraqi WMDs in essence supported Senator Bill Nelson's claim
that all the above statements by members of the Bush White House were indeed false by producing what became known as the Duelfer Report. *USA
Today* wrote a story on the Duelfer Report that stated:

> The 1,000-page report by chief weapons searcher Charles Duelfer, a
> document that President Bush said would represent the last word on
> the issue, confirms earlier findings and undermines much of the
> Bush administration's case about the Iraq weapons threat, though it
> does say Saddam intended to restart his weapons programs once
> United Nations sanctions were lifted.
>
> Using the research of the 1,700-member Iraq Survey Group,
> Duelfer concluded that Saddam ordered his arsenal of chemical and
> biological weapons destroyed in 1991 and 1992 and halted nuclear
> weapons development, all in hopes of lifting crippling economic
> sanctions. "Saddam Hussein ended the nuclear program in 1991
> following the Gulf War," the report states.
>
> The findings were similarly definitive concerning chemical and
> biological weapons: "Iraq unilaterally destroyed its undeclared
> chemical weapons stockpile in 1991" and the survey team found "no
> credible indications that Baghdad resumed production."[156]

In other words, the Bush-appointed Iraq Survey Group found that there were
no nuclear, no chemical, and no biological weapons in Iraq, even though
White House spokesman Ari Fleisher had previously declared, "We went to

war because Saddam Hussein had chemical weapons and had biological weapons."[157]

But the bogus WMD claims were not the only rationale that the Bush administration disseminated to the American public to convince them to support a costly invasion of Iraq. Perhaps the most widely believed threat the Bush administration skillfully manipulated to scare American politicians into voting for the war and frighten the American people was the claim that Saddam Hussein's Socialist-Baathist regime and bin Laden's fundamentalist terrorist organization were one and the same. By invading Hussein's state of Iraq, the American people were told, they could strike at the stateless Al Qaeda terrorists led by bin Laden who had attacked America on 9/11. An analysis of this effort to conflate these two vastly different figures into one sheds light on yet another premise for war that was subsequently proven to be false.

The Myth of "Osama bin Hussein"

As clearly laid out previously, Saddam Hussein was a secular, socialist leader who had systematically dismantled political Islam in his Soviet-allied state as a potential threat (although he did allow for token forms of Islam to return after his 1991 defeat in the Gulf War). Bin Laden, on the other hand, was a Wahhabi fundamentalist from Saudi Arabia who had fought jihad *against* the Soviets back in the 1980s. Other than the fact that two were both ethnic Arabs, they had absolutely nothing in common. In fact bin Laden made his hatred for Hussein known on several occasions calling him, among other things unfit to print, a socialist atheist traitor to Islam.

For his part, Hussein was uninterested in establishing any operational relationship with bin Laden's Sudan- and Afghanistan-based terrorist organization, which sought to overthrow secular regimes like his own and reestablish the caliphate (a pan-Muslim shariah law theocracy). While the average American could not be asked to understand these nuances, the American intelligence community certainly understood such basics, or at least it did prior to 2002.

Such fundamental understandings of the differences between a secular leader who idealized Soviet leader Joseph Stalin and an exiled fundamentalist leader who emulated the Prophet Mohammad were, however, turned on their head by the Bush administration on the eve of the 2003 invasion of Iraq. The Bush White House began a systematic effort to "connect the dots" between Hussein and bin Laden and paint them as one for an undiscerning audience. By painting in broad brush strokes, the Neo-Cons and the Bush White House were able to convince millions of Americans that Iraq equaled Al Qaeda on an operational-ideological level. Britain's *Independent* was to report in 2003, "Ordinary Americans think Bin Laden and Saddam are the same man."[158] This added additional fodder to the campaign to invade Iraq.

The "Osama bin Hussein" disinformation campaign began with an effort to paint the Egyptian Al Qaeda leader of the 9/11 attack, Mohamad Atta, as an Iraqi agent. The White House accusation stated that Atta met with an Iraqi official named Ahmed al Ani in Prague, Czechoslovakia, in April, 2001, presumably to plan the September 11th attack. The *Boston Globe* was to report, "Officials say evidence of the alleged meeting in April 2001 came from a single informant from Prague's Arab community who saw Atta's picture in the news after the Sept. 11 attacks, and who later told his handlers that he had seen him meeting with Ani."[159]

But in a reprise of the bogus Iraqi mobile weapons labs claims made to the German BND by an unreliable source known as Curveball, the source making the Atta claim was subsequently labeled "unreliable."[160] This stemmed in part from the fact that the Czech police stated they had "no evidence that the ringleader of the suicide attacks, Mohammed Atta, met an Iraqi intelligence agent in Prague."[161] In fact the Czech president, Vaclav Havel, felt that it was necessary to call the Bush White House and explain that "there is no evidence to confirm earlier reports that Mohamed Atta, the leader in the Sept. 11 attacks, met with an Iraqi intelligence officer in Prague just months before the attacks on New York."[162]

Such firm rejections of the existence of a meeting between the Al Qaeda operative Atta and the Iraqi agent Ani dovetailed with the CIA's own findings. CIA director George Tenet was to state that "his agency could find no evidence to confirm that the meeting [between Atta and the Iraqi official in Prague] took place."[163] He also stated, "Our Prague office is skeptical about the report. It just doesn't add up."[164] CIA deputy director Michael Morell would state, "The bottom line of the ensuing investigation was that the Czech story did not seem to be true."[165]

FBI director Robert Mueller would similarly discount the claim of a meeting between Al Qaeda operative Atta and Iraqi official Ani stating, "We ran down literally hundreds of thousands of leads and checked every record we could get our hands on, from flight reservations to car rentals to bank accounts" to see if Atta had been in Prague.[166] In the end, the FBI's search found nothing to substantiate the claims. One senior U.S. law enforcement official would later state, "We looked at this real hard because, obviously, if it were true, it would be huge. But nothing has matched up."[167]

In fact the FBI would later confirm that the 9/11 Al Qaeda leader Atta had actually been in Coral Springs, Florida, at the time of the alleged meeting in Prague with the Iraqi agent Ani. Former CIA operative Vincent Cannistraro would emphatically state, "Very early on, both CIA and FBI knew it wasn't true because the FBI had Atta in Florida at the time [of the purported meeting with Ani]."[168] In addition, there were no records showing Atta having left the country to travel to Prague at the time of the supposed 2001 meeting with the Iraqi official Ani.

But the Neo-Cons, who were interested in any rationale that might help them legitimize the invasion of Iraq, were irresistibly drawn to the notion that Atta had met with an Iraqi official in Prague, despite all the evidence to the contrary. They quickly promoted the disproved notion as an established fact. Neo-Con Douglas Feith, for example, created a slide show for the White House that cited the Prague meeting as evidence of an Iraqi–Al Qaeda plot to attack the United States on 9/11. David Corn and Michael Isikoff would later write of the presentation, "Feith's exploitation of the Atta-in-Prague allegation was a case of true believers twisting skimpy intelligence reports to create illusions of proof."[169]

Vice President Cheney then took the discredited story of an Atta meeting with an Iraqi official in Prague to the media on December 9, 2001, and boldly disseminated it to the American people. On *Meet the Press* he was to state, "It's been pretty well confirmed that [Atta] did go to Prague and he did meet with a senior official of the Iraqi intelligence service."[170] Cheney would also state "We have reporting that places him [Atta] in Prague with a senior Iraq intelligence official a few months before the attack on the World Trade Center."[171] In a *New York Times* editorial, top Neo-Con Richard Perle would state, "Evidence of a meeting in Prague between a senior Iraqi intelligence agent and Mohamed Atta, the Sept. 11 ringleader, is convincing."[172] On CNN, Colin Powell would state of a Prague meeting between Atta and Ani, "certainly the meeting took place."[173] Cheney would also state:

> And we spent some time looking into the relationship between Iraq, on the one hand, and the Al Qaeda organization on the other. And there has been some reporting that suggests that there have been a number of contacts over the years. We've seen in connection with the hijackers, of course, Mohammad Atta, who was the lead hijacker, did

apparently travel to Prague on a number of occasions. And on at least one occasion, we have reporting that places him in Prague with a senior Iraqi intelligence official a few months before the attack on the World Trade Center. The debates about, you know, was he there or wasn't he there, again it's the intelligence business.[174]

David Corn and Michael Isikoff reported that the vice president's claims of an Al Qaeda–Iraq meeting in Prague were, however, met with derision by the FBI and CIA, which knew they were bogus. They would write: "CIA officers and FBI agents, however, would roll their eyes whenever they heard an administration official cite the Atta-al-Ani meeting. None, though, would challenge the policy makers. 'Who's going to question the vice president when he keeps espousing this shit?' asked the US counterterrorism official who investigated the Atta issue."[175] CIA deputy director Michael Morell would complain, "Despite our best efforts to un-ring the bell on the Iraqi–al Qa'ida Prague connection, a few in the administration—Vice President Cheney, in particular—repeatedly raised it in public comments."[176]

As with the bogus WMD claims, the Atta-in-Prague story being peddled by the vice president to the American people would, however, ultimately be disproved, this time by the bipartisan 9/11 Commission appointed by Bush. The 9/11 Commission would state that "no evidence has been found that Atta was in the Czech Republic in April 2001." The commission would also report, "There was no reason for such a meeting, especially considering the risk it would pose to the operation. By April 2001, all four pilots had completed most of their training, and the muscle hijackers were about to begin entering the United States. The available evidence does not support the original Czech report of an Atta-Ani meeting."[177] A 2006 Senate Intelligence Committee report on the much-hyped Al Qaeda–Iraq meeting would call it "unverified" and would state, "the most reliable reporting casts doubt on this possibility." It would further state, "Postwar debriefings of al-Ani indicate that he had never seen or heard of Atta until after September 11, 2001, when Atta's face appeared on the news."[178] To compound matters, Congress investigated the meeting between Atta and the Iraqi official Ani and found that not only was Atta not in Prague at the time of the alleged meeting, but neither was Ani. The *Boston Globe* broke this story as follows:

Last week, congressional investigators declared in their major report on the terrorist attacks of Sept. 11, 2001, that after tracing Atta's movements for two years, including trips made under all known aliases, there was no evidence of the Prague meeting. A former intelligence official in the Bush administration told the Globe the CIA obtained evidence soon after the Czech report that the Iraqi agent [al-Ani] was elsewhere at the time of the purported meeting.

"The CIA had proof that Iraqi guy was not in Prague at the time," said the official, who asked not to be named. "The mystery here is why did the CIA allow that story to live when it could disprove it with hard information."[179]

Thus the Atta-in-Prague accusation went the way of the aluminum tubes, the yellowcake, the stockpiles of chemical-biological weapons, the fleets of WMD drones, and the mobile weapons lab indictments and was officially debunked once and for all. This strand of evidence linking Iraq to Al Qaeda turned out to be completely bogus.

But the Atta-in-Prague story was not the only effort the White House made to link Iraq to Al Qaeda. In his now infamous February 5, 2003, speech to the UN, Colin Powell was to attempt to link Al Qaeda to Iraq by citing the migrations of one Abu Musab Zarqawi from Taliban-controlled Afghanistan to the autonomous Kurdish-controlled territories of northern Iraq that had long ago broken away from Hussein's control. Powell would make the case citing the case of Zarqawi, an obscure Jordanian jihadi, as proof of direct link between bin Laden and Hussein as follows:

But what I want to bring to your attention today is the potentially much more sinister nexus between Iraq and the Al Qaida terrorist network, a nexus that combines classic terrorist organizations and modern methods of murder. Iraq today harbors a deadly terrorist network headed by Abu Musab Al-Zarqawi, an associate and collaborator of Osama bin Laden and his Al Qaida lieutenants.

Zarqawi, a Palestinian born in Jordan, fought in the Afghan war more than a decade ago. Returning to Afghanistan in 2000, he oversaw a terrorist training camp. One of his specialities and one of the specialities of this camp is poisons. When our coalition ousted the Taliban, the Zarqawi network helped establish another poison and explosive training center camp. And this camp is located in northeastern Iraq.

Those helping to run this camp are Zarqawi lieutenants operating in northern Kurdish areas outside Saddam Hussein's controlled Iraq. But Baghdad has an agent in the most senior levels of the radical organization, Ansar al-Islam, that controls this corner of Iraq. In 2000 this agent offered Al Qaida safe haven in the region. After we swept Al Qaida from Afghanistan, some of its members accepted this safe haven. They remain there today.

Zarqawi's activities are not confined to this small corner of north east Iraq. He traveled to Baghdad in May 2002 for medical treatment, staying in the capital of Iraq for two months while he recuperated to fight another day.

During this stay, nearly two dozen extremists converged on Baghdad and established a base of operations there. These Al Qaida affiliates, based in Baghdad, now coordinate the movement of people, money and supplies into and throughout Iraq for his network, and they've now been operating freely in the capital for more than eight months. Iraqi officials deny accusations of ties with Al Qaida. These denials are simply not credible.

As I said at the outset, none of this should come as a surprise to any of us. Terrorism has been a tool used by Saddam for decades. Saddam was a supporter of terrorism long before these terrorist networks had a name. And this support continues. The nexus of poisons and terror is new. The nexus of Iraq and terror is old. The combination is lethal. With this track record, Iraqi denials of supporting terrorism take the place alongside the other Iraqi denials of weapons of mass destruction. It is all a web of lies.[180]

Bush would join Powell and would say of Zarqawi's migration to Iraq: "Some al Qaeda leaders who fled Afghanistan went to Iraq. These include one very senior al Qaeda leader who received medical treatment in Baghdad this year, and who has been associated with planning for chemical and biological attacks. We've learned that Iraq has trained al Qaeda members in bomb-making and poisons and deadly gases."[181] There was, however, a major problem with Bush's statement that Zarqawi was a "very senior al Qaeda leader" and Powell's use of Zarqawi in Iraq as evidence of a "sinister nexus" between bin Laden and Hussein; none of it was true. In his masterful account of the War on Terror, terrorism analyst Peter Bergen succinctly stated, "Not only did Zarqawi run a terrorist organization that was separate from and even competitive with Al Qaeda, he was also independent of Saddam

Hussein."[182] To understand the deep flaws in Bush and Powell's claims that
Zarqawi was a link to both bin Laden *and* Hussein, one has to explore the
complex journey of this important figure who was to go on to become a key
player in Iraq after the 2003 invasion.

Zarqawi was a Jordanian thug and criminal who turned to Islam while in
a Jordanian jail. After release from jail, he traveled to Taliban-controlled Afghanistan and organized a militant group known as Jund al Sham (the Army
of the Levant, i.e. Greater Syria). Although most Arab jihadi groups in Afghanistan at the time, including Al Qaeda, were based in the Pashtun lands of
the southeast that gave birth to the Taliban, Zarqawi's group was based in the
northwestern Tajik town of Herat. While Al Qaeda's members primarily
came from Egypt and Saudi Arabia and were interested in overthrowing
those regimes, Jund al Sham's members came from Syria, Jordan, Palestine,
Lebanon, and Kurdish northern Iraq.[183] Jund al Sham's goals were focused on
overthrowing the monarchy in Jordan and the secular-socialist regimes in
Syria and Iraq.

In 2000, Osama bin Laden offered Zarqawi a chance to join his group, but
he "refused for ideological reasons" according to Loretta Napoleoni who has
written a book on Zarqawi.[184] Mary Anne Weaver, who interviewed Zarqawi's
relatives in his hometown and met with some of his jihadi companions,
stated in an article in the *Atlantic Monthly*: "At least five times, in 2000 and
2001, bin Laden called al-Zarqawi to come to Kandahar and pay *bayat*—take
an oath of allegiance—to him. Each time, al-Zarqawi refused. Under no circumstances did he want to become involved in the battle between the Northern Alliance and the Taliban. He also did not believe that either bin Laden or
the Taliban was serious enough about jihad."[185] One arrested member of
Zarqawi's subsequent jihad group that was later based in Iraqi Kurdistan (i.e.,
the autonomous zone that was beyond the reach of Hussein), Al Tawhid wal
Jihad (Monotheism and Holy War), denied that Zarqawi's group was a "collaborator" of bin Laden's as Powell claimed. According to a *Newsweek* article
referencing this member:

> Secret German records compiled during interrogations with a
> captured Zarqawi associate suggest that the shadowy Zarqawi
> headed his own terrorist group, called Al Tawhid, with its own goals
> and may even have been a jealous rival of Al Qaeda. The captured
> associate, Shadi Abdallah, who is now on trial in Germany, told his
> interrogators last year that Zarqawi's Al Tawhid organization was one

of several Islamist groups that acted "in opposition" to bin Laden's Al Qaeda. At one point, Abdallah described how Zarqawi even vetoed the idea of splitting charity funds collected in Germany between Al Tawhid and Al Qaeda.[186]

Bin Laden and Zarqawi were hardly natural collaborators. Zarqawi was an abrasive street thug from Jordan, while bin Laden was a soft-spoken Saudi millionaire who came from an elite family. One Al Qaeda member who was in Afghanistan described the tension between bin Laden's followers and those of Zarqawi as follows: "I understood that they had differences of opinion with bin Laden on a number of issues and positions. . . . From the day al-Zarqawi's group arrived, there were [disagreements]."[187]

In September 2001, the U.S.-led coalition attacked the Taliban regime in Afghanistan and Zarqawi, and his Jund al Sham followers fled to nearby Iran, while most Al Qaeda members retreated to neighboring Pakistan. From Iran, Zarqawi fled to a fundamentalist enclave found in the autonomous Kurdish zones that lay beyond Hussein's control in northern Iraq. This enclave of several villages around the town of Halabja was run by a Kurdish Arab Taliban-style group known as Ansar al Islam (the Supporters of Islam). Ansar al Islam's emir, or commander, was one Mullah Krekar, who was delighted to have Zarqawi's followers boost his ranks. Krekar, as it transpired, was a Kurdish fundamentalist who was at war with both the neighboring secular Kurds and the secular regime of Saddam Hussein and he needed more foot soldiers for his jihad.

Then, on February 5, 2003, America came to know the name Zarqawi, not as an independent Jordanian jihadi who had refused to merge his group with bin Laden's Al Qaeda, but as Powell's evidence of a "sinister nexus" between Al Qaeda and the Iraqi president, Saddam Hussein. In her article on Zarqawi, Weaver writes: "One can only imagine how astonished al-Zarqawi must have been when Colin Powell named him as the crucial link between al-Qaeda and Saddam Hussein's regime. He was not even officially a part of al-Qaeda, and ever since he had left Afghanistan, his links had been not to Iraq but to Iran. 'We know Zarqawi better than he knows himself,' a high-level Jordanian intelligence official said. 'And I can assure you that he never had any links to Saddam.'"[188] As for Mullah Krekar, the *Independent* reported that "he denied links between Ansar al-Islam and Saddam, saying: 'Not in the past, not now and not in the future. I am a Kurdish man, Saddam is our enemy.'"[189] Krekar and his Kurdish jihadis scoffed at the notion conveyed by

Powell to the world that Hussein had an agent in their ranks who controlled them.

Napoleoni would write of Powell's claim that Zarqawi was a "collaborator" with bin Laden and proof of a link between Hussein's regime and Al Qaeda: "The Alliance that Osama bin Laden and al Gharib [Zarqawi] are said to have made in 1999 is one of the many legends which have been constructed around the life of al Zarqawi. No evidence of such an alliance has ever been provided. On the contrary, as early as 2000, one can see the emergence of major strategic differences between the men."[190] In addition to *not* being a member of Al Qaeda, the 2006 U.S. Senate Intelligence Committee on Pre-War Intelligence found that Zarqawi was *not* linked to Saddam Hussein either. In fact Hussein considered Zarqawi a threat and tried arresting him. According to this intelligence report:

> The Iraqi regime wanted to capture Zarqawi. The IIS [Iraqi Intelligence Service] formed a special committee and actively attempted to locate and arrest al-Zarqawi without success, contradicting prewar assessments that the IIS almost certainly had the power to track him. Postwar information from an al-Qaida detainee indicated that Saddam's regime "considered al-Zarqawi an outlaw" and blamed his network operating in Kurdish-controlled northern Iraq for two bombings in Baghdad. . . . Postwar information indicates that Saddam Hussein attempted, unsuccessfully, to locate and capture al-Zarqawi and that the regime did not have a relationship with, harbor, or turn a blind eye toward Zarqawi.[191]

In addition, the CIA found "no conclusive evidence that the [Iraqi] regime harbored Osama bin Laden associate Abu Musab al-Zarqawi."[192] While Hussein's agents were unable to arrest Zarqawi, who had found sanctuary "in a portion of northeastern Iraq that wasn't under Saddam's control," they were able to arrest three of his lieutenants who were found in Iraqi territory they controlled.[193] For his part, Zarqawi, whom Powell erroneously described as a link between Hussein and bin Laden, called Saddam Hussein a "devil" who "terrified people."[194]

Thus not only was Zarqawi not a "connecting dot" to Osama bin Laden as Powell claimed, but he was not a link to Saddam Hussein either. Therefore there was no rationale for Powell to use this non–Al Qaeda operative's existence in Iraq (specifically in Kurdish lands beyond the control of Hussein) as evidence that Iraq was operationally linked to bin Laden in a plot to attack the United States. But even if Zarqawi *had* been linked to Al Qaeda, it must be stressed that he was living in the Kurdish areas of northern Iraq that were effectively at war with Hussein in the south. These areas were not under Hussein's control so there was no need to invade Hussein's Baathist lands in the south.

The Lack of Operational Ties Between
Al Qaeda and Saddam Hussein

Not surprisingly, criticism of the White House's claims that Osama bin Laden was in league with Saddam Hussein came from many directions in the U.S. intelligence community. The Defense Intelligence Agency (DIA) stated its findings as follows: "Saddam's regime is intensely secular and is wary of Islamic revolutionary movements. Moreover, Baghdad is unlikely to provide assistance to a group it cannot control."[195] CIA analyst Michael Scheuer, who led the Agency's bin Laden unit, said Hussein was "never going to give" WMDs to bin Laden "because Al Qaeda would have been just as likely to use them against him as against the United States. They [Al Qaeda followers] hated Saddam."[196]

CIA officer Bob Bauer, who had worked closely on the bin Laden threat, said in 2002, "I'm unaware of any evidence of Saddam pursuing terrorism against the United States."[197] Similarly, Steve Coll, author of *Ghost Wars*, the definitive history of the lead-up to the War on Terror, wrote, "Among some, not all, but many al Qaeda specialists, was a sense of dismay. 'Wait a second, this [Iraq] isn't the enemy. The enemy is over here. Saddam may be a bad guy, but that's not who attacked us on September 11th, and we're not done getting after these [Al Qaeda] guys.'"[198]

Greg Thielmann, the director of the Strategic, Proliferation, and Military Affairs Division in the State Department's Bureau of Intelligence and Research, said, "Based on the terrorism experts I met with during my period of government, I never heard anyone make the claim there was a significant tie between Al Qaeda and Saddam Hussein." He further stated that Bush was "misleading the public in implying there was a close connection."[199]

Another expert stated, "In the Arab world even children laugh at the thought of a relationship between Saddam Hussein and Al Qaeda."[200] One CIA analyst told the Bush administration, "If you want to go after that son of a bitch to settle old scores, be my guest. But don't tell us he is connected to 9/11 terrorism because there is no evidence to support that. You will have to have a better reason."[201] A Jordanian Arab politician who personally knew the notorious Jordanian terrorist Abu Musab Zarqawi similarly stated, "The mentality of al Qaeda simply doesn't go with the Ba'athist one."[202] Gary Schroen, who was head of the CIA's bin Laden station, said: "[CIA director] Tenet, to his credit, had us go back 10 years in the agency's records and look and see what we knew about Iraq and al Qaeda. And I was available at the time and I led the effort. And we went back 20 years. We examined about 20,000 documents, probably something along the line of 75,000 pages of information. And there was no connection."[203] Criticism for the Bush administration's increasingly strident claims that bin Laden and Hussein were one and the same also came from analysts working in Washington, D.C., think tanks. Gene Healy at the CATO Institute gave an almost remedial breakdown of the reasons why Hussein and bin Laden were not collaborators:

> The administration's strongest sound-bite on Iraq is also its weakest argument for war. The idea that Saddam Hussein would trust Al Qaeda enough to give Al Qaeda operatives chemical or biological weapons—and trust them to keep quiet about it—is simply not plausible. Bin Laden, who views the rigid Saudi theocracy as insufficiently Islamic, has long considered Saddam Hussein an infidel enemy. Before Hussein invaded Kuwait in 1990, Bin Laden warned publicly that the Iraqi dictator had designs on conquering Saudi Arabia. When Iraq invaded Kuwait, Bin Laden offered to assemble his mujahedeen to battle Hussein and protect the Arabian peninsula. Last summer, when CNN acquired a cache of internal Al Qaeda training videotapes, they discovered a Qaeda documentary that was highly critical of Hussein. Peter Bergen, the CNN terrorism expert who interviewed Bin Laden in 1998, noted that Bin Laden indicted Hussein, as "a bad Muslim."[204]

As undeterred by the voices rising in protest to the "bin Laden equals Saddam Hussein" accusations as they had been by those voices that contested the bogus WMD accusations, the Bush administration launched a media blitz designed to morph the two distinct leaders into one terrorist threat. It was to be perhaps their most successful public relations campaign to frighten the American public and galvanize them for a war against a secular regime that had no active WMD program nor ties to Al Qaeda Islamic terrorism. Analysis of these claims shows the lengths the Bush White House went to deceive the American people on this issue.

White House Statements Linking bin Laden to Hussein

Some critics attacked Bush and Cheney for *insinuating* that there were ties between Baathist Iraq and fundamentalist Al Qaeda, but an analysis of their actual words shows they did not just insinuate, they outright stated there were direct links. Bush, for example, warned of "the danger of Al Qaida becoming an extension of Saddam's madness."[205] Dilip Hiro has written in his book *Secrets and Lies: Operation Iraqi Freedom and After,* "Bush's strategy was to project Saddam Hussein as an extension of Bin Laden. To do so he needed convincing evidence to establish a link between Al Qaida and Saddam."[206]

Despite the fact that the Zarqawi-as-a-link to both Hussein and Al Qaeda as well as the Atta-in-Prague accusations were both proven false, the Bush administration continued to make assertive statements that directly linked Iraq to bin Laden. President Bush in particular made numerous statements equating the war on Iraq with the war on Al Qaeda in a calculated effort to conflate the two. Below are just a sampling of some of the bold statements by members of the Bush White House that directly painted a picture of Hussein and bin Laden as being in league with one another:

"The reason I keep insisting that there was a relationship between Iraq and Saddam and al Qaeda is because there was a relationship between Iraq and al Qaeda."[207]
—President George Bush

"Evidence from intelligence sources, secret communications and statements by people now in custody, reveal that Saddam aids and protects terrorists, including members of al-Qa'ida."[208]
—President George Bush

"Fragmentary reporting points to possible Iraqi involvement not only in 9/11 but also in previous al Qaida attacks."[209]
—Report prepared by Neo-Con Douglas Feith's Office of Special Plans group titled "Iraq and al-Qaida: Making the Case"

"Saddam Hussein has longstanding, direct, and continuing ties to terrorist networks. Senior members of Iraqi intelligence and Al Qaeda have met at least eight times since the early 1990s. . . . Iraq has also provided Al Qaeda with chemical and biological weapons training."[210]
    —President George Bush

"We know that Iraq and the Al Qaeda terrorist network share a common enemy, the United States of America. We know that Iraq and Al Qaeda have had high-level contacts that go back a decade. We've learned that Iraq has trained Al Qaeda members in bomb-making and poisons and deadly gases."[211]
    —President George Bush

"I continue to believe—I think there's overwhelming evidence that there was a connection between Al Qaeda and the Iraqi government."[212]
    —Vice President Dick Cheney

"The liberation of Iraq is a crucial advance in the campaign against terror. We have removed an ally of al Qaeda and cut off a source of terrorist funding and this much is certain—no terrorist network will gain weapons of mass destruction from the Iraqi regime because the Iraqi regime is no more."[213]
    —President George Bush

"We will have struck a major blow right at the heart of the base, if you will, the geographic base of the terrorists who've had us under assault now for many years, but most especially on 9/11."[214]
    —Vice President Cheney discussing the U.S. invasion of Iraq

"With those attacks, the terrorists and their supporters declared war on the United States and war is what they got. The battle of Iraq is one victory in a war on terror that began on Sept. 11, 2001 and still goes on."[215]
    —President George Bush

"Evidence from intelligence sources, secret conversations, and statements by people now in custody reveal that Saddam Hussein aids and protects terrorists, including members of Al Qaeda. Secretly, and without fingerprints, he could provide one of his hidden weapons to terrorists."[216]
—President George Bush

"The Iraqi intelligence service has a relationship with al-Qaeda that developed throughout the decade of the '90s. That was clearly official policy."[217]
—Vice President Dick Cheney

"There clearly was a relationship. It's been testified to. The evidence is overwhelming."[218]
—Vice President Dick Cheney

"When I talk about the war on terror, I am not just talking about Al Qaida, I am talking about Iraq."[219]
—President George Bush

"We've learned that Iraq has trained al-Qaida members in bomb-making and poisons and deadly gases. And we know that after September 11th Saddam Hussein's regime gleefully celebrated the terrorist attacks on America."[220]
—President George Bush

"We know he [Hussein] is out trying once again to produce nuclear weapons and we know that he has a long-standing relationship with various terrorist groups, including the Al Qaeda organization."[221]
—Vice President Cheney

"We have to recognize that terrorist networks have relationships with terrorist states that have weapons of mass destruction, and they're inevitably going to get their hands on them, and they won't hesitate one minute in using them."[222]
—Secretary of Defense Donald Rumsfeld

"His regime has had high-level contacts with Al Qaeda going back a decade and has provided training to Al Qaeda terrorists."[223]
—Vice President Dick Cheney

"The liberation of Iraq is a crucial advance in the campaign against terror."[224]
—President George Bush

"Imagine those 19 [9/11 Al Qaeda] hijackers with other weapons and other plans, this time armed by Saddam Hussein. It would take one vial, one canister, one crate slipped into this country to bring a day of horror like none we have ever known."[225]
—President George Bush

"You can't distinguish between al Qaeda and Saddam when you talk about the war on terror . . . they're both equally as bad, and equally as evil, and equally as destructive."[226]
—President George Bush

After the U.S. occupation of Iraq in 2003, the Americans captured the majority of Iraq's leaders and interrogated them, usually with lie detectors. Much to the Bush administration's dismay, they quickly realized that, like the mythical WMDs, the much-hyped links between Saddam Hussein's regime and Al Qaeda simply did not exist according to the interrogations. FBI interrogation records, for example, reveal that "Saddam denied ever laying eyes on the 'zealot' bin Laden, bent on striking the U.S. He said he 'did not have the same belief of vision' as the terror kingpin. Saddam never sought Al Qaeda assistance because he feared the terror group would turn on him."[227] Without any WMDs to give to Al Qaeda, a Saudi-led group that it did not have any operational ties to, there was absolutely no rationale for the United States and Britain to launch a full-scale invasion of Iraq to "disarm" it and prevent it from collaborating with Al Qaeda in a chemical-biological attack on the U.S.

In the months following the interrogations of the captured Iraqis, there were many reports in U.S. newspapers that revealed to the American public that this key premise for the invasion promoted by the Bush administration (i.e., that Iraq was tied to Al Qaeda) was false. The *Washington Post* published several headlines on the issue at this time, such as "Hussein's Prewar Ties to

Al Qaeda Discounted," "Al Qaeda-Hussein Link Is Dismissed" and "As Rationales for War Erode, Issue of Blame Looms Large." CNN's Peter Bergen was
to report:

> After the fall of Hussein's regime, no documents were unearthed in
> Iraq proving the Hussein–al Qaeda axis despite the fact that, like
> other totalitarian regimes, Hussein's government kept massive and
> meticulous records. The U.S. Defense Intelligence Agency had by
> 2006 translated 34 million pages of documents from Hussein's Iraq
> and found there was nothing to substantiate a "partnership" between
> Hussein and al Qaeda. Two years later the Pentagon's own internal
> think tank, the Institute for Defense Analyses, concluded after
> examining 600,000 Hussein-era documents and several thousand
> hours of his regime's audio- and videotapes that there was "no
> smoking gun" [i.e., direct connection between Hussein's Iraq and al
> Qaeda].[228]

One story from the *Washington Post* was illuminating and captured the sentiment that many Americans felt at the time as this key rationale for the invasion of Iraq collapsed like the WMD myth before it:

> Captured Iraqi documents and intelligence interrogations of Saddam
> Hussein and two former aides "all confirmed" that Hussein's regime
> was not directly cooperating with al-Qaeda before the U.S. invasion
> of Iraq, according to a declassified Defense Department report
> released yesterday.
>
> "Overall, the reporting provides no conclusive signs of coopera-
> tion on specific terrorist operations," that CIA report said, adding
> that discussions on the issue were "necessarily speculative." It quoted
> an August 2002 CIA report describing the relationship as more
> closely resembling "two organizations trying to feel out or exploit
> each other" rather than cooperating operationally.
>
> The CIA was not alone, the defense report emphasized. The
> Defense Intelligence Agency (DIA) had concluded that year that
> "available reporting is not firm enough to demonstrate an ongoing
> relationship" between the Iraqi regime and al-Qaeda, it said. . . . The
> inspector general concluded that a key Pentagon office—run by
> then–Undersecretary of Defense Douglas J. Feith—had

inappropriately written intelligence assessments before the March 2003 invasion alleging connections between al-Qaeda and Iraq that the U.S. intelligence consensus disputed. . . .

The report said, the CIA had concluded in June 2002 that there were few substantiated contacts between al-Qaeda operatives and Iraqi officials and had said that it lacked evidence of a long-term relationship like the ones Iraq had forged with other terrorist groups.[229]

Congressional studies and reports came soon thereafter that further dismantled this key claim that had been so widely and confidently disseminated by the Bush administration. For example, the Senate Intelligence Committee Report on War and Peace issued a report that found that there were "Iraq–al Qaida contacts, but no complicity or assistance."[230] Further findings of the committee included the following conclusions:

Conclusion 93. The CIA reasonably assessed that there were likely several instances of contacts between Iraq and al-Qaida throughout the 1990s, but that these contacts did not add up to an established formal relationship.

Conclusion 96. The CIA's assessment that to date there was no evidence proving Iraqi complicity or assistance in an al-Qaida attack was reasonable and objective. No additional information has emerged to suggest otherwise.

Conclusion 97. No information has emerged thus far to suggest that Saddam did try to employ al-Qaida in conducting terrorist attacks.

A 2006 congressional Select Committee on Intelligence was equally damning and summed up the findings from interviews with Iraqi leaders on the subject of Al Qaeda as follows:

According to Tariq Aziz [the captured Iraqi foreign minister] "Saddam only expressed negative sentiments about bin Ladin." . . . Aziz underscored Saddam's distrust of Islamic extremists like bin Ladin.[231]

During the FBI's debrief of a top official in Saddam's government, Abid Hamid Mahmoud al Kattab al Tikriti, al Tikriti noted that Saddam Hussein's position was that Iraq should not deal with al Qa'ida.[232]

[Senior Iraq Intelligence official] Hijazi told [FBI] de-briefers that once he returned to Iraq, he wrote a negative report on the meeting with bin Ladin. Hijazi "criticized bin Ladin for his hostile speech and his insistence on the Islamization of Iraq." Hijazi said that he assessed that "working with bin Ladin would damage relations with Arab countries in the region."[233]

A former high-ranking Iraqi official provided information about an unsuccessful attempt by al Qa'ida to meet with Saddam Hussein in Baghdad in 1998. The former Iraqi official stated that in 1998 bin Laden sent al-Qa'ida representative Abu Hafs al-Mauritani to Baghdad in order to request $10 million to be used to continue al-Qa'ida attacks against the West. According to the official, Saddam refused to meet with Abu Hafs and explicitly rejected the request for assistance. Another senior Iraqi official stated that Saddam did not like bin Ladin because he called Saddam an "unbeliever."[234]

Saddam's regime is intensely secular and is wary of Islamic revolutionary movements. Moreover, Baghdad is unlikely to provide assistance to a group it cannot control.[235]

Looking at prewar intelligence on Iraq, the Select Committee on the U.S. Intelligence Community's Prewar Intelligence Assessment on Iraq further concluded that the CIA had accurately assessed that contacts between Saddam Hussein's regime and members of al-Qaeda "did not add up to an established formal relationship."[236] It also stated:

"The Intelligence Community has no credible information that Baghdad had foreknowledge of the 11 September attacks or any other al-Qaeda strike."[237]

Conclusion 93. The Central Intelligence Agency reasonably assessed that there were likely several instances of contacts between Iraq and al-Qaeda throughout the 1990s, but that these contacts did not add up to an established formal relationship.[238]

Conclusion 94. The CIA reasonably and objectively assessed in Iraqi Support for Terrorism that the most problematic area of contact between Iraq and al-Qaeda were the reports of training in the use of non-conventional weapons, specifically chemical and biological weapons.[239]

The final nail in the coffin in the "Osama bin Laden equals Saddam Hussein" myth came from the bipartisan 9/11 Commission, which found "they [tentative contacts between Iraq and Al Qaeda] do not appear to have resulted in a collaborative relationship. Two senior bin Laden associates have adamantly denied that any ties existed between al Qaeda and Iraq. We have no credible evidence that Iraq and al Qaeda cooperated on attacks against the United States."[240] The *Washington Post* was to report of the 9/11 Commission's findings: "The finding challenges a belief held by large numbers of Americans about al Qaeda's ties to Hussein. According to a Harris poll in late April, a plurality of Americans, 49 percent to 36 percent, believe 'clear evidence that Iraq was supporting al Qaeda has been found.'"[241] But the Bush administration had to have been pleased to hear that 49 percent of Americans had bought into the myth that bin Laden had operational ties to Hussein. And far from backing off on the bogus claims in the face of damning government reports that demolished the White House's claims that Iraq was tied to Al Qaeda, members of the Bush administration continued to insinuate that there were in fact operational ties between Iraq and Al Qaeda.

Polls Show That a Majority Americans Bought into the "Osama bin Hussein Myth"

What was the end result of this campaign of disinformation from the White House linking Hussein to bin Laden? Not surprisingly, an overwhelming number of Americans came to believe from 2002 to 2004 that Saddam Hussein had attacked their country on 9/11 or was linked to Al Qaeda in some other nefarious fashion. A 2002 Pew Research Center poll found that a whopping 66 percent of Americans said they believed Saddam Hussein was involved in the 9/11 attacks (that same poll found that 79 percent of Americans believed he also had *nuclear* weapons).[242] A *Washington Post* opinion poll similarly found that 70 percent of Americans believed the Iraqi leader was personally involved in the 9/11 attacks."[243] Not surprisingly, 63 percent also supported the U.S. invasion of Iraq as a response to Hussein's perceived role in the 9/11 attacks.[244]

If this news were not disturbing enough, a Knight Ridder poll found that "half of those surveyed said one or more of the September 11 terrorist hijackers were Iraqi citizens."[245] Of course none of the hijackers were Iraqi citizens; most came from Saudi Arabia (a country that the Bush administration did not accuse of having ties to terrorism, despite the fact that several Saudi princes were known to have given money to extremist causes and members of Osama bin Laden's family still supported him).

The news got worse. A Gallup poll in 2002 found that a total of 86 percent of those surveyed said Saddam was supporting terrorist groups planning to attack the United States. In addition, 53 percent believed he was involved in the 9/11 attacks, and 94 percent said Saddam Hussein either had weapons of mass destruction or was developing them. Another 83 percent of those who said he had weapons of mass destruction said he would use them to attack the United States.[246]

The *Washington Post* published several front-page stories around this time that aimed to disabuse its readers of these false notions being propagated by the Bush White House. Among them was one that stated:

> Nearing the second anniversary of the Sept. 11, 2001, terrorist attacks, seven in 10 Americans continue to believe that Iraq's Saddam Hussein had a role in the attacks, even though the Bush administration and congressional investigators say they have no evidence of this. Sixty-nine percent of Americans said they thought it at least likely that Hussein was involved in the attacks on the World Trade Center and the Pentagon, according to the latest Washington Post poll.
>
> Bush's opponents say he encouraged this misconception by linking al Qaeda to Hussein in almost every speech on Iraq. Indeed, administration officials began to hint about a Sept. 11–Hussein link soon after the attacks. In late 2001, Vice President Cheney said it was "pretty well confirmed" that attack mastermind Mohamed Atta met with a senior Iraqi intelligence official.
>
> But this summer's congressional report on the attacks states, "The CIA has been unable to establish that [Atta] left the United States or

entered Europe in April under his true name or any known alias."
Bush, in his speeches, did not say directly that Hussein was culpable
in the Sept. 11 attacks. But he frequently juxtaposed Iraq and al
Qaeda in ways that hinted at a link.

"You couldn't distinguish between al Qaeda and Saddam Hussein," said Democratic tactician Donna Brazile. "Every member of
the administration did the drumbeat. My mother said if you repeat a
lie long enough, it becomes a gospel truth. This one became a gospel
hit."

The Post poll, conducted Aug. 7–11, found that 62 percent of
Democrats, 80 percent of Republicans and 67 percent of independents suspected a link between Hussein and 9/11. In addition, eight
in 10 Americans said it was likely that Hussein had provided
assistance to al Qaeda, and a similar proportion suspected he had
developed weapons of mass destruction.[247]

But these were not the most alarming polls. The most tragic findings came
from a Zogby poll that found that 8.5 out of every 10 U.S. soldiers serving in
Iraq (i.e., 85 percent) said the United States mission was "to retaliate for
Saddam's role in the 9-11 attacks." A full 77 percent said they believed the
main or a major reason for the war was "to stop Saddam from protecting al
Qaeda in Iraq."[248]

At the time of the poll, news channels featured U.S. aircraft taking off
from aircraft carriers to drop bombs on Iraqi targets. Scrawled on the bombs
were messages such as "Paybacks for 9/11," and "NYPD" or "NYFD" (a trib-
ute to the large numbers of New York Police Department and Fire Department members who lost their lives in the Al Qaeda attack on 9/11).

In other words, thousands of U.S. troops who fought and died or were
wounded in Operation Iraqi Freedom did so mistakenly believing they were
attacking the Iraqi enemy that had attacked their country on 9/11. Many U.S.
soldiers in this theater of action bought into the myth that they were fighting
and dying in the streets of such Iraqi towns as Fallujah, Ramadi, and Baghdad so that that they would not have to fight the Iraqi insurgents/rebels in the
streets of America.

Such gross misunderstandings might help explain why U.S. troops subse-
quently tortured scores of Iraqi detainees in the notorious prison of Abu
Ghraib after the invasion or carried out a massacre of twenty-four unarmed
Iraqi men, women, and children in Haditha in 2005.[249] The U.S. troops in-

volved may mistakenly have thought that they were torturing or killing Iraqis who supported the Al Qaeda terrorists that carried out the 9/11 attacks. Anyone on the streets of Baghdad could be an Al Qaeda terrorist; they were theoretically all in it together.

In the early years of the Iraq war, the vast majority of Americans also continued to believe that there was a "sinister nexus" linking Saddam Hussein to bin Laden. This certainly stemmed in part from the fact that the Bush administration never backed down on its false statements that bin Laden and Hussein were collaborators in terrorism against the United States. On the contrary, even as the media, Senate committees, and numerous best sellers dismantled the White House's pretext for invading Iraq, the Bush administration continued to assert the bin Laden–Hussein "connection."

In a typical interview in 2003 with MSNBC's Tim Russert, Vice President Cheney disingenuously kept the ambiguity on the bin Laden–Hussein myth alive:

> *Mr. Russert:* The *Washington Post* asked the American people about Saddam Hussein, and this is what they said: 69 percent said he was involved in the September 11 attacks. Are you surprised by that?
>
> *Vice Pres. Cheney:* No. I think it's not surprising that people make that connection.
>
> *Mr. Russert:* But is there a connection?
>
> *Vice Pres. Cheney:* We don't know. You and I talked about this two years ago. I can remember you asking me this question just a few days after the original attack. At the time I said no, we didn't have any evidence of that. Subsequent to that, we've learned a couple of things. We learned more and more that there was a relationship between Iraq and al-Qaeda that stretched back through most of the decade of the '90s, that it involved training, for example, on BW [biological weapons] and CW [chemical weapons], that al-Qaeda sent personnel to Baghdad to get trained on the systems that are involved. The Iraqis providing bomb-making expertise and advice to the al-Qaeda organization.
>
> With respect to 9/11, of course, we've had the story that's been public out there. The Czechs alleged that Mohamed Atta, the lead attacker, met in Prague with a senior Iraqi intelligence

official five months before the attack, but we've never been able
to develop anymore of that yet either in terms of confirming it
or discrediting it. We just don't know.[250]

Thus what (along with the WMD myth) was perhaps the most widely circu-
lated and believed lie in U.S. history continued to be propagated by an unrepentant Bush White House. This happened even as tens of thousands of
America's men and women were sent into harm's way to fight an enemy that
they incorrectly believed was both an Al Qaeda terrorist *and* a weapons of
mass destruction threat to their nation. The question many discerning voices
asked at this time was whether the American public would ever wake up to
the fact that their own elected leaders had deliberately misled them.

Will the Record Ever Be Set Straight?

In the aftermath of the invasion of Iraq, as no WMDs or links to bin Laden
materialized, several best sellers came out that systematically demolished the
link between Iraqi WMD and Al Qaeda that had been assiduously propagated by the Bush White House as a case for war. These included: *Hubris: The
Inside Story of the Spin, Scandal, and Selling of the Iraq War*, by Michael Isikoff
and David Corn; *A Pretext for War: 9/11, Iraq and the Abuse of America's Intelligence Communities*, by James Bamford; *The Greatest Story Ever Sold: The
Decline and Fall of Truth in Bush's America*, by Frank Rich; *Secrets and Lies:
Operation Iraqi Freedom and After*, by Dilip Hiro; and *Weapons of Mass Deception: The Uses of Propaganda in Bush's War on Iraq*, by Sheldon Rampton
and John Stauber.

In his book *Bush's Wars*, Terry Anderson summed up the gist of the above
books' findings, stating, "The [Bush] administration's prewar claims in their
rush to war were bogus. Saddam had no WMD program, no stashes of chemical or biological weapons, no UAVs and no links to Al Qaeda."[251]

Hollywood got into the act soon after and produced such movies as *Green
Zone*, starring Matt Damon as a frustrated U.S. soldier trying desperately to
uncover nonexistent WMDs in post-invasion Iraq, and *Fair Game*, starring
Sean Penn as Ambassador Joe Wilson in the notorious Nigerian yellowcake
episode.

The media similarly hammered away at the White House's collapsing case
for war. A Fox News headline declared, "No Iraq WMDs After '91"; A *Washington Post* headline declared, "Iraq's Arsenal Was Only on Paper," while a

CNN headline declared, "No WMD Stockpiles in Iraq." The *Los Angeles Times* reported, "Condoleezza Rice Regrets There Were No WMDs in Iraq," as the *Washington Post* reported, "Al Qaeda-Hussein Link Is Dismissed." *Time* magazine asked, "So, What Went Wrong?" while *USA Today* reported, "Final Report: Iraq Had No WMDs."

The nationally syndicated McClatchy News Service reported, "Exhaustive Review Finds No Link Between Saddam and Al Qaida," and reported:

> An exhaustive review of more than 600,000 Iraqi documents that were captured after the 2003 U.S. invasion has found no evidence that Saddam Hussein's regime had any operational links with Osama bin Laden's al Qaida terrorist network. The Pentagon-sponsored study, scheduled for release later this week, did confirm that Saddam's regime provided some support to other terrorist groups, particularly in the Middle East, U.S. officials told McClatchy. However, his security services were directed primarily against Iraqi exiles, Shiite Muslims, Kurds and others he considered enemies of his regime. The new study of the Iraqi regime's archives found no documents indicating a "direct operational link" between Hussein's Iraq and al Qaida before the invasion, according to a U.S. official familiar with the report.[252]

Nicholas Kristof, writing for the *New York Times*, wrote there were "indications that the US government souped up intelligence, leaned on spooks to change their conclusions and concluded contrary information to deceive people at home and around the world. . . . [This] does matter enormously for American credibility. After all, as [Bush White House spokesman] Ari Fleischer said on April 10 about W.M.D.s 'That is what this war was about.' "[253] Charles Hanley wrote a piece for the Associated Press in 2005 titled "Piecing Together the Story of the Weapons That Weren't," which captured the growing awareness among the public that they had been deceived by their leaders:

> The story of the weapons that weren't there, the prelude to war, was over, but a long post-mortem is still unfolding—of lingering questions in Washington, of revelations from investigations, leaks, and first-person accounts. Some 52% of Americans believe the Bush administration deliberately misled them about the presence of

banned arms in Iraq, according to a *Washington Post*–ABC News poll taken in June. Hans Blix, U.N. inspector, says Washington's "virtual reality" about Iraq eventually collided with "our old-fashioned ordinary reality."[254]

Even Fox News joined in the barrage of attacks on the Bush administration when prime-time anchor Megyn Kelly hammered Cheney, who, unlike President Bush, Rice, and Powell, remained stubbornly unrepentant about the Iraqi WMD fiasco. In a June 2014 interview, Kelly boldly held Cheney accountable, stating to the clearly shocked former vice president, who did not expect to be attacked on the Fox network:

> Time and time again, history has proven that you got it wrong as well in Iraq, sir. You said there were no doubts Saddam Hussein had weapons of mass destruction. You said we would greeted as liberators. You said the Iraq insurgency was in the last throes back in 2005. And you said that after our intervention, extremists would have to, quote, "rethink their strategy of Jihad." Now with almost a trillion dollars spent there, with 4,500 American lives lost there, what do you say to those who say, you were so wrong about so much at the expense of so many?[255]

Further rejection for the premise of the war, however, came from George Bush's own brother, Jeb Bush, a presidential candidate in 2016 and the former governor of Florida, who stated of the missing WMDs, "Knowing what we know now I would not have engaged. I would not have gone into Iraq."[256] But the ultimate rejection of the war came from Republican presidential candidate Donald Trump, who said, "I think it was a mistake. But it was a horrible mistake. Number one, there were no weapons of mass destruction. So did they know there weren't or not? But there were no weapons of mass destruction. Chuck, the war in Iraq was a disaster. We end up with absolutely nothing. Iran is taking over Iraq as we sit here right now."[257]

As news of the truth that there were no WMDs in Iraq or Iraqi links to bin Laden gradually began to trickle down to the masses, opinions in America began to change dramatically. By 2008 the *Washington Post* reported that 57 percent of Americans had come to believe that Bush had "deliberately misled people to make the case for war with Iraq."[258] When asked in a Quinnipiac poll in November 2008, "Do you think going to war with Iraq was the right thing to do?" 58 percent of those polled answered that it was "wrong." A *Time* magazine survey carried out by an Angus Reid poll in 2007 similarly found that 55 percent of Americans felt it was "wrong to go to war in Iraq."[259] By the following year *Time* found that number had risen to 58 percent.[260] A 2008 Gallup poll found that 63 percent of those who were polled said that sending troops to Iraq to be a mistake.[261] By 2014 a CBS poll found that 75 percent of Americans did not feel the war in Iraq was worth the cost.[262] In that poll only 18 percent of Americans felt the war had been worth the cost, making it one of the most unpopular wars in U.S. history.

By 2008 the majority of Americans thus seemed to have turned on the bogus rationales for the war and to have to come to distrust those in the Bush administration that they held responsible for deceiving them. By this time it became widely accepted that the Bush administration had not simply been given bad information by the intelligence community; its members had actually lied, repeatedly, to produce unambiguous, bold statements declaring the existence of Iraqi WMD programs and links between Iraq and Al Qaeda. In 2008, for example, the Associated Press published the findings of a study carried out by the Center for Public Integrity and the Fund for Independence in Journalism on the Bush administration's war statements, which stated:

> A study by two nonprofit journalism organizations found that President Bush and top administration officials issued hundreds of false statements about the national security threat from Iraq in the two years following the 2001 terrorist attacks. The study concluded that the statements "were part of an orchestrated campaign that effectively galvanized public opinion and, in the process, led the nation to war under decidedly false pretenses."
>
> The study counted 935 false statements in the two-year period. It found that in speeches, briefings, interviews and other venues, Bush and administration officials stated unequivocally on at least 532 occasions that Iraq had weapons of mass destruction or was trying to produce or obtain them or had links to al-Qaida or both.[263]

The *Washington Post* similarly reported on a damning 2008 Senate Intelligence Committee report on the issue: "Yesterday's long-awaited Senate Intelligence Committee report further solidifies the argument that the Bush administration's most blatant appeals to fear in its campaign to sell the Iraq war were flatly unsupported. Some of what President Bush and others said about Iraq was corroborated by what later turned out to be inaccurate intelligence. But their most compelling and gut-wrenching allegations—for instance, that Saddam Hussein was ready to supply his friends in al-Qaeda with nuclear weapons—were simply made up."[264]

Bush's chief counterterrorism advisor, Richard Clarke, would reply, when asked whether the Senate Intelligence Committee outlined lies that were made by the Bush administration: "There certainly are and this is a big report. What it says is statements by the president were not substantiated by intelligence. And then it says statements by the president were contradicted by available intelligence. In other words, they made things up. And they made them up and gave them to Colin Powell and others who believed them."[265] Members of the House and Senate similarly came to believe they had been lied to by the Bush administration. Senator Jay Rockefeller, chairman of the Senate Intelligence Committee, for example, stated:

> Before taking the country to war, this Administration owed it to the American people to give them a 100 percent accurate picture of the threat we faced. Unfortunately, our Committee has concluded that the Administration made significant claims that were not supported by the intelligence. In making the case for war, the Administration repeatedly presented intelligence as fact when in reality it was unsubstantiated, contradicted, or even non-existent. As a result, the American people were led to believe that the threat from Iraq was much greater than actually existed.
>
> It is my belief that the Bush Administration was fixated on Iraq, and used the 9/11 attacks by al Qaeda as justification for overthrowing Saddam Hussein. To accomplish this, top Administration officials made repeated statements that falsely linked Iraq and al Qaeda as a single threat and insinuated that Iraq played a role in 9/11. Sadly, the Bush Administration led the nation into war under false pretenses.
>
> There is no question we all relied on flawed intelligence. But, there is a fundamental difference between relying on incorrect intelligence and deliberately painting a picture to the American people that you know is not fully accurate.[266]

Senator Rockefeller was to also state, "In short, we invaded a country, thousands of people have died, and Iraq never posed a grave or growing danger."[267] The 2005 Commission on the Intelligence Capabilities of the United States Regarding Weapons of Mass Destruction agreed with Rockefeller and stated, "It was the United States that put its credibility on the line, making this one of the most public and most damaging intelligence failures in recent American history."[268] Joseph Cirincione, director of the Nonproliferation Project at the Carnegie Endowment for International Peace, similarly concluded that "none of his [Powell's] core assertions about Saddam's growing arsenal of weapons of mass destruction turned out to be true."[269]

But the ultimate refutation of the war, and those who created it, came from George Bush Sr. who, in his 2015 memoir *Destiny and Power*, attacked his son's advisors, secretary of defense Donald Rumsfeld and vice president Dick Cheney. Bush Sr. was to write of Cheney's succumbing to Neo-Con influence: "He just became very hardline . . . just iron-ass. His seeming knuckling under to the real hard-charging guys who want to fight about everything, use force to get our way in the Middle East." As for Rumsfeld, Bush Sr. wrote: "I think he served the president badly. There's a lack of humility, a lack of seeing what the other guy thinks. He's more kick ass and take numbers. I think he paid the price for that."[270]

As the Iraqis watched their country descend into a bloody chaos that would cost the lives of over two hundred thousand people following the U.S. invasion, Baghdad University's president, Nihad Mohammed al-Rawi, despaired to an Associated Press reporter, "A country was destroyed because of weapons that don't exist!"[271] Many of those Iraqis who similarly felt that their country had been unjustly invaded under the White House's false pretenses would of course join the insurgents to fight and kill the American invaders.

But it was not just the Bush White House that was blamed for the WMD or bin-Laden-equals-Saddam-Hussein "misstatements." Several commissions were organized to analyze the failure of the country's intelligence community, which had failed to stand up to the pressure from the Bush administration on producing evidence to legitimize an invasion. The Commission on the Intelligence Capabilities of the United States Regarding Weapons of Mass Destruction, created by President Bush, chaired by Senator Charles Robb and Judge Laurence Silberman, and consisting of several other prominent leaders (including Arizona Republican senator John McCain; Admiral Bill Studeman, the head of the Defense Intelligence Agency; and Charles Vest, the president of MIT; among others), for example, wrote up a damning assessment of the U.S. intelligence community's role in the

intelligence debacle. In light of the importance of this 2005 report's key findings for history, I have reproduced some of them here:

> On the brink of war, and in front of the whole world, the United
> States government asserted that Saddam Hussein had reconstituted
> his nuclear weapons program, had biological weapons and mobile
> biological weapon production facilities, and had stockpiled and was
> producing chemical weapons. All of this was based on the assess-
> ments of the U.S. Intelligence Community. And not one bit of it
> could be confirmed when the war was over.[272] . . .
>
> *These assessments were all wrong.* This became clear as U.S. forces
> searched without success for the WMD that the Intelligence Com-
> munity had predicted. Extensive post-war investigations were
> carried out by the Iraq Survey Group (ISG). The ISG found no
> evidence that Iraq had tried to reconstitute its capability to produce
> nuclear weapons after 1991; no evidence of BW agent stockpiles or of
> mobile biological weapons production facilities; and no substantial
> chemical warfare (CW) stockpiles or credible indications that
> Baghdad had resumed production of CW after 1991.[273]

The commission also listed seventy-four recommendations for reorganizing
the intelligence community in light of its 2002 failures on Iraqi WMDs. But
not before continuing its scathing critique of the intelligence community's
lapses as follows:

> The NIE [i.e., the notorious October 2002 flawed National Intelli-
> gence Estimate] said that Iraq's biological weapons capability was
> larger and more advanced than before the Gulf War and that Iraq
> possessed mobile biological weapons production facilities. This was
> wrong. The NIE further stated that Iraq had renewed production of
> chemical weapons, including mustard, sarin, GF, and VX, and that it
> had accumulated chemical stockpiles of between 100 and 500 metric
> tons. *All of this was also wrong. . . . The Intelligence Community's Iraq
> assessments were, in short, riddled with errors* [emphasis mine].[274]
>
> [Intelligence] collectors and analysts too readily accepted any
> evidence that supported their theory that Iraq had stockpiles and
> was developing weapons programs, and they explained away or
> simply disregarded evidence that pointed in the other direction.[275]

The critique also included:

> We conclude that the Intelligence Community was dead wrong in
> almost all of its pre-war judgments about Iraq's weapons of mass
> destruction. This was a major intelligence failure. Its principal causes
> were the Intelligence Community's inability to collect good informa-
> tion about Iraq's WMD programs, serious errors in analyzing what
> information it could gather, and a failure to make clear just how
> much of its analysis was based on assumptions, rather than good
> evidence. On a matter of this importance, we simply cannot afford
> failures of this magnitude.[276]

More broadly, the Senate Intelligence Committee also found that the "CIA
mischaracterized Iraq WMD and abused its intelligence position." This committee also found that "most of the major key judgments in the Oct. 2002
National Intelligence Estimate [NIE], *Iraq's Continuing Programs for WMD*,
either overstated, or were not supported by, the underlying intelligence reporting. A series of failures led to the mischaracterization of the intelligence."[277] This failure was subsequently described as "groupthink" and the
result of analysts who disagreed with the momentum for war who failed to
stand up to the so-called evidence of WMDs.

By the time the various government committees helped establish the fact
that the "Bush administration knowingly twisted and hyped intelligence to
justify that invasion," it was, however, too late.[278] The "preemptive" war to
"disarm" Hussein and prevent him from collaborating with bin Laden's atomized network hiding out in the remote tribal regions of Pakistan had already
been launched. The United States had invaded Iraq and quickly found itself
caught up in a bloody insurgency that would drag on for many years and cost
the lives of thousands of American who believed their leaders, as well as the
lives of tens of thousands of Iraqis who had nothing to do with 9/11.

As the number of U.S. dead in Iraq eventually surpassed the number of
Americans who died on 9/11 by approximately 50 percent, the war gradually
became a vaguely understood, disquieting backdrop for most Americans'
lives. The only reminder that the war still going on for most Americans was
the section in their daily newspapers that listed the names of the dead. Even
while the war in Iraq gave the American lexicon such acronyms as WMD,
IED (improvised explosive device), UAV (unmanned aerial vehicle, or
drone), EFP (explosively formed projectile), AQI (Al Qaeda in Iraq), and

MRAP (mine-resistant ambush-protected vehicles), it was relegated to the background by most. After years of being on a constant war footing, many Americans became fatigued by the war reporting coming out of the deserts of Iraq.

Those few Americans who did closely follow the Iraq war and counted the dead, coming home in the thousands, were distanced from the events in ways they had not been during the Vietnam era. Many Americans simply tuned the war out and focused on things closer to home. This stemmed largely from the fact that the thousands of Americans who were dying and being maimed in Iraq were professional soldiers, not conscripts drafted from average American households as had been the case in Vietnam. The rare images of American flag–draped coffins being flown home, of funerals in communities across the country, and of thousands of horribly wounded veterans that were broadcast by the media did not make into most Americans' living rooms.

For many Americans the war might not have been happening at all, so disconnected were they from the events in distant Iraq. Few Americans had an overview or macro understanding of the war of the sort that many had developed during World War II. This was in part because there were few major military events, like the D-Day–style invasions or the Battle of Midway, to rally the country around. There were just countless ambushes in backstreets, small skirmishes in out-of-the-way outposts, daily IED mine attacks, and the occasional medium-scale operation in towns with exotic names like Basra, Ramadi, Baquba, Mosul, Tal Afar, and Fallujah, which were hazily understood at best. The contours and course of the Iraq war remained murky to the vast majority of Americans, who simply had a vague understanding that things were not going well in that distant conflict, but not much more.

The following chapter aims to overcome this deficit and bring the course and chronology of the 2003 to 2011 Iraq War to life for those who may have lived through the invasion and resulting insurgency, but did not properly understand its contours at the time. For those who did not experience the conflict, it will provide a history of a war that, for all its false premises, began successfully enough before quickly devolving into a classic guerilla insurgency that was to come perilously close to ending in the first major defeat for the American military since Vietnam.

FIGURE 1. U.S. troops boarding a Chinook helicopter in Afghanistan.

U.S. Army photo by Staff Sergeant Kyle Davis.

FIGURE 2. One of the primary architects of the U.S. invasion of Iraq, Neo-Con deputy secretary of defense Paul Wolfowitz.

Department of Defense photo by Helene C. Stikkel.

FIGURE 3. Donald Rumsfeld, the outspoken secretary of defense who directed the successful U.S. invasion of Afghanistan but deployed too small a force to occupy post-U.S.-invasion Iraq.

Department of Defense photo by Scott Davis, U.S. Army.

FIGURE 4. M1 Abrams U.S. tanks at ceremonial arch built by Hussein in Baghdad.

Photo by Technical Sergeant John L. Houghton Jr., U.S. Air Force.

FIGURE 5. U.S. Marines firing on Iraqi insurgents during the First Battle of Fallujah.

Photo by Corporal Matthew J. Apprendi, U.S. Marine Corps.

FIGURE 6. A car bombing in Iraq, 2005.

Photo by Specialist Ronald Shaw Jr., U.S. Army, DOD Defense Visual Information Center.

FIGURE 7. President George W. Bush speaking to crowds at Ground Zero, the site of the former World Trade Center in the aftermath of the 9/11 attack.

Photo by Sergeant First Class Thomas R. Roberts—FEMA Photo Library.

FIGURE 8. President Hamid Karzai speaks to journalists in Kabul after casting his vote. He said Afghans should vote for the candidate of their choice and called the vote "a step towards progress and democracy."

Photo by USAID Afghanistan.

FIGURE 9. Secretary of State Colin Powell holding a mock vial of anthrax in his famous speech to the UN in February of 2003, where he outlined the threat of Iraqi WMDs to the world.

FIGURE 10. British and American troops in the southern, Taliban-infested province of Helmand, Afghanistan.

Photo released by the U.S. Army, ID 070410-A-9834L-006.

FIGURE 11. An Apache attack helicopter provides air support for U.S. troops in Afghanistan.

Photo by Specialist Mike Pryor, U.S. Army.

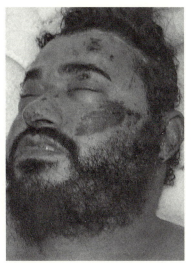

FIGURE 12. Ambassador Paul Bremer, the governor of post-U.S.-invasion Iraq, who disbanded the Sunni-dominated Iraqi army and Baathist Party, thus disenfranchising hundreds of thousands of Sunnis.

Department of Defense photo by Helene C. Stikkel.

FIGURE 13. Jordanian terrorist and creator of AQI (Al Qaeda in Iraq) Abu Musab al Zarqawi after being killed in a U.S. bomb strike.

From "Multi-National Force—Iraq, Situational Update, Maj. Gen. William B. Caldwell, IV," dated June 8, 2006, released by U.S. government.

FIGURE 14. U.S. troops on patrol in Dangam in the hills of eastern Afghanistan.

Photo by Sergeant Brandon Aird, released by the U.S. Army, ID 070725-A-6849A-473.

FIGURE 15. The capture of Saddam Hussein in a "spider hole" near his hometown of Tikrit.

U.S. Army photo.

FIGURE 16. Australian NATO patrol in Tangi, Afghanistan.

Courtesy of ISAF Headquarters Public Affairs Office from Kabul, Afghanistan (flickr// ResoluteSupportMedia).

FIGURE 17. Nouri al Maliki, the controversial Shiite prime minister of Iraq, who antagonized Sunnis after the 2011 U.S. withdrawal of troops and (with President George W. Bush) drove them into the hands of ISIS.

White House photo by Eric Draper.

FIGURE 18. A Syrian rebel fighter from the U.S.-backed moderate Free Syrian Army. Screenshot from "International Military Intervention in Syria Remains Unlikely," video by Voice of America News.

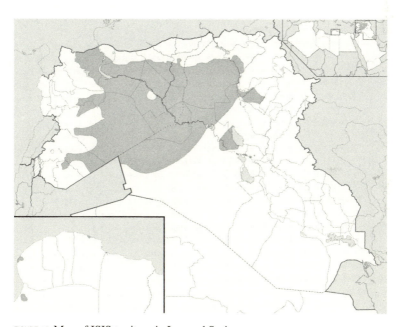

FIGURE 19. Map of ISIS territory in Iraq and Syria.

Created by NordNordWest, Spesh531 [CC BY-SA 3.0 (http://creativecommons.org/licenses/by-sa/3.0)], via Wikimedia Commons. Photo by Sergeant Brandon Aird, released by the U.S. Army, ID 070725-A-6849A-473.

FIGURE 20. Pro-American Uzbek horsemen led by General Dostum gathering to wage war on the Taliban in the Hindu Kush Mountains.

Photo by the author.

FIGURE 21. Northern Alliance general Dostum leading his Uzbek fighters to attack Taliban positions.

Photo by the author.

FIGURE 22. The elite Green Beret Special Forces A-Team code named Tiger 02, which was inserted into the Hindu Kush Mountains of Afghanistan to fight alongside anti-Taliban Uzbek fighters in 2001.

FIGURE 23. U.S. Air Force combat controller Bart Decker riding with Uzbek horsemen in the Hindu Kush after calling in airstrikes on the Taliban.

FIGURE 24. U.S. Special Forces riding on horseback with General Dostum to the front to fight with the Taliban in 2001.

CHAPTER 4

The Invasion and Occupation of Iraq

We will in fact be greeted as liberators.

—Vice President Dick Cheney predicting how U.S. troops
would be welcomed when they invaded Iraq

The Americans have occupied our land under a false pretext, and without
any international authorization. They kill our women and children and old
men.

—Iraqi Sunni insurgent from the Army of Muhammad

Pre-invasion Controversies

In the winter of 2002–3, Saddam Hussein, increasingly fearful of a looming U.S. invasion, allowed the UN to resume the WMD inspections that had
been halted back in 1998 on the eve of Clinton's Operation Desert Fox. As a
potential U.S. invasion seemed a distinct likelihood, a worried Hussein ordered his military leaders to "cooperate completely" with the UN inspectors.[1]
Hussein also told his leaders, "What can they discover, when we have nothing?"[2] His announcement to his generals that Iraq no longer possessed
WMDs was said to have sent their "morale plummeting."[3] Michael Gordon
and General Bernard Trainor have written of Hussein in their history of the
Iraq invasion and have stated that "Saddam was not looking for a war with
the United States and he was not expecting one either. . . . While Saddam believed that revealing the absence of WMD was risky, he discounted the

danger of alarming the United States. According to his associates, he did not consider the United States a natural adversary. He saw no reason why the Americans would want to invade Iraq."[4]

But as the UN inspectors came up empty handed in their search for Iraqi WMDs, the White House grew increasingly frustrated with the UN. Anti-UN sentiment was rife among the Neo-Cons at this time as the UN inspectors seemed to be dismantling the Bush administration's main rationale for launching a preemptive invasion. The IAEA nuclear weapons inspectors who had also been allowed in to resume inspections further infuriated the Bush White House when they stated in February 2003, "After three months of intrusive inspections, we have to date found no evidence or plausible indication of the revival of a nuclear weapons program in Iraq."[5]

There were many Democrats who heeded such news and rejected the Bush White House's case for invading Iraq. Among them was the junior senator from Illinois, Barack Obama. Obama would presciently state, "I suffer no illusions about Saddam Hussein. He is a brutal man. A ruthless man. But I also know that Saddam poses no imminent and direct threat to the United States or to his neighbors. I know that an invasion of Iraq without a clear rationale and without strong international support will only fan the flames of the Middle East, and encourage the worst, rather than best, impulses of the Arab world, and strengthen the recruitment arm of al-Qaeda."[6]

After stating "There is no credible information to connect Saddam Hussein to 9/11," Democrat Senator Robert Byrd of Virginia told Congress, "Today I weep for my country. I have watched the events of recent months with a heavy, heavy heart. No more is the image of America one of strong, yet benevolent peacekeeper. The image of America has changed. Around the globe, our friends mistrust us, our word is disputed, our intentions are questioned."[7]

The Republicans, however, rallied to the Bush White House and lashed out anyone who opposed the march to war, from the U.N. to staunch NATO allies who did not believe the WMD evidence. Neo-Cons and many Republicans grew particularly frustrated with NATO member France, which had supported U.S. operations in Afghanistan after 9/11 and in the First Gulf War, but now came out against Bush's calls for a second invasion to disarm Hussein. The French foreign minister, Dominique de Villepin, summed up the French position stating, "Since we can disarm Iraq through peaceful means, we should not take the risk to endanger the lives of innocent civilians or soldiers, to jeopardize the stability of the region and further widen the gap between our people and our cultures."[8]

Overlooking the fact that United States achieved independence from Great Britain in the Revolutionary War only with crucial French support and fought in both World Wars alongside the French, one Republican representative, Bob Ney, reacted to the French position by having the U.S. House adopt a resolution renaming French fries "Freedom Fries" to punish America's "so-called ally." Across America, fury with the French "betrayal" was manifested in public calls for "dumping in the gutter" of French wine or champagne and televised destruction of French cars such as the Peugeot.

But it was not only France that disbelieved the Bush administration's hype about WMDs in the fateful months leading up to Operation Iraqi Freedom. Other NATO members, including such pro-U.S. stalwarts as Germany and Turkey, both of whom also sent troops to fight alongside the Americans in Afghanistan, came out vehemently against the impending invasion of Iraq. Skeptical parliaments in these countries simply did not subscribe to the case for war that the Bush administration was making. The most crucial NATO member to reject the premise for invading Iraq was actually Turkey, which, after being promised $6 billion in order to let the United States invade Iraq's northern border from neighboring Turkish provinces, voted in parliament to reject the American offer and sit out the war. This meant the entire invasion would have to come from one direction, the south (i.e., the U.S. would be invading Iraq from Kuwait and could not send the Fourth Infantry Division in from the north via Turkey to open a second front). This feud between the U.S. on one hand, and France, Germany, and Turkey on the other, created one of the greatest rifts in NATO's history.

Condemnation also came from Pope John Paul II, who sent a cardinal to meet with President Bush to talk him out of the invasion. The Vatican said that war in Iraq would be a "disaster" and "a crime against peace and a crime against international law." The pope was particularly worried about the fate of the ancient Assyrian Christian community of Iraq should the United States invade (the pope's fears were not exaggerated; this community, one of the oldest in the world, was subsequently destroyed for the most part following the invasion after it was attacked by ISIS militants).

Warnings against the invasion of Iraq also came from America's Arab allies in the Middle East. Egyptian leader Hosni Mubarek, who had assisted Bush Sr. in the First Gulf War of 1991 with troops, warned Bush Jr. against invading Iraq and presciently stated, "We fear a state of disorder and chaos may prevail in the region."[9] Saudi leader Crown Prince Abdullah warned of the unintended consequences of an invasion, "I do not believe it is in the

United States' interests, or the interest of the region, or the world's interest, to do so. And I don't believe it will achieve the desired result."[10] The Saudis refused to let the U.S. invade from their country as they had in the First Gulf War. Even the Israelis warned that destroying Hussein's regime would destabilize Iraq and the surrounding regions.

There were also mass protests across the globe against the war that drew tens of millions of people. One anti–Iraq invasion rally in Rome drew approximately three million people, making it the largest single antiwar protest in history (there were smaller antiwar rallies in Barcelona, Spain, which drew 1.3 million; London, which drew one million; and Melbourne, Australia, which drew half a million). On February 15, 2003, millions of protestors across the globe in over eight hundred cities took part in what the *Guinness Book of World Records* labeled the largest protest in history. Polls across the planet conducted prior to the invasion showed that less than 10 percent of those who were polled in most countries supported the impending war against Iraq.

Such widespread discontent with America's impending invasion of Iraq in 2003 compared drastically with the outpouring of support from NATO and across the globe when it came to launching the 2001 invasion of Taliban-controlled Afghanistan in response to the 9/11 attacks. On that occasion there was even a spontaneous candlelight vigil in Tehran, Iran, to commemorate those who had died in the World Trade Centers, and in France thousands came to place flowers at the gates of the U.S. embassy.[11]

There were also voices being raised against the impending invasion of Iraq in 2003 on the home front as well. Brent Scowcroft, the widely respected Republican elder statesman who had been national security advisor under Presidents Gerald Ford and George Bush Sr. wrote an opinion piece in the *Washington Post* before the invasion titled "Don't Attack Saddam." In it, Scowcroft was to write:

> We need to think through this issue very carefully. We need to analyze the relationship between Iraq and our other pressing priorities—notably the war on terrorism [i.e., against Al Qaeda]—as well as the best strategy and tactics available were we to move to change the regime in Baghdad.
>
> Saddam's strategic objective appears to be to dominate the Persian Gulf, to control oil from the region, or both. That clearly poses a real threat to key U.S. interests. But there is scant evidence to

tie Saddam to terrorist organizations, and even less to the Sept. 11 attacks. Indeed Saddam's goals have little in common with the terrorists who threaten us, and there is little incentive for him to make common cause with them.

He is unlikely to risk his investment in weapons of mass destruction, much less his country, by handing such weapons to terrorists who would use them for their own purposes and leave Baghdad as the return address. Threatening to use these weapons for blackmail—much less their actual use—would open him and his entire regime to a devastating response by the U.S. While Saddam is thoroughly evil, he is above all a power-hungry survivor.

But the central point is that any campaign against Iraq, whatever the strategy, cost and risks, is certain to divert us for some indefinite period from our war on terrorism. Worse, there is a virtual consensus in the world against an attack on Iraq at this time.[12]

But the Bush White House was impervious to such calls for caution from a fellow Republican and the chorus of condemnation from across the globe. In the winter of 2002–3 the White House prepared to launch the war in furtherance of what became known as the "Bush Doctrine" (i.e., the right for America to unilaterally use force against any and all perceived threats before they actually emerged), regardless of the divisions it was causing in NATO. The Bush White House took heart in the fact that at least British prime minister Tony Blair, a staunch U.S. ally, backed the war (although this made him extremely unpopular in Britain, where the media labeled him "Bush's poodle").

As the U.S. military prepared for a full-scale invasion of Iraq designed to prevent WMDs from possibly being transferred in the future from Baathist Iraq to Pakistan-based bin Laden, the man in charge of operations was Secretary of Defense Donald Rumsfeld. At this stage Rumsfeld and his deputy, Paul Wolfowitz, were to make several strategic decisions that were to come to haunt the American effort in the subsequent war and to lead America perilously close to defeat. The primary mistake Rumsfeld made was to send in an invasion force that was far smaller than the one the generals were requesting at the time.

General Tommy Franks, the head of Central Command, had previously come up with a draft plan that called for an invasion army of four hundred thousand troops, while Marine general Anthony Zinni had created a plan for

380,000 troops.[13] Other generals, such as army chief of staff, Eric Shinseki, a decorated war veteran from the Vietnam conflict who took lessons from his postwar military experience in Bosnia, agreed. Based on the Bosnian ratio of number of U.S. troops to population in NATO-occupied Bosnia, General Shinseki felt America needed a large army to occupy Iraq once it had been conquered. Shinseki felt that the so-called Phase IV of the war (occupation) required more troops than the actual combat phase in order to create security and stability and prevent the rise of an insurgency. He feared that America might win the initial invasion but then lose the conflict during the postwar phase if it did not deploy a large army. Shinseki's view has been described as follows:

> Shinseki of the Army drew not only on his experience in the Balkans, trying to administer a fractious region postwar. [He also drew from] all the corpus of evidence that had been produced by the Army War College, by every other group that looked into this, to say that there was a crucial moment just after the fall of a regime when the potential for disorder was enormous. So there would be ripple effects for years to come, depending on what happened in those first days or weeks when the regime went [down]. . . .
>
> The Army War College study had worked out a very detailed checklist for how the military, and the Army in particular, should start thinking about the postwar, well before it actually went to war. One of their conclusions was that it was best to go in heavier than you actually needed to be, so that at the beginning of the postwar period your presence would be so intimidating that nobody would dare challenge you.[14]

Rumsfeld and Deputy Secretary of Defense Wolfowitz, however, publicly scorned Shinseki, in what has been described as "the most direct public dressing-down of a military officer, a four-star general, by a civilian superior since Harry Truman and Douglas MacArthur, 50 years ago."[15] Wolfowitz would rebut Shinseki, stating, "I don't see why it would take more troops to occupy the country than to take down the regime."[16] Vice President Dick Cheney agreed and stated that "to suggest that we need several hundred thousand troops there after military operations cease, after the conflict ends, I don't think is accurate. I think that's an overstatement."[17]

General Shinseki ultimately left the military under a dark cloud.[18] Many in the military came to resent Rumsfeld for this and other acts that they deemed to be arrogant. Military historian Thomas Ricks has written, "Of all the services, it [the army] was the one most at odds with Rumsfeld and other senior Pentagon civilians, distrusting their views, and believing they were interfering on matters in which they were professionally uninformed."[19] In his book on the war, Todd Purdum has written that the generals had "deep misgivings" about Rumsfeld's plans to cut down the size of their invading force to create a lighter, more nimble expeditionary force.[20]

The reasons for the clash between the civilian leadership of the military on the one hand and the generals on the other had everything to do with Rumsfeld's "transformational" visions for a new, lithe, agile military. Rumsfeld had been inspired by the fast, light invasion of Afghanistan in 2001, which had been carried out by small groups of U.S. Special Forces. It had not needed a full-scale invasion to conquer Texas-sized Afghanistan. Since that success, Rumsfeld had been clashing with the military as he tried to cut back on the size of the army and create a battle plan for a more agile invasion force that would be able to defeat the Iraqis with speed and advanced technology, not overwhelming numbers.

Rumsfeld criticized the Powell Doctrine as "old thinking" and stressed that the twenty-first century American military would travel light and fast. The smaller "army of transformation" would not be slowed down by cumbersome logistics units; instead it would engage in a blitzkrieg style of warfare that Rumsfeld labeled "shock and awe." In this sense, Rumsfeld, who had no military experience, saw Iraq as a "great big laboratory."[21]

When it came to the actual invasion of Iraq in March and April of 2003, Rumsfeld's vision of a fast-moving blitz by a small army would be vindicated. Instead of sending in the four hundred thousand troops initially requested by the generals, the invasion force consisted of just 145,000 soldiers (twenty thousand of which came from the UK). This small, fast-moving force would shatter the Iraqis' obsolete army in less than three weeks and conquer Baghdad.

But history would demonstrate that Rumsfeld's transformational army was too small to effectively occupy Iraq during the Phase IV postcombat period. This helped lead to the collapse of Iraqi civil society and rise of a bloody insurgency that almost defeated the small U.S. force occupying this California-sized country. Far from withdrawing troops immediately after the invasion as Rumsfeld had initially called for, the military was forced to send in a later "surge" of twenty-eight thousand additional troops to save the army from defeat at the hands of a deadly insurgency that Rumsfeld had not foreseen.

Military historian Fred Kaplan has written of Rumsfeld's mistake in failing to prepare for the postinvasion occupation of Iraq by sending in enough troops to occupy this large country:"Rumsfeld wasn't interested in postwar Iraq because it couldn't be shaped by transformation and had nothing to do with his broader vision of American power. . . . He didn't plan for a postwar because he didn't want a postwar. It wasn't oversight; it was deliberate."[22]

A major reason for Rumsfeld's failure to prepare for the postwar occupation was that he had subscribed to the Neo-Cons' and Cheney's unrealistically rosy vision of a post-invasion Iraq. After the invasion, Rumsfeld felt the Americans would be greeted as liberators, and a friendly Iraqi government could be quickly put in place to keep the peace. This would then allow the U.S. troops to withdraw in a relatively short period of time

An underlying premise for this vision came from President George Bush and the Neo-Cons' contempt for the concept of "nation building." The Neo-Cons and Bush derided this sort of nation building as "armed humanitarianism," "mutwah" (military missions other than warfare) or "militarized socialism." Prior to the invasion of Iraq, Bush had ridiculed the Clinton administration for previously using U.S. troops to rebuild war-torn societies in the Balkans and Haiti. Bush made it clear that when he became president, U.S. troops would be used only to fight wars, not rebuild shattered societies. In October 2000, presidential candidate George Bush mocked the Clinton-era concept of nation building and the idea that the U.S. military should be involved in reconstructing war-torn nations stating, "Maybe I'm missing something here. I mean, are we going to have some kind of nation-building corps from America? Absolutely not."[23] Bush also said in a debate, "I don't think our troops should be used for what's called nation building."[24]

Fully subscribing to this worldview, Rumsfeld and Wolfowitz planned on quickly beginning the withdrawal of U.S. troops soon after the Iraq invasion, rather than getting bogged down in the distasteful process of Clinton-era-style nation building. Because America would not be occupying and rebuilding postwar Iraq (which they assumed would be peaceful and would use its own oil resources to rebuild itself), Rumsfeld and the White House made no contingency plans for the rise of a deadly postinvasion insurgency like the one that ultimately emerged during Phase IV.

In a breath-taking statement that captured Wolfowitz's complete disconnect from the chaotic reality on the ground that would subsequently emerge after the invasion, he summed up the reasons why a much smaller peace-keeping/occupation force than the one envisioned by General Shinseki would be sufficient. According to Wolfowitz, "there was no history of ethnic strife in Iraq, as there was in Bosnia or Kosovo," and he also stated that "Iraqi civilians would welcome an American-led liberation force that stayed as long as nec-essary but left as soon as possible."[25]

Wolfowitz's remarkable statement overlooks the fact that Iraq's Sunni Arabs had killed thousands of Shiite Arabs and Kurds in the 1980s and again in 1991 after the First Gulf War (as many as 180,000 Iraqi Shiites were killed by Hussein's Sunni regime in 1991 and a similar amount of Kurds in the Anfal campaign).[26] There was a deep reservoir of bad blood in Iraq between Sunni Arabs and Kurds and Shiites that would almost certainly lead to con-flict if the Baathist regime were ever removed. Wolfowitz's statement also re-jected the reality of the situation where a U.S. force would have to stay on in Iraq long after the overthrow of the government to keep order, instead of leaving "as soon as possible."

As a full-blown insurgency and Bosnian-Kosovo-style ethnic strife later erupted from 2003 to 2007 and shattered Rumsfeld's and Wolfowitz's unreal-istic vision of a peaceful postinvasion Iraq, General Eric Shinseki would ulti-mately be vindicated. Rumsfeld would take the blame for the ensuing fiasco and would be fired by Bush when it turned out that the army he had deployed was too small to suppress an unexpected, full-scale insurgency and Bosnian-Kosovo-style civil war. Military historian Thomas Ricks has written, "General [Eric] Shinseki was right that a greater international force contribution, U.S. force contribution and Iraqi force contribution should have been available immediately after major combat operations."[27]

A larger occupying force of the sort originally called for by Shinseki would have helped stabilize postinvasion Iraq by carrying out such vital tasks as guarding borders to prevent foreign fighters from infiltrating the country to fight U.S. troops, protecting government infrastructure that was looted by mobs and oil facilities that were destroyed by insurgents, providing security for average Iraqi civilians who were still "on the fence" about the American occupation, and crushing local insurrections in towns like Fallujah before they metastasized.

It must, however, be said that not all those in the Bush White House were believers in the Neo-Cons' and Rumsfeld's transformational vision of a post-invasion Iraq, where the small American invasion force could quickly disen-gage itself from any occupation role and immediately come home. The one dissenting voice was Secretary of State Colin Powell, who had always been a supporter of using large military forces to minimize risks to troops (the so-called Powell Doctrine). Powell warned Bush, "Iraq is like a piece of crystal. You're going to shatter it. And it's going to be in pieces all over the place."[28] Powell also told the president that, after the invasion, "You are going to be the proud owner of 25 million [Iraqi] people. You will own all their hopes, aspirations, and problems. You'll own it all." He then famously used the Pottery Barn rule and said of Iraq, "You break it, you own it."[29]

Powell argued that if the Americans "broke" Hussein's Baathist government, then the U.S. military would, by necessity, become occupiers to rebuild central authority. The U.S. military would have to act as the de facto government for many years to come while the Iraqi government was rebuilt. In other words, the U.S. military would have to rebuild Iraq and engage in "nation building," something the Neo-Cons and Bush utterly despised. Powell also warned that Rumsfeld's "shock and awe" invasion plan did not have any plans for the aftermath of invasion and did not envision Iraqi resistance.

But Powell was not in charge of the military; that was Secretary of Defense Rumsfeld's job, and Powell's warnings went unheeded.

As all these events were taking place in the Pentagon, Saddam Hussein began to accept that his ultimate nightmare, a full U.S. invasion in search of WMDs he no longer possessed, was inevitable. Realizing that his army, which had deteriorated terribly since the First Gulf War of 1991 because of the arms embargo and sanctions, would probably be defeated in open combat, he made contingency plans. Should his army be vanquished in the field of frontal combat with the American invaders, his fighters would resort to irregular warfare and would fight the militarily superior Americans using asymmetric tactics. In other words, the Iraqi fighters would bog the American occupiers down in a Vietnam-style guerilla war during Phase IV and disrupt Rumsfeld's overly ambitious plans to set up a pro-American government and quickly withdraw. This was exactly the sort of scenario that General Shinseki and Powell had envisioned and that Rumsfeld had deliberately ignored when he called for a too-small invasion force. The Iraqi response to Rumsfeld's "Shock and Awe" might well have been labeled "Grind Down and Dismay."

To bleed the Americans and disrupt their overly optimistic postinvasion plans, Hussein dispatched as many as forty thousand Sunni irregular fighters known as Fedayeen Saddam (Saddam's Men of Sacrifice) to the south and center of the country with large amounts of weapons including landmines, mortars, sniper rifles, automatic weapons, and RPGs (rocket-propelled grenades). There they would blend in with the local civilian population and launch ambushes on invading U.S. troops. These Sunni paramilitary fighters and many others from the wider Sunni community would ultimately turn the deserts of Iraq into a killing zone for American troops, who had been told by Vice President Cheney that they would be "greeted as liberators." In so doing, they would vindicate General Shinseki and Powell, cost Rumsfeld his job, and cost almost forty-five hundred American troops their lives. Thus the seeds to a bloody insurgency, the very thing Rumsfeld had not planned on, were being planted even as the secretary of defense planned on sending in his small army to carry out a clean in-and-out blitz on the Iraqis.

Shock and Awe

On March 17, 2003, President Bush gave a televised speech wherein he demanded that Saddam Hussein and his notorious sons Uday and Qusay leave Iraq within forty-eight hours. The speech had many alarming allusions to Iraq's possession of deadly WMDs and operational links to Al Qaeda. It seemed to convince most Americans that Iraq needed to be invaded for their protection and, in spite of the fact that most of the world was against the invasion, Bush had the backing of Congress, which voted for the war in October of 2002 (including such senators as Hillary Clinton and John Kerry, who later came out against the war once it devolved into a bloody insurgency and no WMDs were found).

Some highlights from Bush's alarmist speech give insight into much of the hyped rhetoric that was emanating the Bush White House that frightened average Americans and convinced even reluctant Democrats to vote in favor of the war to disarm Iraq. Bush was to state in no uncertain terms:

> Intelligence gathered by this and other governments leaves no doubt that the Iraq regime continues to possess and conceal some of the most lethal weapons ever devised. . . . The regime has a history of reckless aggression in the Middle East. It has a deep hatred of America and our friends. And it has aided, trained and harbored terrorists, including operatives of al Qaeda. The danger is clear: using chemical, biological or, one day, nuclear weapons, obtained with the help of Iraq, the terrorists could fulfill their stated ambitions and kill thousands or hundreds of thousands of innocent people in our country, or any other. . . . The United States and other nations did

nothing to deserve or invite this threat. But we will do everything to defeat it. Instead of drifting along toward tragedy, we will set a course toward safety. Before the day of horror can come, before it is too late to act, this danger will be removed. . . . Today, no nation can possibly claim that Iraq has disarmed. And it will not disarm so long as Saddam Hussein holds power. . . . It is too late for Saddam Hussein to remain in power. It is not too late for the Iraqi military to act with honor and protect your country by permitting the peaceful entry of coalition forces to eliminate weapons of mass destruction. . . . Unlike Saddam Hussein, we believe the Iraqi people are deserving and capable of human liberty. And when the dictator has departed, they can set an example to all the Middle East of a vital and peaceful and self-governing nation.[30]

Then, linking Iraq's WMDs to a 9/11-style scenario in the U.S., Bush warned: "The people of the United States and our friends and allies will not live at the mercy of an outlaw regime that threatens the peace with weapons of mass murder. We will meet that threat now, with our Army, Air Force, Navy, Coast Guard and Marines, so that we do not have to meet it later with armies of fire fighters and police and doctors on the streets of our cities." But before the forty-eight-hour deadline was up, the invasion of Iraq, optimistically labeled "Operation Iraqi Freedom," commenced with a decapitation airstrike on a farm outside Baghdad that the CIA thought Saddam was hiding in on the night of March 19, 2003. In an ominous sign of things to come, however, the strike did not kill Hussein, who was not there at the time, and instead it killed or injured Iraqi civilians. They would be the first of tens of thousands of Iraqi civilians to die in Operation Iraqi Freedom.

The actual land invasion by the Marines and U.S. Army (accompanied by a British thrust on the Al Faw peninsula on the night of March 19–20), began on March 20, 2003. The U.S./UK invasion force of roughly 145,000 troops (60,000 Marines, 65,000 U.S. Army troops, and 20,000 British troops) crossed from Kuwait into Iraq in what has been called a "running start." The Marine First Expeditionary force moved northward to the east of the Army's Third Infantry Division along Highway 1, which essentially ran through the center of the Euphrates-Tigris basin.

The first real opposition the invading U.S. force encountered was in the southern Shiite city of Nasariyah, which had strategic importance for the bridges over the Euphrates found in it. The initial advantage went to the Iraqis, who on March 23 ambushed a lost U.S. Army logistics column, the 507th Maintenance Company, and killed eleven U.S. soldiers and captured several others (including a female U.S. soldier named Jessica Lynch, who was later rescued by U.S. troops and became a household name). But the Marines ultimately won the battle against Fedayeen guerilla fighters and took control of the strategic bridges spanning the Euphrates. Approximately four hundred Iraqis and thirty-two Americans died in the fighting, making it the most costly battle for the Americans in their race up the Euphrates-Tigris valley toward Baghdad.

The next major battle was further to the north in the Shiite town of Najaf, which was guarded by a unit of elite Republican Guards. General Tommy Franks, who was in charge of the invasion, decided to attack the Republican Guard with Apache Longbow attack helicopters at night on March 24. This operation, however, failed owing to a barrage of antiaircraft fire, which brought down one helicopter and damaged every single helicopter in the command, forcing the remaining helicopters to return to base. On April 1 the 101st Airborne attacked the center of Najaf in a reconnaissance-in-force probe that was nicknamed a "Thunder Run." The U.S. soldiers came under heavy small-arms fire from Fedayeen dressed in what were described as "black pajamas" but succeeded in capturing the enemy's headquarters.

In many ways the invasion of southern Iraq in 2003 was different from the First Gulf War of 1991. The main difference was that in the first war the fighting was primarily head on combat between tanks, but in the second war it was primarily U.S. troops fighting Fedayeen paramilitaries who engaged in ambushes. There were also no mass surrenders of Iraqi troops as had been the case in the first war, nor any mass Shiite uprising in support of the Americans.

Meanwhile, the British broke into the southern city of Basra after defeating the Iraqis in a major tank fight, the Brits' largest tank battle since World War II (one of the few major tank battles of the war). They then seized the Old Quarter in the heart of the city after battling Fedayeen. The British would try to control this restless Shiite city for most of the duration of the war. They would, however, be ineffective and would be confined to their base outside the city for much of their stay in the south.

The invading American force, meanwhile, broke through the so-called Karbala Gap south of Baghdad after wiping out a defensive Iraqi tank force belonging to the Nebuchadnezzar and Medina divisions using artillery rockets. As these events were occurring in the south, the U.S. Tenth Special Forces

Group (Army Green Berets) and CIA Special Activities Division operatives liaised with pro-American Kurdish rebels in the autonomous Kurdish areas to the north. There they assisted the pro-U.S. Kurds in fighting against a local jihadist group made up of Arabs and radical Kurds known as Ansar al Islam. In a reprisal of the Green Berets' joint campaign with General Dostum's Uzbek horsemen in the opening days of the 2001 Afghan war, the U.S. special operators called in precision bomb strikes on the Ansar al Islam militants in their bases in an enclave in the northeast of Kurdistan known as Halabja. These strikes destroyed the militants' bases and forced the Islamist extremists to flee either across the nearby border into Iran or down into the Sunni areas of Iraq.

Among those who fled at this time to the Sunni Arab lands in Iraq proper was Abu Musab Zarqawi, the Jordanian jihadist who had created his own jihadi group that Colin Powell had erroneously claimed in his speech to the UN was linked to both Al Qaeda and Hussein. This attack on Ansar al Islam's small enclave in the Kurdish north was as close as the United States came to actually confronting Al Qaeda–style jihadists during their invasion of Baathist Iraq (although it must be stressed that Ansar al Islam was *not* part of bin Laden's Al Qaeda, nor was it linked to Saddam Hussein).

The destruction of the Ansar al Islam in their northern enclave freed up the Kurdish Peshmerga fighters to move against Iraqi forces on the so-called Green Line, which separated their lands from Hussein's lands to the southwest. They broke out of their enclave and liberated the important city of Kirkuk, which had always been a prize for the Kurds, who called it their Jerusalem. This northern operation was known as Operation Viking Hammer and distracted tens of thousands of Iraqi troops from fighting the main invasion thrust in the south.

Meanwhile, the main invasion from the south was halted on March 24 owing to a three-day sandstorm known as a *shamal*. But once the storm passed, U.S. mechanized troops poured through the Karbala Gap and seized bridges over the Euphrates that led to Baghdad. The race north had been the fastest moving march by a U.S. military force in history and thrilled Rumsfeld, who called the initial stages of the invasion "Shock and Awe." On the last six days of their northern sprint U.S. troops covered 251 miles in just six days.

From Karbala, the fast-moving U.S. forces seized Baghdad's international airport to the southwest of the city and converted it into a logistic hub on April 4. Everyone realized that the real battle for Iraq would now be fought in the taking of Baghdad, a city of five million people. The great fear was that the Baathist regime would wage house-to-house combat in the streets of Baghdad in defense of their so-called Red Zone. Back in the United States, many Americans who had believed the Bush administration's hype on WMDs also feared that the cornered Hussein regime would use chemical, nuclear, and biological weapons to defend Baghdad.

To test the Iraqis' resolve, the U.S. Army decided to launch a "reconnaissance in force" armed probe into the heart of Baghdad once again known as "Thunder Run." On April 5 a force of twenty-nine tanks and fourteen Bradley fighting vehicles launched a bold attack into the heart of Baghdad and entered a hornet's nest. One eyewitness to the April 5 Thunder Run recorded, "It was an incredible sight! Drivers and tank commanders were firing as fast as they could, and they were flying! They must have been going 50 miles per hour."[31]

Almost every single vehicle in the probing column took a hit by an Iraqi RPG as the fast-moving invaders raced into the town from the south and faced a gauntlet of fire. Despite the odds against them, the raiders were, however, able to reemerge from the firefight having lost only one tank (it was later estimated that two thousand Iraqi fighters and 437 civilian bystanders were killed in the attack).[32] Many of the U.S. armored vehicles returned to the U.S. base at the airport on fire, leaking oil, and blackened from explosions. The Iraqis, who had been previously announcing that the American invaders were being defeated in the south, were as disheartened by this audacious raid into the heart of their capital as the Americans were emboldened by it. The sight of a battalion-sized unit of Americans blazing through the heart of the city shocked Iraqis, who had been fed propaganda that "Fortress Baghdad" was invincible. Prior to this incursion, the Iraqi information minister had announced, "There will be no American infidels in Baghdad. Never!"[33]

On April 6 it was decided to launch an even bolder Thunder Run into the government center of Baghdad, and, instead of retreating, the troops would stay and hold their position by the Republican Palace. Again Bradley fighting vehicles and Abrams tanks raced into the heart of the city facing stiff opposition but were able to seize their symbolic objective despite the intense RPG and gunfire they encountered. There they were forced to fight thousands of Iraqis and the occasional suicide bomber car attacks to hold their prized position. The Americans were almost overwhelmed as they ran out of fuel and ammo. But a resupply column of ten more armored vehicles, ammo truck, and fuel trucks broke through to reinforce their occupation of what would later become known as the Green Zone. For two days the two-battalion-sized occupation force from the army's Third Infantry Division held the center of the enemy's capital and repulsed Iraqi attacks in a bold showing of the flag.

This audacious invasion by just under 975 soldiers and eighty-eight vehicles broke the fighting spirit of the Iraqis just as the Marines approached Baghdad from the east after having fought their way through a dangerous river crossing. With U.S. troops in control of the Iraqi equivalent of the National Mall in Washington, D.C., it was hard for the Iraqi information minister, known as "Comical Ali" by the Americans, to continue to claim that the Americans were "committing suicide on the defenses of Baghdad." To compound matters, on April 9 American troops entered the Firdos Square in the heart of Baghdad and toppled a massive statue of Hussein as foreign journalists from a nearby hotel photographed the event. Local Iraqis then came out and beat the statue with their shoes in an Arabic sign of contempt for their hated dictator.

This event more than any other symbolized the fall of Hussein's regime and the victory of the Americans. As the Marines approached Baghdad from the east and the U.S. Army from the west, thousands of disheartened Iraqi soldiers simply shed their uniforms and went home with their weapons to see what would happen. The Iraqi army had been defeated in conventional war and had lost its fighting spirit (there was of course no Iraqi deployment of unconventional Iraqi chemical, biological, or nuclear weapons because they did not exist). General Tommy Franks, the head of Centcom (Central Command) later estimated that thirty thousand Iraqis had died in the invasion of their country.[34] By contrast the invading American-UK force lost just 172 soldiers.[35]

The April 9 takedown of the Hussein statue in Firdos Square later became seen as the high-water mark of the war in Iraq and led to considerable hubris back in the United States. Fox News's Bill O'Reilly went so far as to predict that "military action will not last more than a week."[36] Even as the victorious Americans spread throughout the country hunting for Hussein and other Baathist leaders who had gone into hiding, the Bush White House prematurely celebrated the end of the war. The ultimate victory lap was carried out by President George Bush who, on May 1, 2003, landed in a Lockheed Viking jet on the deck of the USS *Abraham Lincoln* as it cruised off the coast of San Diego, California, and boldly proclaimed, "My fellow Americans, major combat operations in Iraq have ended. In the battle of Iraq, the United States and our allies have prevailed. Because of you, the tyrant has fallen and Iraq is free."[37] Behind him on the aircraft carrier a massive banner had been hung at the behest of the White House that declared "Mission Accomplished."

But even as the Bush White House prematurely celebrated the end of the war, America began to put several policies in place that would lead it to help mobilize a deadly insurgency of the sort that Rumsfeld and Wolfowitz had not planned for in Phase IV of the war. Far from being "accomplished," America's war mission, which would later cost almost forty-five hundred U.S. lives, had actually just begun. Tragically, history would show that, while the United States had enough troops to conquer Iraq, it did not have enough troops to occupy and control this vast country of thirty-six million people.

The Rise of the Iraqi Insurgency

In the aftermath of the defeat of Saddam Hussein's army, the Iraqi government collapsed, and everyone from forty thousand policemen to the ministers of oil melted away. As civil society collapsed, gangs of Iraqis came out to loot government buildings in Baghdad and across the country. Across Iraq, everything from electrical wiring, to telephones and chairs in government buildings, to police cars, to fire engines, to school desks, hospital equipment, and oil piping was looted. Fires raged, and all government buildings and most ministries were looted or gutted.

Among the looters' first targets in the postinvasion power vacuum was the National Museum in Baghdad, which housed one of the most valuable collections of ancient Mesopotamian artifacts in the world. Without police to maintain order, cars were carjacked, women were raped, people were kidnapped, billions of dollars was looted from banks, stores were burnt, ancient relics were stolen or destroyed, and anarchy prevailed in exactly the sort of scenario General Eric Shinseki had feared, and Rumsfeld had discounted.

At this time, many Iraqis who had disliked Hussein and were sitting on the fence came to associate the anarchy and loss of electricity, water, and security in the aftermath of the invasion with the now distrusted American invaders. When asked by a reporter about the chaos and looting, an unapologetic Rumsfeld dismissed the question by stating flatly that "democracy is messy" and "stuff happens."[38] He also said, "Freedom's untidy, and free people are free to make mistakes and commit crimes and do bad things."[39]

But it need not have been that way had the Americans come with a much larger occupation force to step in and help police and maintain order in the country of the sort called for by Powell and Shinseki. Todd Purdum, author of a history of the Iraq war, described the unfolding Phase IV problems as follows:

> The problems for the Americans was that, after the fall of the statue, there was no order in Baghdad, and they didn't have enough troops on the ground to enforce order. They didn't have enough civil affairs officers. They didn't have enough military policemen. The 4th Infantry was still making its way up from Kuwait. So if Rumsfeld's vision of the war plan was a tactical success, some generals in the Pentagon began to worry if it mightn't have been a strategic failure, because the American forces did not have the capacity to enforce order in the all-important aftermath of the war.[40]

Thomas Ricks, author of a best-selling history of the war in Iraq titled *Fiasco*, agreed and wrote, "The problem is, we had insufficient forces to secure and freeze the situation and capitalize on that moment."[41] To compound matters, the overly optimistic plan was to start withdrawing the too few U.S. troops and bring the number down to a mere thirty thousand by midsummer 2003.[42] Rumsfeld's spokesman summed up the Neo-Cons' plans for Iraq by stating, "We're going to stand up an interim Iraqi government, hand over power to them, and get out of there in three or four months."[43] Nation building was to be avoided at all costs, and U.S. troops were to come home as expeditiously as possible.

As this chaos was unfolding and losing America the hearts and minds of millions of average Iraqis, the White House sent a civilian official named Paul Bremer to take charge of postwar Iraq. On May 11, 2003, Bremer became governor of postwar Iraq in his role as head of the Coalition's Provisional Authority. This made him perhaps the most powerful American abroad since General Douglas MacArthur took control of post–World War II Japan. But Bremer's initial decisions lacked the sagacity of MacArthur's policies during the occupation of Japan.

The architects of Bremer's missteps were the Neo-Cons, who called for total de-Baathification based on the model of de-Nazification in post–World War II Germany. Paul Bremer's first step was Provisional Authority Order Number 1, issued on May 16. Order Number 1 banned the Sunni-dominated Baathist Party, which had run Iraq for decades. The previous temporary governor of Iraq, General Jay Garner, and his staff were appalled by the decision and warned Bremer, "It was too deep."[44] One of Garner's staff recalled saying, "if you do this, you're going to drive 30,000 to 50,000 Ba'athists underground by nightfall. And the number's closer to 50,000 than it is 30,000."[45] The CIA station chief in Baghdad agreed with the number of fifty thousand Baathists being driven underground and said, "In six months you will regret this. . . . Many of the state's competent administrator's were fired overnight."[46] By banning the Baathist Party, which had as many as one hundred thousand members who were used to being in power, Bremer turned this mass of powerful leaders and their dependents against the U.S. occupation overnight.[47]

The majority of those to be disenfranchised with Order Number 1 were of course Sunnis, who had held the grip on power in the country for five centuries. This act had a negative impact on everyone from civil servants to the technocrats who ran government ministries. An Iraqi source claimed, "Thousands of people who had never committed a crime in their lives, including school teachers, engineers, and doctors were fired. . . . Many of the state's most competent administrators were fired overnight, leaving the bureaucracy in a parlous state."[48]

In some Sunni areas, such as Fallujah, there were no schoolteachers left after Order Number 1 was promulgated because most of them were fired as members of the Baath Party.

A total of forty thousand school teachers were fired as were one third of the Ministry of Health and many officials involved in hospitals, communication, universities and electricity. Far from helping to stabilize Iraq, this act led to disruption, unemployment and economic hardship for tens of thousands of average Iraqis who had joined the Baath Party, usually just to get a job, and their dependents.

The process of firing Baath members was simply too broad. Instead of limiting punitive efforts to Baathist members who were found in trials to have been guilty of criminal acts (and there were many of these), everyone in the governing party was in essence collectively punished. This of course turned them against the American occupiers and fed into sectarianism since the majority of those who were fired were Sunnis.

Bremer's second step compounded matters and might have been a play from a manual on how to incite an insurgency. His second step was Order Number 2, which disbanded the Iraqi army, on May 23, 2003. This step went against the suggestions of a group of security experts at the National Defense University, who had also warned against "top down de-Baathification."[49] This group had warned that the Iraqi military was one of the rare unifying institutions in Iraq that stressed overarching national identity.

According to this group of experts, "to tear apart the army in the war's aftermath could lead to the destruction of one of the only forces for unity within the society." The Iraqi military, which consisted of 385,000 men in the army, 285,000 in the Ministry of Defense and 50,000 in the presidential security units, was a much-respected institution in Iraq, and its sudden disbandment shocked Iraqi society. The tens of thousands of Iraqi soldiers who had taken their weapons home instead of fighting the American invasion felt betrayed when they were fired.

This sweeping act created a recruitment pool of armed and disaffected soldiers. In one fell swoop these Iraqi soldiers lost their careers, their paycheck, their pensions, and their source of pride. General Daniel Bolger would claim that de-Baathification "guaranteed Sunni outrage."[50] General Jay Garner would report "We created half a million angry, armed, unemployed Iraqis in 48 hours. That was dumb."[51] Efforts to employ 137,000 members of the Iraqi military who registered with the U.S. Army to engage in reconstruction jobs were terminated. An Iraqi army commander involved in the process said "disbanding and enraging—rather than enlisting all those unemployed Iraqis who were willing to help" was a "stupid decision."[52]

One American colonel was to subsequently recount the almost simultaneous ramp-up in violence following the firing of the Sunni-dominated army as follows: "Who knows how many [Iraqi army] folks got disgruntled and went to the other side? I will tell you this, 72 hours after the decision was made, the first major attack from the airport road took place. And I got two of my military police killed. And it's sort of been downhill from there."[53] Another U.S. Army colonel said, "When Bremer did that, the insurgency went crazy. May was the turning point."[54]

The U.S. military, CIA, and State Department were all against these NeoCon-inspired policies, and one U.S. general furiously said, "You guys just blindsided Centcom. We snatched defeat from the jaws of victory and created an insurgency."[55] Another expert on Iraq stated, "We made hundreds of thousands of people very angry at us and they happened to be the people in the country best acquainted with the use of arms."[56] Prior to this act, the U.S. military had hoped to work with the Iraqi military to rebuild Iraq. Their aim was to provide thousands of Iraqi soldiers with jobs, pride, and a stake in building a new Iraq. That option was now gone.

Dexter Filkins, a journalist who was in Iraq at the time, reported: "I talked to American military commanders who told me that leaders of entire Iraqi divisions (a division has roughly ten thousand troops) had come to them for instructions and expressed a willingness to coöperate. In fact, many American commanders argued vehemently at the time that the Iraqi military should be kept intact—that disbanding it would turn too many angry young men against the United States. But the Bush White House went ahead. Many of those suddenly unemployed Iraqi soldiers took up arms against the United States."[57] *The New Yorker* was to write of the firing of the Sunni-dominated Iraqi army and Baathist Party, "This was probably the single most catastrophic decision of the American venture in Iraq. In a stroke, the Administration helped enable the creation of the Iraqi insurgency."[58] Germany's *Der Spiegel* would similarly write, "Thousands of well-trained Sunni officers were robbed of their livelihood with the stroke of a pen. In doing so, America created its most bitter and intelligent enemies."[59]

The straw that broke the camel's back and added insult to injury was when Bremer's staff then created a provisional government that was dominated by Shiites. One Sunni explained the impact this decision had on his disenfranchised community as follows: "At first no one fought the Americans, not the Baath, not the army officers, and not the [Sunni] tribes. But when the Americans formed the Governing Council [in July 2003] with thirteen Shia [Shiites] and only a few Sunnis, people began to say 'The Americans mean to give the country to the Shia' and then they began to fight, and the tribes began to let Al Qaeda in."[60]

Emma Sky, who worked for the U.S. military at the time, reported of the Shiite-dominated Governing Council's discrimination against the Sunnis. She stated, "The allocation of posts based on ethnicity and sect undermined any hope of building a 'nation,' institutionalizing sectarianism rather than pluralism."[61] In other words, the newly empowered Shiites did not try to bridge communal divides when they came to power and instead "used sectarianism to mobilize constituents." In the new scheme of things, the Sunnis were losers, and the Shiites were on top.

Combined together, Orders Number 1 and 2 essentially fired, disenfranchised and disempowered two million people who had weapons, respect, and built-in communication networks. The Iraqi military was especially furious, and Iraqi soldiers who had lost their jobs, source of pride, and incomes took to holding daily protests at the gates to the Green Zone (i.e., the fortified district in downtown Baghdad that the U.S.-led government occupied). During these protests, one Iraqi officer stated, "We are all very well trained soldiers and we are armed. We will start ambushes, bombings and even suicide bombings."[62] Another humiliated Iraqi would state, "We're against the occupation, we refuse the occupation—not one hundred percent, but one thousand percent. They're walking over my heart. I feel like they are crushing my heart."[63] During one protest against the mass firings, two Iraqi officers were shot by U.S. troops, thus further infuriating this laid-off pool of potential recruits for the insurgency.[64]

These angry Iraqis, a majority of whom were the previously ruling Sunnis, felt they had no stake in the new Iraq that the United States was building and resented what they saw as de-Sunnification. One Sunni's anguished complaint captures the sentiment of this group that felt it had been arbitrarily removed from power by the Americans after ruling Iraq since the advent of Islam in the region. This source stated, "We were at the top of the system. We had dreams. Now we are losers. We lost our positions, our status, the security of our families, stability. Curse the Americans, curse them."[65] Historian Ahmed Hashim has written, "Dissolving the army meant also driving a stake through a Sunni identity that had relied on the armed forces as a primary institutional and symbolic support of identity."[66] Fulfilling the law of unintended consequences, this pool of marginalized Sunnis would become known in U.S. military parlance as POIs (Pissed-Off Iraqis). Many of them would go on to join the Sunni insurgency, which began to take shape in the summer of 2003. The insurgents offered unemployed ex-soldiers or ex-Baathists salaries of up to $100 to shoot Americans or plant landmines. If they filmed the killing of an American they got a bonus.

Within a matter of weeks the Sunni insurgents would begin to wage a classic guerilla war on U.S. patrols via roadside bomb attacks, mortar attacks, sniper ambushes, and suicide bombings. They had no problem accessing weapons and explosives because many of them were previously in the military or the Fedayeen Saddam. One Iraqi general spoke of the decision by scores of fired Iraqi soldiers to join the insurgency and fight the American occupation: "The Americans bear the biggest responsibility. When they dismantled the army what did they expect those men to do? They [the fired Sunni Iraqi soldiers] were out in the cold with nothing to do and there was only one way out for them to put food on the table. . . . They didn't de-Baathify people's minds, they just took away their jobs."[67]

Among the Sunni insurgents' first strategic targets were the Jordanian embassy, which was bombed on August 7, and the UN Mission in Iraq, which was suicide bombed on August 19. These two bombings led the UN, International Monetary Fund, and World Bank to withdraw from the country and convinced most foreign governments (whom the White House had been counting on to assist in the reconstruction of Iraq) to stay away from what was fast developing into a full-blown insurgency.

This withdrawal of world support for the U.S. occupation comported with the wishes of one Abu Musab Zarqawi, the Jordanian jihadi leader who had fled from Afghanistan to Iraqi Kurdistan after 9/11 and now appeared to be head of a newly created Sunni Arab insurgent group known as Tawhid wal Jihad (Monotheism and Holy War). It was his group that claimed the bombings on the UN building and Jordanian embassy. Zarqawi and his fanatical Sunni followers acted as missionaries and recruiters for many previously secular Baathist insurgents who quickly became "jihadified" under their influence. In the ultimate of ironies, Operation Iraqi Freedom was thus leading not the spread of democracy across the Middle East (as the Neo-Cons had envisioned) but to the radicalization of tens of thousands of secular-Baathist Iraqis who had previously had no interest in anti-American holy war.

One Iraqi woman spoke of this radicalization of secular Sunnis: "They speak in the name of God. Before they spoke in the name of Saddam."[68] Prior to the U.S. toppling of Saddam's secular regime, one Iraqi stated, "we were forced to pray in secret. And we could not grow a beard. If we attended mosque too regularly we were thrown into prison."[69] Now, with the overthrow of the secular Baathist Party, it was the Islamist radicals who had emerged to lead the Sunni resistance to the U.S. occupation on the grassroots level. In his book *The Assassins' Gate*, George Packer wrote of this desecularization and radicalization process that took place in Iraq:

> The Iraq War made some of the Bush administration's assertions false, and it made others self-fulfilling. One of these was the insistence on an operational link between Iraq and al Qaeda. In fact, Saddam had always kept a wary distance from Islamist groups; he co-opted conservative Sunni imams in Iraq only to use them as window dressing. But after the [2003] fall of the [Baathist] regime, the most potent ideological force behind the insurgency was Islam and its hostility to non-Islamic intruders. Some Baathist members even stopped drinking and took to prayer.[70]

One Iraqi source said of this process of radicalization that was facilitated by the U.S. invasion, "All of these guys got religious after 2003."[71] Many former Baathists and Iraqi army members joined the insurgency, which was based on radical Islam. Among the most prominent jihadist groups for former Baathists who had rediscovered their religion was the Army of the Naqshbandi Order, which was based on an ancient Sufi Islamic brotherhood.

Baathist Iraq had thus overnight become a breeding ground for a new jihad as disenfranchised Sunnis grew their beards long and joined the Islamist insurgency en masse. The most prominent of the Baathists leading the insurgency against the Americans was Izzet al Douri, a high-ranking Iraqi general who escaped the Americans and directed Sunni insurgents belonging to the Naqshbandi Order from the safety of neighboring Syria.

As the insurgency broke out in central and western Iraq and dozens of U.S. troops were killed in a land they had been told would welcome them, Donald Rumsfeld adamantly refused to acknowledge the rebels' existence. Instead of calling the insurgency what it was (i.e., a classic guerilla-style war against a foreign occupying force), Rumsfeld contemptuously labeled the insurgents "dead-enders" and "the last remnants of a dying cause."[72] He would not allow the military to even use the word "insurgency."[73]

Vice President Dick Cheney similarly constructed an alternative universe where the Iraqi "dead-enders" would be easily defeated and confidently stated, "I think the level of activity that we see today, from a military standpoint, I think will clearly decline. I think they're in the last throes, if you will, of the insurgency."[74] In his history of the Iraq war, Ali Allawi has written: "The denial of the existence of an insurgency permeated the entire CPA-governing apparatus throughout the early period. Underlying their smug indifference was a misplaced confidence in the ability of the Coalition to contain and defeat what were still thought of as desperate acts of the remnants of the defunct regime."[75]

But the military was more forthcoming than the politicians, and General John Abizaid, the new head of Central Command, would state, "we are conducting what I would describe as a classical guerilla-type campaign."[76] General Ricardo Sanchez similarly admitted, "the undeniable fact is that we are still at war."[77]

With the insurgency spreading like wildfire throughout what became known as the Sunni Triangle (i.e., the area in central Iraq dominated by Sunnis, who made up 20 percent of the country), President Bush declared with bravado, "There are some who feel that the conditions are such that they can attack us there. My answer is bring 'em on."[78] One infuriated U.S. soldier in Iraq angrily responded to Bush's invitation to the insurgents saying, "My soldiers and I were searching for car bombs and scanning rooftops for snipers, and our president was in Washington taunting our enemies and encouraging them to attack us."[79] As the insurgency exploded in the following months, a Sunni insurgent group known as the Islamic Army also sent a response to Bush, which read, "Have you another challenge?"[80]

When the insurgency spread in the summer and fall of 2003, U.S. troops responded by carrying out clumsy raids on Iraqi houses to arrest suspected insurgents. They soon had thousands of prisoners and decided to reopen a notorious prison west of Baghdad known as Abu Ghraib, which had previously been used by Saddam Hussein. The United States ultimately imprisoned over seventy-five hundred Iraqis in this facility, which was built to hold just five thousand.

Many of these prisoners would later be deemed to be innocent and to have had no ties to the insurgency. Their arrest was emblematic of a clumsy overreaction that simply played into Zarqawi's insurgents' hands and gave them a recruitment tool. Tragically, an unknown number of these Iraqi prisoners (men and women) were beaten until unconscious, attacked with dogs, urinated on, stripped of their clothes, and raped and sodomized by sadistic U.S. guards. We know this because one American guard unit took unbearably gruesome photos of themselves piling naked Iraqi prisoners on to piles, beating prisoners bloody, attacking them with German shepherds, and humiliating and torturing them in various ways.

When photographs of the grinning U.S. troops torturing and humiliating Iraqi prisoners were leaked to the press and shown on CBS's news show *60 Minutes* in April 2004, it proved to be an unprecedented scandal for U.S. military forces. It was also a recruitment bonanza for the Sunni insurgents. Zarqawi capitalized on the deep outrage among Arab men over the humiliation of their fellow countrymen at the hands of the American "infidel invaders" to convince Sunnis to partake in "defensive jihad of liberation."

The Abu Ghraib scandal also allowed Zarqawi to recruit outraged Arabs from the neighboring Sunni majority in Syria (the Syrian minority government, however, was Alawite Shiite), Jordan, and especially Saudi Arabia. Iraq became a magnet for Islamist fanatics who wanted the chance to kill Americans and make them pay for invading the Muslim world. Soon Iraq was filled with hundreds of fanatical foreign fighters who were known to be willing to die for jihad. Many of these were chosen to be suicide bombers as this new asymmetric tactic spread throughout the previously secular Sunni lands. Fully realizing the negative ripple effect of Abu Ghraib on Iraqis, one U.S. lance corporal grimly stated of the guilty U.S. guards in the prison, "Some assholes have just lost the war for us."[81]

But even as the Sunni insurgency spread, the Americans achieved a major victory on December 13, 2003, by capturing Saddam Hussein, who was hiding in a "spider hole" near his hometown of Tikrit. The former Iraqi leader did not put up a fight when he was discovered, even though he was armed with an AK-47 and a pistol. Instead he announced, "I am Saddam Hussein. I am the president of Iraq. I want to negotiate." A triumphant Paul Bremer announced, "Ladies and gentlemen, we got him!"[82] Later a scruffy-bearded Hussein was photographed in the humiliating position of having his teeth examined by a U.S. military dentist in jail.

Hussein would ultimately be executed by the new elected Shiite-dominated Iraqi government in December 2006. The videotaped footage of him being mocked by his Shiite executioners, who chanted the name of a militant Shiite leader named Moqtada al Sadr, would infuriate many Sunnis after it was televised. A CNN report would also state that when the execution was over there were Shiites chanting in the background and "dancing around the body."[83] In the Shiite holy city of Najaf, Shiites poured out into the streets banging drums to celebrate the death of their people's enemy. For their part, members of the Baath Party who were in hiding among the insurgents proclaimed, "The Baath and the resistance are determined to retaliate in all ways and all places that hurt America and its interests."[84]

Hopes that the arrest of Hussein and subsequent killing of his two notorious sons, Uday and Qusay, in a firefight in Mosul would put an end to the mounting Sunni insurgency were dashed, however, when Islamist guerillas seized control of several towns in Iraq's largest province, the western desert region of Anbar. The town of Fallujah became their de facto capital and was openly dominated by Zarqawi-led Sunni militants who enforced strict shariah law there.

The world came to know the name Fallujah on March 31, 2004, when four security contractors for the U.S. firm Blackwater got lost in the town and were brutally killed by insurgents. The Sunni insurgents then burnt their bodies and hung them from a bridge to the delight of a cheering mob. When footage of the mangled, blackened bodies hanging from a bridge in pieces was broadcast globally, it infuriated the Bush administration, which seemed to take the atrocity personally. It was a bold refutation of Cheney's wishful prediction that "we will be greeted as liberators" and visual rejection of Rumsfeld's claims that there was no insurgency. For many Americans who had felt that their soldiers would be greeted as liberators, the sickening images were also a message that, at least a component of the Sunni segment of

Iraq, which had been dislodged from power, had come to see the U.S. troops as invaders and occupiers.

It was now obvious to many that America was engaged in its first large scale guerilla war since Vietnam as increasing accounts of ambushes, IED attacks, and suicide bombings began to appear on the news. At the time, U.S. newspapers reported that 476 U.S. troops had died in Iraq since the president had hubristically announced the "end of major combat operations" on the aircraft carrier.[85]

The Bush administration decided that a resolute response to the events in Fallujah was needed, but the generals on the ground felt that an "overly kinetic revenge" reaction might be like pouring gasoline on a fire. They felt it would play into Zarqawi's hands. In the end, however, the politicians overruled the generals, and it was decided to launch an attack on Fallujah in April 2004. The Marines would be sent in to crush the rebels in Fallujah in an operation known as "Vigilant Resolve." The Marines subsequently fought a bruising battle that quickly saw them in control of one-third of the city and moving deeper to Fallujah's center.

But the resolve of the Iraqi government, the White House and Paul Bremer collapsed when the Arabic news channel Al Jazeera broadcast images of destroyed mosques, fleeing civilians, and casualties in hospitals. The Bush administration and Iraqi Governing Council came to see the operation as a public relations disaster, and, after the death of twenty-seven American soldiers and wounding of ninety more, the misnamed Operation Vigilant Resolve was called off by the White House. The Marines were furious at the politicians, and Lieutenant General James T. Conway was to state, "When you order elements of a Marine division to attack a city, you really need to understand what the consequences of that are going to be and not perhaps vacillate in the middle of something like that. Once you commit, you got to stay committed."[86]

General Bernard Trainor would similarly state: "The Fallujah battle in particular had been a textbook example of how not to go to war. . . . The Marines had been ordered to attack against the better judgment by superiors who failed to secure the necessary backup from the Governing Council or the UN and then stopped the attack in its tracks just as they were making progress. There had been a yawning disconnect between the battlefield and the Bush administration's political strategy."[87]

With the withdrawal of the Marines from Fallujah, Zarqawi declared victory, and his forces spread throughout the city and the nearby capital of

Anbar Province, Ramadi, enforcing strict shariah law. Among Zarqawi's moves at this time was to behead an American civilian named Nicholas Berg on videotape. Videotaped beheadings of foreign contractors, Iraqi collaborators with the U.S. occupation, and later Shiites, would become a calling card of the Sunni insurgency.

But it was not only the Sunnis who were causing problems for the Americans. In Baghdad and the south the Americans stirred up another beehive among the sectarian group that should have been most appreciative to the Americans for overthrowing Hussein's Sunni-dominated regime, the Shiites. The Neo-Cons had expected the newly liberated Shiites to be a pro-U.S., pro-Israel ally in the Middle East, especially since they had begun to take over key positions in the police, military, and government (including prime minister-ship) in May 2004. But in this, as in so much else, the Neo-Cons were wrong.

It all began in April and May 2003 when the Shiite Islamists took advantage of the collapse of the Baathist regime to sweep into power throughout the Shiite south and neighborhoods of Baghdad they inhabited. Simply put, there were too few U.S. troops to prevent the Shiite radicals from seizing control of most Shiite areas, and some analysts (and of course the disempowered Sunnis) came to see Operation Iraqi Freedom as Operation Shiite Empowerment. This was especially the case when the Shiite radicals created lists of well-known Sunni Baathists and began to kill those on the hit lists. Many of those who were killed were Sunni teachers, doctors, artists, journalists, and others who had been forced to join the Baathist party just to get ahead in Iraqi society under Hussein.

To compound matters, the Shiites, who were often more devout than the Sunnis—many of whom had become secularized to a certain extent under Baathist rule—were far from grateful to the Americans for empowering them. Many of the Shiites' clerics saw the Americans as "infidel occupiers" and demanded that they leave Iraq. Ahmed Hashim states in his history of the insurgency that throughout the Shiite lands, "young Islamist men who had once hidden overt symbols of piety from the [Baathist] regime 'came out of the closet', so to speak."[88] These Shiite radicals then set up ad hoc shariah Islamic law courts to replace the secular courts of the Baathists, and this went against the Americans' plans for Iraq. At the time some Shiite militants threatened to kill any woman who wore makeup or did not wear a head scarf.

Matters came to a head in March 2004 when Bremer decided to close down a newspaper run by a powerful Shiite religious-militia leader named Moqtada al Sadr because it was publishing anti-American diatribes. Dismissing Sadr as a mere rabble-rouser, Bremer underestimated this powerful leader, whose influence spread from the sprawling slums of Sadr City (a Shiite neighborhood of two million people in Baghdad that had been named for his father, a grand ayatollah who had been killed by Saddam Hussein) to the Shiite city of Basra in the south. Sadr spoke for millions of impoverished Shiites who had been marginalized under Hussein.

To compound matters, a warrant was issued for Sadr's arrest for his role in ordering the killing of a more moderate Shiite leader and for speaking against the United States in his sermons. When thousands of members of his militia, the Mahdi Army, heard the news they rose up and began to fight against the Americans and British as well. By early April they had seized the holy cities of Najaf and Karbala and the town of Kut in the south and had taken control of much of Sadr City in Baghdad. These cities were retaken in June by U.S. forces at considerable effort.

Thus the Americans were opposed by many, if not most, Sunni Arabs, who made up 20 percent of the country, and many Shiites, who made up 60 percent of the country. Only the Kurds, who took advantage of the invasion to establish a stable de facto Kurdish state in the mountains of the north, appeared to wholeheartedly welcome the Americans.

Meanwhile, Zarqawi's Sunni insurgents brazenly turned Fallujah into the de facto capital of a jihadist state and used it as a springboard for sending suicide bombers into Baghdad to wreak havoc. By this time they controlled most of Anbar, an area that makes up one-third of Iraq. If this were not enough, in October 2004 Zarqawi boldly announced that his independent jihad group, Tawhid wal Jihad, was joining Al Qaeda and would henceforth be known as Al Qaeda in Iraq (AQI). Thus the Bush administration's 2002 claim that there was an Al Qaeda presence in Iraq became a self-fulfilling prophecy two years later. There was now a bona fide Al Qaeda–linked "franchise" consisting of thousands of Iraqi and foreign terrorists operating in the lands that had been dominated by secular Baathists prior to the 2003 invasion.

This new Iraqi iteration of Al Qaeda dwarfed the original Al Qaeda Central run by bin Laden. It was one step forward, two steps back, although Bush would overlook the fact that the United States had helped create this new iteration of Al Qaeda by stating that Iraq was now "central to the war on terror."[89] Professor Juan Cole was to write of this self-defeating process, "Ironically, by invading, occupying, weakening and looting Iraq, Bush and Cheney brought al-Qaeda into the country and so weakened it as to allow it

[Al Qaeda] actually to take and hold territory in our own time."[90] By this time a classified intelligence report would state that Iraq had become a "cause célèbre for jihadists, breeding a deep resentment of US involvement in the Muslim world and cultivating supporters for the global jihadist movement."[91] Had the U.S. simply limited its military operations to destroying bin Laden's organization in Afghanistan, it would not have "built a bridge too far" and allowed the jihadists to pop up in the heart of the Arab world.

Having stirred up the hornet's nest in Iraq and "jihadified" or "Al Qaedified" the Sunni portions of the country, Bush would then cynically tell the American people, "We will defeat them there so we don't have to face them in our own country."[92] This theory, that Americans were fighting and dying in Iraq to prevent Iraqis from attacking Americans in their own streets and towns, became known as the "fly-paper theory." In this bizarre theory, the Americans were not recruiting insurgents by invading their country on false premises and arresting them for internment in Abu Ghraib. On the contrary, the U.S. troops were acting as "fly-paper" to suck jihadi insurgents into combat in places like Fallujah so they would not attack places like Columbus, Ohio. This assumption overlooked the inconvenient fact that there was no Al Qaeda in Iraq until after the U.S. invaded the country and disenfranchised hundreds of thousands of Sunnis who then went on to create Al Qaeda in Iraq (AQI).

As the situation deteriorated in Fallujah by the fall of 2004, it was finally decided that the Al Qaeda–held city would have to be taken after all, regardless of the public relations fallout. On November 7, sixty-five hundred Marines, fifteen hundred U.S. Army troops, and two thousand Iraqi security forces (roughly three times the size of the force used in the First Battle of Fallujah in April) moved to encircle the roughly three to four thousand Islamist insurgents holed up in the city. The insurgents had dug in to the city and created everything from HBIEDs (house-borne improvised explosive devices, i.e., houses rigged to explode when entered by U.S. troops) to interconnecting tunnels designed to turn the large city into an urban killing zone.

The subsequent Second Battle of Fallujah, known as Operation Phantom Fury, was the bloodiest battle of the entire Iraq War. The Marines, who charged into combat playing Wagner's "Flight of the Valkyries," compared the house-to-house fighting in Fallujah to the 1968 Battle of Hue in Vietnam, and it was a bloody slog. When it was over between one thousand and two thousand insurgents and fifty-four Americans were killed, and one-fifth of the city's fifty thousand houses were destroyed.

In the process, the U.S. troops uncovered twenty-four bomb factories and 455 weapons caches. They also uncovered torture houses used by Zarqawi's followers, including one where the victims' legs had been sawed off, which demonstrated just how depraved and brutal the Sunni insurgents had become.[93] Unfortunately, Zarqawi himself was not among the dead as he had fled the fighting and left his second in command to run the defense of the city.

With the collapse of their capital in Fallujah, the Sunni insurgents fled north to Mosul, Iraq's second largest city and a Sunni stronghold. Thus far this city had been kept calm by Lieutenant General David Petraeus's 101st Airborne Division, which had done a masterful job of winning over the hearts and minds of the local people. But Mosul was almost overrun as thousands of Sunni militants tried taking it over. The insurgents were barely defeated by several U.S. Army Stryker units on November 12, 2004. From Mosul, the insurgents fled to the city of Baquba, capital of Diyala Province, north of Baghdad, and declared it the capital of their state.

By 2005 it was obvious that the United States was essentially playing a game of "Whack a Mole" with Sunni insurgents, who were capitalizing on popular hatred for the Americans that stemmed from their ham-fisted raids on real or perceived insurgents' houses and other clumsy, self-defeating tactics. American troops, many of whom equated average Iraqis with Al Qaeda thanks to the Bush White House's propaganda designed to merge the two, failed to understand how they themselves would react if their roles were reversed and Iraqi invaders occupied their homeland and carried out house searches for American insurgents.

Iraqis also complained of tremendous cultural ignorance among the American troops they encountered. One Iraqi whose house had been targeted for a U.S. raid said: "[U.S. soldiers] searched my house. They kicked my Koran. They speak to me poorly in front of my children. [It's] not that I encourage my son to hate Americans. It's not that I make him want to join the resistance. Americans do that for me."[94] Perhaps the most notorious example of U.S. brute force acting as a catalyst for grievances among Iraqis was the 2005 Haditha Massacre. In this tragedy, a group of Marines burst into Iraqi houses and slaughtered twenty-four Iraqi civilians, many of them children and the elderly, to avenge the death of one of their comrades in an earlier IED strike. While a Pentagon investigation supported "accusations that U.S. Marines deliberately shot civilians, including unarmed women and children," none of the killers was ever sentenced to jail time.[95] The outraged Iraqi government called the massacre a crime against humanity, and the Sunni in-surgents vowed to avenge the dead. Tragically, this was not to be the only massacre of Iraqi civilians by Americans.

There was another killing of seventeen Iraqis by armed contractors work-ing for Blackwater Security. In this case, the Blackwater security guards, members of a vast legion of twenty thousand contractors serving in Iraq, mowed down civilians in a square in downtown Baghdad. As in the Haditha case, Iraqis were outraged when the Blackwater killers were not immediately sent to jail. As these events served as recruitment drives for militants, the number of Sunni insurgent groups seemed to proliferate. U.S. troops were soon fighting such Baathist/Sunni-jihadi groups as Al Qaeda in Iraq (later known as the Islamic State in Iraq or ISI), the 1920s Revolution Brigade (a Baathist group), Jaish al Islam (the Army of Islam), Ansar al Shariah (the Supporter of Islamic Law), the Army of the Naqshbandi (a Baathist Sufi group), and the Army of Mohammad.

Not all U.S. actions, however, had negative side effects. The most success-ful counterinsurgent at this time was JSOC (Joint Special Operations Com-mand) head General Stanley McChrystal, whose task force killed hundreds of top insurgents. Using a combination of advanced surveillance and inter-ception technology and special forces raids, McChrystal became the bane of the terrorists. His SEAL (Sea, Earth, Air, and Land, elite Navy Special Forces) and Delta Forces became feared by the Iraqi insurgents as "ninjas" who would "burst into town then disappear."[96]

But American domestic support for the war nonetheless declined back home as the evening news bombarded viewers with images of seemingly endless combat and loss of American lives. To compound matters, thousands of National Guard troops were called up to duty to fight in Iraq. Many of these part-time National Guard soldiers were teachers, construction workers, restaurant owners, and so on, who had not bargained on fighting and dying in the deserts of Iraq when they enlisted to become "weekend warriors." When these fathers, brothers, and mothers went to war, and often came back in flag-draped coffins or horribly maimed, it had ripple effects on their com-munities. The constant combat was clearly taking a toll on the U.S. military, which ultimately took to involuntarily extending soldiers' service in combat zones through an extension of their war deployments known as "stop loss."

As Bush's project to construct a model Western democracy in the deserts of Iraq foundered, one man gloated: Osama bin Laden. The Al Qaeda leader watched the American efforts that had inadvertently helped mobilize support for terroriststic jihad in the land of his former enemy, Hussein, with undisguised glee. Bin Laden subsequently stated, "Be glad of the good news: America is mired in the swamps of the Tigris and Euphrates. Here he [Bush] is now, thank God, in an embarrassing situation and here is America today being ruined before the eyes of the whole world."[97] Michael Morell, the deputy director of the CIA, would state, "Bin Ladin welcomed the US intervention in Iraq."[98] He would also state, "the Iraq War supported the al Qa'ida narrative and helped spread the group's ideology."[99]

Having been defeated in Afghanistan, what can best be described as "Al Qaedism" had been revived in the deserts of Iraq. Another man also relished the mayhem that destroyed the Neo-Cons' and Rumsfeld's vision of flourishing post-invasion Iraq that would serve as a "beacon of democracy," and that was the sadistic butcher, Abu Musab Zarqawi.

Ironically, Al Qaeda Central, which was hiding out in Pakistan, fretted that the notorious Jordanian jihadi in Iraq was giving their organization a bad name with his butchery. Bin Laden ordered his subordinates "not to publish pictures of prisoners after they were beheaded."[100] The Al Qaeda Central second in command, Ayman al Zawahiri, sent Zarqawi a letter asking him to tone down the gruesome violence, sectarian attacks on Shiites, bloody suicide bombings, and attacks on civilians.[101]

But Zarqawi and his followers had created a cult of death that thrived on videotaped beheadings as well suicide bombings against Shiites and "collaborators with the infidels" (often Iraqis lining up to join the newly formed police). Most important, by 2005 Zarqawi was obsessed with fomenting a jihad and civil war against the Shiite "snakes" whom he accused of working with the Americans to establish a democratic government that was not in line with his calls for a Sunni-dominated shariah law caliphate. Zarqawi seemed hell-bent on launching a civil war between Shiites and Sunnis that would further rend the fabric of the civil society the Americans and the Iraqi government were desperately trying to construct.

Zarqawi summed up the sick logic for his jihad on Shiites as follows:

Shi`ism is a religion that has nothing in common with Islam . . . The Shiites have been a sect of treachery and betrayal throughout history and throughout the ages. It is a creed that aims to combat the Sunnis. When the repulsive Baathist regime fell, the slogan of the Shi`a was "revenge, revenge, from Tikrit to al-Anbar." This shows the extent of their hidden rancor toward the Sunnis.

Targeting and hitting them in [their] religious, political, and military depth will provoke them to show the Sunnis their rabies and bare the teeth of the hidden rancor working in their breasts. If we succeed in dragging them into the arena of sectarian war, it will become possible to awaken the inattentive Sunnis.[102]

But Zarqawi's days as a jihadi emir (commander) were numbered as Mc-Chrystal's special forces tracked his movements around the northern town of Baqubah. Having discovered the identity of Zarqawi's spiritual advisor, JSOC then tracked this individual to a safe house outside of Baqubah in June 2006. After staking it out for six weeks, Zarqawi himself was spotted arriving. U.S. forces then decided to bomb the house with laser guided bombs delivered by F-16s. Remarkably, Zarqawi survived the explosion and stumbled outside, where he then died from lung damage, in the possession of U.S. troops.

Zarqawi was replaced as head of AQI by Abu Omar al Baghdadi and his deputy an Egyptian bomb expert named Abu Ayub al Masri. These two terrorist masterminds subsequently blew themselves up with suicide vests when they were tracked down and surrounded by Iraqi security forces in April 2010. It was at this time that a relatively unknown Islamic scholar named Abu Bakr al Baghdadi took over as the leader of AQI. It was Abu Bakr al Baghdadi who would later achieve fame in October 2006 as the founder of a new umbrella organization/iteration of AQI known as ISI, the Islamic State of Iraq (a bold move towards statehood that Al Qaeda Central did not approve).[103] When this group expanded into Syria in 2013, it changed its name to ISIS.

But the rise of ISIS was still many years away. Meanwhile, back in 2006, with the killing of the notorious Zarqawi, the new Shiite prime minister of Iraq, Nouri al Maliki, triumphantly proclaimed the death of the most wanted man in the country and bane of all Shiites. But the seeds of sectarian hatred that had been fiendishly planted by Zarqawi had begun to grow and flourish even though he was no longer alive to nurture them. Al Qaeda in Iraq continued to foment a civil war against the Shiites, who dominated the newly formed Iraqi government, police, and army, throughout 2006 and 2007.

But the Shiites' main religious leader, Grand Ayatollah al Sistani, ordered his followers not to give into the urge to fight back against the Sunnis, and most of his followers seemed to heed his calls for restraint. That changed on February 22, 2006, when AQI terrorists blew up the gold-domed Al Askari mosque in Samarra, an ancient edifice that is the holiest shrine for Shiites. Devout Shiites across Iraq reacted with outrage to this sacrilege and attacked

Sunnis, killing over a thousand. Sunni mosques across Iraq were also attacked and destroyed by Shiite mobs in the beginning of tit-for-tat violence that came to resemble a civil war. In Baghdad, Shiites began to ethnically cleanse Sunnis from their neighborhood and vice versa, as this previously mixed city descended into a spiral of Balkan-style violence. The Kosovo-style civil war and ethnic cleansing that Deputy Secretary of Defense Paul Wolfowitz had proclaimed would not break out in Iraq had come to pass.

An Iraqi source described this attempt by Shiites to conquer the capital and cleanse it of the opposing sectarian group as follows: "Neighborhoods were attacked as if they were fortresses; within a matter of hours they were surrounded, cut off from the rest of the city, besieged, invaded, and eventually emptied of their inhabitants.... Armed groups set up checkpoints in broad daylight and ruled over the local population with total impunity. People would leave home uncertain if they would make it back alive, or if their houses would still be standing if they did return."[104] An estimated 4.7 million Iraqis were displaced in the process as civil society in Iraq disintegrated.[105]

At this time, Moqtada al Sadr's Shiite militia created death squads, which began to systematically hunt and kill Sunnis in Baghdad and elsewhere. Their most notorious modus operandi was to use power drills to drill holes in the heads of Sunnis who were kidnapped at random. They also set up checkpoints and killed those who did not know the Shiite prayers and rituals. To compound matters, many of Sadr's followers infiltrated the government and essentially took control of the Ministries of Transportation, Agriculture, Interior, and Health. In essence, Sadr's Mahdi Army had "captured the very instruments of state," according to Michael Gordon and Bernard Trainor, and one minister of health was accused of using Health Ministry guards as death squads.[106]

Most important, Sadr's followers took control of the National Police, and this force along with pro-Iranian Shiite group known as the Badr Brigades began to partake in sectarian killings of Sunnis. In one typical example of the Shiite violence, Sadr's followers burst into the Ministry of Higher Education, publicly rounded up over one hundred workers who were Sunni, and executed them in cold blood.

By 2006, U.S. troops were recording roughly three thousand Iraqi deaths a month (i.e., roughly the number killed on 9/11) and more than 250 car bombings and suicide attacks a month.[107] A member of the U.S. Army's EJK (Extra-Judicial Killing) Task Force captured the gruesome nature of the butchery as follows: "I remember those days when we'd have up to one hundred murders a day. It was getting pretty gruesome in terms of bodies getting stacked up in morgues and not being able to burn them in a timely manner. We're talking about bodies stacked six to seven feet high. I don't mean to be gross, this is just what happened. Body fluids would get six to eight inches on the floor."[108] Another U.S. soldier would report, "Every patrol, you're finding dead people. Their eyes are gouged out. Their arms are broken."[109]

A third victim of the civil war was the ancient Christian community in the northern province of Nineveh. For centuries this group had intermingled with surrounding Muslims and had been protected by the Baathist regime in more recent decades. As the civil war unraveled the fabric of Iraqi society, this group experienced murders, ethnic cleansing, and the blowing up of their houses.[110]

As the Americans tried to combat the sectarian violence, they came under attack by Sadr's Mahdi Army followers and Shiites belonging to the pro-Iranian Badr Brigades. It was at this time that Iran, which was all too happy to see fellow Shiites turning neighboring Iraq into a quagmire for the American invaders, got into the act and shipped the Sadrists deadly IEDs known as EFPs (explosively formed penetrators or projectiles). While the U.S. military had developed heavily armored combat vehicles known as MRAPs (mine resistance ambush protected) to resist IEDs, the new EFPs could penetrate even these hardened vehicles. The powerful EFPs deployed by the Mahdi Army were also able to blow up such fighting vehicles as Strykers, Humvees, Bradleys, and even Abrams tanks with their molten copper warheads. The Iranians also provided the Badr Brigades and Mahdi Army with high-powered sniper rifles to kill U.S. troops.

As the insurgency spread into the Shiite lands of Baghdad and the south, a Sunni sniper named Juba posted videos on the Internet of himself picking off U.S. soldiers and was said to have shot thirty-seven Americans.[111] By 2007, the "peaceful and self-governing nation" that President Bush had predicted would be established in Iraq after the invasion had devolved into a bloody quagmire for the Americans.[112] Senator Edward Kennedy would famously call it "Bush's Vietnam."[113]

The mistake of sending in too small a force had been compounded by the firing of tens of thousands of Baathists, the disbanding of the Iraqi army and closing down of Sadr's newspaper. The clumsy U.S. response had compounded matters. The U.S. invasion had, as the Saudis predicted, also opened Pandora's box and released the pent-up demons of Sunni on Shiite violence with a vengeance in this country that had functioned prior to the arrival of the Americans (prior to the war Shiites and Sunnis often inter-married). Tens of thousands of Iraqis had died in the aftermath the U.S. invaded, and millions more had been made refugees. Terry Anderson has written in his book *Bush's Wars*, "No one was safe anywhere. Iraq belonged to militias, the resistance, terrorists, any man with a gun. The roads leading to Baghdad were war zones. Iraqis continued to live in a republic of fear."[114] If this were not enough, electricity in Baghdad, which had once run twenty-four hours a day, was now down to as little as six hours a day. And oil production, which the Neo-Cons had promised would pay for the invasion and rebuilding of Iraq, had plummeted from 2.6 million barrels to 1.1 owing to graft and sabotage by insurgents.[115]

Most Iraqis blamed the Americans for the collapse of their society and felt that the U.S. had invaded Iraq to seize its oil. On one occasion, when President Bush visited Iraq to sign a SOFA (Status of Forces Agreement) and gave a press conference, an Iraqi journalist threw his shoes at him (an Arabic sign of disrespect) and shouted, "This is a gift from the Iraqis; this is the farewell kiss, you dog!" Far from being welcomed as liberators, the Americans were now dying at the hands of both the Shiites and the Sunnis, and the U.S. military had too few troops to crush the insurgency or end the civil war.

Tragically, the invasion had backfired and both the Sunnis and the Shiites had become radicalized by the U.S. invasion and had come to be led by Islamic extremists who were at war with the Americans. The Sunni area to the south of Baghdad had become so dangerous for U.S. troops that it was now nicknamed the Triangle of Death. And most tellingly, the U.S. military was recording one thousand attacks on their troops per week.[116] A 2006 National Intelligence Estimate (NIE) by the country's various intelligence services stated that "the Iraq war has made the overall terrorism problem worse" as Shiites and former Baathist Sunnis become radicalized and joined the militants in their thousands.[117]

The rank-and-file U.S. troops in Iraq realized they were desperately undermanned for confronting the insurgency, terrorism, civil war, and chaos that had predominated during Phase IV (i.e., occupation). In Anbar Province, the Marines were so undermanned they took to putting uniforms on cardboard cutouts to intimidate insurgents who were attacking their positions. One Marine general told a visiting U.S. politician, "Senator, if anybody tells you we have enough troops over there when you get back, tell them to go to goddamn hell."[118] Another U.S. soldier said, "We had momentum going in and had Saddam's forces on the run. But we did not have enough troops."[119] There was, in General Bernard Trainor's words, a "chronic insufficiency of force."[120]

There was at this time a deep tension between the military, which wanted more troops, and the Neo-Cons and their allies in the White House who were opposed to this "mission escalation." An army officer in Iraq, Paul Arcangeli, said of Deputy Secretary of Defense Paul Wolfowitz (whom he described as "dangerously idealistic" and "crack-smoking stupid"), "I blame him for all this shit in Iraq. Even more than Rumsfeld, I blame him."[121] Former Central Command head General Anthony Zinni captured the tension when he said, "I don't know where the neocons came from. Somehow the neocons captured the president, they captured the vice president."[122] Zinni would also say, "I think—and this is just my opinion—that neocons didn't really give a shit what happened in Iraq and the aftermath [of the invasion]. I don't think they thought it would be this bad."[123]

It became increasingly obvious to former Marine general Zinni and to other commanders in the theater of action that more troops were needed to prevent the Shiite and Sunni militants, who had capitalized on the collapse of the Baathist Party to seize vast swathes of the country, from prevailing. America could lose the war if more troops were not urgently deployed to Iraq. This, however, went squarely against the grain of Rumsfeld's vision of a small, lithe army. Rumsfeld had a "fierce position" in opposition to the idea of sending in reinforcements.[124]

But Rumsfeld's position had been weakened considerably since the early days of the Afghan war, when his jocular, folksy press conferences with journalists made him the darling of the media. In April 2006 a group of generals had even called for his dismissal for "disastrously managing the war."[125] General Paul Eton, who served in Iraq, wrote that Rumsfeld was "incompetent strategically, operationally and tactically."[126] Rumsfeld had also become the target of the wrath of many Republicans, who blamed him for their huge defeat in the 2006 midterm elections, which were a sweep for the Democrats, who took control of both houses of Congress. The Democrats had hammered the Republicans for starting the increasingly unpopular war and had pinned the blame for the subsequent insurgency squarely on Bush and Rumsfeld. The Democrats had mocked Bush's 2006 claim that "absolutely we are winning."[127] The Democrats also made a point of reminding the Americans that the fiscally conservative Republicans were paying $1 billion per week to wage a destructive war across the world in Iraq.[128]

By this time polls showed that a majority of Americans believed they had been "intentionally misled" into going to war by the Bush administration.[129] Gallup polls also showed that 59 percent of Americans wanted U.S. troops out of Iraq and 60 percent called the war a mistake.[130] In addition, 51 percent of Americans had come to see "no link between the war in Iraq and the broader antiterror effort."[131]

It was not just average Americans who had turned against Rumsfeld's war; General William Odom, the former head of the National Security Agency, came out and called it "the greatest strategic disaster in American history."[132] Bush's numbers in the polls would plummet too, and he would become ranked as the most unpopular president in the history of polling with just a 28 percent approval rating (i.e., his numbers were even lower than Nixon's after Watergate).[133] At this time, popular bumper stickers on American cars read, "Heal the wounded, Bury the dead, Bring the troops home" and compared Bill Clinton's lie about his affair with Monica Lewinsky with the WMD hype stating "Clinton lied, Nobody died." New York real estate mogul Donald Trump, who would later run for president on the Republican ticket in 2016, would capture the frustrations of many in 2003 when he stated "The war's a mess" and "It wasn't a mistake to fight terrorism and fight it hard, and I guess maybe if I had to do it, I would have fought terrorism but not necessarily Iraq."[134]

On election day, November 7, 2006, Rumsfeld, who had come to be seen as both a lightning rod for increasing dissatisfaction with the war and a liability by the Republicans, offered his resignation (his deputy, Paul Wolfowitz, had already left the Pentagon by this time, as had many of the Neo-Cons who were blamed for the disaster in Iraq). Rumsfeld's replacement, ex-CIA director Robert Gates, came to office promising to change the course of the war. His arrival was roundly welcomed by the military, which saw him as a positive alternative to Rumsfeld. Most important, Gates showed himself much more willing to listen to the generals on the ground in Iraq and proved to be amicable to their pleas for more troops. Thus the pieces were put in place for a wave of U.S. reinforcements that would ultimately combine with unfolding events in Anbar Province to change the course of the war and give the Iraqi government a much-needed breathing space.

The 2007 Troop Surge and the Anbar Awakening

By 2007, a group of intellectuals and military officers led by retired general John Keane had come to the conclusion that Rumsfeld's "light footprint" policy and dependency on "standing up" the Iraqi army to replace the Americans was not working. They felt that more troops were needed to quash the violence in Iraq. When the head of U.S. troops in Iraq, General George Casey, came out against the troop increases, these officers met with Bush and called for the general to be removed.

In a meeting with Bush, this group then convinced the president to "double down" on his bet in Iraq and try to prevent a calamitous takeover of the country by Sunni and Shiite militants. In her history of the 2007 surge, Kimberly Kagan calls Bush's subsequent decision to take the politically unpopular decision of sending further reinforcements into the war in Iraq at a time when Senators Obama and Biden opposed the move, the "boldest stroke of his presidency."[135] Bush would later state: "In earlier operations Iraqi and American forces cleared many neighborhoods of terrorists and insurgents, but when our forces moved on to other targets, the killers returned. This time we will have the force levels we need to hold the areas that have been cleared." Thus was born the famous eighteen-month Bush troop "surge" of over twenty-eight thousand reinforcements (five brigades) that would bring the total number of U.S. soldiers in Iraq to 168,000.

The new man chosen to lead the counteroffensive was General David Petraeus, the former head of the 101st Airborne, who had previously brought a modicum of peace and stability to the northern Sunni city of Mosul. He had done so by limiting the firing of Baathists in his areas and engaging in hands-on construction and security projects with locals. In other words, he had gone his own way and was proudly doing local "nation building" and limiting the de-Baathification called for by Bremer and the Neo-Cons.[136] Petraeus's successful approach was based to a large extent on his previous deployment in Haiti, where he had engaged in Clinton-era nation reconstruction. Petraeus had a plan to do the same thing for all Iraq and implement a new style of warfare that was outlined in a new *Counterinsurgency Field Manual* he had helped create at Fort Leavenworth.

This manual called for a total revision of how the war was to be fought. Thus far U.S. troops had been largely isolated from the Iraqis and confined to massive FOBs (forward operating bases), except when they went out on patrols. While on patrol, U.S. troops had carried out a "kinetic" policy of "kicking in doors," "putting two shots in the chest," and attempting to quash the insurgency by brutally arresting MAMs (military-aged males), aged sixteen to sixty, who might be insurgents. During these patrols, one U.S. colonel said, "we had these dragnet arrests. You'd go into a village and just arrest everybody."[137] One U.S. Army intelligence office said of the Fourth Infantry Division, "The 4th ID was bad. These guys were looking for a fight. I saw so many instances of abuses of civilians, intimidating civilians, our jaws dropped."[138] One Marine officer proudly compared his regiment to a motorcycle gang and said, "We drive around, beat up bad guys, then move to the next town."[139]

These brutal and humiliating U.S. sweeps and mass arrests of Iraqis, many if not most of whom were uninvolved in insurgent activity, acted as a prime recruiter for the insurgency. One Iraqi insurgent was to refer to them as follows in a warning to the U.S. president and people: "Once again we call upon you, if you are serious about looking after the safety of your soldiers, to leave our country immediately, or we will take revenge for every Iraqi killed or humiliated and every house ransacked. You should know by now that the Iraqis are now well aware of the big lie you have told them that you are here to liberate Iraq from dictatorship."[140]

After seeing an U.S. Army unit cordon off an Iraqi village and then go through it kicking in doors and arresting Iraqis, one U.S. general, Jack Keane, said. "We're breeding an insurgency here."[141] Petraeus also felt that this twin policy of keeping the U.S. troops from interacting on a daily basis with the populations they were supposed to be protecting combined with overly aggressive sweep tactics was backfiring and creating more enemies than America could kill. His belief was that "an operation that kills five insurgents is counterproductive if collateral damage (i.e., accidental deaths or destruction) leads to the recruitment of fifty more insurgents."[142] The new COIN (counterinsurgency) manual that would be adapted under General Petraeus warned against an overemphasis on killing and capturing the enemy instead of protecting the population. Among other things it stated:

"The more you protect your force, the less secure you are."
"The more force you use, the less effective you are."
"Sometimes doing nothing is the best reaction."[143]

To a degree, the new "bottom-up" COIN policy would also be based on his own achievements in Mosul and on those of one Colonel H. R. McMaster, whose successful strategy of "clearing, holding and building" in the north-western border town of Tal Afar had begun to be emulated. This new "popula-tion-centric" approach criticized the military for keeping its forces confined to large bases to protect them. The new *Counterinsurgency Field Manual* instead called on U.S. troops to get out of their FOBs and interact with, and protect, the local population, to win them over by living in smaller JSS (joint security stations) with Iraqi soldiers or in COPs (command outposts). This would put a human face on the local U.S. troops and help win hearts and minds.

The counter-insurgency manual also stressed the need to win over and rehabilitate Iraqi insurgents who might have joined the insurgency because of overly aggressive U.S. tactics (i.e., "door kicking" in U.S. military parlance). This latter point actually coincided with previous developments that were happening in the western Sunni province of Anbar at this time that ulti-mately helped Petraeus implement his ambitious COIN plans. As it trans-pired, Anbar, Iraq's largest province, had by 2006 come to suffer under the rule of fanatical AQI insurgents. These Islamist militants had forced women to wear the *abaya* (full veil); outlawed alcohol and cigarettes; taken power from the hands of local tribal leaders known as sheikhs; enforced strict Is-lamic shariah law (they even forbade women from buying phallic shaped cu-cumbers and began cutting the hands off of thieves); taken over mosques; closed schools for teaching secular subjects; taken control of smuggling, (which had previously been controlled by local tribes); and taken to kidnap-ping local girls and women and taking them as their wives.

The AQI operatives had essentially overturned the old tribal order in this region and antagonized the local Sunni sheikhs who had previously wel-comed them. Many Sunni tribal sheikhs came to see the AQI militants who terrorized them on a daily basis as a worse enemy than the Americans in their FOBs. Few saw AQI as worse of an enemy than Abdul Sattar Abu Risha, a tribal leader from the Anbar capital of Ramadi, whose father and two brothers had been killed by AQI. In the fall of 2006, Abu Risha united with several other tribal sheikhs and created the Anbar Sahwa (Awakening). This alliance of Sunni tribes that were threatened by Sunni AQI then took to kill-ing AQI and fighting them for power and resources. Many of the Anbar Awakening fighters were themselves ex-insurgents who had now turned their guns on AQI. The American military were thrilled by this development, which took thousands of their enemies off the battlefield. Most important, Abu Risha declared, "The [U.S.-led] coalition forces are friendly forces, not occupying forces!"[144]

In response to these welcome developments, local American commanders began an ad hoc policy of paying these Anbar Awakening militias to patrol their neighborhoods to keep AQI out and to actively fight against AQI terrorists. The Americans now had thousands of armed, Arab-speaking, local fighter-guides to help them track down AQI operatives in areas the Anbar Sahwa militias knew intimately. The Anbar Awakening fighters became known in U.S. military parlance as "Sons of Iraq" or "Concerned Local Citizens" and were given bright fluorescent orange crossing guard belts to delineate them from AQI insurgents.

In this respect, the U.S. military benefited from fortuitous events beyond its control and took advantage of AQI's arrogance. At this time, the Americans came to have a deeper appreciation of the tribes, a group that Wolfowitz had dismissed as unimportant.[145] Clearly in Anbar, the tribes that had been antagonized by Al Qaeda were the center of gravity.

In response to these developments among the Sunni tribes of Anbar, AQI (which it must be stressed was also Sunni) declared "open war" on the Anbar Awakening for siding with the "filthy crusaders." Ultimately, the AQI terrorists managed to kill Sheikh Abu Risha in a bombing soon after he met with President Bush in September 2007. But by then the U.S. surge reinforcement troops (often at the platoon level) had bolstered the Anbar Awakening fighters and helped them spread to other provinces. As the U.S. surge reinforcements arrived and left their FOBs to live in smaller command outposts and work with the Anbar Awakening fighters, they pushed AQI out of Ramadi and other cities.

In essence, the surge reinforced the Anbar Awakening movement and helped it spread throughout the Sunni lands of central Iraq. By this time the Americans were working under the new principles of Petraeus's COIN, which called on them to protect the local population instead of seeing it as the enemy. One U.S. advisor noticed a drastic change in the attitude of American troops toward the Iraqis and stated, "In '03 the guys were Christian crusaders seeking revenge for 9/11. Today they are advising Iraqis in a way they couldn't back then."[146]

Clearly the Americans had also committed to the long haul now that they had discarded Rumsfeld's plan for a short war. To compound matters, AQI, which had put the cart before the horse and took to arrogantly calling itself the Islamic State of Iraq (ISI), began to clash with other Sunni insurgent groups for power and resources. When its fighters killed members of the Baathist 1920s Brigade, the latter group turned to the United States for help in fighting AQI. The Americans were only too happy to assist the Baathists in this "red on red" violence against AQI. Many insurgents then left the insurgency and created local versions of the Anbar Awakening. These came to include such groups as the Ameriya Knights, Ghazaliya Guardians, Salahuddin Awakening Congress, Baghdad Patriots, The Desert Protectors, and Knights of the Two Rivers.

By mid-2007, the U.S. had approximately 103,000 so-called Sons of Iraq on the payroll and were using these Sunnis to help spot IEDs, hunt AQI, and patrol neighborhoods. This "Sunni Surge" in essence took 103,000 fighters off the enemy's rosters and made them U.S. allies. While the Shiite-dominated government of Prime Minister Maliki was unhappy about the U.S. working with tens of thousands of armed Sunnis, the Anbar Awakening helped stabilize the provinces surrounding Baghdad, and this allowed Petraeus to use his surge troops to directly retake the capital.

Petraeus and AQI knew all too well that Baghdad and its population were the center of gravity in Iraq. Whoever gained control of the capital could control the country. As it was, the United States estimated that 70 percent of Baghdad was under the control of the Mahdi Army or Sunni insurgents. The U.S. military was also aware that AQI and other Sunni insurgent groups were also based in the "belts" of suburban neighborhoods surrounding the capital. In these belts the terrorists produced IEDs and car bombs, stored munitions, and trained fighters. Previously there had been too few U.S. troops to move from the capital into the suburbs. But now with surge reinforcements of five additional brigades, Petraeus finally had the means to attack the Sunni belt sanctuaries and retake the center of the city as well.

The so-called Baghdad Security Plan (known to the supporting Iraqi troops as Operation Farhd al Qanoon—Enforcing the Law), which would take advantage of more than twenty thousand extra troops in the capital, began on February 14, 2007. Petraeus and his number two, General Raymond Odierno, dispersed thousands of troops from their FOBs into Baghdad's neighborhoods to carry out patrols with Iraqi forces. There they began neighborhood-by-neighborhood sweeps designed to flush out Shiite death squads and Sunni insurgents and uncover weapons caches. As expected, the U.S. death toll initially climbed as the U.S. and allied Iraqi troops plunged into some of the toughest neighborhoods in Baghdad to defeat the enemy. But ultimately the violence began to fall off, and the Americans were able to report a 50 percent decline in Iraqi deaths and a 90 percent drop in attacks in Anbar Province. Most important, the Americans were now protecting the Iraqi people instead of bursting into their homes and arresting them.

Part of this success came from a concomitant "surge of concrete" as the U.S. troops constructed vast walls of concrete to keep Shiite and Sunni death squads from entering one another's neighborhoods in Baghdad to butcher one another. While AQI tried preventing the construction of the walls, they failed, and this drastically brought down civilian deaths. These walls also froze the sectarian civil war, which by this time had largely been won by the Shiites, and divided much of this once-unified city into Sunni and Shiite quarters.

Having gained control of much of the city center, the real battle then shifted to the suburban belt safe havens, which were dominated by Sunnis. In June 2007, the United States launched Operation Phantom Thunder, which led to the conquest of the belts and neighboring provinces such as Diyala and Baquba. Now AQI was on the run as they were hunted by Anbar Awakening militias and U.S. and Iraqi army troops (largely Shiites). The U.S. was no longer playing "Whack a Mole." Its troops were now out on the streets occupying neighborhoods and working to protect the local population from the terrorists. The U.S. troops had taken to heart one commander's orders to "Get out of your humvees, get out of your tanks, your Brads, and walk around. Stop commuting to war."[147] U.S. troops sallied out from their FOBs to retake neighborhoods and created numerous new posts in abandoned schools, factories, and apartment buildings. At one point, General David Petraeus even walked the streets of a Baghdad neighborhood ominously known as Jihad without body armor on and freely talked with locals to demonstrate how the new policy was working.[148]

As a semblance of peace settled on many, but not all, neighborhoods in Baghdad and its environs, many Iraqis for the first time came to see the Americans not as "door-kicking" foreign invaders, but as their protectors. The Sunnis in particular had come to see the Americans as their protectors vis-à-vis the Shiites. Petraeus's surge and new COIN tactics had paid off, despite considerable criticism back home, including one attack by the liberal group MoveOn.org, which had labeled him "General Betrayus" in an ad in the *New York Times*.[149] On another occasion, when Petraeus and Iraq ambassador Ryan Crocker sought defend the surge to Congress, a skeptical Senator Hillary Clinton told him in September 2007 that his testimony and reports on the surge's success required "a willing suspension of disbelief."[150]

Having silenced his skeptics and succeeded against all expectations,

Petraeus was feted in America as the man who had saved the war in Iraq and given the Shiite Maliki government in Baghdad a breathing space. No one thought the Sunni insurgents had been totally defeated, but AQI was now no longer an existential threat to the Iraqi government; it had been put on the run by JSOC night raids and Anbar Awakening militias in particular. By 2008, CIA director Michael Hayden would declare that AQI or the Islamic State in Iraq was "near strategic defeat."

If the rise of Anbar Awakening among disgruntled Sunni tribes and the success of the surge were not enough, in August 2007 the militant Shiite leader Moqtada al Sadr called a truce after his followers got into a bloody firefight with Iraqi government troops (mainly fellow Shiites) in Basra and other places that cost scores of lives. Thus the Sunni insurgency, the Shiite insurgency, and the Sunni-Shiite civil war were, to a considerable extent, defused by late 2007. While many Republican and Democrat critics had called for the withdrawal of U.S. troops from the "lost war in Iraq" and had considered Bush's surge to be doubling down on a bad bet, the president and his star general had prevailed in the end. There had been no Saigon-style retreat by U.S. helicopters from a besieged Green Zone in Baghdad as many had predicted. With concrete walls separating the warring parties in Baghdad, Anbar Awakening militias guarding the Sunni neighborhoods and towns, Sadr's followers honoring the truce (Sadr later traveled to Iran for several years to study Islam), and an Iraqi army and police being trained by American advisors, calamity had been narrowly averted. It had been a close thing, but Iraq now had the breathing space it needed to rebuild.

Presidents Bush and Maliki were so confident of success that they signed a Status of Forces Agreement (SOFA) in 2008, which called for U.S. troops to withdraw from Iraq by December 31, 2011 (this was when the infamous incident happened wherein an Iraqi journalist threw his shoes at Bush). Many Republican critics later accused the subsequent president, Barack Obama, of prematurely withdrawing U.S. troops from Iraq in 2011 and "cutting and running." In actuality, however, the treaty that laid the groundwork for this later withdrawal was signed by a war weary Bush and the democratically elected Iraqi government, which wanted an end to the highly unpopular U.S. occupation.

But for all the fact that disaster had been averted (or at least fended off for the time being as history would later show with the rise of ISIS in the summer of 2014) and withdrawal treaty signed, the legacy of the Bush White House's invasion of Iraq was not to be positive. Colonel Tom Greenwood would, for example, describe the new Shiite-dominated Iraq the Americans had installed as "little more than an Iranian proxy," and he would state that "we have destabilized the region worse than Saddam Hussein ever did."[151]

If the creation of an Iranian-allied Shiite government in Iraq was not bad enough, much of central Iraq had almost been transformed into an Al Qaeda in Iraq jihadist state as well. There were still thousands of AQI terrorists operating in Iraq, and they continued to wage a low-level terror campaign. These Sunni militants were just bidding their time. All those involved in the war realized it had also been an incredibly close call and that events beyond the control of the Americans (i.e., the Anbar Awakening 'surge' of 103,000 Iraqi troops, the victory of the Shiites in the civil war, and the calling of a truce by Sadr's forces) had played a key role in turning the tables at the last minute. Military historian Thomas Ricks was to sum up the course of the war in his best-selling history of the Iraq war, *Fiasco*, as follows:

> President George W. Bush's decision to invade Iraq in 2003 ultimately may come to be seen as one of the most profligate actions in the history of American foreign policy. The consequences of his choice won't be clear for decades, but it already is abundantly apparent in mid-2006 that the US government went to war with scant solid international support on the basis of incorrect information—about weapons of mass destruction and a supposed nexus between Saddam Hussein and al Qaeda's terrorism—and then occupied the country negligently. Thousands of US troops and an untold number of Iraqis have died. Hundreds of billions of dollars have been spent, many of them squandered.[152]

In Ricks's opinion, the war had almost been lost owing to the civilian leadership's mistakes, which had then necessitated a belated surge to stave off defeat. Robert Merry, writing for the conservative *National Review*, was even more damning in his succinct critique of the vice president's role in getting America involved in the war in Iraq:

> Cheney was wrong to support the invasion of Iraq in 2003. He was irresponsibly wrong when he assured the nation, without serious evidence, that Iraq's Saddam Hussein possessed weapons of mass destruction. He was wrong to argue that Saddam was in alignment with Al Qaeda leaders. He was wrong when he assured the American

people that U.S. forces would be greeted as liberators rather than invaders. He was wrong to think that Western-style democracy could be planted upon the soil of a culture that contains doctrinal objections to significant elements of Western-style democracy. He was wrong to miss the implications of destroying the balance of power between Iraq and Iran. He was wrong not to see the consequences of the ongoing societal chaos in Iraq that would be unleashed by the invasion.[153]

The new secretary of defense appointed by Bush, ex-CIA director Robert Gates, would subsequently tell West Point graduates, "In my opinion, any future defense secretary who advises the president to again send a big American land army into Asia or into the Middle East or Africa should have his head examined."[154] The consensus in America, even among Republicans who had strongly supported Bush initially, was that the war had not been worth it in terms of lives and money wasted. A 2007 poll found that Bush, whose popularity it will be recalled skyrocketed after the 9/11 attacks, had fallen precipitously. According to a *Newsweek* poll taken in that year, 73 percent of Americans disapproved of Bush's handling of the Iraq war, and 65 percent disapproved of the job he was doing.[155]

The highly unpopular war played a key role in Barack Obama's subsequent victory over Republican candidate John McCain in the 2008 presidential elections. Obama caught the popular mood when he labeled Iraq "a war of choice" and Afghanistan a "war of necessity." He also famously said, "I am not opposed to all wars. I'm opposed to dumb wars."[156] A CNN poll found that 51 percent of Americans agreed with Obama's description of the war in Iraq as "dumb."[157] Obama promised to withdraw U.S. troops from the unpopular "elective war" in Iraq as soon as possible, and this made him popular among his Democratic base and among undecideds (by 2009 a Pew Research poll would show that 76 percent of Americans supported getting U.S. troops out of Iraq).[158] By this time, even Republican politicians had come to see the costly war as a drain on the economy during an economic recession which began in 2008, and there were Republican calls by fiscally conservative members of the party for nation building at home, instead of in the Middle East.

Among the newly elected President Obama's first moves upon taking control of the White House was traveling to Iraq, where he told hundreds of cheering American troops it was time for the Iraqis to "take responsibility for their country and for their sovereignty." Obama followed Bush's SOFA (Status of Forces Agreement) signed with Prime Minister Maliki in December 2008, and all U.S. troops were pulled out of Iraqi cities by June 2009 and combat operations declared over on August 31, 2010.[159]

Obama was to subsequently reject the Bush Doctrine, which called for unilateral, full-scale invasions of nations thought to be harboring terrorists, and the whole interventionist, aggressive mindset of the Neo-Cons. In the summer of 2015, he was to put the era of triumphalism that led to the Bush invasion of Iraq behind him when he boldly stated:

> Now, when I ran for president eight years ago as a candidate who had opposed the decision to go to war in Iraq, I said that America didn't just have to end that war. We had to end the mindset that got us there in the first place. It was a mindset characterized by a preference for military action over diplomacy, a mindset that put a premium on unilateral U.S. action over the painstaking work of building international consensus, a mindset that exaggerated threats beyond what the intelligence supported. Leaders did not level with the American people about the costs of war, insisting that we could easily impose our will on a part of the world with a profoundly different culture and history.[160]

Meanwhile in Iraq, by the summer of 2009 the surge troops had come home, and most remaining U.S. troops had been withdrawn from Iraqi cities, and Iraqi army (primarily Shiite) troops had taken their place. The Americans' role was now to "advise and assist" Iraqi forces that were standing up at this time. The Iraqis now had a breathing space to rebuild their country as the American surge troops came home, the Brits withdrew from Basra, and the U.S. role in the bloody war began to come to an end. That breathing space had been built on the lives of thousands of U.S. troops who had sacrificed their lives in the deserts of Iraq to make the tentative stability possible.

Ironically, as the Americans withdrew from Iraq in fulfillment of the SOFA treaty signed in 2008 by presidents Bush and Maliki, titled "Agreement Between the United States and the Republic of Iraq on the Withdrawal of US Forces from Iraq," it was the Sunnis who were now reluctant to see them go. While Prime Minister Maliki and Shiites celebrated their departure, the Sunnis, including many ex-insurgents, had come to see the Americans as protectors against the now dominant Shiites. The Sunnis had real fears for their future in a country controlled by a Shiite government that appeared to be moving closer to their enemy, Shiite Iran. Few of them saw Maliki as an honest power broker in the way the Americans had ultimately turned out to be.

Tensions were kept under control until the last U.S. forces withdrew to Kuwait on December 18, 2011, in a subdued ceremony commemorating the deaths of an estimated 190,000 Iraqis and almost forty-five hundred Americans in the calamitous war fought to prevent Hussein from providing nonexistent WMDs to Al Qaeda in Pakistan.[161] After eight and a half years, the war that Rumsfeld had predicted would last six months "at the most" was finally over.[162] But even as Obama fulfilled his campaign promise and ended the unpopular war in Iraq, he had to deal with one last major land war in Eurasia that had been bequeathed to him by the Bush administration; the war in Afghanistan.

By the time of the outbreak of the 2006–7 Iraqi civil war, Afghanistan had largely fallen off the American radar screen and was hardly covered by the media. The war against Al Qaeda Central and the Taliban had always been a sideshow for the Bush administration's main objective, the overthrow of Saddam Hussein. This refocus from Afghanistan to Iraq had taken its toll on the original theater of the war on terror. Afghanistan had become widely known in America as the "Forgotten War" and had suffered in terms of troops, finances, and other resources while the United States focused its energies on defeating its newly forged enemies, Baathist-Sunni-Islamist insurgents and Shiites in Iraq.

The distraction of Operation Iraqi Freedom had been welcomed by the down-but-far-from-out Taliban and Al Qaeda Central, who had most definitely *not* forgotten the "forgotten war" in Afghanistan. While Iraq sucked the oxygen out of Central Command (which originally deployed a mere six thousand troops in Texas-sized Afghanistan), the Taliban regrouped in the wild tribal regions of neighboring Pakistan and prepared to launch a full-scale insurgency. By 2003, the Taliban had reawakened their local networks and begun to swarm across the lightly guarded southern Afghan provinces of Kandahar and Helmand. The small number of U.S. troops and unreliable Afghan troops were simply unable to prevent the infiltration and conquest of much of the southeast by a highly motivated Taliban foe. By 2007, the Taliban had moved to within less than an hour's drive from the capital of Kabul. Many observers feared for the survival of the Afghan government of President Hamid Karzai, who had come to be derisively known as the "Mayor of Kabul" owing to the increasingly limited amount of territory he controlled.

An alarmed Obama, who had famously called the war in Afghanistan "the war of necessity" when he was running of president, was convinced by his generals that the democratically elected government that the United States had installed in Kabul was in dire threat of being overrun. Rajiv Chandrasekaran has written a history of the war in the Afghan south and states, "For Obama, Afghanistan had been the good war, the war that began with the two fallen towers, not the war that stemmed from faulty intelligence and exaggerated claims of weapons of mass destruction."[163] Obama had called Afghanistan "the war that has to be won."[164] In Obama's mind it was high time for America to remember the forgotten war in Afghanistan before the Taliban reconquered the country and allowed it to return to being a sanctuary for the Al Qaeda terrorists who had attacked America on 9/11.

This was the background for Obama's decision to refocus the American war effort from Iraq back to the original target of the "War on Terror" and send tens of thousands of U.S. troops to Afghanistan to fight a newly galvanized Taliban, which was on the march. What follows is an analysis of the second round of fighting in Afghanistan that would make the Afghan War the longest conflict in American history. It was this ground war, and a stealthier war fought by CIA drones in the tribal zones of neighboring Pakistan, that would ultimately decide the fate of the man whose actions had originally called forth America's War on Terror: Osama bin Laden.

CHAPTER 5

Remembering the "Forgotten War" in Afghanistan

The war against Iraq was not integral to the GWOT [Global War on Terror] but rather a detour from it.
— Jeffrey Record, U.S. Army War College's Strategic Studies Institute

We have to understand that the situation is precarious and urgent here in Afghanistan, and I believe this has to be the central focus, the central front, in the battle against terrorism.
— Presidential candidate Barack Obama speaking in Kabul, Afghanistan

The Taliban Sanctuary in Pakistan

By 2003 it became clear that predictions that the Taliban had been destroyed in 2001–2's Operation Enduring Freedom and that the relegation of the Afghan campaign to a "manhunt" were premature. Mullah Omar, who had last been seen riding off on the back of a moped as his state collapsed around him in December 2001, appeared to have retained his authority as the Commander of the Faithful. His forces regrouped just across the border in the Pashtun sanctuaries in Pakistan's remote FATA (Federally Administered Tribal Agencies) region and prepared to wage a guerilla jihad against the U.S.-led coalition. Various guerilla fronts were then created in Afghanistan, and these were run by Taliban *shuras* (councils) based in Quetta (capital of the Baluchistan Province of Pakistan) and Wana (the largest city in the FATA province of South Waziristan). As the Taliban retreated across the Afghan-

Pakistani border into the seven Rhode Island–sized provinces of the FATA, this area became known as "Talibanistan."

The Taliban quickly took over this wild, isolated land and enforced their strict brand of Islam among the Pashtun tribesmen of the autonomous region, from the province of Bajaur Agency in the north to their main area of focus, the provinces of North and South Waziristan in the south. There they began to recruit local Pashtun militants, who soon formed their own distinct Pakistani Taliban movement. The *Pakistani* Taliban would ultimately declare war on the Pakistani state in 2007 following the Lal Masjid-Red Mosque siege (to be discussed below), but Mullah Omar and the original *Afghan* Taliban would be protected by America's "frenemy allies," the Pakistanis, and focus their efforts on retaking Afghanistan.

The Americans and the Pakistanis were thus at odds when it came to Mullah Omar and the main Afghan Taliban group he led. One journalist described the Afghan Taliban's sanctuary in Pakistan's Pashtun tribal zones, which include much of north Baluchistan, as follows: "As I traveled through Pakistan and particularly the Pashtun lands bordering Afghanistan, I felt as if I were moving through a Taliban spa for rehabilitation and inspiration. . . . Quetta had become a kind of free zone where strategies could be formed, funds picked up, interviews given and victories relished."[1]

While the Pakistanis officially claimed to be "with" the United States in the war against the Taliban, they were clearly reluctant to move against their former Afghan Taliban clients and blatantly allowed them to regroup on their territory. The Pakistanis were both with and against the U.S. in the War on Terror. In the process, Pakistani leader Pervez Musharraf managed to acquire some US$10 billion in Coalition Support Funds for his country's initial efforts, which were mainly directed against foreign Al Qaeda operatives, not against local Afghan Taliban (the support funds given to Pakistan would later soar to $26 billion). Essentially the Americans bought the Pakistanis to help them against fleeing Al Qaeda (whom they arrested and delivered to the Americans), but they proved to be unreliable allies in the fight against the Afghan Taliban, whom they had midwifed.

In the meantime, the FATA became a cross border sanctuary for the exiled Afghan Taliban and newly formed Pakistani Taliban. The Pakistani army had never entered into this autonomous tribal zone and was reluctant to do so at the behest of the distrusted Americans to fight the Taliban, who had previously been their proxies. This allowed the Taliban to commence a guerilla campaign against the undermanned American forces in neighboring

Afghan provinces of the south and east that were inhabited by fellow Pashtuns (Pashtuns live on both sides of the border).

On several occasions the Americans prodded the Pakistani military to enter the FATA region and destroy the Taliban's insurgent/terrorist sanctuaries in this remote tribal zone. But the Pakistani government's operations were thwarted by a lack of real will and unexpectedly determined resistance by the Pakistani Taliban. On two occasions, the Pakistani army invaded the FATA under U.S. pressure. But ultimately Pakistani troops withdrew in defeat after signing humiliating peace treaties with the Pakistani Taliban, who defined the truces as an act of capitulation on the part of the Pakistani government. Thus the Afghan and Pakistani Taliban created a de facto state in the border regions of Afghanistan and Pakistan and used it as springboard to attack both the U.S.-led coalition in Afghanistan and, ultimately, the Pakistanis as well (in the case of the Pakistani Taliban).

The Taliban reinfiltration into Afghanistan from their Pakistani border sanctuaries typically began when small groups of Taliban vanguard units entered districts in Zabul, Uruzgan, Kandahar, and Helmand Provinces in conjunction with local supporters who had hidden weapons caches. They then threatened and intimidated pro-Karzai government mullahs or elders and killed them if they resisted. Their next step was to set up Islamic "shadow" courts, which administered the sort of swift, uncorrupted justice the conservative Pashtuns favored. These courts often appealed to local Pashtuns who had grown discontented with the corruption found in the President Karzai's Afghan government courts.

Then the Taliban began recruiting local men to join their units. These units engaged in planting land mines, frontal assaults on Afghan police checkpoints, assassinating government officials or anyone suspected of collaborating with the Karzai government, and other insurgent activities. Their terrorist acts ranged from beheading schoolteachers who had begun teaching girls, to killing several Karzai-appointed governors in bombings.

From 2003 to 2004 Taliban units secretly infiltrated a swath of Afghan provinces ranging from Nuristan and Kunar in the northeast to Helmand and Kandahar in the south. With the Americans distracted in Iraq, there were too few troops to prevent the Taliban's infiltration. Local Pashtuns sensed that the tide was turning in favor of the Taliban and, out of fear or sympathy with them, began to assist them. By 2007 (i.e., the year of General Petraeus' surge in Iraq), as much as a third of Afghanistan had fallen to the resurgent Taliban who, like the mujahideen before them, controlled the countryside while the government controlled the towns. At this time, the U.S. presence in such northeastern provinces as Nuristan or Kunar was limited owing to a reluctance on the part of the Bush administration to engage in major nation-building activities in Afghanistan. But it was in the south that the Taliban made their greatest efforts to seize territory.

The southern front was given to a Taliban commander named Mullah Dadullah, who soon became the most feared terrorist in Afghanistan. His story is the story of the Taliban resurrection in Helmand, Zabul, and Kandahar Provinces. Mullah Dadullah was a Pashtun mujahideen fighter in the 1980s. He lost a leg in the Afghan civil war of the 1990s while fighting against Tajik forces in the western town of Herat. For this reason he was sometimes known as Dadullah i Leng (the Cripple). Others have called him the "Afghan Zarqawi" for his penchant for beheading his victims in the fashion of the infamous Iraqi Jordanian terrorist Abu Musab Zarqawi. Dadullah took advantage of the small number of U.S. forces in Kandahar and neighboring Afghan province of Helmand (no more than three thousand U.S. troops were stationed at Kandahar Airport and at a few bases) to reestablish fighting units throughout the vastness of the south. These forces then began to launch swarm attacks on coalition forces in 2005 but sustained heavy losses in this sort of frontal combat and reverted back to mujahideen-style guerilla warfare.

It was not Dadullah's guerilla tactics, however, that gained him fame, but his bloodthirsty acts of terrorism. He seemed to have been impressed by the terror tactics of Zarqawi, who made decapitations his calling card. Inspired by Zarqawi's DVDs (which made their way to Afghanistan via AQI emissaries), Dadullah had himself filmed using a small knife to hack off the heads of suspected "CIA spies." These videos, and others of Dadullah training with his troops and preparing suicide bombers, were soon selling like hotcakes in the Pashtun lands on either side of the Afghanistan-Pakistan border. Many Taliban recruits were drawn to his macabre Iraqi-style executions and cult of martyrdom. In one unbearably gruesome video Mullah Dadullah even guided a twelve-year-old boy in hacking off the head of a man described as a spy.

It is his use of suicide bombings, however, that gained Mullah Dadullah his greatest notoriety. It was Dadullah who transformed Kandahar into the number-one target for suicide bombings by 2006. He recruited hundreds of suicide bombers from the Pashtun madrassas (seminaries) in Pakistan's tribal areas and threatened to release hundreds more on his targets. While suicide bombing was once taboo among the Taliban, Dadullah converted them to this Arab tactic and made it his weapon of choice. One cannot underestimate the impact this fierce commander had on destabilizing the southern Pashtun provinces of Zabul, Uruzgan, Helmand, and Kandahar. His name became a byword for terror, and his penchant for flaunting his power by giving interviews to reporters made him the Taliban's most famous field commander.

But it was this weakness that may have gotten him killed when his movements were reported by a spy. Dadullah's reign of terror came to an end in May of 2007, when he was tracked by British NATO forces as he crossed into Afghanistan from Pakistan. He was subsequently killed in an assault on his compound, and his body was taken to Kandahar. There the jubilant governor showed his one-legged corpse to reporters to prove that the dreaded Dadullah was finally dead.

But by then his tactic of suicide bombing had come to be adopted by the Taliban, who called them "Mullah Omar's missiles." The original impetus for suicide bombings had, however, originally come from Arab Al Qaeda operatives, who carried out two to three bombings per year on Afghan government and U.S. and NATO troops from 2002 to 2004. These demonstrative acts and videos of successful suicide bombings in Iraq seem to have convinced the Taliban to condone this alien tactic. By 2005 the Taliban had launched a tentative suicide bombing campaign that saw as many as twenty-three suicide attacks on Afghan targets, including one powerful bomb in Kandahar that killed the Kabul police chief and twenty others.

In the following year the campaign escalated to over 130 suicide bombings. The destabilizing impact that these attacks had can perhaps best be imagined by those who remember the panic that swept the United States when a domestic terrorist known as the Beltway Sniper stalked Americans in 2002. In the aftermath of bombings, U.S. and coalition troops on "hearts and minds" campaigns came to fear crowds for fear suicide bombers might be in them. In one case, panicked U.S. Marines gunned down innocent civilians after a suicide attack, and foreigners and government officials now began to move more cautiously, knowing that suicide bombers were potentially waiting for them.

Despite the seeming randomness of the attacks, patterns nonetheless began to emerge as I discovered through my own research on the ground in Afghanistan for the CIA's Counter Terrorism Center. It soon became obvious to me that, for all the fact that the Afghan *fedayeen* (suicide bombers) had been inspired by their Iraqi counterparts, they had developed their own targeting characteristics. For example, while Iraqi bombers aimed for high civilian body counts with the aim of shredding the fabric of society, Afghan suicide bombers were more inclined to go after "hard" (government, police, and military) targets rather than "soft" (civilian) targets. This trend seemed to fit the Pashtun warrior code (the bombers tended to be Pashtuns), with its emphasis on acts of martial valor. While Arab suicide bombers in Iraq seemed to have had no compunction about killing unarmed women and children, Afghan Taliban bombers were clearly reluctant to do so. Instead the Taliban bombers tended to go after NATO convoys, government buildings, checkpoints, military bases, policemen, and government installations.[2] This tendency helped explain another bizarre characteristic of the Taliban suicide bombers, their low kill ratio. Hard military targets are harder to kill than soft civilian targets. In many cases the Afghan Taliban bombers killed only themselves and one or two others, usually civilian bystanders. There was also a strange trend whereby Taliban suicide bombers in dozens of cases per year set off their bombs and killed only themselves.

But for all their ineptitude, many bombers succeeded, and in 2007 the country experienced 160 bombings. The primary provinces that were targeted were Kandahar, Khost, and Kabul, with most bombs going off in the Pashtun belt. Surprisingly, there were no bombings in the Hazara Shiite lands, a trend that differentiated the Afghan bombers from their counterparts in Iraq, who targeted Shiites. There have also been three large-scale and deadly suicide bombing attacks in Afghanistan. These have included the November 2007 bombing of a sugar factory in Baghlan Province, which killed seventy-five to one hundred people; the February 2008 bombing of a dog fight in Kandahar, which killed eighty; and the July 2008 bombing of the Indian Embassy in Kabul, which killed eighty-five (this attack was carried out with Pakistani ISI [Inter Service Intelligence] assistance and demonstrated the abiding links between the Afghan Taliban and their former allies the Pakistanis).

Perhaps no Afghan insurgent was more closely linked to the Pakistani ISI than the Afghan fighter Jalaluddin Haqqani and his son Sirajuddin, who took over operations long before rumors spread of his father's reported death in 2015. Haqqani had previously been a Pakistani-sponsored mujahideen in 1980s but had gone over to the Taliban when they approached his eastern Pashtun lands in the provinces of Khost, Paktia, and Paktika in the mid-1990s. When the Taliban regime fell in 2001, he crossed over the border into the FATA of North Waziristan with his followers. There he was welcomed by local Pakistani Pashtun tribes who were linked to him from the 1980s anti-Soviet jihad. He then set up a powerful, semi-independent insurgent network that boldly carried out insurgent attacks and suicide bombings in his former bailiwick of Khost, Paktia, and Paktika Provinces in Afghanistan. His insurgent/terrorists also carried out several brazen terrorist attacks on Kabul itself, including one bombing of a ceremony headed by Karzai, with the backing of the Pakistani ISI. Joint Chiefs of Staff chairman Admiral Michael Mullen called the Haqqani networks a "veritable arm" of the Pakistani ISI intelligence service, so close were the ties between Pakistani and the Haqqanis.

The Haqqani network also made ample use of suicide bombing, kidnapping, and extortion. But for all the American and Afghan governments' remonstrations to the Pakistani government to move against this pro-Taliban terrorist network, the Pakistanis proved to be reluctant to attack what they saw as a strategic asset. The United States was thus forced to take the unilateral step of attacking the Haqqani network in its North Waziristan base using CIA drones (to be discussed below).

But the Pakistanis' efforts to continue to covertly support the Afghan Taliban insurgents in their mounting insurgency against the Americans would ultimately come to haunt them and show that they were playing with fire. In July 2007 militants from a major mosque in the Pakistani capital, Islamabad, known as the Lal Masjid (Red Mosque) began to pour into surrounding neighborhoods and clash with storeowners who they claimed were selling "pornographic" DVDs and videotapes. They also kidnapped local women whom they described as "prostitutes" and seized control of a nearby government building. The militants, who were mainly Pashtuns, then called for the introduction of strict shariah law in Pakistan of the sort that was already being harshly enforced in the FATA provinces by the Taliban. The heads of the Lal Masjid mosque known as the Ghazi brothers also threatened to unleash suicide bombers on the capital if the government refused their demands to introduce shariah law. The Pakistani government had no choice but to act against this blatant challenge to its authority in the heart of the capital and sent troops to surround the mosque.

The Pakistani policy of covertly sponsoring the Afghan Taliban had created what is known in intelligence circles as a boomerang or "blowback" effect. Pakistani troops subsequently stormed the Lal Masjid mosque and madrassa and fought with the militants for several days before gaining control of the building. Ninety-one militants and eleven Pakistani soldiers, including the Pakistani commander in charge of the operation, were killed in the fighting. While this originally seemed like a victory, when word of the siege reached the Pakistani Taliban in their autonomous "emirates" in FATA, they declared an end to the tentative "truce" with the Pakistani government and the beginning of jihad on the Pakistani state. The independent frontier-tribal lands of "Talibanistan" were now at war with the Pakistani state, and Pakistanis could no longer pretend that the war on terrorists was purely in the interest of the Americans. It must be stressed that it was the Pakistani branch of the Taliban, not the Afghan Taliban, who were at war with Pakistan's secular government (the Afghan Taliban, led by Mullah Omar, remained neutral in the conflict and continued to have close links to Pakistan).

Among the Pakistani Taliban's first act was to send scores of suicide bombers against civilian and military targets, killing more than a hundred in less than a week.[3] The death toll from Pakistani Taliban attacks eventually surpassed three thousand a year as Pakistan became the epicenter of a suicide campaign that surpassed that of Iraq's in its intensity. The Pakistani military was thus forced to respond and invaded the FATA region of South Waziristan in 2009, setting off battles that led to the deaths of hundreds of Taliban Pakistani troops and civilians. South Waziristan was ultimately brought under Pakistani control, and, in June 2014, the Pakistani army finally invaded North Waziristan after the failure of peace talks with the Pakistani Taliban and a bold terror assault on Karachi Airport.

This invasion, known as Operation Zarb e Azb, after a holy sword used by the Prophet Muhammad, was a success in driving out the Pakistani Taliban factions that had blatantly ruled the region for over a decade. By 2015 casualties from terrorism in Pakistan had plummeted as the terrorists were put on the defensive even in remote sanctuary fallbacks like the Shawal Valley on the north-south Wazirstan border. But this victory came at a cost, and by 2015 a total of forty-four hundred Pakistani soldiers had been lost fighting against the Pakistani Taliban (i.e., approximately twice the number of U.S. soldiers lost in Afghanistan).[4]

The Pakistani Taliban responded in 2008 to the first Pakistani Army assault on their autonomous territories in Bajaur Agency by invading the so-called settled lands of the Pashtun-dominated neighboring North West Frontier Province (now called Khyber Pakhtunkhwa) and seizing control of the scenic Swat Valley, just one hundred miles to the west of the capital of Islamabad. From there, the Pakistani Taliban began to move into surrounding regions such as Buner and to enforce harsh shariah Islamic law throughout the larger region. A Taliban spokesman declared at the time that "shariah is not only for Malakand division, it is for all humanity, for all Muslims. So we will go more for implementation of Quran, shariah-e-muhammadi, not only in Malakand division but other parts of Pakistan also."[5]

Average Pakistanis, who had always seemed to be bizarrely tolerant of the Taliban, began to wake up to the threat they posed to their secular state when the Taliban in Swat Valley released videos of themselves whipping school girls and torturing those they defined as "bad Muslims" or criminals. It was in the Swat region, incidentally, that the Taliban tracked down and shot an outspoken local school girl named Malala Yousafzai, who dared to go to school despite a Taliban ban. She survived the gunshots to the head and was awarded the Nobel Prize for her bravery in 2014.

As this "creeping Talibanization" was being carried out by the Pakistani Taliban and cross border raids being launched by both the Pakistani and Afghan Taliban into Afghanistan, the CIA and JSOC (Joint Special Operations Command) came up with a solution to the problem of the militant sanctuaries in Pakistan's tribal zones. They began to attack the Taliban and Al Qaeda in their remote FATA hideouts using a lethal new technological innovation known as Predator drones. As early as 2002 the CIA was using Predator drones or "un-manned aerial vehicles" to monitor more than 150 Al Qaeda training facilities and Taliban bases in Pakistan's FATA. Then, two years later, Nek Muhammad, a Pakistani Taliban leader who just two months before had vowed to continue his support of Al Qaeda and jihad against the United States, was killed on June 18, 2004, in a mysterious explosion.

At the time Pakistan's *Dawn* newspaper reported that witnesses had seen a spy drone flying overhead minutes before the missile attack. But in the same article a Pakistani general rejected the claim and insisted that Pakistani forces had carried out the attack. Clearly the Pakistanis did not want the negative public relations fallout that would come from a public acknowledgement of the fact that a foreign power was acting in its own interests to kill Pakistani citizens, on Pakistani soil. It would later be revealed, however, that the Pakistanis had allowed the CIA to establish a drone base in a remote airstrip in Shamsi, Baluchistan, from which it flew its lethal drones. Clearly the unpredictable Pakistanis had secretly allowed the CIA to wage a covert assassination campaign against Al Qaeda and Taliban militants in a counterterrorism/ force-protection capacity.

In 2008 the aerial campaign stepped up considerably, and thirty drone strikes were recorded. The pace of the attacks picked up notably in August of that year after the Bush administration made a unilateral decision to carry out attacks without seeking Pakistani permission first. This diminished the risk of the Taliban or Al Qaeda being tipped off by sympathizers in the Pakistani military or ISI, as had happened on several occasions in the past vis-à-vis the Haqqani network. But by January 2009, Bush's term was up, and a new president, Barack Obama, came to office telling, the Islamic world in his first major overseas talk in Cairo, Egypt, that America was not at war with Muslims. Many Pakistanis wanted to know whether he would continue the controversial drone assassination program.

The answer was a resounding yes. History shows that the number of UAV (unmanned aerial vehicle) strikes in Obama's first year in office exceeded the previous year's total by sixteen. Obama launched a withering fifty-two drone strikes on militants in Pakistan's FATA region in 2009 (all but two drone strikes in the history of this campaign took place in this Taliban-controlled secessionist region). In the following year, the Obama administration launched a record-setting 122 drone strikes. Al Qaeda were in disarray as their commanders were decimated in the drone blitz on their hideouts, and many fled to Karachi or back to their homes in the Arab world. They were now afraid to gather openly to train, exert their power, and launch attacks for fear of the ever-present drones, which could even intercept their phone calls.

Clearly the incoming Obama administration had come to see these drone strikes as a vital component of its war against terrorism in Pakistan and Afghanistan. Like the Bush administration before it, the Obama administration felt that the public relations fallout in Pakistan (where reports of civilian deaths from the drones were wildly exaggerated) was worth the disruptive effect the drones had on Al Qaeda and Taliban, who were planning new terrorist attacks from their FATA sanctuary. In fact Obama (who came to be known as "Obomba" in Pakistan) ordered 353 drones strikes in Pakistan by October 2015, compared to just 48 under President Bush (i.e., Obama launched more than seven times as many as Bush).[6]

While his Republican critics described Obama as "weak" on counterterrorism and accused him of being "anti-war," former Secretary of Homeland Security, Janet Napolitano, pushed back on this notion stating, "President Obama has authorized more military actions in Muslim countries than any previous president and that the most conservative estimate identifies more than 3,000 drone strike fatalities during his tenure, including much of Al Qaeda's leadership. He is the first president since the Civil War to authorize the assassination of another American — Anwar al-Awlaki, himself."[7] Jeffrey Goldberg of the *Atlantic* similarly defended Obama saying "this president who has this reputation [of being weak] is the greatest terrorist hunter in the history of the American presidency. I mean, we just saw in the last week the 150 militants in Somalia wiped out by a U.S. strike. Who ordered that strike?"[8]

Obama's drone campaign decimated the Taliban and Al Qaeda's ranks and kept them wondering who was next and hiding, instead of planning new terrorist outrages.[9] The Taliban and Al Qaeda came to have a tremendous fear for the high-tech drones that struck out of the blue without warning and with uncanny precision. The CIA's ability to hit its targets in Pakistan increased in 2007 with the introduction of a much-improved drone known as the MQ-9 Reaper. The Reaper had a much larger engine, allowing it to travel three times the speed of the earlier drone, known as the Predator, and carry far more armament. This ordnance included GBU-12 Paveway II laser-guided bombs and Sidewinder missiles. Like the more primitive Predator, the Reaper could loiter over its intended target for over twenty-four hours, using high-resolution cameras to track militants' "pattern of life" movements from up to two miles away. Then, when the target was tracked leaving crowded areas, it could fire its deadly mini-missiles (often at targets in moving vehicles) to destroy them in the open and thus avoid civilian bystander casualties known as "collateral damage."[10]

It has also been reported that the Predators and Reapers were aided by secret electronic transmitter chips placed on or near targets by tribesmen working for CIA bounties. These cigarette lighter–sized homing beacons helped account for the drones' success in taking out dozens of high-value Al Qaeda and Taliban targets, while usually avoiding civilians. In essence, the drones' Hellfire missiles could home in on the beacons and precisely destroy Taliban and Al Qaeda cars or buildings where they were meeting.

It was clear from the success rate in killing high-value targets that the CIA had excellent intelligence resources in the tribal areas. These locals tracked the Taliban and Al Qaeda leadership, often for money or out of distaste for the extremists who beheaded many moderate *maliks* (Pashtun tribal heads) and terrorized the population. In addition to killing over a dozen high-ranking Taliban leaders, the strikes have taken out ten of Al Qaeda's top twenty leaders and the heads of the Pakistani Taliban on three separate occasions. Thousands of Taliban foot-soldiers have also been killed.

All this has been achieved with very little civilian bystander or "collateral damage" casualties. The widely respected *Long War Journal* has reported that in this aerial assassination campaign consisting of 389 strikes by October 2015, 2,789 Taliban and Al Qaeda leaders and operatives were killed and just 158 civilians, making this the most precise "bombing" campaign in history (in actuality most of the strikes were carried out by precision-guided Hellfire missiles or even smaller "Scorpions," not clumsy "dumb" bombs as in past bombing campaigns).[11]

Former CIA Director Michael Hayden said of this program "I think it fair to say that the targeted killing program has been the most precise and effective application of firepower in the history of armed conflict. It disrupted terrorist plots and reduced the original Qaeda organization along the Afghanistan-Pakistan border to a shell of its former self."[12]

In 2015 I had the opportunity to interview Lt. General David Deptula, the Air Force commander who led the air campaign against the Taliban in 2001 and became the first Deputy Chief of Staff for ISR (Intelligence, Surveillance, and Reconnaissance) at Air Force Headquarters, on the issue of the drones' unparalleled loitering ability and discerning precision. Deptula captured the drones' sense of "deadly persistence" stating "Remotely piloted aircrafts' ability to fly over one spot for a very long time allows those flying them to observe, evaluate, and act very quickly, or to take all the time necessary to be sure they can do what they really want to do. That precise engagement is simply not available to other types of weapons. Unfortunately, military combat operations do result in civilian casualties—from all sources in all mediums–air, ground, and sea. However, the fewest number of civilian casualties result from air operations, and fewest number by aircraft system type are from UAVs (Unmanned Aerial Vehicles)."[13] While researching my book *Predators: The CIA's Drone War on Al Qaeda* I had the extraordinary opportunity to interview several drone pilots. Far from being cold-blooded killers who "kill civilians 99 percent of the time" as they are described by their critics, I found them focused on avoiding killing civilians at all costs. They are worried about having innocent blood on their hands. As a result of such focus the New America Foundation reported no civilian deaths from 2012 to 2016.

The unpredictable Predator and Reaper attacks on convoys, *hujras* (guest houses), compounds, training camps, and madrassas wreaked havoc in the Taliban and Al Qaeda ranks. As a result, Al Qaeda members were forced to dismantle their training camps in favor of hidden classrooms; they no longer communicated using cell phones for fear of being tracked; they were forced to replace trusted veterans who have been killed with less experienced operatives; and they launched what have been described as "witch-hunts," killing real or perceived spies and traitors. U.S. officials were of course thrilled by the success in wiping out the enemy and disrupting their plans to carry out new attacks on the American mainland or on American troops in Afghanistan. According to a senior U.S. counterterrorism official, "These attacks have produced the broadest, deepest and most rapid reduction in al-Qaeda senior leadership that we've seen in several years."[14]

The strikes have, however, turned many average Pakistanis against America and might thus represent a strategic defeat in the greatest battle in this frontline country, the battle for the hearts and minds of the Pakistani people. For all their popularity among counterterrorism officials in the United States, polls show that 82 percent of Pakistanis find the drone missile strikes to be unjustified.[15]

The fact that Pakistani began to carry out its own drone strikes in the fall of 2015 using its drone the Barraq may change that perception. Fully aware of the unpopularity of the CIA strikes, the Pakistani government sought to distance itself from them. This took the form of a flow of public statements criticizing the attacks and two dressing-downs of the U.S. ambassador. Former Pakistani prime minister Yousuf Raza Gilani described the strikes as "disastrous" and said, "such actions are proving counter-productive to [the government's] efforts to isolate the extremists and militants from the tribal population." In other words, the Pakistani government outwardly condemned the drone strikes as a sop to their people, while covertly allowing them.

The Pakistani government's tacit support for the drone campaign, however, increased with the coming to power of the Asif Al Zardari government in December 2007 (in part owing to the fact that Zardari's wife, former prime minister Benazir Bhutto, had been killed by Pakistani Taliban terrorists). The United States, for example, shared its images from its Predators with the Pakistanis and used them as spy platforms to help the Pakistani military arrest Pakistani Taliban figures. While the U.S. turned down the Pakistani request to let them directly fly the planes themselves for security reasons, the Americans have used the drones to take out targets requested by the Pakistanis.

As the United States and Pakistan increased their cooperation on the drone attacks, the Pakistani public seemed to grow more tolerant of them. I myself found many voices in favor of the drone strikes in the tribal zones of Pakistan where the Taliban were not a mere abstract, as they were in other areas of Pakistan proper where issues of supposed violations of Pakistani sovereignty prevail. Tellingly, when Baitullah Mehsud, the Pakistani Taliban leader responsible for hundreds of suicide bombings that killed average Pakistanis, was killed in an August 2009 drone strike, there was no Pakistani outcry. On the contrary, there was celebration. Nor was there an outcry when his successor, Hakimullah Mehsud, was killed by a drone in 2013. With the Pakistani Taliban posing an ever greater threat to the Pakistani state and people, the previous Pakistani outrage over the strikes seems to have dissipated as the tormented Pashtuns in FATA, and even those in other provinces, have come to see the drone strikes as a necessary evil to help them confront the terrorists. One Pashtun from the FATA region captured this sentiment "The people of Waziristan are suffering a brutal kind of occupation under the Taliban and al Qaeda. It is in this context that they would welcome anyone, Americans, Israelis, Indians or even the devil, to rid them of the Taliban and al Qaeda. Therefore, they welcome the drone attacks."[16]

Even though the Obama administration rejected many of the Bush administration's War on Terror tactics, from waterboarding torture to the use of CIA "black sites" for interrogations and rendition of prisoners (to the point even of trying to close Gitmo, the Guantanamo Bay detention facility), the Obama administration nevertheless settled on drone strikes as its best "worst option" in the campaign against Al Qaeda and the Taliban. Obama took the drone campaign to new levels, and in the process the CIA, which had once been dedicated to spying and espionage, became a "killing machine." Obama was to emphatically state, "the CIA gets what it wants," and its budget went up from $4.8 billion in 1994 to $14.7 billion in 2013.[17]

But for all these developments with the CIA in Pakistan, clearly the main theater of action in Afghanistan and Pakistan was not in the FATA, but on the ground in Afghanistan. With the Taliban literally at the gates of Kabul by the time Obama took office, it was obvious that something had to be done on the ground to save the situation in the "Other War." Millions of Afghans were on the fence, especially in the south and east, where the Taliban had boldly taken control of much of the countryside, and a message of strength was needed to convince them to support the coalition. The new secretary of defense, Robert Gates, warned Obama that the war in Afghanistan had been "neglected" by the Bush administration and that something had to be done to save the deteriorating situation.[18]

By 2009, the Taliban had even managed to spread from beyond their traditional lairs in the Pashtun belt to such northern provinces as Kunduz, Baghlan, and Faryab (this process had been facilitated by the disarmament of local mujahideen and demobilization of Dostum's Uzbek fighters by the Karzai government). In my own travels across Afghanistan I found that zones I had freely traveled across in previous years had become "red zones" that were unsafe to travel. I also found that expats living in the capital were increasingly fearful of going to the wide array of restaurants and bars opened up in Kabul due to urban terror attacks.

Several U.S. outposts in the remote, forested hills of the northeastern Kunar and Nuristan region had also almost been overrun in bold Taliban swarm attacks and the British in the southern province of Helmand were surrounded in their bases by Taliban insurgents. Ultimately, the United States was forced to abandon several of these exposed FOBs and COPs in Nuristan and Kunar to the enemy after suffering unsustainable losses in near daily ambushes. In the deserts of the south, Terry Anderson reported that undermanned battalions of less than a thousand were trying to hold territories larger than U.S. states.[19]

Afghans with their fingers to the wind sensed weakness on the part of the American-led coalition and strength on behalf of the advancing Taliban, who had set up headquarters inside Afghanistan at Marjah and Musa Qala in Helmand Province and in Panjwai and Zhare just outside of Kandahar, their spiritual capital. In the ultimate demonstration of their newfound power, the Taliban had even taken control of most of the new American-built highway that stretched from Kabul to Kandahar, Afghanistan's second-largest city. Travelers going south from Kabul encountered Taliban checkpoints on this road just an hour south of the capital and convoys on this road were regularly being destroyed by insurgents. Clearly the United States and its partners were in danger of losing Afghanistan by 2009.

But the American people were weary of war, and the new vice president, Joe Biden, made it clear that he wanted a more narrowly focused counterterrorism campaign instead of counterinsurgency. Biden advocated a narrow approach focused on Al Qaeda, instead of a ramped up counterinsurgency campaign against the Taliban like the one being requested by the new head of U.S. and NATO forces in Afghanistan, General Stanley McChrystal. As Obama assessed the situation in his first year of office, millions of people from the Pashtun belt to the Iron Belt in America awaited the new president's decision.

History would show that Obama would, in Defense Secretary Robert Gates's words, choose to "own" the "forgotten war" in Afghanistan and refocus Centcom from Iraq to saving the Karzai government and destroying America's original enemies in the War on Terror, Al Qaeda Central and its Taliban hosts.[20]

"Obama's War" in Afghanistan, 2009–14

As the ramped-up drone war under Obama in Pakistan clearly demonstrated, the new president was committed to winning what he called the "war of necessity" in Afghanistan. It was Obama who had promised, "We will kill bin Laden. We will crush al Qaeda. That has to be our biggest national security priority."[21] For too long he felt the original war against the Al Qaeda terrorists responsible for the slaughter on 9/11 had taken a back seat to the "war of choice" in Iraq. To make his case that Afghanistan had been neglected, Obama could point to the fact that the war in Iraq cost almost twice as much as the war in Afghanistan (by 2012 Operation Iraqi Freedom had cost $806 billion, while the war in Afghanistan cost $444 billion).[22] The President was not the only one making this case, and Admiral Michael Mullen, chairman of the Joint Chiefs of Staff, declared the war in Iraq a "distraction" and had revealed that under Bush "my priorities . . . given to me by the commander in chief were: Focus on Iraq first. It's been that way for some time. Focus on Afghanistan second."[23] The insurgent-hunting general appointed in 2009 to lead the NATO mission in Afghanistan, Stanley McChrystal, agreed and said: "Our campaign in Afghanistan has been historically under-resourced and remains so today. Almost every aspect of our collective effort and associated resourcing has lagged a growing insurgency—historically a recipe for failure in COIN. Success will require a distinct 'jump' to gain the initiative."[24] Obama listened to the commanders on the ground, especially McChrystal, and made no secret of his intentions to transfer troops and resources back to the "forgotten war" in Afghanistan when he was running for president back in 2008. In a 2008 speech Obama promised to kill bin Laden and stated:

> We have a difficult situation in Pakistan. I believe that part of the reason we have a difficult situation is because we made a bad judgment going into Iraq in the first place when we hadn't finished the job of hunting down bin Laden and crushing al Qaeda. So what happened was we got distracted, we diverted resources, and ultimately bin Laden escaped, set up base camps in the mountains of Pakistan in the northwest provinces there.
>
> They are now raiding our troops in Afghanistan, destabilizing the situation. They're stronger now than at any time since 2001. And that's why I think it's so important for us to reverse course because that's the central front on terrorism. They are plotting to kill Americans right now. As Secretary Gates, the Defense secretary, said, the war against terrorism began in that region, and that's where it will end.[25]

The process of "finishing the job" in Afghanistan and putting more effort into finding bin Laden began soon after Obama took office, when he quickly

deployed twenty-one thousand troops to Afghanistan to shore up the neglected war effort there beginning in March 2009 (this brought the number of
troops in Afghanistan to sixty-eight thousand). He then received a request for
forty thousand reinforcements from General Stanley McChrystal, the former
head of Joint Special Operations Command who was now in charge in Afghanistan. After much debate in the White House between president and vice
president, Obama decided to send thirty-three thousand surge troops to Afghanistan to bolster the war effort on December 1, 2009. These troops would
buttress the more "silent surge" of twenty-one thousand troops that had earlier been completed. Under the 2010–11 Obama Afghan troop surge the number of U.S. troops would eventually max out at approximately 101,000 troops
(there were an additional forty thousand NATO troops as well).

While it was less than the 168,000 troop level reached by the Iraq surge,
this tripling of the number of troops in Afghanistan was a game changer in
the strategic southern provinces of Helmand and Kandahar, where the Taliban had made their boldest gains (the surge troops did not reinforce the hilly
northeastern provinces). While not politically popular in the United States,
where just 37 percent of those polled supported the war, the reinforcements
were much appreciated by McChrystal and his hard-pressed men on the
ground. McChrystal would subsequently say, "For many years we struggled
to get enough resources to do the mission. We now have enough. . . . For
many years we struggled to get people to pay attention to Afghanistan. Now
everyone is paying attention."[26]

General McChrystal, had the full support of the new U.S. president in
using these surge troops. He also continued his policies from Iraq and called
for an emphasis on protecting the Afghan people, the real center of gravity in
Afghanistan, during the COIN (Counter Insurgency) campaign. After being
deluged with complaints from Afghan president Hamid Karzai about unin-
tentional civilian deaths from NATO bombings, McChyrstal established
strict "rules of engagement" guidelines for the use of airpower. In fulfilling
this "population-centric" mission, which called for "courageous restraint" in
the use of firepower, McChrystal ordered his troops to be extremely cautious
about using artillery and close-air military strikes, because these often killed
Afghan civilians (and were said to drive the surviving Afghans into the hands
of the Taliban). Only in "very limited and prescribed conditions" could
troops in battle call in air or artillery strikes on the enemy. This cautious policy caused some resentment among U.S. troops on the ground, who felt that
their hands were tied in combat with the Taliban, but it did lead to a decline

in civilian deaths. By contrast, the Taliban continued to indiscriminately kill large numbers of civilians, often with suicide bombings and IEDs.

McChrystal used the additional troops given to him by Obama to bolster U.S. forces in contested frontier provinces in the south and east and to help the U.S. Marines fighting the Taliban in Helmand Province. Most important, in February 2010 McChrystal launched the largest military campaign of the entire war, Operation Moshtarak ("Together"). The goal of this operation was to seize the Taliban-controlled town of Marjah in Helmand Province. The town of eighty thousand had been captured by the Taliban and had become their de facto capital inside of Afghanistan. It had also become a center of their opium trade. In following his new COIN policy of protecting civilians, McChrystal decided to warn the Taliban that coalition troops would be invading the town of Marjah. He hoped that this would encourage the Taliban to retreat from the city and thus prevent a large-scale battle in a "civilian-rich" environment. Forewarned that the United States and its allies, including a large Afghan contingent, would be coming, the Taliban withdrew many of their forces but left some scattered around the town to harass the invading allies. Marjah would be no Fallujah-style fight to the death.

On February 13, 2010, a wave of ninety Chinook, Super Stallion, and Cobra helicopters ferrying thousands of coalition troops descended on the town of Marjah. The Taliban fought back sporadically with sniper fire and landmines, but the allies nonetheless succeeded in seizing the town in a short time. Although there was a sizable Afghan contingent in the invading force of fifteen thousand, reporters from the *New York Times* reported that most of the fighting was done by U.S. and NATO troops. Having taken the town with minimal losses and the death of roughly one hundred Taliban, the coalition then flew in what became known as a "government in a box." This consisted of a governor, administrative officials, and policemen. There were high hopes that the incentives offered by this government and the protection offered by the coalition troops would wean the people of Marjah away from the opium trade and the Taliban. Unfortunately, all did not go as planned in Marjah. Taliban insurgents remained scattered among the people and killed those who cooperated with the coalition troops and government.

In essence, the Marjah campaign was an act of micro–nation building, one province at a time. It was also a microcosm of the larger counterinsurgency strategy that posited that if you "cleared, held, and built" you would protect the local population, who would then support you vis-à-vis the Taliban.

Another large U.S. operation was carried out in Kandahar in the summer and fall of 2010. This operation took advantage of twelve thousand reinforcements sent to the province as part of Obama's troop surge. The operation began with an August sweep through the Mehlajat region on the southern fringe of Kandahar city, then proceeded to the Arghandab River valley region to the north. From there, U.S. troops moved into the Zhare District on the western side of Kandahar city. In late October U.S. forces then moved to an area known as the Horn of Panjwai and commenced an airborne assault on the Taliban-controlled villages of Mushan and Zangabad. Along the way the NATO troops destroyed Taliban bases and weapons caches and killed or captured thousands of insurgents in tough, close fighting. This new sustained policy was defined as "holding territory" instead of the previous practice of responding to attacks then moving on, which was described as "mowing the grass." In the process, U.S. casualties increased as the Taliban fought back with small arms and IEDs, and 499 Americans were killed in 2010 in Afghanistan.

Despite these loses, U.S. troops were able to make considerable gains in these operations, in part owing to the use of a new mobile rocket system known as the Himars (High Mobility Artillery Rocket System), which has been described as a "small cruise missile." The Taliban sustained considerable losses in this campaign, which also relied on stepped-up airstrikes. Throughout the summer and fall of 2010, the United States stepped up a massive bombing campaign against the Taliban that began to show results. This aerial campaign was combined with a three-thousand-man CPT unit (CIA-Afghan Counterterrorism Pursuit Team) and Joint Special Operations Command teams. These hunter-killer teams were responsible for killing hundreds of Taliban commanders in the south and forcing much of the leadership to retreat back across the border into Pakistan by the winter of 2010–11. The subsequent 2012 and 2013 Taliban summer offensives were weaker than in past years, and the Taliban began to resort to so-called green-on-blue insider killings of U.S. troops by Taliban infiltrators posing as Afghan government soldiers. Dozens of U.S. troops were killed in these attacks, including one American general, and this caused distrust between the Americans and the Afghan troops they were training and working alongside.

The larger strategic objective of the surge campaign seems to have been to break the Taliban's will to fight a costly war of attrition and push them to the negotiating table. The American military command aimed to drive the Taliban to negotiate before a planned initial withdrawal of some U.S. troops by

September 2012, a date Obama announced to appease antiwar elements in the Democratic Party.

In this respect the plan did not succeed. What it did do was give the Karzai government more time to "train up" its army and police, which had suffered from desertions, drug use, and illiteracy. It also repulsed the Taliban from Kandahar and Helmand, which they had been close to conquering. In June 2011, Obama announced the end of the surge, and these reinforcement troops began to head home.

Interestingly, the top U.S. commander in Afghanistan, General McChrystal, was, however, removed from the scene before the aforementioned operations in Kandahar were completed. McChrystal was removed from his post following the publication in *Rolling Stone* magazine of a controversial interview with him and his staff titled "Runaway General." During the course of the interview, McChrystal's aides (not him though) made disparaging remarks about Vice President Joe Biden and the U.S. civilian leadership in Afghanistan led by Richard Holbrooke. Obama had no choice but to remove the highly successful general, who had become too controversial following the publication of the article. This was a setback for the campaign as McChrystal had had close ties with the often emotionally unstable President Karzai (something that many of his predecessors had not), and he seemed to be winning.

In a brilliant masterstroke, however, Obama chose General David Petraeus, the tremendously popular head of Centcom, as McChrystal's replacement. Petraeus arrived in Afghanistan in July of 2010 and lifted some of the COIN restrictions on bombings and stepped up the special force night raids on the Taliban. During this time, U.S. Special Forces were carrying out fifteen raids a night, and the Taliban came to dread them. Demoralized Taliban fighters refused to take orders on some occasions for fear of being killed by JSOC operatives. This also caused problems with President Karzai, who publicly attacked the U.S. military for alienating Afghans by breaking into Afghan houses in search of insurgents in kill/capture raids and killing innocent civilians in errant bomb strikes. By April 2011, Petraeus had, however, been shifted from Afghanistan to head up the CIA, a job he held until he was forced to step down because of a sex scandal in 2012.

Both generals' efforts were confounded by the fact that the Afghan regime they were fighting to save was accused of widespread corruption. Afghanistan was ranked second to last in the world in an annual corruption survey (only Somalia had worse corruption). Perhaps the most notable example of this corruption was the fraudulent loss of as much as $900 million from the Karzai-linked Kabul Bank in the fall of 2010. The problems clearly stemmed from the top.

In the fall of 2010, the website known as WikiLeaks leaked several classified cables from the U.S. State Department detailing problems with Afghan president Hamid Karzai. He was described in these candid messages as weak, vacillating, and suffering from mood disorders. Although Karzai, who was a polished English speaker, had originally been courted by Washington as a source of hope for Afghanistan, opinion of him had deteriorated considerably, especially in the U.S. military.

Never were the problems with Karzai more apparent than in the August 20, 2009, presidential elections. In the runoff between President Karzai and his chief opponent, Abdullah Abdullah, a half Pashtun, half Tajik leader who had served as an aide for the legendary Massoud, Karzai's supporters were accused of ballot stuffing in many southern Pashtun districts. Hundreds of thousands of votes were illegally cast, particularly in areas of Kandahar controlled by Karzai's brother, Ahmed Wali Karzai. The UN election observers reported on the fraud, and there were calls for a runoff election with Abdullah. In the end, Abdullah chose not to contest the election with Karzai in order to bring peace and consensus to the country.

In September 2014, the unstable Karzai finished his second five-year term as president and was replaced by a Pashtun technocrat named Ashraf Ghani and his vice president, the famous Uzbek general Dostum (although Dostum proved to be restless in Kabul and in the fall of 2015 and winter of 2016 returned to the north to personally lead Uzbek militias in fighting the resurgent Taliban in Faryab and Jowzjan Provinces). Abdullah Abdullah was made chief executive officer, a post created to appease his followers after a close election.

In the meantime, the ultimate American goal was to train the Afghan army and Afghan police so that they could carry on the war once the Americans and their coalition partners completed their withdrawal. In December 2014 America's combat mission in Afghanistan, its longest war since the Revolutionary War, officially came to an end.

But in the fall of 2015, a Taliban force seized the northern town of Kunduz for fifteen days and was repulsed only with the aid of U.S. Special Forces who called in airstrikes on them (tragically, in the heated battle an airstrike by an AC-130 Specter gunship accidentally struck a Doctors Without Borders hospital and killed twenty-two patients and doctors). General John

Campbell used the Taliban conquest of Kunduz, their first seizure of a provincial center, to make the case that the United States should keep more than the previously suggested one thousand troops in Afghanistan after 2016. The Taliban were also able to conquer northern Helmand Province in 2015 forcing Afghan government troops to evacuate the town of Musa Qala in February 2016.

The Takedown of bin Laden

Meanwhile, the man whose actions spawned the two U.S. invasions of Taliban Afghanistan and Baathist Iraq, bin Laden, remained frustratingly at large. In the aftermath of the 9/11 attacks, CIA Counterterrorist Center chief Cofer Black told CIA SAD (Special Activities Division) operatives that were deploying to Afghanistan that he wanted them to "capture Bin Laden, kill him and bring his head back in a box on dry ice." President Obama had made a point of promising the American voters in 2008 that he would get bin Laden.

But bin Laden remained an elusive prey. As has already been pointed out, bin Laden, the focus of the largest manhunt in modern history, was allowed to escape from the eastern mountains of Tora Bora in December 2001. From there, he made his way into Pakistan's remote FATA region and then disappeared into thin air for almost a decade. Every day, week, month, and year bin Laden remained at large served as a victory for Al Qaeda and inspiration for extremists who subscribed to this terror prophet's struggle against the American "*hubal*" (idol of arrogance). His recorded sermons, threats, and mocking were also a finger in the eye to the grieving post-9/11 Americans and source of funds for Al Qaeda and its Taliban allies.

While there were reports of Al Qaeda number two, Ayman al Zawaheri, being active in the tribal agency of Bajaur (which resulted in two attempts to kill him in drone strikes), there was no information on bin Laden's whereabouts in the succeeding years. In one of his numerous videos sent to threaten the West and garner support from followers, bin Laden and Zawaheri were, however, seen walking together on the side of a rocky hill, leading some to speculate that they were both still in FATA. There were several FATA-based Pakistani Taliban commanders who were known to protect Arabs in their midst, so most assumed that bin Laden would not venture out from this protected tribal zone.

But the CIA's drone strikes made this sanctuary insecure, forcing many

Arabs and Taliban leaders to flee the FATA. Several high-ranking Al Qaeda members who earlier left the tribal zone, including Khaled Sheikh Muhammad, the mastermind of the 9/11 attacks, and Ramzi bin al Shibh, the hands-on coordinator of the attacks, were, however, arrested by the Pakistanis and sent to the United States (providing proof that the Pakistanis were with their American allies in the war on terror when it came to Al Qaeda). For this reason, most analysts felt bin Laden was in the FATA, but this was pure speculation because the terror mastermind had proven to be impossible to trace. It quickly became obvious that bin Laden was incredibly security conscious and was not going to make the same mistake as Pakistani Taliban leader Nek Muhammad who was killed by a drone after the U.S. homed in on his cell phone signal. Bin Laden communicated only using couriers. So America's counterterrorist agencies focused on trying to find the identity of bin Laden's couriers. If they could find bin Laden's messengers, it was theorized they might be able to find bin Laden himself.

U.S. counterintelligence officials began to question such high-profile detainees at Guantanamo Bay as Khaled Sheikh Muhammad and former Al Qaeda number three, Abu Faraj al Libi, about the identities of bin Laden's couriers. During this interrogation process, Khaled Sheikh Muhammad and Abu Faraj al Libi refused to give information on one courier whose *kunya* (nickname) had been mentioned by another captive. The interrogators grew suspicious that the courier who Khaled Sheikh Muhammad and Libi were covering up for might be important and might even have direct contact with bin Laden.

In 2007 the real name and identity of the courier was discovered. He was Ahmed al Kuwaiti, a Pashtun who had been brought up in Kuwait. But it proved all but impossible to find the courier in Pakistan, a country of 180 million people. Then, in August 2010, the Kuwaiti Pashtun courier finally tripped up when he incautiously answered a call from another Al Qaeda operative who was already being monitored by the Americans. The courier was quickly traced from the location of his phone call in Peshawar, Khyber Pakhtunkhwa (one of Pakistan's four provinces, previously known as the North West Frontier Province), to a compound in a town in northeast Pakistan known as Abbottabad.

When the American spy satellites began to monitor the compound, the CIA and NSA grew increasingly excited. Ahmed al Kuwaiti was living in a recently built, three-storied, walled concrete compound surrounded by eighteen-foot walls with barbed wire on top. Satellite images of the compound also showed images of a tall man going for walks in the compound garden (bin Laden was said to be around six feet four inches). The compound, which was built in 2005, seemed to have been constructed to house someone important. Most interestingly, the Americans soon discovered that the compound did not have phone or Internet connections that could be tapped and monitored. This seemed bizarre in a mansion worth over $1 million and indicated that its owners clearly had something to hide.

To investigate the matter further, in September 2010 the CIA set up a surveillance safe house near the compound to monitor its inhabitants. The CIA agents quickly began to notice other strange behavior, such as the fact that the compound's inhabitants burnt their trash instead of having it picked up like everyone else in the neighborhood. The inhabitants of the compound also kept to themselves and rarely left it, except to go shopping or to attend Friday prayers at the mosque. The courier and his brother also did not have jobs.

There seemed to be three families living in the compound: the family of the courier Ahmed al Kuwaiti, his brother's family, and a third family that seemed to be roughly the size of the family bin Laden was estimated to have traveling with him. After months of surveillance by spies and satellites, the CIA were said to be at least 60 percent sure that bin Laden was hiding there. This was enough certainty to convince the U.S. president to launch an extremely risky attack on the compound. Obama would later say: "This was still a 55/45 [percent] situation. I mean, we could not say definitively that bin Laden was there. Obviously, we're going into the sovereign territory of another country and landing helicopters and conducting a military operation. And so, if it turns out that it's a wealthy, you know, prince from Dubai who's in this compound and, you know, we've sent special forces in, we've got problems."[27]

By late April 2011, President Obama had held several meetings with his national security team to plan an attack on the Abbottabad compound. While a strike by a Reaper drone seemed to be the most obvious path to take in light of Obama's stepped-up use of drones against Al Qaeda, this was quickly ruled out. The Reaper did not carry enough munitions to totally destroy the strongly built concrete compound. In addition, the slow-moving Reaper drone would have been easily detectable on Pakistani radars. Because the town of Abbottabad was located in the so-called Air Defense Intercept Zone for the Pakistani capital of Islamabad, the drone would have been quickly shot down.

President Obama then consulted with General Bill McRaven, the head of Joint Special Operations Command, the unit tasked with organizing the mission, about the prospect of using B-2 stealth bombers to bomb the compound. But the heavy payload dropped by the bombers would kill all twenty-two people said to be in the compound, including women and children, and possibly neighbors. The bombs would also obliterate bin Laden's body, thus preventing the CIA from getting any DNA proof of his death. Al Qaeda could then claim he was still alive, and Pakistanis would be infuriated by the deaths of so many innocents.

In the end Obama decided to approve a third approach that was fraught with risks, a helicopter-borne "capture or kill" raid on the house. There were two previous debacles stemming from similar heliborne missions that pointed out the dangers of such a risky decision. The first was President Jimmy Carter's fateful decision in 1980 to send in helicopters to free fifty-two U.S. hostages being held in Tehran, Iran, by Iranian militants. Unfortunately, during the operation, known as Eagle Claw, one of the helicopters carrying elite Delta Forces crashed into a fuel transport plane killing eight soldiers and destroying both aircraft. The mission was subsequently aborted, and Iranian news proudly broadcast images of the blackened remains of the aircraft in the Iranian desert. As the man who had taken the risky decision to order the raid, Carter took the blame for the debacle, and the incident contributed heavily to his defeat by Ronald Reagan in the presidential elections held that year.

The second incident that set a dire precedent for Obama was the September 3, 2008, raid by three to five Black Hawk helicopters carrying U.S. Navy SEAL Special Forces on a Taliban-controlled town in the Pakistani FATA tribal agency of South Waziristan. In the ensuing cross border raid as many as twenty people were killed, including women and children. U.S. sources claimed the women who were killed were actively helping the militants. Several suspected Taliban militants were also killed or captured by the U.S. soldiers in the helicopters, who then disappeared into the night. After the raid a local reported, "The situation there is very terrible. People are trying to take out the dead bodies."[28]

As word that innocent Pakistani women and children had been killed in the SEAL raid in Waziristan spread in Pakistan, there were howls of outrage from Pakistani leaders across the board. But it was the Pakistani military that drew the firmest line in the sand. Using bellicose terms more suited for an enemy than an ally, the new head of Pakistan's army, General Pervez Ashfaq

Kayani, stated that Pakistan's territorial integrity would be "defended at all cost." Lest there be any ambiguity, Kayani also stated, "There is no question of any agreement or understanding with the coalition forces whereby they are allowed to conduct operations on our side of the border. . . . No external force is allowed to conduct operations inside Pakistan."[29]

By deploying U.S. boots on the ground in a bold helicopter raid on a town that was just seventy-five miles from the Pakistani capital and home to its most prestigious military academy, without notifying the Pakistanis, Obama was thus taking a huge risk in getting bin Laden. He would be risking his presidency, the lives of the Special Forces, and the already shaky alliance with America's most important strategic partner in the war on Al Qaeda and the Taliban, Pakistan.

But the chance to kill bin Laden, a terrorist who had been hunted by three American presidents, proved to be worth the risks for Obama. The word to launch the raid was given, and President Obama went off to put on a public face and attend an annual correspondents dinner with the media. The mission was kept secret even from America's closest allies. As previously stated, the Pakistanis were not notified because CIA head Leon Panetta worried that "any effort to work with the Pakistanis could jeopardize the mission. They might alert the targets."[30]

After waiting two days for cloudy skies and low moon visibility, four U.S. helicopters, two Black Hawks, and two larger Chinook transport helicopters, carrying an elite Navy SEAL unit of twenty-three members known as Team Six, flew from a U.S. base in eastern Afghanistan at Jalalabad into Pakistani airspace. American Special Forces had now penetrated Pakistani airspace to engage in the first raid since the September 3, 2008, public relations fiasco in South Waziristan. The helicopters arrived at the suspect compound in Abbottabad at 1 A.M. Monday morning (May 2, 2011) Pakistan time, and one of the Black Hawks promptly crashed and rolled over onto its side. Its twelve occupants were, however, unhurt and, together with the twelve soldiers from the other helicopter, breached the compound's walls using explosives.

At around this time, the courier al Kuwaiti fired on the Americans and was killed. His brother was also killed as was a woman (probably the courier's wife) who was caught in the crossfire. One of bin Laden's sons, a twenty-year-old named Khaled, was also killed as the twenty-three SEALs methodically searched the compound, room to room, wearing night-vision goggles.

But SEALs' chief prey, bin Laden, was not found until two commandos burst onto the third floor of the large, unlit home. There they found bin

Laden and his youngest wife, a twenty-nine-year-old Yemeni named Amal al Sadah. When his wife rushed at the SEALs she was shot in the leg, and an unarmed bin Laden was shot in the chest and the head. A SEAL then radioed, "Geronimo E-KIA" (Geronimo being bin Laden's code-name, and E-KIA signifying Enemy Killed in Action).

Cheers swept the White House situation room, where President Obama, Secretary of Defense Robert Gates, and Secretary of State Hillary Clinton were intently following the operation. The SEALs then transported bin Laden's body to the helicopter after his wife had identified it.

From Abbottabad, the helicopters safely flew back over the Hindu Kush foothills and Pashtun tribal lands to their base in Jalalabad, eastern Afghanistan. Incredibly, not one SEAL had been killed or wounded in the stealth attack. Despite the considerable risks, it had been a complete success. Considering the vast distances involved, uncertainty as to who was in the compound, and shaky relations with the Pakistanis, it was the most successful raid in modern U.S. military history and put to rest the demons of the failed 1980 Iranian operation under Jimmy Carter.

Bin Laden's DNA was subsequently confirmed to be matching that of one of his relatives, and his body was then flown to the aircraft carrier the USS *Carl Vinson* and buried at sea after performing proper Islamic rituals in Arabic. While photos of bin Laden's gun-shattered face were taken after his death, President Obama decided not to release them for fear that they would appear on jihadi websites, placards at rallies, and so on to incite hatred and revenge among extremists for years to come. In essence the U.S. made bin Laden, the founder of Al Qaeda and icon for jihadis and militants across the globe, disappear without a trace so he could not become a martyr icon.

While there were of course conspiracy theorists and doubters who did not believe he was dead (the Taliban and Pakistani Islamist groups initially rejected the claims of his death), Al Qaeda subsequently announced his death. After seeing the broadcast images of thousands of jubilant Americans spontaneously celebrating the death of bin Laden in Times Square, at the White House, and at the site of the World Trade Centers, Al Qaeda announced on its webpage, "Soon, God willing, their happiness will turn to sadness. Their blood will be mingled with their tears." One jihadist website known as Islamic Awakening captured the sentiment of many Al Qaeda supporters when it declared, "God damn you Obama!"

The American public was more supportive of the raid, and Obama's subsequent 11:30 P.M. address to the American people was the most watched presidential address in a decade (fifty-seven million Americans watched it). In his speech, Obama declared, "I can report to the American people and to the world that the United States has conducted an operation that killed Osama bin Laden, the leader of the terrorist organization who's responsible for the murder of thousands of innocent men, women, and children."[31]

Not surprisingly, Obama's poll numbers went up, and he received a 9 percent bump in approval ratings in a poll carried out by Pew Research Center and the *Washington Post*. Support for his handling of the war in Afghanistan went up seventeen points, and his handling of terrorism went up twenty-one points. (At this time 67 percent of those polled said they approved of Obama's handling of handling of terrorism.)[32] Two-thirds of those polled considered the killing of bin Laden to be a "major achievement."[33]

Similar spikes were recorded by George H. W. Bush following the successful completion of Operation Desert Storm in 1991 and following the 9/11 attacks for George W. Bush. The killing of Osama would certainly help Obama (who had been labeled a "Muslim" born in Indonesia by New York mogul/Republican presidential candidate Donald Trump and other conspiracy theorists known as "birthers") in the 2012 presidential election. Referring to Obama's bail-out of the auto industry during the recession, Vice President Joe Biden would triumphantly proclaim, "Osama is dead, and General Motors is alive," and this became the mantra on the election trail.

With official recognition of bin Laden's death coming from Al Qaeda, there were limited protests in Karachi and other Pakistani cities organized by the country's Islamist parties, and the Taliban threatened revenge. But most important, there were no widespread protests in the Arab world. By the time of his death the world that had produced bin Laden and his Egyptian number two, Ayman al Zawaheri, had been radically transformed by the so-called Arab Spring. This was a popular revolt that began in Tunisia in the winter of 2011 leading to the overthrow of its dictator, President Ben Ali. This was followed by the overthrow of the secular Egyptian dictator Hosni Mubarek, a leader who al Zawahiri and his Egyptian Al Qaeda followers had long dreamed of toppling in a jihadist revolution.

But Al Qaeda's dream of establishing a jihadist caliphate, governed by shariah law, in Egypt, home to eighty million Arabs, was preempted by the overthrow of the regime by young, largely secular Arab youth. These young Arabs who rallied on Facebook and Twitter demanded democracy, not shariah law. They resoundingly rejected bin Laden and his increasingly shrill calls for jihad. He was seen by many as an embarrassment to Arabs and Islam, especially after the Arab-on-Arab bloodshed and mayhem in Iraq caused by AQI after 2005. In essence, bin Laden's death marked the passing of an era that had begun with Al Qaeda's attacks on the U.S. embassies in Africa in 1998. By 2016 Al Qaeda Central in Pakistan had been decimated by the withering campaign of drone strikes launched by Obama and the mantle for jihad had passed to ISIS (the Islamic State in Iraq and Syria) and the Al Qaeda affiliate in Yemen.

While there are bound to be further Al Qaeda attacks, the odds are that these will be by lone wolves like Faisal Shahzad, the Pakistani who attempted to set off a car bomb in Times Square in May 2010, or ISIS-inspired self-starters like the San Bernardino terrorists who killed fourteen people in 2015. The most dangerous jihadist group in the world may are now ISIS and the "Al Qaeda in the Arabian Peninsula" splinter group based in Yemen.

The Yemeni offshoot of Al Qaeda Central has carried out several bold terrorist plots, including two attempt to blow up Fed Ex and UPS cargo planes with bombs hidden in them and an attempt to kill Saudi prince Muhmmad bin Nayef with a suicide bomb. It has also seized considerable territory in Abyan Province in southern Yemen. The overthrow of the Yemeni government in 2014 by Shiite Houthi rebels also created a vacuum that allowed Al Qaeda in the Arabian Peninsula to expand. While it suffered a setback in June 2015 when its leader, Nasir al Washiri, was killed in a drone strike ordered by Obama, it remains the most deadly terrorist group in the world that is actively planning mass casualty terror strikes such as blowing up commercial airliners. In fact by 2015 the CIA was forced out of Yemen by the collapse of the Yemeni government and Al Qaeda in the Arabian Peninsula increased its numbers from three hundred to more than a thousand.

An Al Qaeda franchise also emerged in northwest Africa known as Al Qaeda in the Islamic Maghreb (AQIM). This branch conquered a Texas-sized territory in northern Mali before being pushed out by French forces from 2013 to 2014. Having lost control of its territory, AQIM turned to terrorism. In January 2015 terrorists from the group attacked a hotel and restaurant in Ouagadougo, the capital of Burkina Faso, and killed thirty (in conjunction with terrorists from an Al Qaeda affiliated group known as Mouribatoun). The two groups also attacked a hotel in Bamako, the capital of Mali in November 2015 and killed twenty hostages. AQIM struck again in March 2016 killing sixteen in the resort town of Grand Bassam in the Ivory Coast. There were theories at the time that AQIM was trying to compete with ISIS and stay relevant by wracking up body counts that made headlines.

But for all the importance Al Qaeda's franchises in Africa and Yemen gained, bin Laden's death in 2011 of course had more important implications for the war in what increasingly became known as the Af/Pak (Afghanistan-Pakistan) theater. Many U.S. congressmen felt that bin Laden could not have been living so close to Pakistan's most prestigious military school, the Kakul Pakistani Military Academy, in Abbottabad, had he not been protected by elements of the Pakistani military, ISI, or government. While the Pakistanis were angered by this accusation and pointed out the difficulties the United States had in finding criminals on the FBI's Most Wanted List, one poll showed that 84 percent of Americans believed that high-level Pakistanis knew where he was hiding all along. Congressmen on both sides of the aisle called for a cutting-off of the billions of dollars of aid the U.S. was giving the Pakistanis to help it in the War on Terror. Many pundits called on the U.S. to begin treating Pakistan not as an ally, but as an enemy.

In defense of the Pakistanis, it should be noted, however, that Al Qaeda and its Pakistani Taliban allies had killed thousands of Pakistani soldiers (twice as many Pakistani troops were killed fighting the Taliban than American soldiers). The Pakistani Taliban also made several attempts on the lives of presidents Musharraf and Zardari, and the Pakistanis had arrested the number three in Al Qaeda, Khaled Sheikh Muhammad, and over six hundred other Arab Al Qaeda fighters or terrorists fleeing Afghanistan to Pakistan after 2001's Operation Enduring Freedom.

It should also be noted that President Zardari's wife, Benazir Bhutto, had been killed by these terrorists, as had thousands of average Pakistanis (up to three thousand in one year). The Pakistani government, which was humiliated by the raid, carried out an investigation on the killing of bin Laden known as the Abbottabad Commission Report, which concluded that bin Laden was able to live in Pakistan without detection or arrest for nine years "because of widespread incompetence among military and intelligence authorities."[34]

Seen in this light, it seems highly unlikely that bin Laden would have trusted his security to the Pakistanis who were working with the CIA in this environment of hate and distrust, nor that the Pakistanis, who had received more than US$26 billion since 2001 to fight the common enemy, would have risked angering America and the West by harboring the world's most wanted fugitive. Most important, former President Musharraf had secretly given President Bush the permission to launch a raid on bin Laden should he ever be found on Pakistani soil.[35]

While the Pakistanis were certainly humiliated by the unexpected raid on their country that killed bin Laden (and threatened that a repeat of the incursion would be seen as an attack on their sovereignty), their leader had tacitly approved it back in 2001. After the raid, they continued to cooperate with the Americans and allowed them to interrogate bin Laden's wives who were arrested by the Pakistanis at the compound.

It should also be noted that NATO convoys continued to supply troops in Afghanistan via Pakistan's strategically important Khyber Pass. For all its obvious flaws and deep levels of distrust, the partnership with the Pakistanis was America's most important alliance in the war against Al Qaeda and the Taliban, with perhaps the exception of the American alliance with the Karzai government in Afghanistan.

This brings us to the impact of bin Laden's death on the war in Afghanistan. The death of bin Laden was celebrated by many Afghans, especially those belonging to the Northern Alliance opposition, who had been fighting his forces and warning the West of his terrorism since the late 1990s. In the Pashtun south, opinions were more mixed. While the Taliban threatened revenge for bin Laden's death (which is ironic considering it was his terrorist attack on the United States that led to the punitive American destruction of their regime when the Taliban refused to turn him over), his demise may have removed one of the primary reasons for their alliance with Al Qaeda, namely Mullah Omar's promise to offer bin Laden melmastiia (the Pashtun honor obligation to offer sanctuary to a guest). Some argued that bin Laden's death would essentially allow the Taliban to divorce from Al Qaeda now that their personal obligations had been removed. They also speculated that the Taliban would resent fighting against the Americans, who were killing them in the thousands, while bin Laden (the catalyst for the invasion of their lands) lived in relative security in a mansion far from the battlefront.

For their part, many average Afghans who had benefited from the NATO occupation feared that, with bin Laden's death, the Americans and their allies would argue that the rationale for U.S. troops being in Afghanistan had been removed. In this assumption they were not disappointed. Both Democrats and Republicans began to argue that bin Laden's death and the dismantlement of Al Qaeda's sanctuary in Afghanistan meant that America had achieved the original goals of Operation Enduring Freedom.

There were even rumors that the reclusive Mullah Omar, who had not been seen for over a decade, was dead (rumors that were confirmed in the summer of 2015 when the Taliban conceded that he had been dead since

April 2013 and they had kept the fact a secret). Democrat senator John Kerry allied with Republican senator Richard Lugar to a call for an end to the war. Kerry stated, "We should be working toward the smallest footprint necessary, a presence that puts Afghans in charge and presses them to step up to the task. Make no mistake, it is fundamentally unsustainable to continue spending $10 billion a month on a massive military operation with no end in sight."[36] These calls of course overlooked the fact that a precipitous drawdown of U.S. troops would embolden the Taliban, who had not renounced their ties with Al Qaeda nor their maximalist desire to reconquer all of Afghanistan.

To allay Afghan fears of such an outcome, U.S. ambassador to Afghanistan Karl Eikenberry promised that "this victory will not mark the end of our effort against terrorism" and pledged that "America's strong support for the people of Afghanistan will continue as before."[37] For the Afghan government and millions of Afghans who have moved back to Afghanistan since 2001 with the aim of rebuilding their lives, his comments were cause for hope.

Meanwhile, the massive American war effort in Afghanistan began to come to a gradual halt as American troops came home in waves and Afghan troops who had been trained by NATO forces took over much of the fighting. By 2012, the Obama surge troops had come home, and the number of U.S. troops in the country fell to around sixty thousand. By 2014 the number had fallen to thirty-two thousand, and Obama promised that the number of U.S. troops would remain at ninety-eight hundred in 2015 and 2016. While there had been plans for a total drawdown of U.S. troops, the White House had learned from the chaos in post-U.S. Iraq and decided residual troops were required in Afghanistan.

In September 2014 the newly elected Afghan president, Ashraf Ghani, signed a Bilateral Security Agreement with the United States to keep the residual ninety-eight hundred troops in Afghanistan (plus three thousand NATO troops). There would be no replay of the failure of Obama and Iraqi prime minister Maliki to sign a new SOFA (Status of Force Agreement) in 2011 (to be discussed in the next chapter). Having seen the rapid rise of ISIS in post-U.S.-withdrawal Iraq, the Afghan and U.S. governments worked together to keep residual forces in Afghanistan to prevent such an occurrence in that country.

On December 28, 2014, Operation Enduring Freedom officially came to an end after more than thirteen years, and a new phase known as Operation Resolute Support began. This phase officially involved the Americans and NATO forces primarily training and supporting Afghan troops. But this did not mean a complete end to the active U.S. war effort in Afghanistan. While there had been plans in place for an end to all combat missions for U.S. troops after 2014, the example of the rise of ISIS in post-U.S. Iraq convinced Obama to order a more expansive mission for the U.S. military in 2015 than originally planned. President Obama's new December 2014 orders allowed U.S. troops to carry out "discretionary" missions against Taliban fighters who threatened them or the Afghan government and authorized U.S. bombers and drones to support Afghan troops on combat missions.[38] They were also authorized to act in a counterterrorism role defined as tracking remnants of Al Qaeda. The remaining U.S. troops would officially act as "combat enablers" (i.e., they would be involved in providing occasional air support, communications, and intelligence gathering for Afghan troops).

Officially U.S. troops could not wage combat with the Taliban in this new phase, except in a "force protection" role. But in April 2015 the *New York Times* reported that the remaining U.S. troops were still engaged in an "aggressive range of military operations against the Taliban."[39] In particular, it was reported that Special Forces were still engaged in raids on Taliban targets, months after the official end of the combat mission. Most important, the new Afghan president, Ashraf Ghani, lifted the previous restrictions on U.S. bombings and night raids that had been implemented by the previous president, Karzai. As mentioned previously, U.S. combat controllers were also deployed to expel the Taliban from the town of Kunduz in October 2015.

This continuing military involvement in Afghanistan by a U.S. president whose foreign policy had come to be defined for critics by the word "retrenchment" was necessitated, in part, by the resurgence of the Taliban. The year 2014 was the deadliest in the Afghan war for civilians, with a death toll of 3,188. By this time thirty-five hundred foreign troops had been killed in Afghanistan, twenty-two hundred of them American.[40]

By early 2015 it was apparent that the Taliban had taken heart from the U.S. withdrawal and had gone on the offensive, especially in the northern, ethnically mixed Tajik, Pashtun and Uzbek province of Kunduz. In April 2015, the Taliban came close to taking the provincial capital of Kunduz and were repulsed only by Afghan army reinforcements rushed to this strategic province, which has a large number of Pashtuns (the ethnic group that makes up the bulk of the Taliban). As late as the summer of 2015, the Afghan army was able to hold nearly all four hundred district centers in the country (with an exception in northern province of Badakshan), but by the summer Afghan soldiers' death rate was already exceeding that of the previous year, and the Taliban appeared to be on the offensive on all fronts. In the fall of 2015 the UN rated the threat level in about half of the country's administrative districts as either "high" or "extreme," more than at any time since the American invasion toppled the Taliban in 2001.[41]

While the Taliban shura (ruling council) appeared to be deeply divided over the choosing of Mullah Mansour in the summer of 2015 to replace Mullah Omar as the Commander of the Faithful (Mullah Omar was said to have died in Pakistani hospital in Karachi in 2013), most rank-and-file Taliban fighters accepted him as their new leader. The brief two-week Taliban conquest of Kunduz in the fall of 2015 seemed to have strengthened his hand and solidified his rule. There was nonetheless grumbling from many Taliban rank-and-file about the fact that Mullah Mansour had kept word of Mullah Omar's death hidden for two years and fears of his close ties to Pakistan. Mullah Omar's son, Mullah Yaqoub, and a rebel faction led by the slain Mullah Dadullah's brother which pledged allegiance to ISIS, fought briefly against Mullah Mansour, but were defeated in 2015.

For his part, Mullah Mansour vowed to continue the struggle begun by his predecessor Mullah Omar to fight until shariah law prevailed in Afghanistan. He chose as his deputy Sirajuddin Haqqani, the leader of the feared semi-independent Haqqani network. Thus the Taliban appeared to be dedicated to continuing the jihad insurgency, even though peace talks had been briefly mooted in Doha, Qatar, in the spring of 2015 (a move that seemed to have divided the Taliban). As for Mullah Mansour, his rule was short-lived and Obama ordered a drone strike that killed him in the Pakistan province of Baluchistan in May 2016.

For its part, the Obama administration, alarmed by the Taliban's bold conquest of Kunduz for two weeks in the fall of 2015 and looking at the chaotic precedent in post-U.S. Iraq, decided in October 2015 to reverse its earlier decision to withdraw all but one thousand troops by the end of 2016. Instead, Obama chose to leave ninety-eight hundred troops in Afghanistan through 2016 (i.e., into the presidency of his successor) and then drop the number to fifty-five hundred in 2017.

Obama would explain his decision, which disappointed antiwar activists, by saying: "While America's combat mission in Afghanistan may be over, our commitment to Afghanistan and its people endures. I will not allow Afghanistan to be used as a safe haven for terrorists to attack our nation again. . . . The bottom line is, in key areas of the country, the security situation is still very fragile, and in some places there is a risk of deterioration. . . . The modest but meaningful extension of our presence—while sticking to our current, narrow mission—can make a real difference. It's the right thing to do."[42]

Obama would compare his decision to keep troops in Afghanistan with his decision to withdraw them from Iraq by saying that in Afghanistan he had a clear mission for the troops, the full support of the local government, and legal agreements that protected U.S. troops. He would state, "In the Afghan government we have a serious partner who wants our help."[43] By contrast, John Earnest, the White House press secretary, would state, "In 2011 we did not have the effective cooperation from the Iraq government."[44]

The U.S. troops would continue to be based in three forward operating bases: at Bagram (north of Kabul), at Jalalabad (in the east); and at Kandahar (in the south). Troops in these bases had repeatedly been called into fights utilizing special ops and to call in air strikes in the past and were most likely to continue such missions. In February 2016 a battalion of as many as 700 soldiers was deployed to the Taliban-besieged southern province of Helmand to support Special Operations forces operating in the area. This was the largest new deployment of American soldiers outside a forward operating base since the official end of the combat mission in December 2014. Evidence of Central Command's continuing role in the fighting in post-Operation Enduring Freedom Afghanistan came in January 2016 when two U.S. soldiers were wounded and one killed fighting in Helmand. These deployments were a response to the fact that the Taliban had conquered more than half of the province by early 2016.

While many in the White House had called for a complete end to the war in Afghanistan, Obama was to declare, "it's harder to end wars than it is to begin them."[45] There was to be no precipitous withdrawal of U.S. forces as had been the case in Iraq in December 2011. The lesson from that chaotic postwar outcome had been learned, and neither the new Afghan president, Ashraf Ghani (who was far more willing to work with the Americans and Pakistanis than his recalcitrant predecessor, Karzai) nor the U.S. military wanted a complete withdrawal of U.S. forces.

President Ghani, who was the polar opposite of the troublesome Karzai (who had gone so far as to call the Taliban his "brothers" and put a halt to U.S. Special Forces night raids), was at pains to express his gratitude to the American people for their sacrifices. Ghani declared, "We will never forget your sons and daughters who have died on our soil. They are now our sons and daughters."[46]

As the Afghan War officially wound down from its most active combat phase (at least for the Americans and their NATO allies), President Obama was to declare, "It's time to turn the page on more than a decade in which so much of our foreign policy was focused on the wars in Afghanistan and Iraq."[47] By this time the United States had spent more than $104 billion in Afghanistan, a number that surpassed the Marshall Plan to rebuild post–World War II Europe, and made it the most expensive foreign assistance ever offered to another country (when adjusted for inflation in today's dollars).[48]

As the Americans and NATO allies drew down most of their forces in 2014, the Taliban stepped up their offensives on Afghan army and police units, and casualties rose. Afghan security forces lost roughly five thousand men fighting an emboldened Taliban in 2014.[49] Without constant U.S. close air support by Apache attack helicopters, B-1B bombers, F-16s, A-10 Warthogs, and other aircraft that had long proven to be the deciding factor in battles with the Taliban, the insurgents appeared to be more confident. While the Taliban usually stopped fighting in the winter months, they kept up their offensive during the winter months of 2014–15 and were less afraid to mass for offensives. The Taliban were in essence testing the Afghan fighting forces to see if they could hold their ground without the Americans to support them as actively as before. While the Taliban did make some gains in remote provinces in the east and south, for the most part the 350,000 Afghan security forces and thirty thousand Afghan local police militias held their own. The Taliban proved incapable of permanently taking any regional capitals as some had predicted they would (although they briefly took Kunduz province's capital and almost took Maimana, the capital of Faryab Province in the fall of 2015). Isolated Afghan army forces did, however, withdraw from the northern Helmand districts of Nawzad and Musa Qala in February 2016 in the face of determined Taliban attacks.

This was as much as the American generals and the Obama White House could ask for. By this time, America's bold plans of crushing the Taliban and building a secure democracy in Afghanistan had been replaced by the so-called "Afghan good-enough" policy. This policy essentially accepted the fact that the Taliban could not be beaten down or negotiated with to create a peace treaty and that compromises in America's grand ambitions had to be made. In fact the Obama administration even proved willing to compromise its policy of not negotiating with terrorists and released five top Taliban commanders in return for the release of a captured U.S. Army private named Bowe Bergdahl in 2014 (the Obama administration defended the action by pointing out that the Taliban were not officially listed by the State

Department as a Foreign Terrorist Organization). By this time, all parties concerned realized that the only way to end the Taliban insurgency was through negotiations that were being carried out in Qatar that might lead to reconciliation with the resilient insurgents.

But the new American willingness to compromise on its ambitious goals for Afghanistan did not mean that the United States and its coalition allies did not make tremendous gains in Afghanistan in their fourteen-plus years of warfare in the country. The world that the U.S. and its NATO allies created in Afghanistan included a tremendously increased gross national product; schools for millions of newly enrolled children (including 3.1 million girls), which teach math, science, literature, geography, and so on, instead of strict shariah Islamic topics; a bustling capital swelled by over a million newcomers; wide ownership of cell phones and Internet access, and numerous television channels (the Taliban had banned television and Internet); new dams; a free press; new government buildings; beauty shops, which were banned in the Taliban times; DVD stores; jobs; a massive army and police force built to the tune of $65 billion; democracy; women in parliament; several skyscrapers in Kabul; newly built wells; expanded electricity service; unveiled women in the capital and Hazara region; hospitals and clinics; electricity plants; hundreds of miles of tarmac roads filled with millions of new cars; demined fields; an end to weekly shariah law public executions and floggings; and on and on.

This world was inadvertently made possible by bin Laden. In a roundabout way, many average Afghans, especially the women and girls who make up half the population and the Northern Alliance Uzbeks, Hazaras, and Tajiks (i.e., the majority of the country) who fought to be freed from Al Qaeda's Taliban allies, owe bin Laden a debt of gratitude. Had he not attacked the distant United States on 9/11, the improvements in their lives would not have been possible.

For better or worse, perhaps bin Laden's most lasting legacy in Afghanistan was the emergence of a post-Taliban generation of Afghans who grew up in this new environment, instead of suffering under the misrule of the most oppressive, fundamentalist regime in Eurasia. Thus the war in Afghanistan, which has settled into a precarious stalemate since the situation was stabilized by the Obama troop surge, achieved many of its objectives (including the main objective of denying Al Qaeda a sanctuary and killing up to 70 percent of its leaders) but failed in others (mainly decisively defeating the Taliban insurgency).

Meanwhile, the Taliban remain a resilient enemy and are determined to carry out the war to its successful conclusion, which means the overthrow of the American-backed Afghan government and reestablishment of a strict Taliban theocracy. While the Taliban took heavy losses during the Obama troop surge, they are resilient and resourceful. The newly elected Taliban leader Mullah Mawlawi Haibatullah Akhundzada's followers, like the mujahideen before them, are tough fighters who are fanatically devoted to their cause. They are fired by their devotion to jihad and aim to duplicate the expulsion of the Soviets and the British before them. The Taliban take heart in the memory of their people's previous defeats of invaders and sum up their continuing resolve, and America's waning interest in Afghanistan, by proclaiming, "Americans might have the watches . . . but we have the time."[50]

CHAPTER 6

The New War on ISIS

We will follow them [ISIS] to the gates of hell.
—Vice President Joe Biden in a speech following
the beheading of a U.S. journalist

Know, oh Obama, that we will reach America. Know also that we will cut off
your head in the White House and transform America into a Muslim
province.
—ISIS spokesman, seconds before beheading
a captured Shiite soldier

The Fissuring of Post-U.S. Iraq

It was clear to Barack Obama when he was running for president back in
2008 that the American people were tired of the costly war in Iraq, which for
over half a decade had filled the news with endless images of carnage, bloodshed, and destruction. On the campaign trail he had promised to end the
unpopular war "responsibly."

But in actuality, when Obama became president in January 2009, the
terms for the withdrawal of U.S. forces had already been put in place by president Bush and Iraqi prime minister Nouri al Maliki with their 2008 "Agreement Between the United States of America and the Republic of Iraq on the
Withdrawal of United States Forces from Iraq." This bilateral agreement
called for U.S. forces to be out of Iraq by December 31, 2011. Thus Obama

was not really creating a new framework to get U.S. troops out early (i.e., "cutting and running" in the terms of his hawkish critics who later blamed him for "abandoning" Iraq); he was simply carrying out a pre-existing Status of Forces Agreement (SOFA) signed by the Bush administration in December 2008. Bush and Iraqi prime minister Maliki jointly signed the pact at a conference in the Green Zone in Baghdad on December 14, 2008, and Obama carried out its pre-existing stipulations.

But the Pentagon wanted to retain a small residual force of some sort in Iraq beyond the planned withdrawal date of December 31, 2011. While the 2008 Bush-Maliki SOFA had called for U.S. troops to be withdrawn from Iraq by the end of 2011, there was an informal agreement that some troops would be left behind. Numbers from three thousand to twenty thousand residual troops were bandied around at the time, and new SOFA negotiations were begun in October 2011 as the U.S. withdrawal deadline approached. Secretary of Defense Robert Gates and Joint Chiefs of Staff chairman Admiral Michael Mullen wanted to leave sixteen thousand troops in Iraq, but the Obama administration convinced them to lower the number to ten thousand.[1] This number was later whittled down by Obama to about five thousand troops and a half dozen F-16s.[2]

Obama agreed that some U.S. troops needed to be left behind to train and advise Iraqi forces, but Prime Minister Maliki told the American president that he needed to "line up political allies" in parliament to gain support for such a potentially unpopular move.[3] The Iraqi president was under pressure from many Shiite factions to complete the total withdrawal of all U.S. forces and return full sovereignty to Iraq. As the December 31, 2011, withdrawal deadline approached, both sides assumed an agreement would be made to leave a residual U.S. training force in Iraq.

It was at this time that the American side brought up the thorny issue of immunity for U.S. residual troops from prosecution in Iraqi courts. Should U.S. residual troops break Iraqi laws, the United States did not want to have them tried in an Iraqi court. But with the memory of the Haditha massacre, the Abu Ghraib prison abuse scandal, and the Blackwater shooting of civilians in downtown Baghdad still fresh in their minds, the Iraqi side balked at this request. The notion of having gun-toting American soldiers acting with impunity in post–U.S.-occupation Iraq was seen by the Iraqis as an unacceptable infringement on their sovereignty. The Maliki side felt it was being pressed too hard on this issue and refused to allow U.S. residual troops to be given immunity. Maliki would later say at an October 2011 conference,

"When the Americans asked for immunity, the Iraqi side answered that it was not possible."[4]

Without this immunity, the Americans decided they could not continue to base U.S. troops in Iraq. The issue of legal protection for U.S. troops in post-2011 Iraq was essentially a deal breaker. Thus there was no new SOFA, and the U.S. troops were brought home, except for a contingent of several hundred troops and contractors guarding the massive U.S. embassy in Baghdad (the largest in the world). Obama would later blame the collapse of the talks for a new SOFA on Maliki and the Iraqi government.[5] Republicans since this time have criticized Obama for "cutting and running" and surrendering Iraq and Syria to ISIS. As Dominic Tierney observed in the *Atlantic* in January 2016:

> When Republicans berate Obama for withdrawing American troops, they neglect to mention that Obama inherited a timetable negotiated by the Bush administration for a complete U.S. exit. Could Obama have convinced the Iraqis to switch direction and accept a follow-on force? Here, opinion differs widely. It's fair to say that the White House was internally divided about a successor force, and didn't push as hard as it could have. But a rising tide of Iraqi nationalism made striking such a deal extremely challenging. When I interviewed John Abizaid, the former head of Central Command, for my book on U.S. military failure, he told me that an American successor force was "not in the cards at all." Republicans also vastly embellish what an American successor force might have accomplished. In the GOP's imagination, these troops have grown into supermen who could have held off extremism in the Middle East—as if Obama pulled the Spartans out of Thermopylae. But if 150,000 U.S. troops couldn't salve Iraq's sectarian divisions [during the surge], why would 10,000 soldiers have solved the puzzle? And these troops would almost certainly not have prevented the emergence of ISIS, which mainly arose across the border in Syria.

Regardless of who was to blame, it is doubtful, had the Obama administration been able to work out a new SOFA deal with Maliki to keep three thousand to five thousand U.S. trainers in Iraq, that this small force of advisors could have militarily prevented the rise of the terrorist group ISIS (the Islamic State in Iraq and Syria) in the sprawling Sunni lands in 2014. The U.S. trainers-advisors would not have had a mandate to return to wage full-scale battles and counterinsurgency in places like Fallujah or wider Anbar Province. Their presence might have, however, moderated the anti-Sunni, sectarian tendencies of Shiite prime minister Nouri al Maliki, which emerged right after the U.S. troops departed (to be discussed below). With no U.S. troops remaining in the country, America's influence and leverage over Maliki was tremendously reduced, and he quickly gave in to his anti-Sunni, authoritarian impulses. Maliki was to launch a campaign of Sunni arrests that was to incite rebellions among this sectarian group. Many of these Sunni rebels would subsequently go on to join ISIS, which positioned itself as the voice of repressed Sunnis. In this respect, Obama can be faulted for not forcing this issue of leaving residual American troops in Iraq to possibly be used as leverage against Maliki's subsequent anti-Sunni policies.

Either way, Obama was glad to put the war behind him and thus fulfill his campaign promise to the American people, while Maliki could claim to have restored full Iraqi sovereignty. For an Iraqi leader who was closely aligned to the Shiite Iranians, who hoped to extend their influence in post-U.S. Iraq, this was a victory. For his part, Obama somewhat optimistically declared that the "tides of war are receding" and "the last American soldiers will cross the border out of Iraq with their heads held high, proud of their success, and knowing that the American people stand united in our support for our troops. That is how America's military efforts in Iraq will end."[6]

There were grounds for Obama's optimism as most of the final thirty-nine thousand U.S. combat troops rolled out of Iraq and into Kuwait by mid-December 2011. Al Qaeda in Iraq (AQI) had been shattered and pushed to the far reaches of Anbar Province by the Anbar Awakening, pro-U.S. Sunni tribesmen, and the surge of twenty-eight thousand reinforcement troops under General Petraeus in 2007. The Shiite prime minister, Nouri al Maliki, had promised the departing Americans he would overcome the distrust between the Shiites, who had been put into power by the invasion, and the recently disempowered Sunnis. Most important, Maliki promised the Americans he would put many of the 103,000 Anbar Awakening Sunni militiamen on the government payroll and integrate Sunnis into the army and police forces.

The Americans had left behind a million-man Iraqi security force (350,000 soldiers and 650,000 police), trained to the tune of $25 billion, that was intended to act as a force of unification and defense against the down, but not out, AQI (also known as the Islamic State in Iraq). The Iraqi army, which was armed with everything from attack helicopters to Humvees and MRAPs, was constructed to reflect Iraq's diversity and included Shiites, Sunnis, and Kurds.

The United States had also bequeathed Iraq with a secular constitution, democratic elections, and a 274-member parliament (with a quarter of the seats occupied by women). America had done its best to build up a stable, democratic Iraq, and, after almost forty-five hundred U.S. deaths and eight years of bloody war, it was time for the Americans to end the hemorrhaging of American blood in the sands of Iraq and let the Iraqi state stand on its own.

But even as Obama appeared to kick the dust off from the long war in Iraq and to focus on carrying out a thirty-thousand-strong troop surge to save the deteriorating situation in Afghanistan, the seeds for the unraveling of post-U.S. Iraq began to be laid. In fact it did not take the Iraqi leader a full twenty-four hours after the departure of the last Americans to begin to plant the seeds of discord.

The last American troops left on December 18, and on December 19 Prime Minister Maliki (a Shiite) put out an arrest warrant for his Sunni vice president, Tariq al Hashimi. Seven of Hashimi's bodyguards had been arrested, and subsequently claimed that the vice president had ordered them to plant IEDs and carry out assassinations of Shiites.[7] But the guards had all been severely beaten before making their confessions, and one of them had actually been beaten to death.[8] Knowing his arrest was imminent, Hashimi, who claimed his imprisoned bodyguards had been tortured into making false statements, fled to the autonomous Kurdish north, where he found sanctuary. He proclaimed his innocence from Kurdistan and traveled abroad, where he was received as the vice president of Iraq by surrounding Sunni states.

Maliki also began arresting former Baathist members, mainly Sunnis. One Western analyst said of this process, "Baathism here is a symbol Maliki uses as his bogeyman. It gives him the leeway to go around arresting people. It's about a climate of fear."[9]

The Obama White House, which had been quietly celebrating the withdrawal of the last U.S. troops from Iraq, was alarmed by this unsettling development. All their previous optimism faded as the suspicions and distrust of the 2006–7 civil war period once again rose to the surface now that the Americans were not there to mediate the conflict. At the time, the *New York Times* reported:

> The accusations against Vice President Tariq al Hashimi underlined
> fears that Iraq's leaders may now be using the very institutions
> America has spent millions of dollars trying to strengthen—the
> police, the courts, the media—as a cudgel to batter their political
> enemies and consolidate power. . . .

To government critics, the charges [against Hashimi] seemed to be part of a wide-reaching consolidation of power by Mr. Maliki. Amid the anxiety stirred by the American departure and unrest in neighboring Syria, Mr. Maliki, a Shiite, has tightened his grip on this violent and divided nation by marginalizing, intimidating or arresting his political rivals, many of whom are part of Iraq's Sunni minority.[10]

Reidar Visser, an expert on Iraqi politics, said: "Any leading Sunni politician seems now to be a target of this campaign by Maliki. It seems that every Sunni Muslim or secularist is in danger of being labeled either a Baathist or a terrorist. He [Vice President Hashimi] was someone who tried to be conciliatory with the Shiite Islamists at a time when others did not do so. Now, Maliki is going after him."[11] Fox News reported that the arrest warrant for Vice President Hashimi "raised suspicions that Prime Minister Nouri al-Maliki, a Shiite, ordered the arrest of Vice President Tariq al-Hashimi as part of a campaign to consolidate his hold on power out of a fear that Sunnis in and out of Iraq are plotting against him."[12] Western observers seemed to feel that the charges against the Sunni vice president Hashimi by the paranoid Shiite prime minister, Maliki, were politically motivated. They were simply a continuation, by other means, of the sectarian conflict that had rent the fabric of Iraqi society during the civil war of 2006–7. Maliki, who had been based in Shiite Iran for seven years and had spent much of his life as an exiled dissident leader striving to overthrow the Sunni-dominated Baathist Party, was now showing his true colors.[13]

The White House called for reconciliation, but Prime Minister Maliki was not in the mood for compromise, and Vice President Hashimi was ultimately sentenced to death in absentia. Maliki also ordered the arrest of more than six hundred Sunnis whom he accused of being involved in an improbable plot to overthrow his government and reestablish the Baathist Party.[14] In response to these developments, which were perceived as anti-Sunni by Sunnis, Sunni lawmakers walked out of parliament and began to accuse Maliki of being a sectarian dictator. Maliki's actions enraged Sunni tribesmen across the board, especially in Anbar Province, where many felt betrayed. The 103,000 "Sons of Iraq" Anbar Awakening militiamen who were not given jobs in the Iraqi security forces, as had been promised earlier by Maliki, were outraged. The Shiite prime minister broke his word to the Sunnis and, instead of integrating them into the army and police, cut off payments to the Anbar Awakening militias and essentially fired them.[15]

Maliki even went so far as openly arrest Anbar Awakening militiamen.[16] This was in continuation of a policy of arrest and killing of Anbar Awakening militiamen that the increasingly paranoid Maliki, who believed they were plotting a coup, had begun even before the Americans left Iraq.[17] In addition to moving against these Sunni Anbar militias who had helped defeat Al Qaeda in Iraq in 2007–8, Maliki moved to purge Sunnis from the army. Many of those Sunnis who were purged were professionals who had been trained by the U.S. Army during the occupation.

Meanwhile the Obama administration had completely disengaged itself from Iraq in the political sense and no longer felt it had the right or power to intervene in what was now a sovereign state. One Sunni complained of the Obama administration's disengagement vis-à-vis Prime Minister Maliki and his anti-Sunni policies as follows: "It's not that you can't intervene—we've watched you intervene all around the world to remove long-standing dictators. What we hear you say is that you won't intervene to stop a rising dictator right here and restore the democracy which you bought to us."[18]

Maliki, who then took direct control of the Iraqi army through his newly created post of commander in chief, and brought in Shiite loyalists from his Dawa Party to replace the fired Sunnis. He also purged the Iraqi National Intelligence Service of Sunnis.[19] In essence, Maliki further "Shiiteified" the armed forces, intelligence services, and police and turned them into a Shiite force that began to be used against real or perceived Sunni or Kurdish threats. Promotion in this army depended not on professionalism, but on Shiite credentials and cronyism (a point that would come back to haunt Maliki when he had to use this very force to hold on to Sunni-dominated Mosul when ISIS came to conquer it in June 2014). The Iraqi president proved not to be a president of Iraq, but of the Shiites, and his policies of promoting Shiite loyalists alienated the Sunnis and weakened his army.

Maliki continued his authoritarian-sectarian policies by going after key Sunni political figures who had spoken out against him. Among them was Rafe el Essawi, the popular Sunni finance minister, and sixteen of his bodyguards, who were arrested in December 2012. The *New York Times* reported, "The targeting once again of a Sunni leader by the Shiite-dominated central government threatened to further hinder Iraq's halting process of sectarian reconciliation."[20] As frustrated Sunnis took to the streets to protest, one stated of the arrest warrant against Finance Minister Essawi, "[Vice President] Hashimi is gone, now Essawi, and we have no Sunni leader left to follow," while another stated, "This is targeting all the Sunnis. It was Hashimi first. Essawi now. Who knows who it will be next? The conspiracy against the Sunnis will never stop. We will not keep silent for this."[21] Al Jazeera reported, "The bigger picture is that Sunnis feel that they are not a part of this country any more."[22]

Thousands of Sunnis took to the streets of Fallujah and Ramadi in Anbar Province to protest Maliki's arrest of Sunni politicians. There, the Sunni rhetoric against the Shiite-dominated Maliki government grew increasingly hostile as protest camps were constructed in January 2013. In Ramadi, Sunni protestors raised black jihadi flags of the sort flown by AQI, and one man shouted, "We are a group called Al Qaeda!" Another shouted, "We will cut off heads and bring justice!" as the crowd cheered.[23] Even at this early stage there was a tendency for the increasingly embittered Sunnis to express their frustration by announcing an allegiance to Al Qaeda in Iraq/ISI (Islamic State in Iraq) militants. Although the Al Qaeda/ISI militants remained in the background during the anti-government protests, they were positioning themselves to take advantage of the rising Sunni fury against Maliki's policies.

In response to these protests, Maliki went on television and told the protestors to disband: "This [protest] site has become a base for Al Qaeda" and is filled with "killers and criminals."[24] He further stated, "There will be no negotiations while the [protest] square is still standing." Maliki warned of a sectarian war and of the return of the Baathists. Incautiously, he also brought up ancient battles in Islam that created the Sunni-versus-Shiite rift and portrayed the developments in Fallujah and Ramadi as a manifestation of the medieval-era sectarian war for the fate of Islam.

But the Sunni protestors in Anbar and many other towns in the Sunni west and north of Baghdad did not back down and demanded the release of thousands of Sunnis who had been arrested under Maliki's stringent Counterterrorism Law. They also demanded the removal of the Shiite-dominated Iraqi army from their towns and an end to harsher strictures of de-Baathification. Some Sunnis even began to call for the resignation of Prime Minister Maliki and an end to Iranian influence in Iraq.

Tensions came to a head on April 19, 2013, when Sunni protesters in the town of Hawija, north of Baghdad, marched to a local army garrison and got into a clash with Shiite troops, which led to the death of one soldier and one marcher. In response, Iraqi troops attacked a protest encampment in Hawija, killing dozens of protesters. The army claimed it attacked the camp only after being fired on by militants belonging to the Baathist Sunni insurgent group: the Naqshbandi Army.

In response, local Sunni militants began to attack army checkpoints in the surrounding area, killing soldiers and planting IEDs on roads traveled by the Shiite-dominated army. Sunni militants also set off car bombs in Shiite towns and neighborhoods in Baghdad, and Shiites responded in kind. As protests spread, Sunni tribesmen blocked roads in an effort to prevent army troops from reaching encampments, subsequently prompting firefights, which led to more deaths. Sunni protesters also began to overrun police stations as preachers used their mosques to call on Sunnis to fight Shiites.

By late April 2013, the fighting had spread to the Sunni-dominated town of Mosul in the north and to all Sunni provinces. It was as if all the gains of the Anbar Awakening and the surge were being rolled back, and Iraq was once again descending into sectarian civil war. Tellingly, during the tit-for-tat killings, which spread from Mosul to Tikrit to Fallujah, members of the Anbar Awakening were killed by Shiite security forces. In the three months following the Hawjah incident, three thousand Iraqis were killed in what amounted to the worst sectarian violence since the 2007 civil war.[25]

Tensions were exacerbated when, six months later in December 2013, Iraqi troops arrested a prominent Sunni firebrand and member of parliament named Ahmed al Alwani on terrorism charges. Alwani had earlier called Maliki the "snake of Iran," infuriating the prime minister, who had revived Baathist-era laws allowing him to arrest anyone who criticized the prime minister. While resisting arrest, Alwani's brother and five of his bodyguards were killed. Two Iraqi troops were also killed in the exchange of fire. They were but a handful of the eight thousand people killed in the year 2013, the worst year of violence since the end of the 2007 civil war.[26] To compound matters, Sunnis (including women) were arrested and sent to jail without trials. Clearly the peace that had been achieved in Iraq during the 2007 surge was unraveling, and American hopes that post-U.S. Iraq was healing from this sectarian conflict were collapsing.

By the end of the disastrous year of 2013, Maliki's troops had destroyed a protest camp in the capital of Anbar Province, Ramadi, infuriating tens of thousands of Sunnis. One of the most active tribes in fighting the Shiite Maliki government was the Dulaim tribe of the recently arrested member of parliament, Ahmed al Alwani. As a situation verging on warfare swept the Sunni lands, Maliki launched a bombardment of Fallujah and Ramadi and besieged these two bastions of Sunni power. Then, unexpectedly, on December 31, 2013, he decided to give into one of the Sunnis' demands and remove Iraqi army troops from the encircled towns of Fallujah and Ramadi. His hope appears to have been to calm the situation down and prevent a full-scale Sunni versus Shiite civil war.

But Maliki's belated attempt to compromise with the Sunnis was too late, and his withdrawal of security forces from Fallujah and Ramadi left a vacuum at a time of intense fury among disenfranchised Sunnis, who felt betrayed by the Maliki Shiite-dominated government. That vacuum was quickly filled on January 3, 2014, by a new force of hundreds of masked fighters arriving in pickups under the black jihad banner formerly flown by Al Qaeda in Iraq/Islamic State of Iraq. Only the mysterious fighters, many of whom came from across the border in war-torn Syria, had a new name for their organization; they now called themselves the fighters of ISIS, the Islamic State of Iraq *and* Syria.

The Rise of ISIS

The rise of ISIS or ISIL (the Islamic State in Iraq and the Levant, Levant being another name for greater Syria), or Daesh (an acronym for the Islamic State of Iraq and Sham/Syria that is usually used in a pejorative sense—Arabs who hate ISIS call it Daesh because it sounds like the word *daess* which means to stomp on or crush someone), or simply IS, the Islamic State, as it became known in the summer of 2014, is a direct outcome of the overthrow and disempowerment of the ruling Sunnis by the United States in 2003. The further disenfranchisement of the Sunnis by the Shiite-dominated Maliki government following the U.S. withdrawal of 2011 and the repression against Syrian Sunnis by the Alawite (a syncretic Shiite offshoot) Assad government since 1970 also contributed to its rise. To understand the terrorist group's meteoric ascent to power in a vast swath of Iraq and Syria roughly twice the size of Israel or equal to the size of Pennsylvania or Britain, one has to follow the career of its founder, Abu Bakr al Baghdadi.

Al Baghdadi, whose real name is Ibrahim Awad Ibrahim al-Badr, was born in 1971 near the northern Iraqi town of Samarra, in what is the Sunni heartland. He later attended the Islamic University in Baghdad, where he earned a Ph.D. in shariah Islamic law. He then became the imam for a mosque in Tobchi, a neighborhood in western Baghdad in the late 1990s. This was the secular times of Saddam Hussein's Baathist Party, and al Baghdadi, like many Islamists among the Sunnis and Shiites who had been silenced during this period, rebelled against the perceived lax morality of the era. On one occasion he broke up a wedding in his neighborhood where men and women were dancing together.[27] As a scholar of Islam, al Baghdadi's goal was to teach Islamic law, and Joby Warrick has written in his book on ISIS, "had it not been for the U.S. invasion of Iraq, the Islamic State's greatest butcher would likely have lived out his years as a college professor."[28]

When the United States fatefully invaded Iraq in 2003, al Baghdadi formed his own insurgent group north of Baghdad and was arrested by the Americans, who accused him of being involved in the insurgency. He was thrown into a U.S. prison for insurgents called Camp Bucca in 2005. In this camp, al Baghdadi met with other imprisoned insurgents and began to adhere to their extreme views on terroristic jihad. This experience, especially interacting with insurgents who were tied to Zarqawi's Al Qaeda in Iraq, seems to have further radicalized him and brought him into the ranks of AQI.

The Americans, who had more than twenty-five thousand Iraqi prisoners at the time, did not know that al Baghdadi would one day become a key player in AQI. After his release he became the AQI commander in the Syrian frontier town of Rawa, where he was known for his extreme brutality in enforcing shariah law. In April 2010, AQI leaders Abu Omar al Baghdadi and his deputy, an Egyptian bomb expert named Abu Ayub al Masri, blew themselves up when they were tracked down and surrounded by Iraqi security forces. It was then that AQI's ruling shura (council) met and nominated Abu Bakr al Baghdadi to be the new leader of the terrorist organization, which by this time had taken to calling itself the Islamic State in Iraq (ISI).

This was a low point in AQI/ISI's fortunes. The 2007 surge and Anbar Awakening had pushed them out of their strongholds in Anbar and the provinces north of Iraq, and the Shiite-dominated security forces had taken control of such Sunni strongholds as Fallujah, Ramadi, Tikrit, and Mosul. By 2010, General Ray Odierno was able to announce that the United States had killed thirty-four of the top forty-two leaders of AQI/ISI.[29] But as Prime Minister Maliki marginalized the Sunnis in 2012 and 2013, ISI leader al Baghdadi sensed that the opportunity had come to revive his shattered organization by recruiting disenfranchised Sunnis. AQI/ISI became a major alternative to the Shiite-led Maliki government, which was, by 2012, arresting Sunnis and attacking their protest camps.

Al Baghdadi announced the revival of AQI/ISI by declaring a new campaign against the Maliki government known as "Breaking the Walls." Among its top priorities was breaking imprisoned Sunnis, many of them AQI insurgents, out of jail. At the time al Baghdadi announced to Sunnis, "I urge you to send your sons to join the ranks of the mujahideen [fighters] in defense of your religion and honor. The majority of the Sunnis in Iraq support al-Qaida and are waiting for its return."[30]

Al Baghdadi lost no time in translating his threats into action and launched an attack on Abu Ghraib prison only July 21, 2013, that freed approximately five hundred imprisoned Sunni insurgents. This prison break, which showed AQI/ISI's military abilities shocked the nation, and was followed by seven more prison breaks that freed more hard-core AQI insurgent veterans, many of them on death row. AQI/ISI also began waging an IED, suicide-bombing, and car-bombing campaign that brought casualty levels up to the point of the worst insurgent violence in the 2007–8 period. This led to more than one thousand casualties per month in 2013.[31] Many of those who died were Shiites who were targeted in suicide bombing attacks that were reminiscent of the worst terrorism of the pre-surge times. As the campaign unfolded, al Baghdadi promised that AQI/ISI would retake its old strongholds in the Sunni lands, from Anbar in the west to Mosul in the north.

The Iraqi government responded by launching a campaign of its own known as "Revenge of the Martyrs," which saw mass arrests of Sunnis, thus further exacerbating the Sunni-Shiite divide and playing into ISI's hands. Simultaneously, Iranian-backed Shiite militias were also mobilized to fight against the Sunni insurgents; this was akin to pouring gasoline on the fire. One of the main grievances of the Sunnis was Shiite Iran's growing influence in post-U.S. Iraq. Thus AQI/ISI had succeeded in enhancing the preexisting problems created by Maliki and creating further Sunni-versus-Shiite cleavages. This had always been a goal of Zarqawi prior to his death in 2006, and it had been taken up again by al Baghdadi with a vengeance.

As all these events were happening in the Sunni lands of western and northern Iraq from 2011 to 2013, neighboring Syria collapsed into its own sectarian conflict, which pitted the ruling President Bashar al Assad regime and its Alawite Shiite supporters (12 percent of the Syrian population) against the majority Sunni population that had long been repressed. The problems began in March 2011 when Syrian Sunnis joined the so-called Arab Spring protests that were overthrowing governments from Yemen to Egypt to Tunisia, and began to peacefully march for greater freedoms and rights. As in Libya, Egypt, and Tunisia, where these Arab Spring protests against local strongmen overthrew secular governments and gave Islamists an opening (the same could be said for post-Hussein Iraq and post-U.S.-intervention Libya), in Syria the initially peaceful protests led to the rise of a virulent form of Sunni jihadism.

It all began in March 2011 when Sunni students who sprayed anti–President Assad graffiti on a wall in the Syrian town of Daraa proclaiming "the people want to topple the regime" were arrested, beaten, and tortured (including having fingernails pulled out). Later the corpse of a thirteen-year-old Syrian boy who had been arrested was returned to his parents with his genitals cut off and other signs of torture. The people of the Daraa and other Sunni towns began marching for the arrested students to be freed and refused to be cowed. The Assad regime responded to this civic unrest with brute force and began to arrest, beat, and kill protestors. Obama was infuriated by the slaughter of thousands of civilians by Assad's troops. At the time the Shiite–Alawite Assad regime also began deploying Shiite death squads known as the Shabiha ("ghosts") against Sunni protestors. In response, there were many defections from the government in 2012 by Sunni military officers who joined the Free Syrian Army resistance based in neighboring Turkey.

Quickly the rebellion took on sectarian overtones. The Assad regime would later end up using approximately five thousand Shiite Hezbollah fighters from neighboring Lebanon to fight in the south against rebelling Syrian Sunnis as well as up to twenty-one hundred Iranian troops.[32] The Iranians also deployed thousands of Shiite Hazaras who were living as refugees in Iran to fight in Syria after promising them citizenship and threatening to deport them if they did not fight. Clearly the Iranians and Shiite Hezbollah felt that they had a stake in defending the Alawites in Syria who adhered to a hybrid Shiite offshoot sect that had many syncretic aspects. In fact, Hezbollah fighters played a key role in defending an important Shiite shrine in southern Syria, known as the Tomb of Zaynab, from Sunni rebels in 2013. And Iran, which provided an economic lifeline to the Assad regime, sent hundreds of advisors who trained a pro-government militia known as the National Defense Forces.

The Syrian Sunni opposition forces, which at this stage were relatively moderate and non-sectarian, responded by creating an armed rebel group based in neighboring Turkey known as the Free Syrian Army. At the time Senator John McCain called for arming the Free Syrian Army and other rebels who were fighting against a brutal regime that ultimately used everything from UN-banned chemical weapons to barrel bombs against its opponents. McCain, who actually traveled to Syria and met with moderate rebels, said, "We need to have a game-changing action. No American boots on the ground [but] establish a safe zone, and protect it and supply weapons to the right people in Syria."[33]

The Syrian Assad regime ended up killing tens of thousands of people (far more than ISIS later would) and driving millions of them abroad as refugees, primarily to Turkey, Lebanon, and Jordan. By 2016 ten percent of Syria's population had been killed, eleven million had fled. Some 2.6 million fled to Turkey, 1.4 million to Jordan, 1.4 million to Lebanon, and between 360,000 and 573,00 to Germany (this was Europe's largest refugee crisis since World War II). The Assad regime used starvation and bombing of civilian packed neighborhoods as a tool to break the back of the Sunni resistance. At one point in August 2013, Obama threatened to attack Assad for having "crossed a red line" by deploying sarin chemical weapons against Sunni civilians in a Damascus neighborhood known as Ghouta. But Obama backed down from his threat when Congress refused to authorize airstrikes, the British parliament rejected supporting American actions, and ultimately Russian president Vladimir Putin convinced the Syrian government to dismantle its banned WMDs. This prevented the Americans from directly involving themselves in a war against the Syrian regime that few in America wanted. The Sunni rebels were, however, crushed by America's decision not to attack the Assad regime. But the mantra in the White House and in Western governments was still that Assad had to go in order for a transition government to be created.

The United States and its NATO allies were not alone in their opposition to the brutal Syrian Assad regime. Turkey and the Sunni Arab countries called for creating a no-fly zone against Syrian air force bombers in the northwest and arming the Sunni rebels. A no-fly zone would serve as a designated area or "bubble" where Syrian government aircraft would be shot down by U.S. fighter jets if they passed into it carrying out bombings of Syrian Sunni rebels. Secretary of State Hillary Clinton also called for a no-fly zone in the northwest and for arming Syrian rebels.[34] With CIA director Leon Panetta supporting her, she said that if America "was willing finally to get in the game, we could be much more effective in isolating the extremists and empowering the moderates in Syria."[35]

But President Obama was not initially confident that U.S.-supplied weapons would not end up in the hands of an increasing number of jihadi extremist Sunni groups that had joined the Sunni rebellion against the Shiite Assad regime, and he resisted McCain and Clinton. Obama pointed to the dangerous precedent of the U.S. arming of the mujahideen Afghan freedom fighters in the 1980s and the fact that the most heavily armed and funded mujahideen commander, Gulbuddin Hekmatyar, later turned against his U.S. sponsors and joined the Taliban-led insurgency. If weapons sent to the rebels ended up in the hands of extremists or terrorists, it was also felt the Republicans would make political hay out of it.

Obama also initially did not feel that shifting from non-lethal aid, which was being provided to the rebels, to weapons would tip the balance in their favor. He stated, "I don't think anybody in the region . . . would think that U.S. unilateral actions, in and of themselves, would bring about a better outcome."[36]

Jeffrey Goldberg summed up Obama's cautious approach to putting U.S. troops in harm's way in an April 2016 article in the *Atlantic* entitled "The Obama Doctrine." He wrote, "The message Obama telegraphed in speeches and interviews was clear: He would not end up like the second President Bush—a president who became tragically overextended in the Middle East and whose decision filled the wards of Walter Reed [military hospital] with grievously wounded soldiers. . . . Obama would say privately that the first task of an American president in the post-Bush international arena was 'Don't do stupid shit.'"

It was only later, in 2014, that the Obama administration began training "vetted moderate" Sunni rebels in Turkey and Jordan via a program that ultimately cost $500 million. But these fifty-four hundred Pentagon-trained rebels were ordered to fight the ISIS terrorist group, not Assad. These restrictions for what amounted to a U.S.-backed fighting force in Syria doomed the train-and-equip program, as the Sunni rebels were far more interested in fighting the Assad regime (which was massacring their people) than ISIS, which was made up of fellow Sunnis. In fact, many moderate Sunni rebels went on to join the Al Qaeda–linked Al Nusra Front group because it was most effective at fighting the Assad regime.

Al Nusra, or Jabhat al Nusra l' Ahl as Sham (the Support Front of the People of Greater Syria), was officially formed in January 2012 and quickly became the most effective Sunni rebel group in the war against the Assad regime, a regime that was condemned by the United States for war crimes and blamed for instigating the rise of Sunni extremism as a response. The Al Nusra Front, which included many AQI/ISI members who were sent over from Iraq to support this fellow Sunni insurgent movement starting in August 2011, carried out several spectacular terrorist bombings against Assad regime targets in such Syrian towns as Damascus and Aleppo. ISI's Al Nusra offshoot also proved to be the most effective fighting force in the Sunni rebels' conquest of much of Syria's largest town, Aleppo, and the northern province of Idlib. Many smaller or more moderate groups merged with Al Nusra as its numbers and success grew. It was said to have between six thousand and ten thousand fighters by November 2012.[37] At this time, the United States infuriated many Sunni rebels by declaring Al Nusra an Al Qaeda–linked terrorist group, despite its relative pragmatism and undeniable success against the detested Assad regime.

In April 2013, AQI/ISI leader al Baghdadi, who was at that time carrying out the earlier-mentioned stepped-up terror campaign against the Shiite Maliki regime in Iraq, announced that the Nusra Front was an extension of his own Iraqi group ISI. He also announced that AQI/ISI had actually dispatched the Al Nusra leader, Abu Muhammad al Jawlani (a Syrian member of AQI/ISI), to neighboring Syria to lead that group in its jihad against the Syrian Assad regime. Al Baghdadi shared the news that AQI/ISI had been funding Al Nusra and providing it with fighters from the start. He then proclaimed that Al Nusra and AQI/ISI would merge to form a new group known as the Islamic State in Iraq *and* Syria (ISIS). This was electrifying news and signified the unification of the Sunni jihadists in Syria and Iraq.

But the very next day Al Nusra leader al Jawlani rejected al Baghdadi's proclamation of a merger and stated, "We inform you that neither the al-Nusra command nor its consultative council, nor its general manager were aware of this announcement. It reached them via the media and if the speech is authentic, we were not consulted." Jawlani also said, "Al Nusra Front's banner will remain, nothing will be changed in it."[38] This dispute caused tensions between the two Sunni jihadist groups in Iraq and Syria. Many members of Al Nusra, mainly Iraqis sent by al Baghdadi to fight in Syria, began to defect from Nusra to the newly created ISIS umbrella group, which began to create separate military forces in Syria. In one Syrian province, Idlib, 70 percent of Nusra's fighters were said to have left the group to join ISIS.[39] These defections led to open fighting between Al Nusra and newly created ISIS that caused hundreds of deaths. ISIS also used suicide bombers to target members of other more moderate Sunni rebel groups for assassination.[40] In fact ISIS fighters at times seemed more intent on waging a war against Al Nusra and other moderate rebel forces than against the Assad regime. ISIS quickly gained a reputation for extreme brutality in this intra-rebel fighting and was seen by the other rebel groups as focused on seizing territory, not overthrowing Assad. In fact ISIS soon began making considerable money selling oil from its lands to the Assad regime (for its part, the Assad military rarely attacked ISIS, which controlled territory primarily in the eastern desert away from the Alawite homeland in the west).[41] Ultimately, ISIS was forced out of Aleppo and the province of Idilb by a coalition of other more moderate Syrian insurgent groups but retained its power in its capital of Raqqa in the east and the eastern region of Deir es Zor.

As these disputes were occurring between ISIS and the other Sunni rebel groups, Al Qaeda Central leader Ayman al Zawahiri (who was hiding out in Pakistan, but still retained authority as the leader of the original Al Qaeda group) issued orders for ISIS to remain in Iraq and for Al Nusra to lead the jihad in Syria. He said it was "wrong" for ISIS leader al Baghdadi to have tried to merge the two groups without consulting him. Zawahiri declared that al Baghdadi's unilateral takeover of Nusra was "damaging to all jihadists."[42] Zawahiri also called for ISIS to be abolished and return to being just ISI (the Islamic State in Iraq).[43] He then put al Baghdadi on "probation" for a year.

But far from heeding Zawahiri's orders, al Baghdadi made the momentous decision to break from Al Qaeda Central and declared that he would not take orders from anyone but Allah. In response, Al Qaeda Central cut its ties to ISIS and stated that ISIS was "not a branch of al Qaeda" and emphatically added "[Al Qaeda Central] has no connection with the group called the ISIS, as it was not informed or consulted about its establishment. Therefore, it is not affiliated with al-Qaeda and has no organizational relationship with it. Al-Qaeda is not responsible for ISIS's actions."[44] Thus Al Qaeda Central found itself without an affiliate in Iraq for the first time since the founding of Al Qaeda in Iraq by Zarqawi back in 2004.

Among the newly formed ISIS's first steps was seizing control of the north Syrian city of Raqqa in January 2014. Raqqa was the first provincial Syrian capital to fall to the Syrian Sunni rebels and had been ruled jointly by several rebel factions including Al Nusra. But ISIS forced the other groups out and made it its capital. Then the ISIS Hisbah religious police began the public crucifixion of enemies and the beheading of Alawites. ISIS also enforced strict shariah law in the town, including forcing women to wear headscarves, banning the playing of soccer and smoking, cutting off the hands of thieves, stoning adulterers, forcing boys and girls into separate schools, setting up shariah law courts, public executions on Fridays for those who broke religious laws, and brainwashing young boys to be ISIS fighters in youth camps.

ISIS's estimated ten thousand fighters, many of them foreigners, began to take control of checkpoints on the borders with Iraq and Turkey and of oil wells in the eastern deserts of Syria. This gave ISIS access to up to a million dollars a day in oil funds and allowed it to construct a proto-state in northeastern Syria. ISIS's stated goal was the creation of a "caliphate" (the word *caliph* means "successor to the Prophet Muhammad" and refers to the rulers of the medieval Islamic empire, which stretched from Morocco to its capital in Baghdad to Pakistan). ISIS thus proved to be more adept at conquering territory from other, more moderate groups and constructing a state than at fighting the Assad regime, which it sold oil to.

It was ISIS's goal of creating a utopian caliphate, which conjured up the era of Islam's greatest heyday, that brought to it the attention of foreign fighters, who began to travel via Turkey in droves to join its ranks. Many of these were Sunni Arabs from Tunisia, Saudi Arabia, and Libya who went to fight against the tyrant Assad, whose war crimes against Sunnis were broadcast on Arab television and the Internet. ISIS skillfully used the Internet, including YouTube, Twitter, and Facebook, to spread its message around the world in many languages. It began to appeal to fanatics, disaffected Muslims, Muslim adventurers, and those Islamic extremists who dreamed of living under shariah law. It also appealed to those who were moved by stories of the Shiite Assad regime's extreme brutality against Sunnis.

By October 2014, the UN was to report that fifteen thousand foreign jihadi volunteers from ninety countries had traveled primarily via Sunni Turkey (which initially supported the flow of fighters through its southern lands to join the war against the Shiite Alawite Assad regime) to join ISIS.[45] By October 2015, U.S. intelligence officials would raise that number to thirty thousand.[46] These sources would report that ISIS was replenishing its ranks with one thousand fighters a month.[47] The flow of foreign fighters to join ISIS in Syria surpassed even the volunteer jihad in Afghanistan in the 1980s that had drawn bin Laden to that country. The notion of living in a pure shariah law Islamic state known as the *dawla* (the state) appealed to many Muslim dreamers, revolutionaries, misfits, fanatics, and those who were lost in their own societies. ISIS proved to incredibly adept at luring Muslims living in the West, including women known as the "brides of jihad," to come to Syria to partake in the construction of a new society. What proved most appealing to many was the message of strength. ISIS was an Islamic army on the march, and this had a tremendous appeal.

Ultimately, 3,000 Tunisians; 2,500 Saudis; 1,500 Moroccans; 900 French (France has Western Europe's largest Muslim population); at least 800 Russians (mainly Chechens and Dagestanis from the Muslim north Caucasus); 750 Brits (half of whom returned home, raising fears of domestic terror strikes); 450 Belgians; 100 Danes; and 250 Americans joined ISIS.[48] Many more fighters came from Iraq to help ISIS as it spread out from Raqqa and conquered most of Deir es Zor Province, including Al-Omar, Syria's largest oil field.

As a result, many Syrians came to see ISIS as a foreign group intent on conquering their land, while Al Qaeda–linked Al Nusra was seen as a more moderate local option (incidentally, Al Nusra has also denied that it had any intention to carry out terror attacks against the West).[49] Nusra even made a point of protecting local Syrian churches to show that it was not a fanatical foreign *takfiri* jihadist organization (takfiris are Muslim extremists who declare other Muslims to be "apostates" or "infidels" and thus worthy of killing).[50] In another ironic twist, the moderate Syrian rebel groups such as Ahrar ash Sham (the Free Men of Syria) would claim that they diverted as much as half of their forces from fighting Assad to fighting against ISIS.[51]

Western governments were concerned that many of the battle-hardened Islamic extremist jihadis who flocked to Syria to join ISIS would return to their home countries and wreak mayhem in an example of what is known as "blowback." Foreign fighters had already been involved in suicide bombings in Iraq and Syria, including two Brits who blew themselves up in Ramadi in 2015.[52] There was also a fear that home-grown or self-radicalized "lone wolves" who were unable to travel to Syria might carry out their own attacks after being inspired by ISIS messaging. ISIS leader al Baghdadi had in fact issued a declaration in 2015 that declared that every Muslim needs to "migrate to the Islamic state . . . or fight in his land wherever that may be." An ISIS spokesman similarly declared: "If you are not able to find an IED or a bullet, then single out the disbelieving American, Frenchman, or any of their allies. Smash his head with a rock, of slaughter him with a knife, or run him over with your car, or throw him down from a high place, or choke him, or poison him. . . . If you are not able to do so, then burn his home, car or business. Or destroy his crops. If you are unable to do so, then spit in his face."[53] Lest his audience be inclined to reject his calls for jihad at home or abroad, Baghdadi then stated, "O Muslims. Islam was never for a day the religion of peace. Islam is the religion of war. Your Prophet was dispatched with the sword."[54] During the June 2015 Ramadan, an ISIS spokesman issued a similar message, which said, "Muslims embark and hasten towards jihad. O mujahideen everywhere, rush and go to make Ramadan a month of disaster for the infidels."[55]

This represented a different sort of terrorist threat than Al Qaeda sleeper cells that were aiming for mass-casualty terror attacks like blowing up buildings or commercial aircraft. Fears that Muslims living in the West would heed Baghdadi's calls were magnified in January 2015 when two Belgian Moroccan terrorists who had been to fight in Syria were killed in a shootout with police in Verviers, Belgium, while planning an attack on police.[56] There was also the case of a French Muslim who had fought in Syria with ISIS who returned to Europe and killed four people at a Jewish museum in Brussels, Belgium, in May 2014. One of the January 2015 Paris terrorists, Amedy Coulibaly, declared his loyalty to ISIS before taking and executing Jewish hostages at a kosher deli in support of the Charlie Hebdo cartoon attack (although he never actually traveled to Syria to fight for ISIS).

In June 2015, a French Muslim who was inspired by ISIS attacked a U.S.-owned chemical plant near Lyons, France, with a homemade bomb. He decapitated his boss, stuck the boss's head on a fence, and hung a black ISIS banner reading "There is no God but Allah and Mohammad is his Prophet" on a fence surrounding the plant. On that same day a terrorist inspired by ISIS opened fire on a beach in Sousse, Tunisia, killing thirty-nine predominantly British tourists, including children, in cold blood as they swam or lay on the beach. In Canada, in October 2014, a convert to Islam drove his car into two soldiers, killing one of them, as a protest against Canada's support for the U.S. air war on ISIS. In Australia, police arrested fifteen Muslims who were planning to randomly behead Australian citizens and wrap their bodies in ISIS flags for public display. In Kosovo, five people were arrested for plotting to poison the water supply in fulfillment of an order from ISIS in July 2015. And in October, twelve Chechen terrorists trained by ISIS were arrested in Russia while preparing a homemade bomb to be detonated in Moscow's transport system. By August 2015, there were also fears that ISIS terrorists might be hidden among the hundreds of thousands of war refugees, most of them young men, fleeing into Europe via the Balkans from Syria and Iraq.

The most infamous ISIS-inspired attack was the November 13, 2015, massacre of 130 people in Paris, France, in the deadliest terrorist attack in Europe since the 2004 Madrid train bombings. In this attack, seven European Muslims exploded suicide bomb vests, shot down Parisians in outdoor cafes with AK-47 assault rifles, and massacred eighty-nine people they were holding hostage at a concert by an American metal band at the Jewish-owned Bataclan theater. The terrorists in the Bataclan theater mowed the concert-goers down at random with Kalashnikovs and hand grenades before blowing themselves up when the police stormed the theater. Three of the suicide bombers also blew themselves up outside the Stade de France soccer stadium during a game between France and Germany that was being watched by President François Hollande. The terrorists, who were all European Union citizens except for one who was a Syrian refugee, claimed to be attacking Paris for the French role in the bombing campaign against ISIS and for its "perverse" culture. At least half of the perpetrators who attacked in three squads had undergone some sort of centrally organized training with ISIS in Syria.

France responded to the attack by launching airstrikes on the ISIS capital of Raqqa three days later and by tracking down and killing the head of the massacre, Abdelhamid Abaaoud, in a Paris shootout. Abaaoud, a Belgian Moroccan from the Brussels neighborhood of Molenbeek, home to a community of radicalized Muslims, had traveled to Syria to fight with ISIS. A video emerged from Syria of him loading a truck with bloodied corpses and telling the camera, "Before we towed jet skis, motorcycles, quad bikes, big trailers filled with gifts for vacation in Morocco. Now, thank God, following God's path, we're towing apostates, infidels who are fighting us."[57] Abaadoud was also involved in an August 2015 terror attack on a train traveling from Amsterdam to Paris that failed when the terrorist's gun jammed and he was jumped and restrained by three off-duty American soldiers.

A group of terrorists linked to the cell that previously carried out the Paris attack also carried out suicide bombings in Brussels in March 2016 killing thirty-one and injuring two hundred and seventy people at a metro stop near EU buildings and in a terminal at the city's airport. The location of the attack surprised few, and terrorism experts have described Belgium as "Belgistan" ever since the 1990s. The Brussels neighborhood of Molenbeek, a hotbed of jihadism that is 80 percent Muslim (most being immigrants from Algeria and Morocco), had a large population of un-integrated/radicalized Muslims and the November 2015 Paris attack was most likely planned there. After the Paris attack, Belgian authorities conducted dozens of raids, combed whole neighborhoods for militants and locked down the capital for days. Belgian authorities suspected that there was an "ecosystem" or "milieu" that protected the militants, but scores of suspected terrorists with links to ISIS were nonetheless arrested in these raids.

Salah Abdeslam, the only surviving member of the ten-man terror team that attacked Paris in November 2015 (he backed out of blowing himself up as several of the attackers did), not surprisingly fled to Brussels after that attack. Europe's most wanted man was finally captured in March 2016 in the neighborhood of Molenbeek after being shot in the knee by local security forces while fleeing. The authorities reported that he then cooperated with them, providing them potentially valuable insights into how ISIS terror cells operated. His capture most likely accelerated the timetable for the March 21, 2016, Brussels attack four days after his arrest as the plotters feared that Abdeslam might reveal their plot.

More than one hundred Belgian Muslims returned to the country after traveling to Syria, making Belgium per capita the greatest supplier of ISIS jihadis in Europe, and they remained a security threat (many of them were, however, subsequently arrested). In March 2016 it was reported that ISIS had trained four hundred terrorists working in interlocking cells like the one that carried out the Paris bombings to infiltrate Europe and carry out terror plots, and few doubted that Brussels was among their potential targets.

One of the brothers who carried out the March 2016 bombings in Brussels, Brahim el-Bakraoui, was reported to have been caught in Turkey in June 2015 and deported to the Netherlands. Turkish president Recep Tayyip Erdogan said Turkey warned both Belgium and the Netherlands that Bakraoui was "a foreign fighter." Erdogan subsequently dropped a bombshell and stated, "Despite our warnings that this person was a foreign terrorist fighter, Belgium could not establish any links with terrorism."[58] It was later confirmed that he had been arrested in the southern Turkish city of Gaziantep and deported to the Netherlands before being passed to Belgium. But the Belgians failed to confirm his links to terrorism and he was subsequently released.

A third suicide bomber involved in the Brussels attack, Najim Laachraoui, was suspected of having traveled to Syria for training in bomb making. It was later reported that his family had reported his radicalization and trip to Syria to the authorities, but he was not arrested. The other bombers, Brahim el Bakraoui and his brother Khalid also acted as facilitators for the Paris attackers by operating a safe house for them and providing them with weapons. A fourth suicide bomber caught on CCTV escaped after his bomb failed to explode in the airport terminal and the so-called "man in white" became the most wanted man in Europe. In the aftermath of the attack one suspect linked to the attack was arrested in Germany and a bombing attack said to be at an advanced stage was disrupted in France.

After the Brussels attack, police subsequently found an explosive device, detonators, nails to be used for a bomb, "chemical products," and an ISIS flag in raids on an apartment in the Schaerbeek district of Brussels tied to the bombing. ISIS claimed the attack was to punish Belgium for being part of the anti-ISIS coalition and promised, "What is coming is worse and more bitter."[59] An ISIS member sent out a message after the attack stating, "We have come to you with slaughter" while the hashtag #Brusselsonfire was used by ISIS supporters praising the slaughter in a similar wording to the #Parisonfire which trended after the French capital was attacked.[60]

The attack, like the one in Paris, caused widespread fear in the United States. Republican presidential candidate Ted Cruz ignited controversy at the time by stating, "We need to empower law enforcement to patrol and secure Muslim neighborhoods before they become radicalized," and added, "For years, the West has tried to deny this enemy exists out of a combination of political correctness and fear. We can no longer afford either. Our European allies are now seeing what comes of a toxic mix of migrants who have been infiltrated by terrorists and isolated, radical Muslim neighborhoods."[61]

This statement was criticized by many who pointed out that the vast majority of American Muslims living outside of Dearborn, Michigan (which had a high concentration of Muslims) were integrated and assimilated into American society in a way that one did not find in Muslim ghettos like Molenbeek or impoverished Muslim banlieues (neighborhoods) in Paris.

But America was not immune to ISIS's appeal for Muslims living in the West to wage terrorist jihad at home. There was, for example, the case of the May 6, 2015, attack on a deliberately provocative Mohammad cartoon exhibit in the Dallas suburb of Garland by two American Muslims who had pledged their loyalty to ISIS that ended with the death of the two gunmen at the hands of a policeman. In June 2015, a Boston Muslim who had planned to behead police officers after being radicalized by ISIS online propaganda was shot and killed when he was approached by two Joint Terrorism Task Force officers and refused to drop his knife. There were also preemptive arrests in July 2015 of a cell in New York and New Jersey that was taking orders from the *dawla* (state) of ISIS to carry out a pressure-cooker-bomb terror attack in New York.[62] One of the conspirators who was arrested in this case told his parents they could either let him go off to fight alongside ISIS "or you watch me kill non-Muslims here."[63] As of October 2015, the United States had criminal cases against fifty foreign fighter suspects.[64] Among them was a Malaysia-based Kosovar hacker who hacked a Phoenix-based hosting company and provided the names, photographs, and addresses of over one thousand U.S. service members to ISIS. Specifically, he provided them to Junaid Hussain, the head of ISIS's hacking division, who was recently killed by a drone after proclaiming, "O Crusaders . . . know that we are in your emails and computer systems, watching and recording your every move . . . and . . . will strike at your necks in your own lands."[65]

One of the most notorious cases of ISIS supporters carrying out an attack in America was the December 2, 2015, terror attack in San Bernardino, California, by an American-born Pakistani Muslim named Syed Rizwan Farook and his Pakistani wife, Tashfeen Malik. In this massacre, the couple stormed a holiday party being held at a county health department (a center that treated people with disabilities and where Syed worked that had recently had a baby shower for his wife) and killed fourteen people in cold blood. They stalked the building in tactical gear and masks, systematically slaughtering people with semiautomatic rifles and pistols. Later that afternoon, they were chased down in their vehicle and killed in a hail of bullets after a shootout with police. Police subsequently found that Tashfeen had declared her *bayat* or loyalty to ISIS leader Abu Bakr al Baghdadi on Facebook as the attack began, and that the couple had thousands of rounds of ammunition and several pipe bombs in their home. The most infamous jihadi attack (and America's worst gun massacre), however, took place in a gay club in Orlando, Florida, known as the Pulse in June 2016. On this occasion an Afghan American named Omar Matteen pledged allegiance to ISIS on the phone while killing 49 people.

ISIS responded by calling the couple "supporters," but not members who were ordered to carry out the attacks. The FBI found no evidence of direct ISIS command and control in the case, which was described as homegrown "DIY (do it yourself) terrorism" of the sort that was harder to detect and preempt. Jeh Johnson, the secretary of Homeland Security, said of the attack, the deadliest in America since 9/11, "We have moved to an entirely new phase in the global terrorist threat and in our homeland security efforts." Terrorists have "in effect outsourced attempts to attack our homeland. . . . This requires a whole new approach, in my view."[66]

If these were not cause for concern, there were several cases (including one involving three girls from Colorado, one involving a convert to Islam who was an Air Force veteran, and one involving two American Uzbeks and a Kazakh from Brooklyn) where American Muslims were intercepted and arrested on their way to join ISIS. Law enforcement officials claim that 250 American Muslims have nonetheless traveled to Iraq and Syria to fight.[67]

But the odds were higher that the foreign volunteers who left their countries and made it to Syria to "join the caravan of the Knights of the Islamic State" would be "martyred" in combat against heavily armed Assad government troops than return home to carry out terror attacks. The Assad regime proved to be more resilient than anyone had figured, and its heavy weapons gave it an advantage over the more lightly armed Sunni rebels. Thousands of the Sunni volunteers from abroad began to die for the cause of jihad in the bloody wars in Syria (which, by 2015, had led to the death of approximately 250,000 people according to the U.N. and 470,000 by 2016 according to the Syrian Center for Policy Research). According to Jordanian sources, approximately six thousand foreign fighters were killed in fighting in Syria between 2011 and late 2013 alone.[68]

Among the most militarily effective foreign volunteer fighters in Syria were indisputably the Chechens, a Muslim highlander people from Russia's Caucasus Mountains who fought two bloody wars against the Russian Federation, from 1994 to 1996 (which they won against tremendous odds) and from 1999 to 2009 (which they lost after a long and bitter struggle). The out-numbered Chechens had attained an almost mythical status for defeating the massive Russian Federation in open combat, and for years U.S. troops had (without a shred of proof) claimed that mysterious Chechen "brigades" were traveling across Eurasia to defend the Pashtun Taliban. While the Chechen defense of the distant Taliban was a myth, a few hundred of these legendary warriors did, however, openly travel to Syria to fight under the command of Umar al Shishani (a.k.a. Umar the Chechen), who was appointed military commander of ISIS.[69] These tough mountain warriors, who were fighting as much against the Russian-sponsored Assad regime as for ISIS, proved to be "force multipliers" owing to their expertise in warfare. The Chechens' elite units often spearheaded ISIS attacks. Word that Chechens were in the enemy ranks was said to have terrified Assad regime fighters.

As ISIS and its foreign fighter vanguard conquered as much as one-third of Syria (mainly in the north and east) in 2013, it began to make inroads in Iraq's Sunni-dominated Anbar Province in the first week of January 2014. It will be recalled that Maliki's Shiite government troops had been attacking Sunni protestors and militants in Ramadi and Fallujah, but the Iraqi prime minister had abruptly withdrawn his Shiite government forces on December 30, 2013. This gave ISIS an opening, and on January 3, 2014, black-clad AQI/ISIS fighters swarmed in and seized control of most of Fallujah and much of Ramadi and drove out or executed Iraqi government officials and policemen. The militants then raised the black banner of ISIS above the government buildings and police stations in these cities that had been conquered with such bloodshed by American Marines back in 2004 and 2007. From the mosques the militants called on Sunnis to join ISIS and proclaimed they were establishing "Allah's rule on earth." The ISIS fighters declared Fallujah and Ramadi to be part of their Islamic State and pronounced in a mosque, "We are here to defend you from the army of Maliki and the Iranian Safavids."

Pro-government Sunni tribesmen and Maliki government forces fought to retake control of Fallujah and Ramadi for the next few weeks, but the ISIS fighters fought back ferociously, on occasion using suicide bombers. One Maliki government fighter reported of the fighting, "When we first entered Ramadi, it was like hell opened a door. They were shooting at us from every-where. For me, I have one idea in my mind—that I have to fight with no mercy, or I will die."[70] Ultimately, the Iraqi army and pro-government Sunni tribal troops ceded control of most of Fallujah to ISIS by late January 2014. They were, however, able to retake much of Ramadi.

Having gained control of Fallujah, ISIS then created a Taliban-style morality police force known as the Committee for the Promotion of Virtue and Prevention of Vice. Many of the gains of the 2007–8 surge and Anbar tribal awakening were thus swept away in Anbar in just a few days in January 2014. From Fallujah, ISIS fighters then conquered other Anbar towns, including the strategic border town with Syria, Qaim, and Haditha and Abu Ghraib. ISIS's success came in part from the fact that Baathists and Sunni former members of Saddam Hussein's army had joined it and lent their military expertise to the militants, who had come to be seen as the main force to stand up to Maliki and the Shiite-dominated government. A former member of Saddam Hussein's army known as Al Bilawi was to become ISIS's number two military commander in Iraq while another Baathist named Samar al Khlifawi was described as "the strategist chiefly responsible for the Islamic State's early military success."[71] This infusion of ex-Baathist Sunnis gave ISIS tremendous military potential that it would later put to good use. The Baathist-ISIS alliance was known as the "Coalition of Revenge," and observers noted, however, that there was a possibility for a fissure between these two distinct Sunni groups once they had achieved their shared objective of overthrowing Shiite rule.

ISIS also gained support from Sunni tribes who resented Maliki's policies toward them. As many as eighty Sunni tribes had joined ISIS by 2014.

In the aftermath of this catastrophe, Maliki asked the United States for help and was given one hundred Hellfire missiles to be used by his helicopters, thousands of M4 and M16 rifles and ten Scan Eagle reconnaissance drones, but not much else. While the conquest of Anbar by ISIS militants sent shockwaves throughout Iraq, it did not cause much of a stir back in America, where most people seemed to have put the war behind them. A back-page story in the *New York Times* recorded the conquest of Fallujah and Ramadi as follows: "For the United States, which two years ago withdrew its forces from Iraq as officials claimed the country was on track to become a stable democracy, Anbar holds historical significance. It was the place of America's greatest losses, and perhaps its most significant success, of the war. Nearly one-third of the U.S. soldiers killed during the war died trying to pacify Anbar, and Americans fought two battles for control of Fallujah, in the bloodiest street-to-street combat U.S. troops had faced since Vietnam."[72] While American troops who had served and sacrificed in Anbar grumbled at the ISIS conquest of the places they had fought so hard to pacify in 2007, no one was calling for U.S. troops to be sent back to reconquer Anbar in a seemingly endless blood feud between Sunnis and Shiites in the desert. At this stage war fatigue still dominated, and what would later be described as "ISISphobia" had yet begun to panic average Americans, as ISIS's conquests did not make headlines. And the Obama administration was comforted by the fact that ISIS rebels were halted at Abu Ghraib to the west of Baghdad and did not have the strength to challenge the Maliki government for control of this Shiite-dominated capital city. In many ways the parceling of Iraq into a Sunni-dominated Anbar, Shiite-dominated center and south, and a Kurdish north was the de facto fulfillment of a partition plan mooted by Senator Joe Biden many years earlier.

And thus ISIS was able to consolidate its hold over most of Anbar Province in the winter and spring of 2014. While Iraqis who suffered from ISIS's continuing suicide bombing campaign were aware that the Sunni terrorist group posed a threat to their country, the group remained under the radar from January to June 2014 for most Americans. But it later became clear that ISIS was plotting a bold "Breaking the Walls"–style assault on Iraq's second-largest city, the northern Sunni town of Mosul. It was ISIS's conquest of this large northern city and its looming threat to the oil-rich region of Kirkuk and Kurdistan that was to draw a reluctant President Obama back into the sands of Iraq and, ultimately, into the bloody Shiite-versus-Sunni civil war in Syria as well.

The June 2014 ISIS Blitz and U.S. Military Response

The Maliki government had warnings that ISIS was contemplating an attack on the large northern city of Mosul prior its June 2014 conquest by the Sunni terrorists. After arresting and interrogating seven ISIS members, for example, a general in that city warned the Iraqi government that an attack was imminent. But government officials scoffed at the notion of ISIS storming a town of 1.8 million people. As a result, reinforcements were not sent north.[73] On June 5, 2014, ISIS, however, hinted at its plans and launched an attack on the northern town of Samarra. Samarra, it will be recalled, was home to the Al Askari gold-domed mosque, which was blown up by AQI terrorists back in 2006. The June 5 ISIS attack was repulsed, however, by government troops, who were determined to protect this important Shiite shrine.

Then, before dawn on June 6, 2014, hundreds of pickup trucks carrying ISIS fighters raced out of the desert and began attacking checkpoints to the west of Mosul. These militants were bolstered by Sunni sleeper cells in the city, who rallied supporters to their cause. Their aim was to set off powerful bombs downtown, overrun several districts, then retreat before the Iraqi army could destroy them.[74] It was meant to be a bold raid designed to make a statement and show that Prime Minister Maliki could not maintain security in Mosul. But as the ISIS militants overran several checkpoints, they found to their shock that Iraqi army troop units were undermanned and often fled their positions. While on paper there were said to be four divisions made up of twenty-five thousand troops guarding Mosul, in reality there were only about ten thousand troops.

There were a couple of reasons for this shortage in troops. One was that thousands of Iraqi government troops and most of Mosul's tanks had already been sent to fight ISIS in Anbar. The Iraqi army had forty-two thousand men fighting to retake Anbar in June. The other reason was that many of the government troops in Mosul were so-called ghost troops (i.e., soldiers who paid their corrupt commanders half of their salaries to stay at home).

Then there was the fact that Mosul was not a Shiite town; it was primarily Sunni. As Mosul's army defenders, most of whom were Shiites, confronted the approximately two thousand ISIS invaders, their hearts were not in the fight for this town they did not see as theirs. When the ISIS militants overran checkpoints, suicide bombed any resistance points, and infiltrated deeper into the city, they hanged captured soldiers and set their bodies on fire, crucified them, or torched them on the hood of their U.S.-supplied Humvees.[75] This, and the use of a massive suicide bombing attack on the Iraqi army's headquarters that shook the center of Mosul, spread panic among the Shiite defenders, who were already disinclined to fight for a Sunni town. The governor of Nineveh Province, for which Mosul was the capital, urged residents to "stand firm," but within hours he was forced to flee as his provincial headquarters was overrun by hundreds of ISIS fighters armed with RPGs, sniper rifles, and machine guns.[76]

Stunned by the attack, Mosul's defending generals retreated to the east of the city to set up their headquarters, and this move led to further panic among rank-and-file government soldiers. After four days of fighting, the government defenses collapsed on June 10, and thousands of Iraqi army soldiers discarded their uniforms and fled southward with fleeing civilians. Half a million people were reported to have fled the ISIS advance, fleeing southward toward Baghdad or toward the relatively stable sanctuary of Kurdistan to the east. Among them were most of Mosul's ancient Christian population of Assyrians, Chaldeans, and Syriac Orthodox that had lived in the region for over sixteen hundred years. This community was given the choice of converting to Islam, paying *jizya* tax on non-Muslims, or "facing the sword." An account of ISIS's treatment of this indigenous Christian population stated: "The Assyrian

International News Agency reported that ISIS terrorists entered the home of a Christian family in Mosul and demanded that they pay the *jizya* (a tax on non-Muslims). According to AINA, 'When the Assyrian family said they did not have the money, three ISIS members raped the mother and daughter in front of the husband and father. The husband and father was so traumatized that he committed suicide.'"[77] As a result of such treatment, the Christian population of Mosul fled in panic. Hundreds of thousands of Christians from the plains of Nineveh Province abandoned their ancestral lands and one bemoaned the fate of his people saying "We're afraid our whole society will vanish."[78] ISIS also carried out efforts to destroy Iraq's ancient Christian cultural heritage. Among the many Christian edifices destroyed by ISIS was the fourteen hundred year old St. Elijah Monastery. The destruction of this ancient culture that had long enriched northern Iraq and coexisted peacefully with its Muslim neighbors since the Middle Ages was a blow to this previously diverse region.

But not everyone greeted the conquest with panic. Many Sunni inhabitants of Mosul welcomed ISIS, and one stated, "I hope God supports them and makes them victorious over the oppression of al-Maliki."[79] Another Sunni in Mosul stated, "The Arab Iraqi people want Maliki to go to prison. He is a traitor. Fourteen Daesh [ISIS] members come, and the whole Iraqi army flees. The people of Mosul do not want the Iraqi Army in Mosul. I'm an old man, and they [the Iraqi army] stopped me for one hour at a checkpoint, using bad language."[80] The BBC reported that local Sunnis stoned Iraqi government troops as they fled Mosul.[81] For their part, the Sunni ISIS fighters seem to have tried to reassure the local Sunnis that they represented them and would defend their interests vis-à-vis Maliki and the Shiites.

As the small number of stunned ISIS fighters took control of the large city of Mosul, they freed hundreds of prisoners from jail, many of them fellow terrorists, and these were seen wandering the streets in their orange prison suits. But hundreds of Shiite prisoners were massacred in cold blood by the militants.[82] With the Iraqi army fleeing southward, the ISIS fighters also seized hundreds of millions of dollars of U.S. supplies, including seven hundred Humvees, several Stryker vehicles, helicopters, ammunition, and weapons.[83] They then took control of government buildings in the city and in short time had placed the ISIS symbol on police cars that began to patrol Mosul.

Having seized the largest city in northern Iraq, the ISIS militants warned women not to go outside unless it was necessary, banned alcohol and cigarettes on pain of public lashing, ordered residents to attend mosque five times a day, burnt books on secular topics in the libraries, and beheaded local Shiite policemen and placed these grisly trophies in rows.[84] The ISIS terrorists also destroyed the Tomb of Jonah, an ancient shrine of the Old Testament prophet that was frequented by both Muslims and Christians for centuries. As strict Salafist puritans, the ISIS militants also demolished ancient mosques with tombs in them because they were opposed to the worship of saints. But not all was strictly Islamist in the new scheme of things, and, in a sign of the importance of Baathists in the ISIS conquest of Mosul, a former general in Saddam Hussein's army was made governor of the city.

As a bizarre sense of normalcy returned to the streets of Mosul following the conquest, the world's attention shifted to the southeast. There the Kurds reacted to the stunning events by moving from their autonomous region and seizing the strategic oil-rich town of Kirkuk, which had been abandoned by Iraqi government troops as they fled ISIS. Kirkuk had been a bone of contention between Iraq's Arab and Kurdish populations ever since Saddam Hussein ethnically cleansed tens of thousands of Kurds from the town in the 1980s. Now the Kurdish Peshmerga fighters were taking advantage of the crisis to stake their claim to what they called "the Kurdish Jerusalem." As Iraqi government control collapsed in the region, these long-suffering Kurds dared to dream of having their own state. The Kurds for the time being were content to use their 160,000-man-strong Kurdish Peshmerga force to hold the line on a 640-mile border with the ISIS state in northern Iraq.

Meanwhile, the ISIS militants continued their momentum and surged south and captured the town of Baiji, home to Iraq's largest oil refinery. But Iraqi troops guarding the refinery located outside of the town held off ISIS attacks. They fought an on-and-off battle for control of this vital asset until October 2015, when they regained control of it from the militants. From Baiji, the ISIS fighters took control of Tikrit, a symbolically important town because it was home to Saddam Hussein. At this time ISIS fighters massacred seventeen hundred fleeing Shiite soldiers who were captured at a former U.S. base there (Camp Speicher). ISIS fighters also attacked the shrine town of Samarra and advanced southward to within sixty miles of Baghdad. There they were finally stopped not by Maliki's government troops, but by Iranian-linked Shiite militias such as the Kataib Hezbollah and Badr Organization, which showed more willingness to fight than the army. These Shiite volunteers were fighting not for Iraq, but as Shiites against their Sunni enemies.

There were widespread reports at the time that members of Iran's Al Qud's force (an elite unit of the Revolutionary Brigades) were assisting their fellow Shiites in the defense of Baghdad and cities to the north of it from the

Sunni ISIS militants. The Iranian units were led by General Qassam Sulei-mani, the head of the Al Quds force, and ultimately stopped ISIS at the town of Amerli, a hundred miles north of Baghdad, with the help of U.S. air sup-port. The *Los Angeles Times* commented at the time on the irony of the United States working with the Iranian Revolutionary Guard's elite unit (which had previously trained Iraqi Shiite insurgents to kill Americans) to repulse ISIS and save the Shiite Turkmen population of Amerli.[85]

While the Iraqi army subsequently tried to retake Saddam's hometown of Tikrit, it was repelled, leaving ISIS in control of most of the Sunni lands north and west of Baghdad. For the next twenty-five days ISIS consolidated its rule and then on June 29, 2014, issued a remarkable statement declaring the creation of a new caliphate. The declaration called on all jihadi groups to recognize the Ca-liphate of the Islamic State (IS), as ISIS now took to calling itself to stress its reach beyond all borders (i.e., it was no longer limited to just Syria and Iraq). It also declared al Baghdadi (now called Caliph Ibrahim) to be the new caliph. A few days later, on July 1, al Baghdadi/Caliph Ibrahim declared, "Let the world know that we are living today in a new era. . . . Muslims today have a loud, thundering statement. A statement that will cause the world to hear and understand the meaning of terrorism."[86]He also issued threats against "crusaders, atheists and Jews" and said support for the caliph was a religious obligation of all Muslims.

On July 4, 2014, al Baghdadi/Caliph Ibrahim then took the bold step of com-ing out of hiding and openly giving a filmed sermon on the *minbar* (pulpit tower) in Mosul's Grand Mosque (also known as the Nouri Mosque) while wear-ing a black robe and turban of the sort worn by the medieval Abbasid caliphs. There, the man who had a $10 million U.S. bounty on his head boldly proclaimed to all Sunni Muslims, "I am your leader who presides over you," and called on them to "obey" him and fight jihad for the sake of Allah. This brazen act by a man who had appeared in only two photos prior to this embarrassed the Maliki government and threw down the gauntlet to Al Qaeda Central and all other ter-rorist groups seeking to claim authority over the global jihad movement.

Not surprisingly, al Baghdadi's claim to the caliphate was rejected by most Muslims in the following month. The imam of the Al Azhar Mosque in Cairo, one of Islam's most prestigious Islamic institutions, called ISIS "satanic." Per-haps the most interesting rejection, however, came from Yusef al-Qaradawi, the spiritual guide of the Muslim Brotherhood. This Qatar-based scholar said, "We look forward to the coming, as soon as possible, of the caliphate. But the declaration issued by the Islamic State is void under sharia and has dangerous consequences for the Sunnis in Iraq and for the revolt in Syria."[87] He added that the nomination of al Baghdadi as caliph, by a group "known for its atrocities and radical views," failed to meet strict conditions dictated by shariah law.

Interestingly, many Muslim extremists also rejected ISIS's later claims to be the legitimate caliphate. The most deadly Al Qaeda chapter, Al Qaeda in the Arabian Peninsula, which was based in Yemen, criticized ISIS for its "barbaric" acts and said "filming and promoting it [beheadings] among people in the name of Islam and jihad is a big mistake and not acceptable whatever the justifications are."[88] The emir of Al Qaeda in the Islamic Maghreb (North Africa) also rejected ISIS's claims to the caliphate and declared, "we still adhere to our pledge of allegiance to our sheikh and emir, Ayman al Zawahiri. It is obvious for the Muslims and all Jihadi organizations that follow the correct method, that the announcement of such a serious step [meaning the establishment of the caliphate], will not happen until after the expansion of consultation."[89] The Pakistani Taliban also rejected al Baghdadi's claim to be caliph and stated that he "did not achieve 0.1% of the requirements of a Caliphate."[90]

As the rift between Al Qaeda Central and its Yemeni and Algerian chapters, on one hand, and ISIS, on the other hand, indicated, there was growing division between the older Al Qaeda generation and the more radical ISIS generation. One ISIS fighter captured this dichotomy, and the surge in interest among the new generation of Muslim radicals for ISIS, by stating, "Al Qaeda is an organization and we are a state. Osama bin Laden, God have mercy on him, was fighting to establish the Islamic state to rule the world, and—praise God—we have achieved his dream."[91]

There were, however, numerous reports of radical Islamic militants in other countries declaring allegiance to the ISIS caliphate. In Egypt's restless Sinai desert, the terrorist group Ansar Beit al Maqdis, for example, changed its name to ISIS in the Sinai Province in 2014 and sent representatives to Syria requesting financial support, weapons, and tactical support for their struggle against the secular Egyptian government.[92] In that same year an ISIS-linked group in Algeria calling itself the Caliphate Soldiers in Algeria beheaded a French hostage to punish France for joining the war on ISIS. In June 2015, the Caucasian Emirate, a terror group operating in the northern Caucasus Mountains of Russia, swore loyalty to ISIS and declared itself the Caucasian Province of the Caliphate. In the Philippines, the Abu Sayyaf jihadi group also declared its allegiance to ISIS.

In January 2015, an ISIS-affiliated Libyan group known as the Tripoli Province of the Islamic State also declared allegiance to ISIS and attacked a luxury hotel in the Libyan capital of Tripoli and carried out a suicide bombing in the town of Qubah that killed forty-two. In February of that year, Libyan jihadists who swore allegiance to ISIS took control of the Libyan port city of Sirte (Surt) and the town of Derna and created an ISIS-like ministate. They then captured and beheaded twenty-one Egyptian Coptic Christians and sent the video of their killing to ISIS for propaganda purposes.

Then in April 2015, two Libyan groups linked to ISIS calling themselves the Barqa Province of the Islamic State and the Fezzan Province of the Islamic State filmed themselves beheading and shooting to death thirty Ethiopian Christians. One of the executioners proclaimed, "To the Nation of the Cross, we are back again!" and warned that for those who refused to convert to Islam, "we owe nothing except the edge of the sword."[93] The fact that ISIS's Furqan Network then displayed the Libyan videos, which were mixed with their own footage, seemed to indicate some sort of contact with their distant ISIS "provinces" in Libya. There was also the case of ISIS sending a dozen fighters to Libya to assist the extremist group Ansar al Shariah with technical support.[94] Al Baghdadi came to exert more control over the ISIS branch in Libya than any other arm of ISIS. Operatives from Syria organized Libyan ISIS operations. In January 2016 Libyan ISIS members carried out the deadliest terror attack in Libyan history in a suicide bombing at a police station in Zliten that killed sixty.

ISIS members from Libya gained widespread notoriety for attacking targets in neighboring Tunisia. The United States has said that ISIS had between five thousand and six thousand five hundred fighters in the hundred and fifty mile strip they controlled on the Libyan coast. The United States was so alarmed by this development that it launched an airstrike on an ISIS jihadi camp in the town of Sabratha on the coast that was for training primarily Tunisians in February 2016 killing forty nine. They also killed the head of ISIS in Libya, Abu Nabil, in an airstrike in November 2015.

In March 2015, a group calling itself Jund al Khilafah (the Army of the Caliph) attacked a museum in the Tunisian capital, killing twenty-two tourists who were described as "citizens of Crusader countries" in the name of Caliph Ibrahim. At the time, the Jund al Khilafah terrorists announced, "Surely, the security of Tunisia will see horror, and surely you will see assassinations and explosions."[95] This was followed by a pledge of allegiance to ISIS from the Nigerian Islamic terrorist group Boko Haram, which had previously gained notoriety for kidnapping dozens of local school girls. In Gaza, a group calling itself the Islamic State in Jerusalem also engaged in gun battles with Hamas in June 2015. In response to the rise of ISIS in eastern Afghanistan, Obama ordered commando raids on their hideouts. The leader of ISIS in

Afghanistan was killed in February 2015 in a drone strike. By January 2016 special force raids had killed 100 of the estimated 1,000 ISIS members in Afghanistan. By the summer of 2016 it was reported that Obama had dispatched special forces to assist local anti-ISIS forces against the estimated 4,000 to 6,000 ISIS fighters in that country.

In January 2015, a splinter Pakistani Taliban group declared its allegiance to ISIS and beheaded a Pakistani government soldier to demonstrate its loyalty. There have also been cases of disaffected Afghan Taliban commanders swearing allegiance to ISIS, and in April 2015 a group calling itself the ISIS Wilayat Khorasan (the Province of Greater Afghanistan) set off a bomb in a bank, killing thirty-four, in the eastern town of Jalalabad. This group also took control of several valleys in the eastern province of Nangahar and killed dozens of captured opponents by having them blown up in a trench. In the north Afghan province of Kunduz, fanatical ISIS fighters were also reported to be fighting alongside local Taliban according to local sources.[96] In the east, however, fighters claiming allegiance to ISIS have attacked the Taliban and in one instance beheaded ten of them.[97]

While the distances between these various groups in North Africa, Russia, and Central and South Asia, and the Philippines on one hand, and ISIS on the other, precluded any direct command and control, these symbolic declarations of allegiance highlighted the tremendous appeal ISIS's caliphate had to extremist Muslim militants from Sub-Saharan Africa to the Caucasus to Pakistan to the Pacific.

But ISIS's global reach was to be more than symbolic. In a sign of things to come, ISIS carried out its first direct terror attack beyond the borders of Iraq and Syria by dispatching two suicide bombing against Shiite mosques in Saudi Arabia in May 2015, killing twenty-five. In June 2015 ISIS struck again and claimed a suicide bombing of a Shiite mosque in Kuwait, which killed twenty-five Shiite worshippers. In October of that year an ISIS gunman opened fire on a Shiite meeting hall in Saudi Arabia, killing five people it described as "apostate polytheists." ISIS also carried out three bombings against Houthi Shiites in Yemen in the spring and summer of 2015, killing dozens. Continuing its attacks on Shiites, in October 2015 ISIS operatives carried out a bombing of a traditional Shiite march in Bangladesh, a country that had little history of sectarian violence. In January 2016 four ISIS-directed militants carried out an attack in the Indonesian capital of Jakarta which led to four deaths. In addition, in two separate bombings in May and June 2016, ISIS killed 78 Yemeni soldiers.

In July 2015 a Turkish terrorist who had been trained by ISIS carried out a bombing in Suruc in southern Turkey, killing thirty-three, mostly Kurds, at a socialist rally. This attack, however, backfired and led Turkey to join the war on ISIS and offer the Incirlik Airbase in southern Turkey near Syria for U.S. aircraft. Sadly, it also led to renewed violence between the PKK Kurdish terrorist group, which erroneously blamed the Turkish government for the bombing, and Turkey (the PKK and the Turkish government had previously had a two-year truce). In October 2015, the Turkish government blamed the brother of the Suruc bomber for an ISIS bombing at a Kurdish peace rally in the Turkish capital of Ankara that killed ninety-nine, in that country's worst terrorist attack.[98] ISIS also carried out a suicide bombing in the heart of Istanbul's historic Sultan Ahmet district in January 2016 which killed ten German tourists. I visited the usually bustling tourist site as workers cleaned the blood off the pavement a few hours later and found it empty of the usual throngs of tourists. This bombing, and another ISIS attack on Istanbul's Ataturk international airport in June 2016 that killed more than forty people, were clearly aimed at Turkey's tourism industry.

But all these terrorist attacks across the globe were to come in the weeks and months following the initial June 29, 2014, bold declaration of ISIS's caliphate in Mosul, which was to subsequently galvanize the above-mentioned Muslim extremists. Back in the summer of 2014, when ISIS initially stormed onto the world stage and declared its state, few experts expected such a global reaction.

As if emboldened by its initial proclamation of the caliphate in June of 2014, ISIS/IS then began an offensive to the southeast against the autonomous Kurdish zone (the Kurdistan Regional Government) and against Yazidis in the west in the Mount Sinjar area near the Syrian border. This summer 2014 ISIS offensive began with the August 1 conquest of the remote town of Sinjar, home to 350,000 people, most of them Yazidis. Tragically, the Kurdish Peshmerga forces, which had grown complacent since the overthrow of Hussein in 2003, abandoned the Yazidis of Sinjar to the ISIS fighters. The Yazidis, a Kurdish group of approximately half a million, who practice a syncretic faith that weaves together elements of ancient Persian Zoroastrian faith and long forgotten Mesopotamian religions, including the worship of the sun and a fallen angel named Melek Tawwus (the Peacock Angel), Islam, Judaism, and Christianity, were declared "devil worshippers" by ISIS. Thousands of them were slaughtered in cold blood and as many as two hundred thousand Yazidis fled the ISIS militants. Thousands of Yazidis fled from their villages seeking sanctuary in the heights of the holy Mount Sinjar where they believe Noah's ark landed. There they faced starvation as the ISIS militants besieged the mountain and enacted a blockade. Others fled to the holiest shrine at Lailish in the hills just beyond the Kurdish Regional Government's frontlines. There, in the stone halls of the temple built on the spot where Yazidis believe the Peacock Angel landed on earth, I subsequently met with their second highest leader, Baba Chawish (the Father Guardian) and he told me "we faced the latest in a long string of over seventy genocides. Our community is based on these ancestral lands and we were being slaughtered, enslaved and scattered from the lands that are sacred to us. We prayed for survival and peace for all mankind."

To compound matters, the ISIS fighters then raped thousands of captured Yazidi women and kidnapped and sold them in markets as *sabiyya* (Koranlegitimized human spoils of war). They claimed that the Koran gave them the right to take the Yazidi women and girls as young as twelve to be "concubines" as they were infidels and idolaters. Videos of laughing ISIS fighters shooting off their weapons and distributing captured Yazidi females whose husbands and fathers had been massacred went viral on the Internet and brought the true nature of the terrorists' barbarity to viewers around the world. The videos and promises of Yazidi "brides" also attracted many extremists to travel to Syria to acquire one. ISIS fighters who were reported to have raped girls as young as twelve claimed that raping "unbelievers" brought them closer to God.

On August 6, 2014, ISIS fighters captured the Mosul Dam, the largest dam in Iraq and that country's most important source of water and electricity. Experts feared that ISIS could destroy the dam and unleash a sixty-five-foot wave down river from the dam, killing thousands. As ISIS surged in an eastward direction they also came to within twenty-five miles of Erbil, the flourishing capital of the thus far peaceful, pro-American Kurdish Regional Government. Hundreds of Americans worked in Erbil in oil-related jobs, and the White House worried about their safety. Obama stated of the traditionally moderate Kurds who had a long history of protecting local Christians and Yazidis, "The Kurdish region is functional in the way we would like to see. It is tolerant of other sects and other religions in a way that we would like to see elsewhere. So we do think it is important to make sure that that space is protected."[99]

Appalled by the plight of the Yazidis and fearful of an ISIS conquest of Erbil, the Obama administration heeded Kurdish authorities' pleas for help, and on August 8 began a bombing and airdrop campaign designed to push back ISIS and head off a humanitarian disaster. The airdrops provided desperately needed food and water to Yazidis, who were dying of starvation and dehydration on Mount Sinjar and destroyed some ISIS positions and convoys. The

U.S. bombing halted the ISIS offensive against the vaunted Kurdish Peshmerga fighters, who had failed to live up to their reputation as indomitable fighters. Most important, the bombing broke the ISIS siege of the Yazidis and allowed tens of thousands hiding on the mountain in appalling conditions to flee to the safety with the help of PKK and YPG Kurdish fighters by August 13, 2014.

It was in response to America's intervention on behalf of the beleaguered Kurds of northern Iraq that ISIS was to carry out a barbaric act that was to bring it to the attention of the American public, which had not been too concerned by its actions thus far. On August 19, 2014, an American freelance journalist named James Foley, who had been captured in Syria, was beheaded on film by a black-clad, British ISIS terrorist dubbed "Jihadi John." The ISIS executioner threatened America saying that the United States was fighting not insurgents, but an "army" and a "state that has been accepted by a large number of Muslims worldwide." He then threatened: "Any aggression towards the Islamic State is an aggression towards Muslims from all walks of life who have accepted the Islamic Caliphate as their leadership. So any attempt by you, Obama, to deny the Muslims their rights of living in safety under the Islamic Caliphate will result in the bloodshed of your people."[100] Thus America was, for the first time in almost three years, back at war in the sands of Iraq, this time against a new, more powerful iteration of its previous AQI Sunni terrorist enemy from the Iraq War. A State Department Iraq expert was to describe ISIS as "worse than Al Qaeda" and a "full blown army."[101] ISIS fighters, often driving in pickup trucks with guns mounted in the back known as 'technicals', would commence their attacks with suicide bombings and were not afraid to die as martyrs in combat.

But the Obama administration realized all too clearly that the bombings were a tactic that had saved the Kurds from the immediate ISIS threat, but were not a strategy that could deal with the underlying grievances that had driven thousands of disgruntled Sunnis to support the ISIS militants' sweeping conquests. To deal with the deeper issue of Sunni distrust of the Shiite-dominated Iraqi government that had repressed them for years, it was obvious that Prime Minister Maliki would have to go. The Americans and other world leaders called on Maliki to be replaced by a leader who could mend ties with the rebellious Sunnis. By now even members of Maliki's own Dawa Party had come to see him as lightning rod for dissatisfaction among Sunnis. On August 14, 2014, a beleaguered Maliki stepped down from the premiership and was replaced by a more conciliatory figure, Haidar al Abadi. Abadi, also a Shiite, promised to include Sunnis in the government and military and to mend the fissures in Iraqi society that had been caused by Maliki's previous anti-Sunni policies.

Referring to the Sunnis, Prime Minister Abadi struck a conciliatory note and stated, "We have to listen to the grievances, some of which are right and some of which are false."[102] Among Abadi's first steps as prime minister was reaching out to the alienated Kurdish Regional Government of the north by allowing the Americans to arm them to fight ISIS. He also reached out to the Sunnis and appointed seven ministerial posts to them. He then lifted the death sentence against a prominent Sunni politician and fired several generals appointed by Maliki who had tens of thousands of "ghost soldiers" under their command.[103]

As the Obama administration worked to prevent ISIS from expanding into Kurdistan and to create a more inclusive Iraqi government, the terrorists responded yet again with another direct provocation. On September 2, 2014, the masked British terrorist seen in the Foley beheading again beheaded another American on video and threatened Obama directly. As he beheaded war correspondent Steve Sotloff, the ISIS executioner stated, "I'm back, Obama, and I'm back because of your arrogant foreign policy towards the Islamic State.... As your missiles continue to strike our people, our knife will continue to strike the necks of your people."[104]

The videotaped execution of Foley and Sotloff caused a sensation back in the United States, with politicians on both sides of the aisle calling on Obama to retaliate against ISIS. U.S. secretary of state John Kerry described the group as "ambitious, genocidal, territorial-grabbing, caliphate-desiring quasi state with an irregular army."[105] Obama said of ISIS: "In a region that has known so much bloodshed, these terrorists are unique in their brutality. They execute captured prisoners. They kill children. They enslave, rape and force women into marriage. They threatened a religious minority with genocide. And in acts of barbarism, they took the lives of two American journalists."[106] Obama then declared war on ISIS and stated, "Our objective is clear, and that is: to degrade and destroy ISIS so that it's no longer a threat, not just to Iraq but also to the region and to the United States."[107]

Obama, who had seemingly built his legacy on ending the war in Iraq, was, however, clearly a reluctant warrior. Instead of returning U.S. troops to places like Fallujah, Ramadi, or Mosul, to "reoccupy Iraq," Obama would outline a policy designed to defeat ISIS through an air campaign and support for local allies. He would state on September 11, 2014, "Our objective is clear: we will degrade, and ultimately destroy, ISIL through a comprehensive and sustained counter-terrorism strategy. First, we will conduct a systematic campaign of airstrikes against these terrorists.... Second, we will increase

our support to forces fighting these terrorists on the ground."[108] Obama, who
described himself as "an admirer of the foreign policy realism of George
H. W. Bush," would elaborate further on his policy on September 17 to troops
at MacDill Airbase, stating:

> As your Commander-in-Chief, I will not commit you and the rest of
> our Armed Forces to fighting another ground war in Iraq. After a
> decade of massive ground deployments, it is more effective to use
> our unique capabilities in support of partners on the ground so they
> can secure their own countries' futures. And that's the only solution
> that will succeed over the long term.
>
> We'll use our air power. We will train and equip our partners. We
> will advise them and we will assist them. We will lead a broad
> coalition of countries who have a stake in this fight. . . .
>
> Some nations will help us support the forces fighting these
> terrorists on the ground. And already Saudi Arabia has agreed to host
> our efforts to train and equip Syrian opposition forces. Australia and
> Canada will send military advisors to Iraq. German paratroopers will
> offer training. Other nations have helped resupply arms and equip-
> ment to forces in Iraq, including the Kurdish Peshmerga. Arab nations
> have agreed to strengthen their support for Iraq's new government
> and to do their part in all the aspects of the fight against ISIL. And our
> partners will help to cut off ISIL funding, and gather intelligence, and
> stem the flow of foreign fighters into and out of the Middle East.[109]

Obama lost no time in launching a wider air campaign against ISIS that would,
for the first time, come to include bombing raids in Syria as well. On September 22, the United States launched strikes against ISIS positions in Iraq and
Syria with bombers (including the first deployment of the stealth F-22 Raptor)
and forty-seven ship-launched Tomahawk cruise missiles. This blitz was also
aimed at an Al Nusra–linked group in Syria known as Al Khorasan, which was
said to be plotting terror attacks on U.S. airliners with non-metallic devices
such as explosives in toothpaste (Al Nusra furiously denied that the group existed, but the U.S. continued to hunt its members with drones into 2015).
Planes from America's new anti-ISIS coalition members, including such Arab
states as Jordan, Bahrain, Saudi Arabia, and the UAE, took part in the attacks.
Targets in Syria included ISIS headquarters, a finance center, supply trucks,
training camps, and combat vehicles in the ISIS capital of Raqqa, while targets

in Iraq included ISIS positions in Mosul, Sinjar, and near the Haditha Dam, which the militants were threatening. Local sources in Syria claimed that seventy ISIS fighters were killed in the strikes and three hundred wounded.[110]

The embattled Shiite Alawite government of President Assad in Syria, which had seen its area of control limited to the capital of Damascus and the western coast Alawite heartland, was understandably delighted to see its Sunni enemies being targeted by the United States and its Arab allies. It claimed that the U.S. had warned them in advance of the airstrikes. As U.S. airstrikes continued in Syria, targeting ISIS oil wells in the east and positions around the city of Aleppo, the Syrian government and Kurds in northern Syria, who had been threatened by the militants, applauded.

By this time the world's attention shifted to the three Kurdish enclaves made up of Kobane, Afrin, and Jazira with approximately 2.2 million inhabitants in northern Syria along the Turkish border known collectively as Rojava. In the initial stages of the Syrian War, Syrian government troops had pulled out of these three separate Kurdish enclaves effectively ceding control over them to the PKK-linked socialist Kurdish YPG (People's Protection Units). But in October 2014, ISIS militants began to encroach on the central Kurdish enclave based on the Turkish-Syrian border city of Kobane. As three hundred thousand Syrian Kurds fled to neighboring Turkey, ISIS fighters fought fierce battles with Kurdish YPG fighters to conquer this strategic border town. Among the Kurdish defenders were many women, who had long been deployed by the YPG. One Middle East observer was to note of this secular Kurdish region, "Rojava is the only region in the world where women have organized themselves to ideologically and physically fight Islamist forces to protect civilians from fanatic religious rule."[111]

With the world watching, the seesawing battle for Kobane became a test for Obama's new strategy of confronting ISIS by supporting local forces with arms and bombings. To prevent the threatened city from falling to ISIS fighters, who had captured much of Kobane, the United States pushed its reluctant ally, Turkey (an enemy of the Kurds), to let Kurdish Peshmerga fighters from northern Iraq cross its territory to bolster Kobane's defenders. The U.S. also air-dropped weapons to Kobane's Kurdish defenders and launched waves of precision bombing runs that killed hundreds of ISIS fighters. In all, the U.S. hit more than one thousand targets in and around Kobane.

As their losses became unsustainable, ISIS finally pulled back by January 2015 and acknowledged that its forces had been defeated in the four-month battle for Kobane. As the militants retreated, Kurds who had been watching the battle from less than a mile away from the hills of Turkey joyously poured into the city to celebrate its liberation. A senior U.S. State Department official triumphantly proclaimed of the hard-fought victory, "The entire notion of this organization that is on the march and the inevitable expansion and inevitable momentum has been halted at Kobane."[112] Admiral John Kirby, the Pentagon press secretary, summed up the success of the new approach, stating, "I think the air strikes helped a lot. It helped when we had a reliable partner on the ground in there who could help us fine-tune those strikes."[113]

Following the successful defense of Kobane, the YPG Kurds went on the offensive and moved farther south and east against ISIS and captured the key ISIS-controlled border city of Tal Abyad, which had separated the two eastern-most northern Kurdish enclaves. In the winter of 2016 the YPG Syrian Kurds went with their momentum and also moved westward against several Sunni Arab rebel groups who had received U.S. assistance. The unification of Kurds in northern Syria caused concerns in Turkey that they might be creating a de facto Kurdish state on their southern border that would be allied to the PKK (a socialist Kurdish rebel group fighting in eastern Turkey for independence since the 1980s). It was in part to prevent such an occurrence that Turkey finally joined the war on ISIS in July 2015 and allowed the United States for the first time to base its bombers at Incirlik Airbase in southeastern Turkey. Turkey felt that this move would give it more input into the U.S.-led campaign. Regardless of Turkey's fears, in October 2015 the U.S. airdropped fifty tons of small arms ammunition and grenades to a joint Kurdish Sunni, Arab Assyrian, Turkmen and Christian force in northeastern province of Al Hasakah.[114] The American aim with these direct supplies of ammunition to twenty-five to thirty thousand battle-tested Syrian Kurds and three to five thousand Arabs from the Syrian-Arab-Turkmen-Kurdish coalition was to bolster the alliance known as the Syrian Democratic Forces in its efforts to march south and attack the ISIS capital of Raqqa.[115] At the time there were rumors that U.S. Special Forces had taken control of an airfield known as Rmeilan in this Kurdish-dominated region to be used for support operations.

There were other victories as well. In October 2014, Kurdish forces backed by American airpower seized the Mosul dam and by February 2015 had gone on the offensive. Their aim was to cut off supply lines linking areas north of Mosul to the city. By January 2015 U.S. Centcom was to report that it had killed approximately six thousand ISIS fighters in its bombing campaign, which by October had become known as Operation Inherent Resolve.[116] By the summer of 2015 this number had been raised to ten thousand

ISIS members said to have been killed in over 5,827 airstrikes by coalition aircraft (78 percent of them by U.S. aircraft).[117] By September 2015 the number of airstrikes on ISIS has risen to seven thousand. By June 2016 the Pentagon reported approximately 13,000 strikes, 9,000 of which were in Iraq. The United States claimed to have attacked twenty-six hundred ISIS targets by October 2015.[118] By October 2015 the number of slain ISIS members had been reported to be as high as twenty thousand by two Pentagon sources.[119]

Among those killed was said to be the ISIS governor of Mosul, who was killed on December 25, 2014, in an airstrike. In February 2015, Jordanian forces responded to ISIS's brutal burning to death in a cage of one of their downed pilots by launching a flurry of bombings that killed scores of ISIS fighters, including a top commander known as the "Prince of Nineveh."[120] U.S. Special Forces also killed a top ISIS leader, Abu Sayyaf, the organization's top financier, in a raid in eastern Syria in May 2015. In August 2015 ISIS's number two leader, Abu Muslim al-Turkomani (aka Haji Mutazz), a former colonel in Saddam Hussein's intelligence directorate and the commander in charge of ISIS operations in Iraq, was killed in a drone airstrike. In August 2015, three British members of ISIS who were said to be plotting terror strikes in the UK were also killed by U.S. and British drones. Others killed in airstrikes included Tariq bin Tahar al Awni al Harz, a top ISIS leader in charge of moving fighters and weapons from Syria to Libya and "Jihadi John" (Mohammad Emwazi), the Brit responsible for beheading foreign hostages. In March 2016 the Pentagon said that it had killed ISIS's finance minister, Abd al-Rahman Mustafa al-Qaduli, whom many analysts consider the group's number two leader. He was killed in Syria when U.S. commandos swooped in in helicopters and attacked a vehicle he was traveling in in an attempt to capture and interrogate him. Secretary of defense Ashton Carter announced at the time, "We are systematically eliminating ISIL's cabinet," adding it was "the second senior ISIL leader we've successfully targeted this month."[121]

Today, ISIS cannot move openly in convoys for fear of being targeted by coalition aircraft; its leaders move cautiously, fearing death at the hands of unseen U.S. drones; its oil production has been seriously curtailed through systematic bombings of its facilities in eastern Syria; and it has been repulsed in its much-hyped effort to take Kobane. Its much-touted "inevitable expansion" has been ground to a halt, and it retreated even in its core lands in western Iraq and eastern Syria. Peter Neumann, an expert on ISIS, has stated, "ISIS no longer has the momentum in its core territory of Syria and Iraq. It's no longer the ever-expanding jihadist utopia that it seemed to be."[122]

ISIS has also lost over two hundred villages in northern Syria to the YPG Kurds, including the previously mentioned strategic town of Tel Abyad on the Turkish border. In November 2015, Kurdish Peshmerga forces operating in conjunction with United States aircraft and PKK/YPG fighters from Turkey and Syria recaptured the Yazidi-dominated town of Sinjar in northwestern Iraq from ISIS. This gave them control of a strategic road linking Iraq to Syria and made it difficult for ISIS fighters to travel between the Iraqi city of Mosul and the ISIS capital of Raqqa. A newly created coalition of Kurds and local Arabs known as the Syrian Democratic Forces also went on the offensive against ISIS in northeastern Syria's Hasakah Province and received fifty tons of weapons and ammo in air drops from the United States. In February 2016 the Syrian Democratic Forces took the strategic town of Al Shaddadi from ISIS further disrupting their communication between Iraq and Syria. By the summer of 2016 approximately 300 U.S. special forces were said to be "advising and assisting" the Kurdish-dominated Syrian Democrat forces which seized the strategic town of Manbij from ISIS.

The British think IHS Jane's calculated that ISIS lost fifteen percent of its territory in 2015, while the Syrian Kurd YPG People Protection forces tripled the lands they controlled in northern Syria along the Turkish border (much to the consternation of the Turks who began shelling the PKK-linked YPG Kurds in February 2016 to prevent them capturing the town of Azaz and moving to unite their three northern provinces of Jazira, Kobane and Afrin into a proto-state to be known as Rojava).[123] According to IHS Jane's ISIS's territory shrank five thousand square miles down to thirty thousand square miles in 2015 and the expansion of Kurdish YPG territory on the Turkish border cut off its supply routes to Turkey. Coalition spokesman Colonel Steve Warren announced in January 2016 in reference to Iraq, "We have retaken 40 percent of territory that ISIL once held. The enemy is weaker and on the defensive. They have not gained one inch in Iraq since May [2015]. And Syria . . . we think it's about 20 percent." Its army had also declined to between 18,000 and 25,000 from a high of 31,000.[124]

To compound matters, in late March 2016, Syrian government troops backed by Russian aircraft launched an offensive to retake Palmyra in central Syria. By June 2016 the Syrian army had recaptured Palmyra and celebrated its liberation with a concert in the city's ancient stadium.

In addition, ISIS suffered early defeats in Iraq when it lost the Haditha and Mosul dams in the summer of 2014, and was repulsed at Amerli, Ayn al Asad Airbase, Mount Sinjar, and other places. In December 2015, Iraqi Army forces retook the Anbar town of Ramadi from ISIS after three months of encirclement by a much larger Shiite-dominated Iraqi force. In June 2016 Iraqi special forces took Fallujah from ISIS after a brief siege. ISIS fighters who fled Ramadi to Mosul were reported to have been burnt alive as punishment for retreating.[125] It was hopeful sign that Sunni tribal forces joined the Iraqi Army offensive to retake Ramadi, the capital of Sunni-dominated Anbar Province. U.S. and coalition aircraft have actively supported successful Iraqi army ground operations in Tikrit, Baiji, Fallujah, and Ramadi, they have destroyed ISIS command and control facilities in Syria and Iraq, and they patrol the skies hunting for "pop-up targets" of opportunity. By the summer of 2016 the Iraqi government was to report that ISIS-controlled lands in Iraq had dwindled from 30 percent to 14 percent.

In January 2015 the United States bombed an ISIS "cash collection and distribution point" in Mosul blowing up millions of dollars to pay ISIS fighters. At that time the United States also began targeting ISIS oil trucks in what was known as Operation Tidal Wave II. Hundreds of oil tankers were destroyed in November 2015 in an attempt to cut off ISIS's vital oil trade. In one day alone, November 18th 2015, more than three hundred tankers were destroyed. ISIS was formerly making $140 million a month on oil, but after the U.S. bombings of their facilities and tankers lined up for oil they are only making a fraction of that. White House officials would declare that ISIS oil production had been reduced ninety percent by the end of 2015.[126] The situation had become so dire that in January 2016 ISIS announced it would be cutting the salaries of its fighters in half. Charles Lister was on the ground in Iraq and Syria in December 2015 and reported, "There are signs that the Islamic State is under stress in critical areas. Its oil production, refining, and transport operations are being pummeled. Resupplying its crown jewel, the Iraqi city of Mosul, is becoming more arduous. Nearly 1.5 million people in the city live in deteriorating circumstances; those with relatives trapped there speak of growing paranoia among Islamic State officials, shortages, and price inflation."[127]

The White House announced in August 2015, "We have seen significant progress in terms of rolling back ISIL [ISIS] gains inside of Iraq, and the latest statistic is that up to 25 percent of the populated area that was previously controlled by ISIL is now [an area] where ISIL can no longer enjoy freedom of movement."[128] U.S. Air Force lieutenant general John W. Hesterman III has said of the U.S. air campaign that is killing as many as one thousand ISIS fighters a month, "we kill them whenever we find them."[129] As of December 2015 the U.S.-led coalition had carried out almost nine thousand bombings on ISIS. In February 2015 U.S. Central Command stated that it had destroyed or damaged twenty one thousand five hundred and one targets ISIS targets in Iraq and Syria, including six thousand seven hundred and twenty "fighting positions," one thousand two hundred and sixteen pieces of "oil infrastructure" and one thousand forty three "staging areas."[130]

In the territories where its soldiers hold sway, ISIS has also proven to be a poor government when it comes to everything from picking up garbage, to running schools that teach boys and girls something other than shariah Islamic law (boys and girls are now forced to study in separated schools). This may ultimately backfire in its struggle to maintain its support among Sunnis, especially secular ex-Baathists. Its economy remains fragile because of international containment efforts and is unsustainable in the long term. This may compound matters and expose its internal contradictions, especially between secular Baathists and jihadists. But ISIS is nonetheless learning and adapting, and in some areas it controls, it has made successful efforts to win hearts and minds by providing basic services, as well as order and security to the people in war zones in Syria.

At its height, ISIS had as many as thirty-one thousand fighters in its ranks and as much as $1 billion in its coffers.[131] It previously financed much of its military operations by earning $1.5 million a day from selling oil. By all accounts, ISIS was replacing fighters as fast as they were killed, trying to maintain the "cult of the offensive."[132] With up to a thousand foreign fighters a month joining its forces and new recruits being drafted from local men (and even from brainwashed boys in areas it controls) ISIS seemed to be un-cowed and in control of an area of 138,000 square kilometers of land stretching from the Turkish-Syrian border at Jarabolus to Mosul. It also ruled over eight million people, taxing and regulating them as a proto-state.

As of fall 2015, the war on ISIS was, on balance, "tactically stalemated," in the words of General Martin Dempsey, chairman of the Joint Chiefs of Staff. By June 2016 U.S. officials would declare that ISIS's "caliphate" had begun to "unravel and crumble." But even as the tide turned against ISIS, it remained a potent expression of Sunni frustration.

Never is this Sunni empowerment more evident than in the fact that Sunni members of Hussein's Iraqi army and Baathist Party, who were fired by the Americans back in 2003, play a key role in ISIS, despite the seeming contradiction between its Islamic goals and their secular backgrounds. The *Washington Post* has reported, "almost all of the leaders of the Islamic State are former Iraqi officers, including the members of its shadowy military and security committees, and the majority of its emirs and princes."[133]

Compounding matters, U.S. efforts to train five thousand "vetted, moderate" Syrian forces to combat ISIS in Saudi Arabia were called off in October 2015 and deemed to be a failure. In 2014, the Nusra Front attacked and dismantled the CIA's two main moderate fighting groups: the Syrian Revolutionaries Front, and Harakat Hazm. In July 2015, Al Nusra Front also attacked a small U.S.-trained moderate force called Division 30 in northern Syria and succeeded in capturing its commander, before subsequently being driven off by U.S. aerial bombardments.

In addition, millions of dollars worth of weapons sent to Jordan to be dispatched to Sunni rebels were stolen and sold on the black market.

As many as twenty-six hundred U.S. trainers and advisors were nonetheless working in 2016 with Iraqi army forces and Kurdish Peshmergas to plan an eventual offensive to retake Mosul and Anbar. In late March 2016 the much awaited offensive, dubbed Operation Conquest, began in Makhmour to the east of Mosul. A small number of U.S. troops were based in the region and one of them, a member of the elite Marine Raiders, was killed at the time by an ISIS shelling of an American fire base. This made him the second U.S. casualty in Iraq since the commencement of Operation Inherent Resolve.

But it remains to be seen how much of an impact this small number of U.S. trainers and support troops can have on the desertion-plagued Iraqi army, which was already trained for many years at the cost of billions of dollars by thousands of troops during the eight-year U.S. occupation. The idea of this unreliable force reconquering heavily defended Mosul in addition to other Sunni strongholds may not be realistic in the near future.

Most important, the Kurdistan Regional Government is facing bankruptcy due to falling oil prices and a cut off of funds from Baghdad due to its decision to directly sell its oil to Turkey. I met with Peshmerga General Sirwan Barzani, the commander of Sector Six facing ISIS in January 2016 in his frontline base near Mosul, and he listed off the problems facing his embattled force. They lacked the heavy weapons ISIS has acquired, they had not been paid salaries in months due to the financial crisis, and they had not trusted the Iraq Army. Masrour Barzani, the Chancellor of Kurdish intelligence, similarly told me that the Kurds felt threatened by the ISIS state on their borders, but were worried about taking heavy losses in a fight to retake Mosul for the Iraqi government.

As for the Syrian front, the movement to retake Deir es Zor province and the ISIS capital of Raqqa has been slow, but progress had been made. The CIA has been arming several moderate Syrian rebel groups and has stepped up weapons airdrops to them since October 2015; this is a start. But most of the non-ISIS Sunni rebel groups, which are part of the joint Army of Conquest, are focused on fighting the Assad regime in the northwestern regions of Idlib, Homs, and Hama. History would seem to indicate that Obama's containment approach has been highly successful and ISIS has begun to retreat under a combination of U.S.-led Coalition airstrikes and advances by local allies on the ground in Iraq and Syria.

But Obama had his critics. Former British MI6 intelligence chief, John Sawers, described Obama as "cautious, possibly to a fault. I think he's been hesitant to get back involved in military engagements in the Islamic world, for example, scarred by what had happened in Iraq and Afghanistan."[134] Obama's deep reluctance to redeploy U.S. troops to the region and "reoccupy" Iraq has, not surprisingly, left him open to attack from hawks in the Republican Party. After the fall of the Iraqi city of Ramadi and the Syrian city of Palmyra to ISIS in May 2015, Senator John McCain, for example, spoke of the Obama administration's "indecisive policy, inadequate commitment, and incoherent strategy."[135] There was a sense among his critics that Obama was dithering and not doing enough to defeat the ISIS threat to the "world order."[136] South Carolina senator Lindsey Graham has said, "This is not a replacement for a strategy to deal with an existential threat to the homeland" and has even called on the president to put up to ten thousand troops in Iraq and Syria to combat ISIS on the ground in those countries. To support his calls for troops on the ground in Iraq and Syria, Graham melodramatically warned, "They [ISIS] will open the gates of hell to spill out on the world. This is ISIL versus mankind. They're intending to come here. This president needs to rise to the occasion before we get killed back here at home."[137] Republican presidential candidate Donald Trump hinted that he would put "20 to 30,000" troops in Iraq and called for a ban on Muslims traveling to America (although he made an exception for the Muslim mayor of London).

Republican candidates and commentators also blasted Obama for cautiously avoiding the term "Islamic extremists" to describe ISIS or other Muslim terrorist groups (which he did describe as "jihadists"). Republican Candidate Ted Cruz captured the sentiment of many Republicans who were eager to define the enemy as "Islamic" when he described Obama as "an apologist for radical Islamic terrorists."[138]

But Obama stood his ground, and in January 2015 explained why he chose to use terms like "thugs" and "killers" to define ISIS, instead of calling them "Islamic extremists," stating, "Groups like ISIL are desperate for legitimacy. They try to portray themselves as religious leaders and holy warriors who speak for Islam. I refuse to give them legitimacy. We must never give them that legitimacy. They're not defending Islam. They're not defending Muslims. The vast majority of the people they kill are innocent Muslim men, women and children."[139]

President Obama has also scoffed at his Republican critics' ambiguous and often blustery plans for solving the multisided ethnic-sectarian civil war in Syria, which has cost 250,000 lives and seen the collapse of society and the displacement of half the country's population. In October 2015, for example, he said, "When I hear people offering up half-baked ideas as if they are solutions, or trying to downplay the challenges involved in the situation, what I'd like to see people ask is, specifically, precisely, what exactly would you do and how would you fund it and how would you sustain it? And typically, what you get is a bunch of mumbo-jumbo."[140] Here he was referring to comments like those from Republication presidential candidate Ted Cruz, who threatened to "carpet bomb" ISIS and make the sands of the Middle East "glow in the dark" (as if after a nuclear strike). In October 2014, Dr. Jonathan Stevenson, professor of strategic studies at the Naval War College, and Steve Simon, the former director for the Middle East on the National Security Council, published an important article that weighed in on this debate in the influential journal *Foreign Affairs*. In it, they stated:

> The Obama administration has clearly pulled back from the United States' recent interventionism in the Middle East, notwithstanding the rise of the Islamic State (also known as ISIS) and the U.S.-led air war against it. Critics pin the change on the administration's aversion to U.S. activism in the region, its unwillingness to engage in major combat operations, or President Barack Obama's alleged ideological preference for diminished global engagement. But the reality is that Washington's post-9/11 interventions in the region—especially the one in Iraq—were anomalous and shaped false perceptions of a "new normal" of American intervention, both at home and in the region. The administration's unwillingness to use ground forces in Iraq or Syria constitutes not so much a withdrawal as a correction—an attempt to restore the stability that had endured for several decades thanks to American restraint, not American aggressiveness. . . .
>
> The military-centric interventionism [in the Islamic world] of the past 14 years was an aberration from a longer history of American restraint; it must not harden into a new long-term norm.[141]

There were many such voices in Washington, D.C., think tanks and the military, including those of former secretary of defense, Robert Gates, who spoke of the dangers of "imperial overreach" and spoke out in favor of a pullback from U.S. military intervention in the Islamic world. As Republicans called for Obama to launch a war against Assad in Syria for his use of banned WMDs, Gates said, "Shouldn't we finish the two wars we have before we look for another?" There was also a growing awareness in the military that the insurgencies in Iraq and Afghanistan were not beatable without at least a thirty-year occupation of the sort the American people did not have the stomach for. Lieutenant General Daniel Bolger, a senior Army commander in Iraq, summed up this sentiment in an opinion piece for the *New York Times* on November 10, 2014:

> Here's a legend that's going around these days. In 2003, the United States invaded Iraq and toppled a dictator. We botched the follow-through, and a vicious insurgency erupted. Four years later, we surged in fresh troops, adopted improved counterinsurgency tactics and won the war. And then dithering American politicians squandered the gains. It's a compelling story. But it's just that—a story.
>
> The surge in Iraq did not "win" anything. It bought time. It allowed us to kill some more bad guys and feel better about ourselves. But in the end, shackled to a corrupt, sectarian government in Baghdad and hobbled by our fellow Americans' unwillingness to commit to a fight lasting decades, the surge just forestalled today's stalemate. Like a handful of aspirin gobbled by a fevered patient, the surge cooled the symptoms. But the underlying disease didn't go away. The remnants of Al Qaeda in Iraq and the Sunni insurgents we battled for more than eight years simply re-emerged this year as the Islamic State, also known as ISIS.
>
> The surge legend is soothing, especially for military commanders like me. We can convince ourselves that we did our part, and a few more diplomats or civilian leaders should have done theirs. Similar myths no doubt comforted Americans who fought under the command of Robert E. Lee in the Civil War or William C. Westmoreland in Vietnam. But as a three-star general who spent four years trying to win this thing—and failing—I now know better.
>
> We did not understand the enemy, a guerrilla network embedded in a quarrelsome, suspicious civilian population. We didn't understand our own forces, which are built for rapid, decisive conventional

operations, not lingering, ill-defined counterinsurgencies. We're made for Desert Storm, not Vietnam. As a general, I got it wrong. Like my peers, I argued to stay the course, to persist and persist, to "clear/hold/build" even as the "hold" stage stretched for months, and then years, with decades beckoning. The American people had never signed up for that.

And certainly the small number of ten thousand troops proposed by Lindsey Graham would seem woefully insufficient to combat ISIS in the vast deserts of Syria *and* Iraq when it took 168,000 U.S. surge troops allied with 103,000 Anbar Awakening Sunni fighters to defeat the insurgents in just Iraq back in 2007–8. The reintroduction of a small, division-sized U.S. Army presence in the vast deserts of Iraq might actually play into the hands of ISIS recruiters, who are vitally interested in casting their struggle as one between the warriors of Islam and the American "defenders of the cross." Al Baghdadi seemed to relish the idea of fighting Americans in an apocalyptic battle in places like Fallujah when he said, "You should know, you defender of the cross, that getting others to fight on your behalf will not do for you in Syria as it will not do for you in Iraq. And soon enough, you will be in direct confrontation—forced to do so, God willing. And the sons of Islam have prepared themselves for this day. So wait, and we will be waiting, too."[142]

While one of the original architects of much of the chaos in Iraq, former vice president Dick Cheney, capitalized on the rise of ISIS in June 2014 to excoriate Obama for "abandoning" Iraq (and thus conveniently overlooking the fact that it was Bush who signed the treaty for a 2011 withdrawal of all U.S. troops back in 2008), polls at the time showed that Americans did not support U.S. direct military intervention in the bloody sectarian war in the deserts of Iraq or neighboring Syria. After the loss of almost forty-five hundred American lives in Operation Iraqi Freedom in hellholes like Fallujah, only 36 percent of Americans favored U.S. intervention against Syria in 2013, and only 22 percent supported returning troops to intervene in Iraq according to a 2014 poll.[143]

By February 2015, the mood had, however, shifted in the face of constant news of ISIS atrocities, and CBS News was to report in a poll that a majority of Americans (57 percent) supported sending ground troops into Iraq and Syria to confront the terrorist group.[144] By this time 84 percent of Americans had come to see ISIS as a "critical threat" to the United States.[145]

Republicans continued to criticize the seeming inactivity of Obama, who had once dismissed ISIS in early 2013 as a "junior varsity squad" and admitted in 2014, "we don't have a strategy yet" to defeat ISIS. But most Republican candidates for the 2016 presidential elections were cautious when it came to calling for a return of U.S. troops to the sands of Iraq for fear that they would lose voters who were tired of the endless wars in the deserts of the Middle East. Republican presidential candidate Rand Paul went so far as to say that the only boots on the ground in Iraq should be those of the Arabs. He further stated, "If the Iraqis are not willing to fight for their country, I don't think I would send more American GIs."[146]

But by March 2015, Obama could point to the fact that Iraqi Shiite forces had finally gotten their act together and gone on the offensive against ISIS. In mid-March, an Iraqi force of thirty thousand reconquered Tikrit, the capital of Saluhudin Province, a major Sunni center north of Baghdad that had been conquered by ISIS in June of the previous year. It was also symbolic in that it was Hussein's hometown. At the time Vice Presidnet Joe Biden would triumphantly announce, "ISIS's aura of invincibility has been pierced."

But even as Iraqi television showed hundreds of Iraqi fighters celebrating the liberation of the town, critics pointed out the fact that as much as 80 percent of the Iraqi force involved in the conquest of Tikrit was made up of "popular mobilization" Shiite militias that had been trained by Iran's Revolutionary Guard Al Quds Force.[147] Sunnis feared that Shiite militias, estimated to have 120,000 paramilitary fighters, were unaccountable to the government. The Revolutionary Guard leader General Qassam Suleimani was said to have overseen Shiite militia operations, and there were fears that this would fan the fears of Sunnis, who feared both the Shiite militias and the Shiite Iranians. Critics also pointed to the fact that, while the Iraqi government deployed Shiite "popular mobilization" militias, it failed to create Sunni militias. Simply put, alienated Sunni tribesmen in the Tikrit region refused to fight in large numbers against Sunni ISIS on behalf of the distrusted Shiite government in the way the Sunni Anbar Awakening fighters had earlier done during the 2007 troop surge. Thus the odds of Iraq seeing a second Sunni Anbar Awakening to north or west of Baghdad remained slim, as Shiite militias occupied Sunni lands in Saluhhudin Province and in some cases destroyed the Sunnis' villages to prevent their return.

But in a potentially positive sign, in June 2015, displaced Sunnis from Tikrit were escorted back to the town by Shiite forces. And most important, there was no revenge killing of Sunnis by Shiite militias, which had, by this time, become somewhat more professional. This had potentially positive implications for Sunni relations with the Shiite-dominated government of Prime Minister Abadi, which had pledged to end sectarianism.

But not all went smoothly under the new Iraqi prime minister. The Abadi Shiite Iraqi government has been loath to arm and pay the salaries for local Sunni tribal forces in Anbar Province to the west of Baghdad that were fighting ISIS, and thus contributed to the ISIS conquest of the capital of Anbar Province, Ramadi, in May 2015.[148] This was compounded by a reluctance among local Sunnis to allow Iraqi army troops (Shiites for the most part) into Ramadi to help with the defense.

This lack of trust between anti-ISIS Sunnis and Shiites in Anbar proved to be disastrous. After eighteen months of fighting for the Ramadi town center, ISIS forces took advantage of a sandstorm (which grounded U.S. support aircraft) to launch a blitz on Ramadi on May 17, 2015. Their fighters proclaimed to the city's Sunni population, "ISIS is here to save you from the apostates [Shiites]."[149] Their advance into Ramadi was led by a wave of thirty unprecedentedly large "mega suicide bombings" on enemy targets by vehicles such as captured Humvees and a bulldozer. These suicide bombings, which were said to be more powerful than the Oklahoma City bombing, took out whole city blocks, broke through concrete defensive walls in the city center, and broke the nerve of the city's numerically superior Iraqi army defenders.

As in Mosul in the previous year, the defenders' sudden retreat led to the ISIS capture of large stores of U.S.-supplied equipment, including tanks and artillery, and the execution of hundreds of locals who were seen as collaborators with the Shiite-dominated government. A frustrated U.S. secretary of defense Carter was to subsequently level an uncharacteristically harsh rebuke of the Iraqi government forces, stating that the Iraqi troops "had no will to fight" and that "they were not outnumbered. In fact, they vastly outnumbered the opposing [ISIS] force and they failed to fight and withdrew from the site. That says to me . . . that we have an issue with the will of the Iraqis to fight ISIL, to defend themselves."[150] As Carter's statement indicated, Iraqi Shiite government troops seemed increasingly unwilling to fight and die to keep together a country that was unraveling into de facto Shiite, Sunni, and Kurdish sub-states.

At roughly this same time, ISIS also made gains in central Syria when it conquered the ancient city of Palmyra. The world was horrified by the May 2015 capture of this city, which was home to spectacular Roman-era ruins that had been declared a UNESCO World Heritage site by the U.N. There were fears that the ISIS militants would destroy this city that had once been ruled by the legendary Queen Zenobia, just as they had destroyed the ancient capital of the Assyrian empire at Nimrud outside Mosul in the previous year. One ISIS fighter summarized the logic of this culturecide as follows: "These antiquities and idols behind me were from people in past centuries and were worshiped instead of God. When God almighty orders us to destroy these statues, idols and antiquities, we must do it, even if they're worth billions of dollars." [151] As if to confirm the local population's worst fears, ISIS carried out the public execution of captured Syrian government soldiers in Palmyra's Roman amphitheater soon after their conquest. But they then provided bread and electricity to the local population and promised not to destroy the beloved historic site in an effort to win over the local Sunni population. In a popular and symbolic gesture, ISIS fighters also blew up a notorious government prison in the town that had been used by the Assad regime to hold Sunni prisoners.

Such unexpected hopes for tolerance on the part of what the UN has called "cultural cleansers" were shattered in August 2015 when ISIS members beheaded the eighty-one-year-old archeologist and director in charge of Palmyra, hung his body from a Roman column, and put his head on a pole. They then blew up the temple Baalshamin, another UNESCO World Heritage showpiece in Palmyra, dedicated to an ancient god of the sky, which was built almost two thousand years ago. They also blew up a triumphal Roman arch and a temple to the god Baal in October 2015, as well as ancient funeral towers.

ISIS has proven capable of carrying out large-scale terrorist attacks in both Iraq and Syria. In January 2016 ISIS bombers and gunmen attacked a mall in a Shiite neighborhood of Baghdad and killed seventeen. A few hours later they killed twenty three in the eastern Shiite town of Muqdadiya. In the spring of 2016 ISIS launched a blitz of suicide bombings on Shiite neighborhoods in Baghdad. But their bloodiest attacks were in Syria on February 22, 2016. In what was to be the deadliest terror attack thus far of the Syrian civil war, one hundred and twenty were killed in ISIS bombings near the Shiite shrine of Zaynab in a Shiite-dominated neighborhood of southern Damascus and sixty nine were killed by bombs in a pro-Assad regime neighborhood of Al Zahraa in the city of Homs that had been hit by ISIS bombs in December 2015.

Thus despite ISIS's defeat at Kobane, Baiji, and Tikrit, they proved to be deadly, resilient, adaptable, and able to expand in other areas to compensate for its losses, inflicting damage on both people and priceless historical sites. Whenever it was defeated on one front, it would strike in another area. And ISIS proved to incredibly adept at using IEDs when on the defensive and battlefield suicide bombings when on the offensive. Kurdish Peshmerga general Badal Bande, whom I interviewed in his forward operating base facing ISIS lines near the Mosul dam, claimed that the greatest threat his troops faced came from ISIS VBIEDs (vehicle-borne improvised explosive devices or car-driven suicide bombers) that drove into his forces. To defeat them, General Bande's troops deployed anti-tank guided missiles. But the suicidal ferocity of the ISIS fighters, nonetheless, intimidated the Kurds.

But for all the times that ISIS showed unexpected resilience, Obama continued to be reluctant to involve U.S. boots directly on the ground to support the Iraqi government in combat. The U.S. ground role in the war on ISIS was initially limited to trainers at five bases in Iraq. Obama did not see ISIS as a threat to core U.S. interests and scoffed at the alarmist rhetoric of some of his Republican critics, saying, "ISIS is not an existential threat to the United States . . . and they're not coming here to chop our heads off." This bothered some U.S. military officers, who felt the U.S. troops could make an impact on the battlefield if they were not restricted to training bases. One of them stated, "We are risk adverse, we are not putting the enablers where we need them."[152]

The closest Obama initially came to putting U.S. troops in harm's way occurred in June 2015 when he deployed 450 U.S. Army trainers to an Iraqi operation centers base in Anbar Province at Al Taqqadum. Strict policies from the White House prevented U.S. troops from combat operations on the ground in Iraq and Syria. But U.S. Special Forces, nonetheless, were used on occasion for special missions. For example, U.S. troops did come into direct combat with ISIS when they were involved in a raid to free seventy prisoners being held in an ISIS prison in Hawija, northern Iraq, in October 2015. One Delta Force member was killed in this operation; the first American to die in Iraq since the war ended in 2011. A second American, a Navy SEAL, who was part of a quick reaction force sent to rescue Kurdish Peshmergas being attacked by ISIS, was killed in May 2016. This Delta Force raid and the SEALs' support for the Peshmergas were seen as potential signs of things to come, and Secretary of Defense Ashton Carter announced afterward that "there will be more raids."[153] A special force raid was also launched to free hostages in the Raqqa region of Syria in 2014. Analysts theorized that the commandos who carried out the raid belonged to Task Force 27 based in Erbil which was tasked with killing or capturing ISIS high-value targets.

By the spring of 2016, the U.S. had roughly three thousand seven hundred troops in Iraq and some of them were deployed near ISIS lines in the Mosul vicinity in the Nineveh Operations Center. It was speculated at the time that these troops would be embedded or "integrated" with local forces to support a joint Iraqi Army/Kurdish Peshmerga offensive to retake Mosul. But the

Obama administration was adamant that these troops would not be fighting and refused to call these soldiers "boots on the ground." Army Lt. Gen. Sean MacFarland finessed the issue stating "Some would call them [the troops] 'accelerants' to the campaign that would allow us to increase the pressure on the enemy. Now, that doesn't necessarily equate to boots on the ground."[154]

While some (including myself in the *Los Angeles Times*) called on Obama to insert U.S. Air Force "Combat Controllers" armed with SOFLAMs (Special Operation Forces Laser Acquisition Markers) directly into front-line Iraqi forces and Syrian rebel units to call in precision bomb strikes from aircraft on ISIS positions, Obama initially saw this as dangerous escalation or "mission creep" and did not allow it.[155] Kurdish fighters in Syria were nonetheless given equipment to call in air strikes and the Chancellor of Kurdish Intelligence, Masrour Barzani told me in January 2016 that U.S. special forces were closely coordinating airstrikes with Kurdish Peshmerga forces on the frontlines.

But as pressure mounted from Republicans and Democrats alike to do more on the ground to defeat ISIS, in October 2015 the White House announced that it would be deploying "less than fifty" Special Operations troops to northern Syria to help coordinate local Kurdish ground forces. But the White House issued a caveat stating, "These forces do not have a combat mission."[156]

In December 2015, U.S. defense secretary Ashton Carter, however, announced that the United States was deploying a new force of special operations troops to Iraq to conduct raids against Islamic State there and in neighboring Syria. Carter said of the deployment of the new "specialized expeditionary targeting force," "These special operators will over time be able to conduct raids, free hostages, gather intelligence and capture ISIL leaders. This force will also be in a position to conduct unilateral operations into Syria." Thus, despite the risk of "mission creep" escalation and charges of "incrementalism," Obama began to put a limited number of "boots on the ground" in Syria and Iraq in the latter part of his presidency.

The risk of an escalation increased in late September 2015 when the unpredictable Russian leader, Vladimir Putin, suddenly involved his nation in the Syrian conflict on the side of Moscow's longtime ally, the embattled Assad regime. Russia had long been a key supporter of the Syrian Baathist-Socialist regime, which provided Russia with its only naval base outside of former Soviet territory, at Tartus, since 1971. Moscow was concerned by the growing threat to Assad posed by a new alliance of non-ISIS Sunni rebel groups in the northwest known as Jaish al Fatah (the Army of Conquest). This alliance conquered Idlib Province in northwestern Syria soon after its formation in March 2015 and began to encroach on the Alawite coastal homeland toward Latakia. In response, in late September of that year, approximately two thousand Russian military personnel were flown into a Syrian army base known as Hmeimim, near the Assad regime–controlled stronghold of Latakia on the northwest Mediterranean coast of Syria near Turkey (they would also operate later from a base known as Shayrat near Homs). The Russians also dispatched up to fifty aircraft (primarily Su-25 Frogfoot ground attack planes, new Su-34 Fullback medium bombers, and Su-24 Fencer fighter jets) and several Mil 24 Hind attack helicopters to the base. These aircraft were later supported by larger Tu-22M3 strategic bombers and Tu-160 Blackjack and Tu-95MS bombers.

Then, in a move that caught America and its allies by surprise, on September 30, 2015, the Russians began an intensive bombing campaign against what they claimed were ISIS targets. On October 7, 2015, the Russians also fired twenty-six new Kalibr cruise missiles against Sunni rebel targets in Raqqa, Aleppo, and Idlib from warships nine hundred miles away in the Caspian Sea. But it quickly became clear that the vast majority of Russian bombings were in the west, against the Jaish al Fatah (Army of Conquest) alliance of Sunni rebel groups that was threatening Assad regime territory from territories they had recently conquered in the northwestern provinces of Idlib. The Russians also attacked CIA-trained rebels in Hama and Homs Province to the south. Among the Russians' targets were several U.S.-backed Sunni groups in the Sunni rebel alliance, such as the Free Syrian Army, Sham Legion, Jund al Aqsa, Jaish al Sunna, Ahrar ash Sham, and Division 13. One U.S.-backed rebel leader whose base was bombed by Russian aircraft bemoaned the toll of the airstrike as follows: "We are on the front lines with Bashar al-Assad's army. We are moderate Syrian rebels and have no affiliation with ISIS. ISIS is at least 100 kilometers from where we are."[157]

In what resembled a proxy war between Russia and the Americans, the U.S.-backed Free Syrian Army (which had previously been marginalized in the Army of Conquest) initially fought back ferociously against a Syrian army ground offensive being supported by the Russian aircraft using American-supplied TOW (tube-launched, optically tracked, wire-guided missiles) to destroy Russian-built Syrian tanks in October 2015. But the Russians adjusted and began using helicopters, which could not be brought down by TOW missiles instead and they proved to be effective. The CIA-backed rebels, who were forced to retreat, requested antiaircraft missiles to shoot down Russian and Syrian jets and attack helicopters, but they were not delivered for fear of escalating the proxy conflict further. One Free Syrian Army fighter stated, "We can have most of the weapons we want. But nothing to shoot down the planes."[158] At this time the advancing rebels were forced on the defensive and began to retreat on various fronts.

At this time, Putin declared that he had arranged an intelligence-sharing agreement with Iran, Iraq, and Syria, and it appeared as if the demoralized Syrian regime, which was low on manpower, would be bolstered by an alliance of Russia, Hezbollah, and Iran (although at roughly this time an Iranian brigadier general advising the Assad regime was killed in fighting in the east, and several Russians were killed, demonstrating the risks of involvement in the war). Putin, who decried the chaos and "social disaster" that filled the vacuum after the overthrow of autocratic leaders in Iraq, Syria, Egypt, Yemen, and Libya, felt that Assad needed to be bolstered as a bulwark against "terrorists" (he lumped all Sunni rebel groups into this category alongside ISIS). Interestingly, Putin directly blamed the United States for "creating the conditions in which the Islamic State terrorist state was born" and said, "Tens of thousands of militants are fighting under the banners of the so-called Islamic State. Its ranks include former Iraqi servicemen who thrown out on to the street after the invasion of Iraq in 2003."[159]

Tragically, the Russian bombing appeared to weaken the U.S.-backed moderate rebels in the Aleppo Province sufficiently for ISIS to make some advances in the northern areas of the region.[160] They also allowed Assad government troops to clear Sunni rebels out of the Alawite home region of Latakia. In February 2016, Russian aircraft supported Assad regime troops bolstered by Hezbollah and Iranian fighters in encircling neighborhoods of eastern Aleppo that had been controlled by Sunni rebels since 2012. In the process, the revived Assad regime forces were able to cut off the rebels' supply lines to Turkey in their most successful offensive of the war. This decisive offensive also broke a three year siege of several pro-government neighborhoods in the region and caused a mass panicked flight of Sunni refugees. As the Russians and Syrian air force indiscriminately bombed rebel areas causing hundreds of casualties, the Syrian Army starved rebel-controlled neighborhoods. A Russian airstrike just prior to this also killed Zahran Alloush, a powerful Sunni rebel commander who led the Army of Islam.

Syrian Army forces were able to go on the offensive against Sunni rebels belonging to the Free Syrian Army-dominated Southern Alliance in the south due to Russian air support. In essence, the Russian intervention propped up the crumbling Assad regime and allowed it to maintain control over the western corridor where most Syrians live. With Russian support, the

Assad regime aimed to add the prize of Aleppo, previously Syria's largest city, to the core areas it controlled, including the capital of Damascus and Homs.

Prior to the Russian intervention, Assad's forces were said to be so depleted that the government was weighing a retreat from Damascus to the coastal heartland of the Alawites near Latakia and Tartus.[161] While the Syrian Army had once had 220,000 troops (mainly Sunni conscripts lead by Alawite commanders) it had dwindled to an Alawite-led core of 65,000 personnel.[162] Putin decided to bolster both the endangered regime and his own popularity in Russia, where foreign wars have a rallying effect similar to that found in the United States. Another Russian goal appeared to be to establish new "facts on the ground" and thus allow Assad to negotiate from a position of strength before any talks about a transition government were begun. This could be done by destroying or weakening the more moderate Sunni rebel groups in Idlib, which the government lost in 2012, and leaving the American-led coalition with a stark choice between supporting Assad or ISIS. Putin's calculus for his country's first military intervention beyond the borders of the former Soviet Union since the fall of Communism also seemed to be to reassert his country as a major player on the world stage for the first time since it was isolated following its March 2014 invasion of the Crimean Peninsula. While Obama called Putin's five-month intervention in Syria a "blunder," Russia's limited campaign allowed Putin to reshape the battlefield in his favor with few casualties.

But Putin's policy was clearly fraught with risks as best demonstrated by a Turkish air force F-16's shoot-down of a Russian Su-24 fighter bomber that strayed for seventeen seconds into the southern Turkish province of Hatay after bombing Turkish-supported anti-Assad Turkmen rebels in northern Syria in November 2015. In addition, in the previous month the ISIS affiliate in the Sinai Desert blew up a Russian charter plane flying from the resort town of Sharm el Sheikh to St. Petersburg with a bomb, killing all 224 people on board. This was the deadliest disaster in Russian aviation history, and ISIS gloated by posting a picture online of the small bomb that was used to bring down the plane.

But despite these setbacks, Russian support bolstered the Assad regime and allowed it to make gains on the ground that were to be frozen by a cease-fire signed on February 27, 2016. It remains to be seen whether this ceasefire (which did not include ISIS or the Nusra Front) would bring an end to the conflict and lead to a negotiated solution.

While the Republicans took advantage of the Russian entrance into the Syrian conflict to attack Obama for "disengaging" and having "surrendered the Middle East to Putin," Moscow's intervention was not as large, sustained,

effective, or systematic as the U.S.-led campaign known as Operation Inherent Resolve, which halted and pushed back ISIS on several fronts, including
Tikrit, Kurdistan, Baiji, Haditha, and Kobane. The United States, it should be
noted, had approximately forty-five thousand troops in the region and deep
ties to countries from Morocco to Pakistan, while Russia had two thousand
troops, and its only close partner was the embattled Syrian regime, which
controlled only the west of Syria. As for fears that Russia and the U.S. would
become involved in a Cold War–style proxy war or direct confrontation in
Syria, these appeared to be overblown. Obama said, "This is not some superpower chessboard contest," and both superpowers made considerable efforts
to "deconflict" their involvement in Syria.

While the Russian "boots on the ground" intervention in the fall of 2015
on behalf of its longtime Syrian ally helped it protect and enlarge the endangered Alawite heartland on the western coastal strip and the capital of Damascus, the Russians ultimately found the best they could do was create
"facts on the ground" that strengthened the Assad regimes hand before a
cease fire declared in February 2016 froze them. Their best hope was to protect the rump Alawite state on the Mediterranean coast of Syria and perhaps
help it control a corridor that included parts of Aleppo, the Alawite homeland, the cities of Homs and Hama and Damascus the capital. The Obama
administration did not officially seem to be too worried by Putin's intervention in Syria initially and seemed to underestimate the Russians' ability to
shape the battlefield. One official said, "if he wants to jump into that mess,
good luck," while another sarcastically said, "knock yourself out."[163]

As for the American boots on the ground in Syria, this seemed a remote
prospect, regardless of Putin's gambit in support of the Assad regime. Robert
Ford, the former U.S. ambassador to Syria who made a name for himself for
bravely criticizing Assad's attacks on civilians, made this clear when he emphatically stated, "After the Iraq war, the last thing we're going to do is send
the military to Syria. It will never, ever happen."[164]

As ISIS's "caliphate" began to crumble and lose vast swathes of land by the
summer of 2016, Obama clearly felt vindicated in his approach. At the loss of
just three American soldiers killed in combat he had succeeded in his stated
goal of "degrading" ISIS by using surrogates, local allies and bombings. All this
had been achieved at a cost of just $7.5 billion. Obama summed up his posi-
tion on returning U.S. troops to the war-torn deserts of the Middle East when
he stated in a May 2014 speech at West Point, "For the foreseeable future, the
most direct threat to America, at home and abroad, remains terrorism, but a

strategy that involves invading every country that harbors terrorist networks is naive and unsustainable."[165] Obama defined his approach as one defined by "strategic patience and persistence," involving such tactics as preventing the flow of foreign fighters to the region; cutting off ISIS's access to finances through the selling oil; supporting local anti-ISIS forces such as the Kurds, the Army of Conquest, and Iraqi Army; and direct aerial bombings.[166]

On February 11, 2015, Obama further summed up his approach to the stalemated sectarian war in Iraq and Syria in a historic speech where he (unsuccessfully) asked Congress for a new AUMF (authorization to use military force). In his speech, Obama sounded both defiant and upbeat as he summed up America's successes and drew limits to future long-term involvement on the ground in the region:

> Today, as part of an international coalition of some 60 nations—
> including Arab countries—our men and women in uniform continue
> the fight against ISIL in Iraq and in Syria. More than 2,000 coalition
> airstrikes have pounded these terrorists. We're disrupting their
> command and control and supply lines, making it harder for them to
> move. We're destroying their fighting positions, their tanks, their
> vehicles, their barracks, their training camps, and the oil and gas
> facilities and infrastructure that fund their operations. We're taking
> out their commanders, their fighters and their leaders. In Iraq, local
> forces have largely held the line and in some places have pushed
> ISIL back. In Syria, ISIL failed in its major push to take the town of
> Kobane, losing countless fighters in the process—fighters who will
> never again threaten innocent civilians. And we've seen reports of
> sinking morale among ISIL fighters as they realize the futility of
> their cause. . . . Now, make no mistake—this is a difficult mission,
> and it will remain difficult for some time. It's going to take time to
> dislodge these terrorists, especially from urban areas. But our
> coalition is on the offensive, ISIL is on the defensive, and ISIL is
> going to lose.
>
> The resolution we've submitted today does not call for the
> deployment of U.S. ground combat forces to Iraq or Syria. It is not
> the authorization of another ground war, like Afghanistan or Iraq.
> The 2,600 American troops in Iraq today largely serve on bases—
> and, yes, they face the risks that come with service in any dangerous
> environment. But they do not have a combat mission. They are

focused on training Iraqi forces, including Kurdish forces. . . . As I've said before, I'm convinced that the United States should not get dragged back into another prolonged ground war in the Middle East. That's not in our national security interest and it's not necessary for us to defeat ISIL. Local forces on the ground who know their countries best are best positioned to take the ground fight to ISIL— and that's what they're doing. . . . Finally, this resolution repeals the 2002 authorization of force for the invasion of Iraq and limits this new authorization to three years. I do not believe America's interests are served by endless war, or by remaining on a perpetual war footing. As a nation, we need to ask the difficult and necessary questions about when, why and how we use military force.[167]

Obama then optimistically stated, "We all agree that one of our weapons against terrorists like ISIL—a critical part of our strategy—is the values we live here at home."

Regardless of the "kinetic" military approach proposed by Obama, it seems doubtful that the values of the United States (the very country that invaded Iraq and disempowered the ruling Sunnis back in 2003) will be seen as appealing for this emboldened sectarian group, which broke free of hated Shiite rule under the leadership of ISIS in 2014. For better or worse, a significant portion of Iraq and Syria's armed Sunni powerbrokers appear to have aligned themselves with ISIS to empower their sectarian groups vis-à-vis the ruling Shiites of both countries. Few Americans understand that this is a key underlying, unifying factor for the coalition of secular and Islamist Sunnis who have united to create ISIS, regardless of their differing backgrounds. One of those who grasped the importance of this foundational issue, Major General Michael K. Nagata, commander of American Special Operations forces in the Middle East, captured this point succinctly when he said, "We do not understand the movement, and until we do, we are not going to defeat it. We have not defeated the idea. We do not even understand the idea."[168]

ISIS's idea of erasing the artificial state borders drawn by the colonial British and French after World War I and creating a Sunni-dominated theocracy in the heart of the oil-rich Middle East has tremendous appeal to many in the region and throughout the wider Sunni Muslim world. To its adherents, the ideas offered by ISIS are more than just that of a "death cult" or "hateful ideology"; they are a Sunni jihadi empowerment movement and a revolution against dominant Shiites. As one ISIS member described the movement (which seems to have morphed from its origins as a response to the Sunnis' disempowerment back in 2003 by Coalition Order Numbers 1 and 2 to a bold dream of reestablishing a caliphate), "This can't be stopped now. . . . Not [by] Baghdadi, or anyone else in his circle. . . . This is out of the control of any man."[169] Until the Shiite-dominated governments in Baghdad and Damascus overcome years of mistrust and warfare and win the trust of the Sunnis in both Iraq and Syria, ISIS will be able to exploit a deep pool of support in both countries. This will make it incredibly difficult to defeat without U.S. troops on the ground.

Having achieved what Al Qaeda only dreamed of doing (i.e., building a Salafi jihadi state in the heart of two formerly Baathist-secularist countries), ISIS will also continue to appeal to a new generation of increasingly radical global jihadists who believe in its efforts to establish a transnational caliphate. The fact that this proto-state controls land makes it far more appealing to foreign fighters than Al Qaeda was, which hid in the shadows. Thus there are two distinct layers to ISIS, one based on Sunni empowerment and one on militant jihadism, that would seem to ensure that the battle to destroy its ideas could take years, decades, or even generations. Even as the ISIS "caliphate" that held the dream of so many Sunni jihadists collapses and puts a lie to its boastful claim to be "remaining and expanding," the roots of its rage remain. As the ISIS state lost five of its ten towns and 45 percent of its territory by the summer of 2016, it reminded its Shiite enemies that it still had the capacity to strike them with the largest suicide bombing in Iraq's history, the July killing of 250 in Baghdad.

The net result of all this for an American people who voted Obama into power, in part, on his bold calls for ending the "war of choice" in Iraq, may mean a long-term U.S. involvement in the shifting sands of the Middle East that have bedeviled and bogged down many states and empires over the centuries. As ISIS digs in deeper and prepares to defend its hard-won gains from Raqqa to Mosul, victory for the United States and its allies in this clash of ideas and values in the deserts of the Middle East is far from assured.

For further works by the author on issues covered in this book and photographs and videos from various war zones in the Middle East, Central Asia, and the Balkans, see brianglynwilliams.com.

NOTES

Epigraphs: Jessica Stern and J. M. Berger, *ISIS: The State of Terror* (New York: HarperCollins, 2015), 96. "U.S. General Strongly Defends Air Campaign Against ISIS," Fox News, June 7, 2015.

Preface

1. "ISIS Viewed as Threat to the United States, Poll," *Forbes*, February 16, 2015; "Poll: Two Thirds of Americans Fear ISIS Threat," *Newsmax*, August 28, 2014.

2. For more on Dostum and his Mongol horsemen's war against the Taliban alongside U.S. Special Forces, see Brian Glyn Williams, *The Last Warlord: The Life and Legend of the Warrior Who Led U.S. Special Forces in Toppling the Taliban Regime* (Chicago: Chicago Review Press, 2013).

3. Mark Thompson, "The Five Trillion Dollar War on Terror," *Time*, June 29, 2011.

Chapter 1. Planting the Seeds for a Global Conflict

Epigraphs: "Bin Laden Claims U.S. Plane Bombing Attempt," *Reuters,* January 24, 2010. "Bin Laden's Voice on Al Qaeda Video," BBC, September 10, 2002.

1. "Fate of Deir Yassin Spurred Palestinians to Flee," *New York Times,* August 2, 1988.

2. Jodi Rudoren, "Israel Defies Allies in Move to Bolster Settlements," *New York Times,* December 20, 2012.

3. Ibid.

4. Bruce Riedel, *What We Won: America's Secret War in Afghanistan* (Washington, D.C.: Brookings Institute, 2015).

5. For more details on this brutal war, see Brian Glyn Williams, *Afghanistan Declassified: A Guide to America's Longest War* (Philadelphia: University of Pennsylvania Press, 2012).

6. *9/11 Commission Report*, 89. http://www.9-11commission.gov/staff_statements/911_TerrFin_Monograph.pdf.

7. Peter Bergen, *Holy War Inc.: Inside the Secret World of bin Laden* (New York: Simon and Schuster, 2002), 80.

8. Helen Metz, *Iraq: A Country Study*, "The Ottoman Period" (Washington, D.C.: Library of Congress, 1988). http://countrystudies.us/iraq/18.htm.

9. Ibid.; "Republican Iraq." http://countrystudies.us/iraq/21.htm.

10. "Regrets Only?" *New York Times*, October 7, 2007.

11. For examples of Hussein's brutality, see the video at http://fdd.typepad.com/fdd/files/1.wmv.

12. "Why Saddam Hussein Cast Himself as the Godfather of Baghdad," *Telegraph* (UK), May 26, 2012.

13. For more on the issue of U.S. support for Iraq, see Kenneth Timmerman, *The Death Lobby: How the West Armed Iraq* (New York: Houghton Mifflin, 1991).

14. *He Has Gassed His Own People*, History News Network, January 22, 2007.

15. Ibid.

16. Richard Clarke, *Against All Enemies* (New York: Free Press, 2004), 266.

17. "Kuwait: Organization and Mission of Forces," Library of Congress. http://lcweb2.10c.gov/cgi-bin/query/r?frd/cstdy:@field%28DOCID+kw0058%29.

18. Dilip Hiro, *War Without End: The Rise of Islamist Terrorism and the Global Response* (New York: Routledge, 2002), 157 and 159.

19. "The Unfinished War: A Decade Since Desert Storm; Gulf War Facts." http://web.archive.org/web/20080317110507/http://www.cnn.com/SPECIALS/2001/gulf.war/facts/gulfwar/.

20. Ibid.

21. Norman Schwarzkopf, *It Doesn't Take a Hero* (New York: Bantam Books, 1992), 579.

22. "Cheney Changed His View on Iraq," *Seattle Post Intelligencer*, September 28, 2004.

23. "The Apparent Heir," *New York Times*, October 31, 2004.

24. "Approval Highs and Lows," *Washington Post*, July 2007.

25. CNN.com, In Depth Specials, "Gulf War Facts." http://web.archive.org/web/20080317110507/http://www.cnn.com/SPECIALS/2001/gulf.war/facts/gulfwar/.

26. "UN Resolution 687 (1991)." http://www.fas.org/news/un/iraq/sres/sres0687.htm.

27. Ibid.

28. United Nations Special Commission. http://www.un.org/Depts/unscom/General/basicfacts.html#MANDATE.

29. "U.S. Spied on Iraq via UN," *Washington Post*, March 2, 1999.

30. Bob Drogin and John Goetz, "How the US Fell Under the Spell of Curveball," *Los Angeles Times*, November 20, 2005.

31. "Key Targets in Iraq," Center for Strategic and International Studies. http://csis.org/files/media/csis/pubs/iraq_targets.pdf.

32. "UNSCOM Main Achievements." http://www.un.org/Depts/unscom/Achievements/achievements.html.

33. UNSCOM, "Chronology of Main Events." http://www.un.org/Depts/unscom/Chronology/chronologyframe.htm.

34. "On this Day: 1981, Israel Bombs Baghdad Nuclear Reactor," BBC.co.uk, June 7, 2005.

35. "Iraq WMD Timeline: How the Mystery Unraveled," NPR.org, November 15, 2005.

36. "Transcript of Part One of Correspondent Brent Sadler's Exclusive Interview with Hussein Kamel," CNN.com, December 12, 1995.

37. Sheldon Rampton and John Strauber, *Weapons of Mass Deception: The Uses of Propaganda in Bush's War on Iraq* (New York: Penguin, 2003), 00n31.

38. "Interview with Scott Ritter," Federation of American Scientists. http://www.fas.org/news/iraq/1999/07/990712-for.htm.

39. "U.S. Strikes Aimed at Iraqi Weapons of Mass Destruction," *American Forces Press Service*, December 17, 1998.

40. Thomas Ricks, *Fiasco: The American Military Adventure in Iraq* (New York: Penguin, 2006), 19.

41. "Desert Fox Target Toll Climbs Past 75 Iraqi Sites," *Government Executive*, December 19, 1998.

42. Tom Clancy with General Tony Zinni and Tony Koltz, *Battle Ready* (New York: G. P. Putnam's and Sons, 2004), 18.

43. "Lessons of Desert Fox," *Boston Globe*, February 14, 2006.

44. Ricks, *Fiasco*, 21.

45. Ibid.

46. Ibid.

47. Ibid., 22.

48. "PR Push for Iraq War Preceded Intelligence Findings, 'White Paper' Drafted Before NIE Even Requested," National Security Archive Electronic Briefing Book No. 254. Posted August 22, 2008. http://nsarchive.gwu.edu/NSAEBB/NSAEBB254/index.htm#8.

49. Amaztia Bara, "Deterrence Lessons from Iraq," *Foreign Affairs*, July–August 2012, 87.

50. "Comprehensive Report of the Special Advisor to the DCI on Iraq's WMD with Addendums," *Iraq Survey Group*. https://www.cia.gov/library/reports/general-reports-1/iraq_wmd_2004.

51. Michael Morell, *The Great War of Our Times* (New York: Twelve, 2015), 106.

52. Hiro, *War Without End*, 163.

53. Bergen, *Holy War Inc.*, 81.

54. "So Far Saudis Shrug at Revelation of Secret US Drone Base," *Washington Post*, February 11, 2012.

55. Steve Coll, *Ghost Wars: The Secret History of the CIA, Afghanistan, and bin Laden, from the Soviet Invasion to September 10, 2001* (New York: Penguin, 2004), 250.

56. "We've Hit the Targets," *Newsweek*, September 12, 2001.

57. "How Do We Know that Iraq Tried to Assassinate President George H.W. Bush?" History News Network, March 6, 2007.

58. "Bush Calls Saddam 'the Guy Who Tried to Kill My Dad,' " *CNN*, September 27, 2002. http://edition.cnn.com/2002/allpolitics/09/27/bush.war.talk/, September 27, 2002.

59. 9/11 Commission Report. http://www.9-11commission.gov/report/911Report.pdf.

60. "George Tenet: At the Center of the Storm," CBS News, April 25, 2007. http://www.cbsnews.com/news/george-tenet-at-the-center-of-the-storm/, April 30, 2007.

61. 9/11 Commission Report. http://www.9-11commission.gov/hearings/hearing3/witness_yaphe.htm.

62. Peter Bergen, *The Osama bin Laden I Know: An Oral History of Al Qaeda's Leader* (New York: Free Press, 2006), 111.

63. Ibid., 112.

64. Dilip Hiro, *Secrets and Lies: Operation Iraqi Freedom and After* (New York: Nation Books, 2004), 28.

65. Ibid.

66. Samia Nakhoul, "Bin Laden Labels Saddam an Infidel—Jazeera TV," Reuters, February 11, 2003.

67. Bergen, *The Osama bin Laden I Know*, 111.

68. "Vanity Fair Excerpt from the Book 'The Osama bin Laden I Know,' " *Vanity Fair*. http://web.archive.org/web/20090216031256/ http://www.peterbergen.com/bergen/articles/details.aspx?id=233.

69. Ibid.

70. Daniel Benjamin, "Saddam Hussein and Al Qaeda Are Not Allies," *New York Times*, September 30, 2002.

71. Hiro, *Secrets and Lies*, 121.

72. "Saddam Hussein and Al Qaeda Are Not Allies," *New York Times,* September 30, 2002.

73. David Froomkin, "The Propaganda Campaign Dissected," *Washington Post*, June 6, 2008.

74. "A President Finds His True Voice," *Newsweek*, September 23, 2001.

75. "Look at the Place! Sudan Says, 'Say Sorry,' but U.S. Won't," *New York Times*, October 20, 2005.

76. Bergen, *Holy War Inc.*, 127.

77. Coll, *Ghost Wars*, 502–3.

78. See the actual suggestion made by Richard Clarke in the recently declassified memo in "A Comprehensive Strategy to Fight Al-Qaeda?" National Security Archive, 9. http://www.gwu.edu/~nsarchiv/NSAEBB/NSAEBB147/index.htm.

79. Terry Anderson, *Bush's Wars* (Oxford: Oxford University Press, 2011), 52.

80. Clarke, *Against All Enemies*, 225–26.

81. Ibid., 229.

82. Ibid., 231.

83. "Two Months Before 9/11 an Urgent Warning to Rice," *Washington Post*, October 11, 2001.

84. "Transcript: Bin Laden Determined to Strike in the US," CNN.com, April 10, 2004. http://www.cnn.com/2004/allpolitics/04/10/august6.memo/.

85. "A Warning, but Clear? White House Tries to Make the Point That New Details Add Up to Old News," *New York Times*, April 11, 2004.

86. "Bush: August 6th Brief Didn't Foretell 9/11," NBC, April 11, 2004. http://www.nbcnews.com/id/4700899/ns/us_news-security/t/bush-aug-briefdidnt-foretell/#.VsdoKdDOCsg , April 11, 2004.

87. "Excerpts from April 8, 2004, Testimony of Dr. Condoleezza Rice Before the 9/11 Commission Pertaining to the President's Daily Brief of August 6, 2001," National Security Archive. http://www.gwu.edu/~nsarchiv/NSAEBB/NSAEBB116/testimony.htm.

88. Roy Gutman, *How We Missed the Story: Osama bin Laden, the Taliban, and the Hijacking of Afghanistan* (Washington, D.C.: United States Institute of Peace, 2008), 250.

89. Ibid.

90. Paul Thompson, *The Terror Timeline* (New York: Harper Collins, 2004), 50.

91. Bergen, *Osama bin Laden I Know*, 281.

92. Ibid., 308.

93. Carlotta Gall, *The Wrong Enemy: America in Afghanistan, 2001–2014* (Boston: Houghton Mifflin Harcourt, 2014), 53.

94. Thompson, *Terror Timeline*, 46.

95. Ibid., 47.

96. Ibid.

97. "Taleban Warned U.S. of Huge Attack," *BBC*, September 7, 2002. http://news.bbc.co.uk/2/hi/south_asia/2242594.stm.

98. Steve Coll, "Flawed Ally Was America's Best Hope," *Washington Post*, February 23, 2004.

99. Document 31, Defense Intelligence Agency, Cable, "IIR [Excised]/the Assassination of Massoud Related to 11 September 2001 Attack," November 21, 2001, Secret, p. 4–5, National Security Archive. http://nsarchive.gwu.edu/NSAEBB/NSAEBB97/.

100. On September 4, 2001, the Bush administration belatedly agreed to provide the Northern Alliance with $125 million in assistance, a paltry sum that Ahmed Rashid calls "pocket money" in his masterful work *Descent into Chaos* (New York: Viking, 2008), 60–62.

101. Brian Glyn Williams, *The Last Warlord: The Life and Legend of Dostum, the Afghan Warrior Who Led U.S. Special Forces to Topple the Taliban Regime* (Chicago: Chicago Review Press, 2013).

102. Thompson, *Terror Timeline*, 53.

103. Ibid.

Chapter 2. America Goes to War in Afghanistan

Epigraph: "Osama Bin Laden: Famous Quotes," *Telegraph,* May 2, 2011.

1. Frank Rich, *The Greatest Story Ever Sold: The Decline and Fall of Truth in Bush's America* (New York: Penguin, 2006), 230.

2. "Video Showing Atta, bin Laden Is Unearthed," October 1, 2006. www.msnbc.com.

3. The Arab news network *Al Jazeera* released a video of bin Laden meeting with the 9/11 hijackers and discussing their upcoming attack against the U.S. months before it took place. "Al Qaeda Takes Credit for 9/11," Al Jazeera, September 10, 2006. http://www.libertypost.org/cgi-Bin/readart.cgi?ArtNum=158086.

4. Peter Bergen, *The Osama bin Laden I Know* (New York: Free Press, 2006), 304–5.

5. Jonathan Mahler, *The Challenge: Hamdan vs. Rumsfeld and the Fight over Presidential Power* (New York: Farrar, Straus and Giroux, 2008), 10.

6. "One 9/11 Tally, 3.3 Trillion," *New York Times*, September 8, 2011.

7. "Text of Bush's Address," CNN, September 11. 2001.

8. "President George W. Bush Visits Ground Zero," NBC, September 14, 2001.

9. "Poll: Bush Approval Rating 92%," ABC News, October 10, 2001.

10. "Six Days After 9/11 an Anniversary Worth Honoring," *New York Times,* September 7, 2012.

11. Richard Clarke, *Against All Enemies* (New York: Free Press, 2004), 13.

12. James Bamford, *A Pretext for War* (New York: Doubleday, 2004), 54.

13. "Bin Laden Rejoiced on Sept. 11," ABC News, December 13, 2001.

14. "9/11 Conspiracy Theories Won't Stop," CBS News, September 11, 2007.

15. "Bin Laden Told Mother to Expect Big News," Telegraph.co.uk, October 2, 2001.

16. "Video Shows Laughing Hijackers in Afghan Hideout," CNN.com, October 1, 2006.

17. "Video Shows bin Laden, 9/11 Hijackers," CBS News, September 10, 2009.

18. "New Usama bin Laden Video Shows Attackers Last Testament," Fox News, September 11, 2007.

19. Paul Thompson, *The Terror Timeline* (New York: Harper Collins, 2004), 190.

20. Bergen, *Osama bin Laden I Know*, 309.

21. "Email Sent to Flight School Gave Terror Suspect's Goal," *New York Times,* February 8, 2002.

22. Ibid., 319.

23. "Father of Lead Hijacker Defends Son," MSNBC.com, September 11, 2004.

24. "9/11 Conspiracies Won't Stop," CBS News, September 11, 2007.

25. Ibid.

26. "Rabid Speculation: The Arab and Iranian Media Reaction to 9/11," *National Review,* September 11, 2006.

27. Ellen Crean, "The Big Lie," CBS News, September 10, 2009.

28. "Secretary of Truth: 9/11 Truther, Prominent Democrat Running for Statewide Office in Missouri," *Washington Free Beacon*, July 10, 2012.

29. Henry Crumpton, *The Art of Intelligence* (New York: Penguin, 2012), 188.

30. Pat Buchanan, *Where the Right Went Wrong: How the Neoconservatives Subverted the Reagan Revolution and Hijacked the Bush Presidency* (New York: St. Martin's, 2005), 47.

31. Rebecca Leung, "Clarke's Take on Terror," CBS News, December 5, 2007.

32. Bob Woodward, *Bush at War* (New York: Simon and Schuster, 2002), 83–84.

33. "Plans for Attack Began on 9/11," CBS News, September 4, 2002.

34. Woodward, *Bush at War*, 84.

35. "Bush: No Link to 9/11 Found," Seattlepi.com, September 17, 2003.

36. Woodward, *Bush at War*, 85.

37. "Woodward Shares War's Secrets," CBS News, December 5, 2007.

38. Rupeter Cornwell, "Taliban Are Given an Ultimatum: Hand Over bin Laden," *Independent* (UK), September 17, 2001.

39. Ed Vulliamy, "The March to the Brink of Battle," *Observer*, September 23, 2001; Luke Harding and Rory McCarthy, "War-Weary Afghans Flee in Fear," *Observer*, September 16, 2001.

40. Bergen, *Osama bin Laden I Know*, 317.

41. Ibid., 315.

42. Clarke, *Against All Enemies*, 23.

43. "Bush Announces Strikes Against Taliban," *Washington Post*, October 7, 2001.

44. Bob Woodward and Dan Baltz, "Combating Terrorism: 'It Starts Today,'" *Washington Post*, February 1, 2002.

45. "Bring Me the Head of bin Laden," BBC.co.uk, May 4, 2005.

46. It was convincingly argued in Congress prior to the U.S. invasion that "Bin Laden's fighters are intertwined with the Taliban, and any effort to remove Bin Laden from Afghanistan by necessity means the removal of Mullah Omar in the inner core of the Taliban leadership." *Al Qaeda and the Global Reach of Terrorism: Hearing Before the Committee on International Relations*, October 3, 2001. http://commdocs.house.gov/committees/intlrel/hfa75562.000/hfa75562_0.HTM.

47. Ismail Khan, "Mazar Falls: Taliban Says They're Re-Grouping," *Dawn*, November 10, 2001.

48. Kathy Gannon, "Opposition Begins Push on Taliban Stronghold," Associated Press, October 29, 2001.

49. Salah Nasrawi, "Bin Laden Lieutenant Ran Terrorism Camps," Associated Press, November 17, 2001.

50. Rohan Gunaratna, *Inside Al Qaeda* (London: Hurst, 2002), 119.

51. "As-Sahab Media Presents a Video Interview with Sheikh Mustafa Abu al Yazid AKA Sheikh Saeed, Emir of Al-Qaeda in Afghanistan," *SITE Institute*, May 26, 2007.

52. Tamim Ansary, "Bomb Afghanistan to Stone Age? It's Been Done," *CommonDreams.org* September 19, 2001.

53. Sid Jacobson and Ernie Colon, *After 9/11: America's War on Terror, (2001–)* (New York: Hill and Wang, 2008), 14.

54. George Tenet, quoted in ibid., 186.

55. See the actual suggestion made by Richard Clarke in the recently declassified memo "A Comprehensive Strategy to Fight Al-Qaeda?" National Security Archive, 9. http://www.gwu.edu/~nsarchiv/NSAEBB/NSAEBB147/index.htm.

56. Hy Rosenthein, *Afghanistan and the Troubled Future of Unconventional Warfare* (Annapolis: Naval Institute Press, 2006), 176.

57. "A Comprehensive Strategy to Fight Al-Qaeda?" National Security Archive. http://www.gwu.edu/~nsarchiv/NSAEBB/NSAEBB147/index.htm.

58. From [Excised] to DIA Washington, D.C. [Excised], Cable, "[Excised]/Pakistan Interservice Intelligence/Pakistan (PK) Directorate Supplying the Taliban Forces," October 22, 1996, Secret, p. 1 [Excised]. National Security Archive. http://www.gwu.edu/~nsarchiv/NSAEBB/NSAEBB227/index.htm#15.

59. Pervez Musharraf, *In the Line of Fire: A Memoir* (New York: Free Press, 2006), 201.

60. Document 29, Defense Intelligence Agency, Cable, "IIR [Excised]/Veteran Afghanistan Traveler's Analysis of Al Qaeda and Taliban Military, Political and Cultural Landscape and its Weaknesses," October 2, 2001, Secret, pp. 4–6. http://www.gwu.edu/~nsarchiv/NSAEBB/NSAEBB97/index.htm#doc5.

61. Romesh Rattnesar, "Into the Fray," *Time*, October 29, 2001.

62. Brian Glyn Williams, *The Last Warlord: The Life and Legend of Dostum, the Afghan Warrior Who Led U.S. Forces to Topple the Taliban Regime* (Chicago: Chicago Review Press, 2013).

63. Ibid.

64. Ibid.

65. Ibid.

66. For a history of this remarkable campaign, see ibid.

67. Ibid.

68. Ibid.

69. Dalton Fury, *Kill bin Laden* (New York: St. Martin's, 2008), 233.

70. Michael Moran, "The Airlift of Evil," MSNBC.com, November 29, 2001.

71. Williams, *Last Warlord*.

72. "Secretary Rumsfeld Interview with CNN Live Today," March 8, 2002. http://www.defense.gov/transcripts/transcript.aspx?transcriptid=3071.

73. "Taleban Leader Warns of Long Guerilla War," *Gulf News,* October 21, 2001.

74. "A Surge of Special Forces for Afghanistan Likely," *Christian Science Monitor,* December 23, 2008. See graphic for troop numbers in Afghanistan from 2002 to 2008.

75. "Senator Bob Graham Remarks to Council of Foreign Relations," *Council of Foreign Relations,* March 26, 2004.

76. "U.S. Shifts Spy Planes to Afghan War," *USA Today,* August 23, 2009.

77. "An Axis of Evil," PBS.org, Frontline, http://www.pbs.org/wgbh/pages/frontline/shows/tehran/etc/evil.html

78. "Bush Holds Press Conference," http://georgewbush-whitehouse.archives.gov/news/releases/2002/03/20020313-8.html.

79. Bergen, *Osama bin Laden I Know,* 179.

Chapter 3. Hype

Epigraphs: Cheney quoted in George Tenet, *At the Center of the Storm: My Years at the CIA* (New York: Harper Collins, 2007), 315; Hussein quoted in James Gordon Meek, "Former Iraqi Leader Saddam Hussein Bluffed About WMDs Fearing Iranian Arsenal, Secret FBI Files Show," *Daily News,* June 24, 2009.

1. Marc Sageman, *Understanding Terror Networks* (Philadelphia: University of Pennsylvania Press, 2004), and *Leaderless Jihad* (Philadelphia: University of Pennsylvania Press, 2008).

2. For more on El Kaida Turka, see Brian Glyn Williams, "El Kaida Turka: Tracing an Al Qaeda Splinter Cell," *Terrorism Monitor* 2, no. 22 (November 18, 2004).

3. Craig Whitlock, "Europeans Probe Secret CIA Flights," *Washington Post,* November 17, 2005.

4. Michael Morell, *The Great War of Our Times: The CIA's Fight Against Terrorism—from Al Qa'ida to ISIS* (New York: Twelve, 2015), 94–95.

5. Ibid., 87.

6. Seymour Hersh, "The Stovepipe," *New Yorker,* October 27, 2003, 2.

7. Ibid.

8. Michael Gordon and General Bernard Trainor, *Cobra II: The Inside Story of the Invasion and Occupation of Iraq* (New York: Random House, 2006), 121.

9. "Lie by Lie: A Timeline of How We Got into Iraq," *Mother Jones,* October 2006.

10. "In Their Own Words, Who Said What When," PBS. http://www.pbs.org/wgbh/pages/frontline/shows/truth/why/said.html.

11. Morell, *Great War of Our Times,* 98.

12. James Bamford, *A Pretext for War: 9/11, Iraq and the Abuse of America's Intelligence Communities* (New York: Doubleday, 2004), 262.

13. Ibid.

14. "A Clean Break: A New Strategy for Securing the Realm." This remarkable document can be found at http://www.israeleconomy.org/strat1.htm.

15. Brian Whitaker, "Playing Skittles with Saddam," *Guardian,* September 3, 2002.

16. Patrick Buchanan, "Whose War?" *American Conservative,* March 24, 2003.

17. Patrick Buchanan, *Where the Right Went Wrong: How the Neoconservatives Subverted the Reagan Revolution and Hijacked the Bush Presidency* (New York: St. Martin's 2006), 48.

18. Bamford, *Pretext for War,* 266–67.

19. Ron Suskind, *The Price of Loyalty: The George W. Bush White House and the Education of Paul O'Neill* (New York: Simon and Schuster, 2004), 74.

20. Ibid., 73.

21. Bamford, *Pretext for War,* 289.

22. "PR Push for Iraq War Preceded Intelligence Findings, 'White Paper' Drafted Before NIE Even Requested," National Security Archive Electronic Briefing Book No. 254. Posted August 22, 2008. http://nsarchive.gwu.edu/NSAEBB/NSAEBB254/index.htm#8.

23. Bamford, *Pretext for War*, 290.

24. Ibid., 298.

25. "Revealed: The Secrete Cabal with Spun for Blair," *Sunday Herald*,(Scotland) June 8, 2003.

26. "The "Downing Street Memos," July 23, 2002, meeting of Tony Blair and his senior staff. http://downingstreetmemo.com/memos.html.

27. Robert Dreyfuss and Jason Vest, "The Lie Factory," *Mother Jones*, January–February 2004.

28. Thomas Ricks, *Fiasco: The American Military Adventure in Iraq* (New York: Penguin, 2006), 55.

29. Gordon and Trainor, *Cobra II*, 146.

30. Bamford, *Pretext for War*, 298–304.

31. Michael Isikoff and David Corn, *Hubris: The Inside Story of Spin, Scandal, and the Selling of the Iraq War* (New York: Three Rivers, 2007), 98.

32. David Ensor, "Fake Iraq Documents 'Embarrassing' for U.S.," CNN, March 14, 2003.

33. James Risen, "The Reach of the War: Senate Report; How Niger Uranium Story Defied Wide Skepticism," *New York Times*, July 14, 2004.

34. Peter Eisner, "How Bogus Letter Became a Case for War: Intelligence Failures Surrounded Inquiry on Iraq-Niger Uranium Claim," *Washington Post*, April 3, 2007.

35. National Security Archive. http://www.gwu.edu/~nsarchiv/NSAEBB/NSAEBB129/part2-niger.pdf.

36. Isikoff and Corn, *Hubris*, 86.

37. Senate Intelligence Committee, "Report on the US Intelligence Community's Prewar Intelligence Assessments on Iraq," July 7, 2004. http://nsarchive.gwu.edu/NSAEBB/NSAEBB254/doc12.pdf.

38. Ibid., 91.

39. Ibid., 95.

40. National Security Archive. http://www.gwu.edu/~nsarchiv/NSAEBB/NSAEBB129/part2-niger.pdf.

41. Ibid.

42. Isikoff and Corn, *Hubris*, 91.

43. National Security Archive. http://www.gwu.edu/~nsarchiv/NSAEBB/NSAEBB129/part2-niger.pdf.

44. Hans Blix, *Disarming Iraq* (New York: Pantheon Books, 2004), 234.

45. Hersh, "The Stovepipe," 2.

46. Isikoff and Corn, *Hubris*, 99.

47. Ibid., 307.

48. Eisner, "How Bogus Letter Became a Case for War."

49. "Tenet Admits Error in Approving Bush Speech," CNN, December 25, 2003.

50. "Top Bush Officials Push Case Against Saddam," CNN, September 8, 2002.

51. Ibid.

52. "Transcript: Colin Powell on Fox News Sunday," Fox News, September 8, 2002.

53. "Statements by President Bush: United Nations General Assembly, UN Headquarters, New York, 12 September 2002." http://www.un.org/webcast/ga/57/statements/020912usaE.htm.

54. "President Bush Outlines Iraqi Threat," October 7, 2002. http://georgewbush-whitehouse.archives.gov/news/releases/2002/10/20021007-8.html.

55. "The Lies That Led to the Iraq War and the Myth of 'Intelligence Failure,'" *Foreign Policy Journal*, September 8, 2012.

56. National Security Archive. http://www.gwu.edu/~nsarchiv/NSAEBB/NSAEBB129/part3-icnuclear.pdf.

57. Michael Gordon, "Agency Challenges Evidence Against Iraq Cited by Bush," *New York Times*, January 10, 2003.

58. Marge Michaels, "Q and A with the Top Sleuth," *Time*, January 12, 2003.

59. Jeremy Hammond, "The Lies That Led to the Iraq War and the Continuing Myth of 'Intelligence Failure,'" *Foreign Policy Journal*, September 8, 2012.

60. October 2002 NIE: Key Judgments; Iraq's Continuing Program for Weapons of Mass Destruction. http://www.fas.org/irp/cia/product/iraq-wmd.html.

61. Ricks, *Fiasco*, 53.

62. "CIA Whites Out Controversial Estimate on Iraq Weapons," National Security Archive. http://www.gwu.edu/~nsarchiv/NSAEBB/NSAEBB129/.

63. Ricks, *Fiasco*, 53.

64. Hammond, "Lies that Led to the Iraq War," 4.

65. David Kohn, "Selling the Iraq War to the U.S.," CBS News, February 11, 2009.

66. James Moore, *Bush's War for Reelection* (Hoboken, N.J.: Wiley, 2004), 32.

67. James Pfiffner and Mark Phythian, *Intelligence and National Security Policymaking on Iraq: British and American Perspectives* (Manchester: Manchester University Press, 2008), 220.

68. Hammond, "Lies that Led to the Iraq War," 4.

69. Isikoff and Corn, *Hubris*, 307.

70. Hammond, "Lies that Led to the Iraq War," 4.

71. Isikoff and Corn, *Hubris*, 307.

72. "Judging Intelligence: The Senators' Views and Excerpts from the Report on Iraq's Assessment," *New York Times*, July 10, 2004.

73. "Senate Intelligence Committee Report on War and Peace." http://www.ontheissues.org/Archive/Senate_Intel_War_+_Peace.htm.

74. CIA Report, *Iraq WMDs 2004: Nuclear*, CIA website. https://www.cia.gov/library/reports/general-reports-1/iraq_wmd_2004/chap4.html.

75. "Iraqi Drones May Target US Cities," Fox News, February 24, 2003.

76. Terry Anderson, *Bush's Wars* (Oxford: Oxford University Press, 2012), 123.

77. Ibid.

78. Report of the Select Committee on Intelligence on the Intelligence Community's Prewar Intelligence Assessments on Iraq, July 9, 2004, 225. https://fas.org/irp/congress/2004_rpt/ssci_iraq.pdf.

79. "Iraqi Drone Looks More Like Model Plane," Associated Press, March 12, 2003.

80. "Iraqi Drones Not for WMD," CBS News, February 11, 2009.

81. Ibid.

82. Colum Lynch, "U.N.: Iraqi Drones Were No Threat; Aircraft Could Not Deliver Weapons," *Washington Post*, September 5, 2004.

83. Connor Friederdorf, "The Bizarre Story of How Drones Helped Us Get into the Iraq War," *Atlantic*, October 16, 2012.

84. "Text of Bush's 2003 State of the Union Address," *Washington Post*, January 28, 2003.

85. "Intervention in Iraq?" PBS.org, February 6, 2003.

86. "Full Text of Colin Powell's Speech," *Guardian*, February 5, 2003.

87. Bob Drogin and John Goetz, "How U.S. Fell Under the Spell of 'Curveball,'" *Los Angeles Times*, November 20, 2005.

88. Isikoff and Corn, *Hubris,* 182.

89. Drogin and Goetz, "How U.S. Fell Under the Spell of 'Curveball.'"

90. Ibid.

91. Isikoff and Corn, *Hubris*, 129.

92. Joby Warrick, "Lacking Biolabs, Trailers Carried Case for War," *Washington Post*, April 12, 2006.

93. Joby Warrick, "Warnings on WMD Fabricator Were Ignored, Ex-CIA Aide Says," *Washington Post*, June 25, 2006.

94. Isikoff and Corn, *Hubris*, 189.

95. George Packer, *The Assassins' Gate: America in Iraq* (New York: Farrar, Straus and Giroux, 2005). 117.

96. Dilip Hiro, *Secrets and Lies: Operation Iraqi Freedom and After* (New York: Nation Books, 2004), 134.

97. Drogin and Goetz, "How U.S. Fell Under the Spell of 'Curveball.'"

98. "I was Shocked by Poor Weapons Intelligence—Blix," *Guardian*, June 6, 2003.

99. Hiro, *Secrets and Lies*, 112.

100. Ibid.

101. "Interview of the President by TVP, Poland," White House Archives. http://georgewbush-whitehouse.archives.gov/g8/interview5.html.

102. *Capital Report*, CNBC, June 3, 2003.

103. Hiro, *Secrets and Lies*, 127.

104. "Iraqi Mobile Labs Have Nothing to Do with Germ Warfare, Report Finds," *Observer*, June 14, 2003.

105. Drogin and Goetz, "How U.S. Fell Under the Spell of 'Curveball.'"

106. Ibid.

107. Carolyn Lochhead, "Ex-Inspector: Intelligence to Blame for Claim on Iraq / Kay Says Bush Team Didn't Push Analysts," *San Francisco Chronicle*, January 29, 2004.

108. Warrick, "Lacking Biolabs, Trailers Carried Case for War."

109. Ibid.

110. Drogin and Goetz, "How U.S. Fell Under the Spell of 'Curveball.'"

111. "Man Whose WMD Lies Led to 100,000 Deaths Confesses All," *Independent* (UK), April 1, 2012.

112. "Defector Admits to WMD Lies That Triggered the War," *Guardian*, February 15, 2011.

113. Drogin and Goetz, "How U.S. Fell Under the Spell of 'Curveball.'"

114. Warrick, "Warnings on WMD 'Fabricator' Were Ignored."

115. "Powell Says Bad Data Misled Him on Iraq," *San Francisco Chronicle*, April 3, 2004.

116. "Colin Powell on Iraq, Race, and Hurricane Relief," ABC, September 8, 2005.

117. "Powell Rips CIA over Sham WMD Source," *Newsmax*, February 16, 2011.

118. Morell, *Great War of Our Times*, 98.

119. "Unclassified Version of the Commission on Intelligence Capabilities of the United States Regarding Weapons of Mass Destruction." http://www.gpo.gov/fdsys/pkg/GPO-WMD/content-detail.html.

120. Hiro, *Secrets and Lies*, 80.

121. "A Policy of Evasion and Deception," *Washington Post*, February 5, 2003.

122. Anderson, *Bush's Wars*, 109–10.

123. "State of the Union: Collecting Proof; Bush's Speech Puts New Focus on State of Intelligence Data," *New York Times*, January 29, 2003.

124. "Powell, Saddam Speak. CBS News. February 4, 2003. http://www.cbsnews.com/news/powell-saddam-speak-on-i60ii-i/

125. Hiro, *Secrets and Lies*, 75.

126. "Transcript: David Kay at Senate Hearing," CNN, January 28, 2004.

127. David Kay, "Weapons That Never Were, a War That Never Was," NPR, May 29, 2011.

128. Carol Brightman, *Total Insecurity* (London: Verso, 2004), 201.

129. Christopher Sullivan, *Colin Powell: A Political Biography* (Lanham: Rowman and Littlefield, 2009), 188.

130. "Yes, Iraq Definitely Had WMD, Vast Majority of Polled Republicans Insist," *Huffington Post*, January 21, 2012.

131. "George Bush Had a Sickening Feeling over the WMD Lack," BBC, November 2, 2010.

132. "Bush Admits Intelligence Was Wrong," *Guardian*, December 14, 2005.

133. "Bush 'Not Insulted' by Thrown Shoes," ABC, December 14, 2008.

134. "Bush Takes Heat for WMD Jokes," CNN, May 3, 2004.

135. "President Bush Holds a News Conference," *Washington Post*, August 21, 2006.

136. Ewan MacAskill, "Donald Rumsfeld Book Admits 'Misstatements' over WMD Sites," *Guardian*, February 7, 2011.

137. "The Intelligence Business," *New York Times*, May 7, 2006.

138. "Rumsfeld Questions Saddam–bin Laden Link," BBC, October 5, 2004.

139. Adam Blenford, "Rice Admits Doubts on WMD," *Guardian*, January 30, 2004.

140. "Iraq's Chemical Warfare Program," CIA. https://www.cia.gov/library/reports/general-reports-1/iraq_wmd_2004/chap5.html.

141. "Detailed Preliminary Assessment of Chemical Weapons Findings https://www.cia.gov/library/reports/general-reports-1/iraq_wmd_2004/chap5_annxF.html.

142. Katherine Shrader, "New Intel Report Reignites Iraq Arms Fight," *Washington Post*, June 22, 2006.

143. Ibid.

144. Donald Rumsfeld, *Known and Unknown* (New York: Sentinel, 2011), 712.

145. Shrader, "New Intel Report Reignites Iraq Arms Fight."

146. Ibid.

147. "Thousands of Iraq Chemical Weapons Destroyed in Open Air, Watchdog Says," *New York Times*, November 23, 2014.

148. Walter Pincus, "Munitions Found in Desert Renew Debate," *Washington Post*, July 1, 2006; "A Policy of Evasion and Deception," *Washington Post*, February 5, 2003.

149. "Expert: Iraq WMD Find Did Not Point to Ongoing Program," NPR, June 22, 2006.

150. Douglas Jehl, "Report Further Erodes Case on Iraqi Weapons," *New York Times*, October 7, 2004.

151. "Notes from Saddam in Custody," *Time*, December 14, 2003.

152. Meek, "Former Iraqi Leader Saddam Hussein Bluffed About WMDs."

153. Nicholas Kristof, "Missing in Action, Truth," *New York Times*, May 6, 2003.

154. "Comprehensive Report of the Special Advisor to the DCI on Iraq's WMD, with Addendums (Duelfer Report)." https://www.cia.gov/library/reports/general-reports-1/iraq_wmd_2004.

155. "New Information on Iraq's Possession of Weapons of Mass Destruction," *Congressional Record*, January 28, 2004 (Senate), S311–S312. http://www.fas.org/irp/congress/2004_cr/s012804b.html.

156. "Final Report: Iraq Had No WMDs," *USA Today*, October 6, 2004.

157. "White House Daily Briefing, July 14, 2003." http://www.fas.org/irp/news/2003/07/wh071403b.html.

158. Paul Lashmar and Raymond Whitaker, "Ordinary Americans Think bin Laden and Saddam Are the Same Man, *Independent*, February 2, 2003.

159. Brian Whitmore, "A 9/11 Legacy: Confusion over a Name; Czechs Find Error in Tracking Atta," *Boston Globe*, September 19, 2004.

160. Ibid.

161. "Iraq Link to Sept. 11 Attack and Anthrax Is Ruled Out," *Telegraph* (UK), December 18, 2001.

162. James Risen, "Threats and Responses: The View from Prague; Prague Discounts an Iraqi Meeting," *New York Times*, October 21, 2002.

163. Ibid.

164. Ron Suskind, *The One Percent Solution* (New York: Simon and Schuster, 2006), 23.

165. Morell, *Great War of Our Times*, 81.

166. "No Link Between Hijacker, Iraq Found, US Says," *Washington Post*, May 1, 2002.

167. Michael Isikoff, "The Phantom Link to Iraq," *Newsweek*, April 28, 2002.

168. "Bush's War," *Frontline*, PBS, March 24, 2008. http://www.pbs.org/wgbh/pages/frontline/bushswar/etc/script.html.

169. Isikoff and Corn, *Hubris*, 103.

170. Dana Milbank and Claudia Deane, "Hussein Link to 9/11 Lingers in Many Minds," *Washington Post*, September 6, 2003.

171. "Vice President Dick Cheney Discusses the War on Terrorism, the Violence in the Middle East and the Economy," *Meet the Press*, December 9, 2001. http://www.nbcnews.com/id/3080244/ns/meet_the_press/t/transcript-sept/.

172. Richard Perle, "The U.S. Must Strike at Saddam Hussein," *New York Times*, December 28, 2001.

173. "Interview on CNN's Late Edition, Secretary Colin L. Powell, Washington, DC, December 2, 2001," *Department of State*. http://2001-2009.state.gov/secretary/former/powell/remarks/2001/dec/6613.htm

174. Frank Rich, *The Greatest Story Ever Sold: The Decline and Fall of the Truth in Bush's America* (New York: Penguin, 2006), 244.

175. Isikoff and Corn, *Hubris*, 105.

176. Morell, *Great War of Our Times*, 81.

177. *9/11 Commission Report*, chapter 7, "The Attack Looms."

178. "Report of the Select Committee on Intelligence on Postwar Findings About Iraq's WMD Programs and Links to Terrorism and How they Compare with Prewar Assessments," September 8, 2006, 110–11. http://www.intelligence.senate.gov/pub109thcongress.html.

179. Peter S. Canellos and Bryan Bender, "Questions Grow over Iraq Links to Qaeda," *Boston Globe*, August 3, 2003.

180. "A Policy of Evasion and Deception," *Washington Post*, February 5, 2003.

181. "President Bush Outlines Iraqi Threat." http://georgewbush-whitehouse.archives.gov/news/releases/2002/10/20021007-8.html.

182. Peter Bergen, *The Longest War* (New York: Simon and Schuster, 2011), 144.

183. Loretta Napoleoni, *Insurgent Iraq: Al Zarqawi and the New Generation* (New York: Seven Stories, 2005), 98.

184. Ibid., 95.

185. Mary Ann Weaver, "The Short Violent Life of Abu Musab Zarqawi," *Atlantic Monthly*, July/August 2006, 3.

186. Michael Isikoff, "Distorted Intelligence?" *Newsweek*, June 25, 2003.

187. "Saudi Al-Qaeda Terrorists Recount Their Experiences in Afghanistan on Saudi TV and Arab Channels," *MEMRI*, December 7, 2005, dispatch no. 1042.

188. Weaver, "Short Violent Life of Abu Musab Zarqawi," 4.

189. Lashmar and Whitaker, "Ordinary Americans Think bin Laden and Saddam Are the Same Man."

190. Napoleoni, *Insurgent Iraq*, 96.

191. "Report of the Select Committee on Intelligence on Postwar Findings About Iraq's WMD Programs," September 8, 2006, 109. https://www.congress.gov/congressional-report/109th-congress/senate-report/331/1.

192. Warren P. Strobel, Jonathan S. Landay, and John Walcott, "Fresh CIA Analysis: No Evidence Saddam Colluded with Al-Qaida," *Knight Ridder Newspapers*, October 5, 2004.

193. Ibid.; and Jean-Charles Brisard, *Zarqawi: The New Face of Al Qaeda* (New York: Other Press, 2006), 119.

194. Peter Bergen, *The Longest War: The Enduring Conflict Between America and Al Qaeda* (New York: Free Press, 2011), 144.

195. Douglas Jehl, "Report Warned Bush Team About Intelligence Suspicions," *New York Times*, November 6, 2005.

196. *Ibid.*

197. "White House 'Exaggerating Iraqi Threat,'" *Guardian*, October 8, 2002.

198. "Interview Steve Coll." Frontline. http://www.pbs.org/wgbh/pages/frontline/darkside/interviews/coll.html.

199. Canellos and Bender, "Questions Grow over Iraq Links to Qaeda."

200. Anderson, *Bush's Wars*, 124.

201. Tenet, *At the Center of the Storm*, 307.

202. Loretta Napoleoni, *Insurgent Iraq*, 118.

203. Schroen quoted in "Bush's War."

204. Gene Healy, "Why Hussein Will Not Give Weapons of Mass Destruction to Al Qaeda," CATO Institute, March 5, 2003.

205. Hiro, *Secrets and Lies*, 76.

206. Ibid., 60.

207. "Cheney Blasts Media on Al Qaeda–Iraq Link," CNN, June 18, 2004.

208. Lashmar and Whitaker, "Ordinary Americans Think bin Laden and Saddam Are the Same Man."

209. R. Jeffrey Smith, "Hussein's Prewar Ties to Al-Qaeda Discounted," *Washington Post*, April 6, 2007.

210. Canellos and Bender, "Questions Grow over Iraq Links to Qaeda."

211. "US Leaders' Statements on Iraq, Al Qaeda, Associated Press, June 17, 2003.

212. Ibid.

213. "Threats and Responses in Bush and Cheney's Words," *New York Times*, February 8, 2003.

214. "Bush Administration on Iraq 9/11 Link," BBC, September 18, 2003.

215. David Sanger, "Bush Declares One Victory in the War on Terror," *New York Times*, May 2, 2003.

216. Canellos and Bender, "Questions Grow over Iraq Links to Qaeda."

217. "Transcript for September 14, 2003, Guest: Dick Cheney, Vice President; Tim Russert, Moderator," *Meet the Press*, September 14, 2003. msnbc.msn.com/id/3080244/default.htm#.UNHsfrbuZ5s.

218. "Cheney Blasts Media on Al Qaeda–Iraq Link."

219. Hiro, *Secrets and Lies*, 139.

220. "In Their Own Words, Who Said What When."

221. Rich, *Greatest Story Ever Sold*, 266.

222. Anderson, *Bush's Wars*, 100.

223. Ibid., 255.

224. Scott Shepard, "Bush: No Iraq Link to 9/11 Found," Seattlepi.com, September 17, 2003.

225. "Text of President Bush's 2003 State of the Union Address," *Washington Post*, January 28, 2003.

226. "Bush's Top Ten Flip Flops," CBS News, February 11, 2009.

227. Meek, "Former Iraqi Leader Saddam Hussein Bluffed About WMDs."

228. "Bush's Toxic Legacy in Iraq," *CNN,* June 16, 2014.

229. Smith, "Hussein's Prewar Ties to Al-Qaeda Discounted."

230. A copy of the report can be found at http://www.ontheissues.org/Archive/Senate_Intel_War_+_Peace.htm.

231. "Report of the Select Committee on Intelligence on Postwar Findings About Iraq's WMD Programs." 72.

232. Ibid., 71.

233. Ibid., 75.

234. Ibid., 76.

235. Ibid., 80.

236. "2004 Senate Report of Pre-War Intelligence on Iraq." National Security Archive, pp 8–9. http://nsarchive.gwu.edu/NSAEBB/NSAEBB456/docs/specialPlans_45a.pdf.

237. Ibid., 346.

238. Ibid.

239. Ibid.

240. *9/11 Commission Report*; also in Walter Pincus, "Al Qaeda–Hussein Link Is Dismissed," *Washington Post*, June 17, 2004.

241. Pincus, "Al Qaeda–Hussein Link Is Dismissed."

242. Bamford, *Pretext for War*, 377.

243. "Poll: 70% Believe Saddam, 9-11 Link," Associated Press, September 6, 2003.

244. Ibid.

245. Ibid.

246. Rich, *Greatest Story Ever Sold*, 240.

247. Milbank and Deane, "Hussein Link to 9/11 Lingers in Many Minds."

248. John Zogby, "On a New Poll of U.S. Soldiers During Their Service in Iraq," *Mother Jones*, February 28, 2006.

249. Ellen Knickmeyer, "In Haditha, Memories of a Massacre," *Washington Post*, May 27, 2006.

250. "Transcript for September 14, 2003, Guest: Dick Cheney," *Meet the Press*, September 14, 2003.

251. Anderson, *Bush's Wars*, 182.

252. Warren Strobel, "Exhaustive Review Finds No Link Between Saddam and Al Qaida," Mc-Clatchy News Service, March 10, 2008.

253. Kristof, "Missing in Action."

254. Charles J. Hanley, "Piecing Together the Story of the Weapons That Weren't," Associated Press, September 2, 2005.

255. "Megyn Kelly vs. Dick Cheney: An Accountability Moment for the Ex-Veep," Fox News, June 20, 2014. http://www.foxnews.com/politics/2014/06/20/megyn-kelly-vs-dick-cheney-accountability-moment-for-ex-veep/.

256. "Asked Again, Bush Says No on Invasion of Iraq," *New York Times*, May 15, 2015.

257. "I Think People Knew There Were No WMD in Iraq," *Breitbart*, February 14, 2016.

258. E. J. Dionne Jr., "Another Set of Scare Tactics," *Washington Post*, November 15, 2005.

259. "The War in Iraq Wrong for 55% of Americans." http://www.angus-reid.com/polls/3725/war_in_iraq_wrong_for_55_of_americans/.

260. *Time* poll. http://www.pollingreport.com/iraq2.htm.

261. Gallup Poll, http://www.gallup.com/poll/1633/iraq.aspx.

262. "Most Americans Say Iraq War Was Not Worth the Cost: Poll," CBSNews.com, June 23, 2014. http://www.cbsnews.com/news/most-americans-say-iraq-war-wasnt-worth-the-costs-poll/.

263. "Study: Bush Led US to War on 'False Pretenses,'" Associated Press, January 23, 2008.

264. Dan Froomkin, "The Propaganda Campaign Dissected," *Washington Post*, June 6, 2008.

265. "Casus Belli," *Countdown with Keith Olbermann*, MSNBC. http://www.msnbc.msn.com/id/3036677/vp/24994797#24994797.

266. Ibid.

267. "Final Report."

268. "Official Government Edition: The Commission on the Intelligence Capabilities of the United States Regarding Weapons of Mass Destruction; Report to the President of the United States March 31, 2005." http://www.gpo.gov/fdsys/pkg/GPO-WMD/pdf/GPO-WMD.pdf.

269. Glen Kessler and Walter Pincus, "Misfires of a 'Smoking Gun' in Iraq Debate," *Washington Post*, February 1, 2004.

270. "George H.W. Bush Slams 'Iron Ass' Cheney, 'Arrogant' Rumsfeld in New Biography," *Washington Post,* November 5, 2015.

271. Hanley, "Piecing Together the Story."

272. "Official Government Edition," 3.

273. Ibid., 45.

274. Ibid., 9.

275. Ibid., 10.

276. Ibid., 3.

277. "Senate Intelligence Committee Report on War and Peace."

278. "The Truth About the War," *New York Times*, June 6, 2008.

Chapter 4. The Invasion and Occupation of Iraq

Epigraphs: Cheney quoted in E. J. Dionne Jr., "Dick Cheney Reveals His Chutzpah in Op-Ed," *Washington Post*, June 18, 2014; insurgent quoted in Ahmed Hashim, *Insurgency and Counter Insurgency in Iraq* (Ithaca, N.Y.: Cornell University Press, 2006), 104.

1. "Operation Desert Fox: Effectiveness with Unintended Consequences," *Air and Space Power Journal*, July 13, 2005.

2. Ibid.

3. Michael Gordon and Bernard Trainor, *Cobra II: The Inside Story of the Invasion and Occupation of Iraq* (New York: Random House, 2006), 136.

4. Ibid.

5. "The Status of Nuclear Inspections in Iraq: An Update," IAEA.org. http://www.iaea.org/newscenter/statements/2003/ebsp2003n006.shtml.

6. "The Obama Doctrine," *Atlantic,* April 2016.

7. "Senator Robert Byrd, RIP," *Mother Jones,* January 28, 2010.

8. "Bush's War," PBS, *Frontline*, http://www.pbs.org/wgbh/pages/frontline/bushswar/etc/script.html.

9. Brian Whitaker, "Playing Skittles with Saddam," *Guardian*, September 3, 2002.

10. Michael Gordon, "Saudis Warn Against Attack on Iraq by the United States," *New York Times*, March 17, 2002.

11. Joe Klein, "Shadow Land: Who Is Winning the Fight for Iran's Future?" *New Yorker,* February 18, 2002.

12. Brent Scowcroft, "Don't Attack Saddam," *Wall Street Journal*, August 15, 2002.

13. Fred Kaplan, *The Insurgents: David Petraeus and the Plot to Change the American Way of War* (New York: Simon and Schuster, 2013), 56; Gordon and Trainor, *Cobra II*, 158.

14. "Interview: James Fallows," PBS, *Frontline,* http://www.pbs.org/wgbh/pages/frontline/shows/invasion/interviews/fallows.html.

15. Ibid.

16. Thomas Ricks, *Fiasco: The American Military Adventure in Iraq* (New York: Penguin, 2006), 121.

17. "Dick Cheney Reveals His Chutzpah in Iraq in Op-Ed," *Washington Post*, June 18, 2014.

18. Eric Schmitt, "Pentagon Contradicts General on Iraq Occupation Force's Size," *New York Times*, February 28, 2003.

19. Ricks, *Fiasco*, 68.

20. Todd Purdum, *A Time of Our Choosing: America's War in Iraq* (New York: Times Books, 2003), 97.

21. Jesse Singal, "Shock and Awe," *Time*, March 19, 2010.

22. Kaplan, *Insurgents*, 58–59.

23. "Bush a Convert to Nation Building," *Washington Times*, April 7, 2008.

24. "Presidential Debates," American Presidency Project. http://www.presidency.ucsb.edu/ws/?pid=29419.

25. Schmitt, "Pentagon Contradicts General on Iraq Occupation Force's Size."

26. "Uncovering Iraq's Horrors in Desert Graves," *New York Times*, June 5, 2006.

27. Thomas Ricks, "Abizaid Says Withdrawal Would Mean More Unrest," *Washington Post*, December 13, 2006.

28. "Bush's War."

29. Bob Woodward, *Plan of Attack* (New York: Simon Schuster, 2004), 150.

30. "President Says Saddam Hussein Must Leave Iraq Within 48 Hours," George W. Bush White House Archives. http://georgewbush-whitehouse.archives.gov/news/releases/2003/03/20030317-7.html.

31. Terry Anderson, *Bush's Wars* (Oxford: Oxford University Press, 2011), 135.

32. Gordon and Trainor, *Cobra II*, 444.

33. Anderson, *Bush's Wars*, 134.

34. "Secretary of Defense Interview with Bob Woodward—23 Oct, 2003," United States Department of Defense, news transcript. http://web.archive.org/web/20060730192251/http://www.defenselink.mil/transcripts/2004/tr20040419-secdef1362.html.

35. "Operation Iraqi Freedom." http://www.icasualties.org/Iraq/ByMonth.aspx.

36. Anderson, *Bush's Wars*, 134.

37. "Bush Makes Historic Speech Aboard Warship," *CNN*, May 1, 2003.

38. "Donald Rumsfeld, You're No Robert McNamara," *Guardian*, February 3, 2011.

39. Sean Loughlin, "Rumsfeld on Looting in Iraq: 'Stuff Happens': Administration Asking Countries for Help with Security," CNN, April 12, 2003.

40. "Interview with Todd Purdum." PBS, *Frontline*. http://www.pbs.org/wgbh/pages/frontline/shows/invasion/interviews/purdum.html.

41. Ricks, *Fiasco*, 146.

42. Ibid., 221.

43. Anderson, *Bush's Wars*, 141.

44. "Interview with General Jay Garner," conducted on Aug. 11, 2006, *Frontline*, "Lost Year in Iraq," http://www.pbs.org/wgbh/pages/frontline/yeariniraq/interviews/garner.html.

45. "Bush's War: Night Two," PBS, *Frontline*. http://www.pbs.org/wgbh/pages/frontline/bushswar/etc/script2.html.

46. Ricks, *Fiasco*, 159.

47. Ibid.

48. Zaid al Ali, *The Struggle for Iraq's Future* (New Haven, Conn.: Yale University Press, 2014), 68.

49. Ibid., 73.

50. Daniel Boulger, *Why We Lost* (New York: Houghton Mifflin, 2014), 161.

51. "An Iraq Reckoning," *Globe Magazine,* March 11, 2016.

52. Ibid.

53. "Bush's War."

54. Thomas Ricks, *The Gamble: General David Petraeus and the American Military Adventure in Iraq, 2006–2008* (New York: Penguin, 2009), 164.

55. Ibid., 163.

56. Anderson, *Bush's Wars*, 156.

57. Dexter Filkins, "Did George W. Bush Create ISIS?" *New Yorker*, May 15, 2015.

58. Ibid.

59. "The Terror Strategist," *Der Spiegel*, April 18, 2015.

60. Joel Rayburn, *Iraq After America: Strongmen, Sectarians, Resistance* (Washington, D.C.: Hoover Institution Press, 2014), 105.

61. Emma Sky, *The Unraveling: High Hopes and Missed Opportunities in Iraq* (New York: Public Affairs, 2015), 153.

62. Ibid., 164.

63. Ibid., 177.

64. Ali Allawi, *The Occupation of Iraq* (New Haven, Conn.: Yale University Press, 2007), 158.

65. Ibid., 240.

66. Hashim, *Insurgency and Counter Insurgency in Iraq*, 94.

67. "The Hidden Hand Behind the Islamic State Militants? Saddam Hussein," *Los Angeles Times*, April 4, 2015.

68. George Packer, *The Assassins' Gate: America in Iraq* (New York: Farrar, Straus and Giroux, 2005), 251.

69. Hashim, *Insurgency and Counter Insurgency in Iraq*, 119.

70. Packer, *Assassins' Gate*, 309.

71. Ben Hubbard, "Military Skill and Terrorist Technique Fuel Success of ISIS," *New York Times*, August 27, 2014.

72. "Rumsfeld Downplays Resistance in Iraq," Fox News, June 18, 2003.

73. Kaplan, *Insurgents*, 229.

74. "Bush's War."

75. Allawi, *Occupation of Iraq*, 176.

76. Ricks, *Fiasco*, 184.

77. Amy Waldman, "U.S. 'Still at War,' General Declares; G.I. Dies; 20 Hurt," *New York Times*, July 4, 2003.

78. "Dangerous Incompetence," *New York Times*, June 30, 2005.

79. Anderson, *Bush's Wars*, 161.

80. Ricks, *Fiasco*, 172.

81. Ibid., 290.

82. "Ladies and Gentlemen, We Got Him!" *Time*, December 14, 2003.

83. "Hussein Executed with Fear in His Face," CNN, December 30, 2006.

84. "Baathists: Grave Consequences If Saddam Is Hanged," CNN, December 26, 2006.

85. "Marines, Iraqis Join Forces to Shut Down Fallujah," CNN, April 6, 2004.

86. "Key General Criticizes April Attack in Fallujah, Abrupt Withdrawal Called Vacillation," *Washington Post*, September 13, 2004.

87. Michael Gordon and Bernard Trainor, *The Endgame: The Inside Story of the Struggle for Iraq, from George W. Bush to Barack Obama* (New York: Pantheon, 2012), 66.

88. Hashim, *Insurgency and Counter Insurgency in Iraq*, 115.

89. Anderson, *Bush's Wars*, 164.

90. Juan Cole, "The Fall of Mosul and the False Promises of Modern History," *Informed Comment*, June 11, 2014. http://www.juancole.com/2014/06/promises-modern-history.html.

91. Mark Mazzetti, *The Way of the Knife: The CIA, a Secret Army and a War at the Ends of the Earth* (New York: Penguin, 2013), 138.

92. Ibid., 174.

93. Gordon and Trainor, *Endgame*, 118.

94. Hashim, *Insurgency and Counter Insurgency in Iraq*, 101.

95. "Evidence Suggests Haditha Killings Deliberate: Pentagon Source," CBC News, August 2, 2006.

96. Joby Warrick, *Black Flags: The Rise of ISIS* (New York: Doubleday, 2015), 248.

97. Jesse Singal and Christine Lim, "Seven Years in Iraq: An Iraq War Timeline; Enter bin Laden," *Time*, March 19, 2010.

98. Michael Morell, *The Great War of Our Times: The CIA's Fight Against Terrorism—from Al Qa'ida to ISIS* (New York: Twelve, 2015), 109.

99. Ibid., 78.

100. "Osama Bin Laden Letters Warned Against Pillars of ISIS Strategy," *Newsweek,* March 2, 2016.

101. "Al Qaeda Tells Ally in Iraq to Strive for Global Goals," *New York Times*, October 7, 2005.

102. "Zarqawi Letter." *U.S. Department of State Archive.* http://2001-2009.state.gov/p/nea/rls/31694.htm.

103. William McCants, *The ISIS Apocalypse* (New York: St. Martin's), 16.

104. al Ali, *Struggle for Iraq's Future*, 105–6.

105. Ibid., 108.

106. Gordon and Trainor, *Endgame*, 220. See also Rayburn, *Iraq After America*, 89.

107. Kimberly Kagan, *The Surge: A Military History* (London: Encounter Books, 2009), 196. Peter Bergen, *The Longest War: The Enduring Conflict Between America and Al Qaeda* (New York: Free Press, 2011), 285.

108. Gordon and Trainor, *Endgame*, 228.

109. Daniel Bolger, *Why We Lost: A General's Inside Account of the Iraq and Afghanistan Wars* (New York: Houghton Mifflin, 2014), 229.

110. Ali, *Struggle for Iraq's Future*, 186.

111. Brian Glyn Williams, "We Had Sniper Chris Kyle: The Enemy Had Juba the Sniper of Baghdad," *History News Network,* March 27, 2015.

112. "President Says Saddam Hussein Must Leave Iraq Within 48 Hours."

113. Anderson, *Bush's Wars*, 164.

114. Ibid., 190.

115. Ibid., 191.

116. "The Road to the Surge," *Washington Post*, November 2, 2009. http://www.washingtonpost.com/wp-srv/nation/specials/war-within/surgechart.html.

117. "Spy Agencies say Iraq War Worsens Terrorism Threat," *New York Times,* September 24, 2006.

118. Packer, *Assassins' Gate*, 246.

119. Anderson, *Bush's Wars*, 169.

120. Gordon and Trainor, *Endgame*, 65.

121. Ricks, *Fiasco*, 17.

122. Pat Buchanan, *Where the Right Went Wrong: How the Neoconservatives Subverted the Reagan Revolution and Hijacked the Bush Presidency* (New York: St. Martin's, 2005), 37.

123. Ricks, *Fiasco*, 87.

124. Kaplan, *Insurgents*, 206.

125. "Revenge of the Battered Generals," *Times* (UK), April 18 2006.

126. Ricks, *Gamble*, 13.

127. Ibid., 116.

128. Anderson, *Bush's Wars*, 170.

129. Ibid., 191.

130. Ibid., 199.

131. "Polls Show Shift in Opinion on War Effort," *New York Times*, August 23, 2006.

132. Anderson, *Bush's Wars*, 190.

133. Ibid., 212.

134. "Donald Trump and the Iraq War." *Factcheck.org.* February 19, 2016.

135. Kagan, *Surge*, 28.

136. Kaplan, *Insurgents*, 72, 75.

137. "Bush's War."

138. Ricks, *Gamble*, 108.

139. Kaplan, *Insurgents*, 168.

140. Zaki Chehab, *Inside the Resistance: The Iraqi Insurgency and the Future of the Middle East* (New York: Avalon, 2005), 10.

141. Ibid., 229.

142. Ibid., 194.

143. Ricks, *Gamble*, 27.

144. Bergen, *Longest War*, 267.

145. Ricks, *Gamble*, 219.

146. Ibid., 163.

147. Ibid., 166.

148. Sky, *Unraveling*, 209.

149. Jake Tapper, "MoveOn.org Ad Takes Aim at Petraeus," ABC News.com, September 10, 2007.

150. "Clinton Spars with Petraeus on Credibility," *New York Sun,* September 12, 2007.

151. Ricks, *Gamble*, 296.

152. Ricks, *Fiasco*, 3.

153. "Who Is More Responsible for the Rise of ISIS? Bush or Obama?" *National Review*, September 17, 2014.

154. Thom Shanker, "Warning Against Wars Like Iraq and Afghanistan," *New York Times*, February 25, 2011.

155. "How Low Can He Go?" *Newsweek*, June 21, 2007.

156. "Transcript: Obama's Speech Against the Iraq War," NPR, January 20, 2009.

157. "CNN Poll: Americans Agree on Bringing Troops Home from Iraq," CNN, December 21, 2011.

158. "Pew Research Poll," March 9–12, 2009. http://www.pollingreport.com/iraq2.htm.

159. Sky, *Unraveling*, 273.

160. "Full Text: Obama Gives Speech About Iran Nuclear Deal," *Washington Post*, August 5, 2015.

161. "Iraq War: 190,000 Lives, $2.2 Trillion," Costs of War Project. http://news.brown.edu/pressreleases/2013/03/warcosts.

162. Boulger, *Why We Lost*, 161.

163. Rajiv Chandrasekaran, *Little America: The War Within the War for Afghanistan* (New York: Alfred Knopf, 2012), 10.

164. Ibid.

Chapter 5. Remembering the "Forgotten War" in Afghanistan

Epigraphs: Record quoted in Thomas Ricks, *Fiasco: The American Military Adventure in Iraq* (New York: Penguin, 2006), 309; Obama quoted in Carlotta Gall, "In Kabul, Obama Calls Afghan Front 'Central' to War on Terror," *New York Times*, July 20, 2008.

1. "In the Land of the Taliban," *New York Times*, October 22, 2006.

2. Brian Glyn Williams, "Mullah Omar's Missiles: A Field Report on Suicide Bombers in Afghanistan," *Middle East Policy*, 15, no. 4 (Winter 2008): also available at brianglynwilliams.com, under "publications."

3. "Scores Killed in Pakistan Attacks," BBC.co.uk, July 19, 2007.

4. "South Asia Daily Brief," Foreign Policy.com, February 20, 2015.

5. "Taliban Vow to Enforce Shariah Law Through All of Pak," *Indian Express*, April 20, 2009.

6. "Drone Wars Pakistan: Analysis," New America Foundation. http://securitydata.newamerica.net/drones/pakistan-analysis.html.

7. "Janet Napolitano Reviews Peter Bergen's 'United States of Jihad,'" *New York Times,* February 1, 2016.

8. "The Obama Doctrine: Examining the White House Foreign Policy," NPR, March 10, 2016.

9. Brian Glyn Williams, "The CIA's Covert Drone War in Pakistan 2004–2010: The History of an Assassination Campaign," *Studies in Terrorism and Conflict,* 33 (2010); also available at brianglyn williams.com.

10. Brian Glyn Williams, *Predators: The CIA's Drone War on Al Qaeda* (Washington, D.C.: Potomac, 2013).

11. *Long War Journal.* http://www.longwarjournal.org/pakistan-strikes.php.

12. "To Keep America Safe, Embrace Drone Warfare," *New York Times,* February 19, 2016.

13. "The Drone Campaign Against Al Qaeda and ISIS, Interview with Lt. General David Deptula (Ret.)," *Perspectives on Terrorism* 9, no. 3 (2015).

14. Brian Glyn Williams, *Afghanistan Declassified: A Guide to America's Longest War* (Philadelphia: University of Pennsylvania Press, 2011), 220.

15. For a history of the CIA drone war, see Williams, *Predators.*

16. Williams, *Predators,* 169.

17. "Mission Unstoppable," *Foreign Policy,* May 18, 2015.

18. Robert Gates, *Duty* (New York: Alfred A. Knopf, 2014), 198.

19. Terry Anderson, *Bush's Wars* (Oxford: Oxford University Press, 2011), 212.

20. Ibid., 361.

21. "Obama Administration to Ratchet up Hunt for Bin Laden," CNN, November 12, 2008.

22. It's Time to Use the $10 Billion a Month Spent in Afghanistan to Rebuild America," *Business Insider,* June 11, 2012.

23. *Gates, Duty,* 203; "Obama Shifts the Foreign Policy Debate," *Washington Post,* July 23, 2008.

24. Rajiv Chandrasekaran, *Little America: The War Within the War for Afghanistan* (New York: Alfred A. Knopf, 2012), 76.

25. "In 2008 Obama Vowed to Kill Osama bin Laden," *St. Petersburg Times,* May 1, 2011.

26. Chandrasekaran, *Little America,* 140.

27. "Obama: Bin Laden Raid was 55/45 Situation," CNN, May 9, 2011.

28. "At Least Twenty Killed in American Attack in Pakistan," *Boston Globe,* September 4, 2008.

29. "Pakistani Intelligence Chief Warns U.S. to Keep Troops Out," *Reuters,* September 10, 2008.

30. "CIA Director Panetta Feared Pakistan Would Jeopardize Mission to Kill Bin Laden," *Weekly Standard,* May 3, 2011.

31. "Osama Bin Laden Dead," Whitehouse.gov, May 2, 2011. https://www.whitehouse.gov/blog/2011/05/02/osama-bin-laden-dead.

32. "CNN Poll: Killing of Bin Laden Gives Obama a Boost on Terrorism and Afghanistan," CNN, May 3, 2011.

33. Ibid.

34. "The Mysteries of Abbottabad," *New York Times Magazine,* October 18, 2015, 56.

35. "Osama Bin Laden Mission Agreed in Secret 10 Years Ago by US and Pakistan," *Guardian,* May 9, 2011.

36. "After Bin Laden, US Assesses Afghan Strategy," *New York Times,* May 10, 2011.

37. Williams, *Afghanistan Declassified,* 233.

38. "In a Shift, Obama Extends U.S. Role in Afghan Combat," *New York Times,* December 21, 2014.

39. "U.S. Campaign in Afghanistan Surpasses Vow," *New York Times,* April 30, 2015.

40. "Civilian Deaths in Afghanistan Reach New High in 2014," Reuters, December 19, 2014.

41. "Afghan Taliban's Reach Is Widest Since 2001, UN Report," *New York Times,* October 11, 2015.

42. "In Reversal, Obama Says US Troops Will Be Staying in Afghanistan to 2017," *New York Times*, October 16, 2015.

43. "Statement by the White House on Afghanistan." https://www.whitehouse.gov/the-press-office/2015/10/15/statement-president-afghanistan.

44. "Obama's Afghan Pivot Tied to Iraq Meltdown," *New York Times*, October 16, 2015.

45. Statement by the White House on Afghanistan." https://www.whitehouse.gov/the-press-office/2015/10/15/statement-president-afghanistan.

46. "Transition Ceremony Kicks off Resolute Support Mission," Nato.int, December 28, 2014, http://www.nato.int/cps/en/natohq/news_116351.htm.

47. "Statement by President on Afghanistan," Whitehouse.gov, May 27, 2014. https://www.whitehouse.gov/the-press-office/2014/05/27/statement-president-afghanistan

48. "The United States Has Outspent the Marshall Plan to Rebuild Afghanistan," *Foreign Policy*, July 30, 2014.

49. "Taliban Push into Afghan Districts That U.S. Had Secured," *New York Times,* December 22, 2014.

50. "CNN Poll: Americans Are Starting to Think the Terrorists Are Winning," CNN, December 28, 2015.

Chapter 6. The New War on ISIS

Epigraphs: "Biden: We Will Follow Them to the Gates of Hell," CNN, September 3, 2014. "ISIS Threatens to Behead Obama in the White House," *Daily Mail*, January 27, 2015.

1. "In U.S. Exit from Iraq Failed Efforts and Challenges," *New York Times*, September 22, 2012.

2. Ibid.

3. "Despite Difficult Talks, U.S. and Iraq Had Expected Some American Troops to Stay," *New York Times*, October 21, 2011.

4. "In U.S. Exit from Iraq Failed Efforts and Challenges."

5. Ibid.

6. "President Obama Has Ended the War in Iraq," October 21, 2011, https://www.whitehouse.gov/blog/2011/10/21/president-obama-has-ended-war-iraq.

7. "Arrest Warrant Issued for Iraqi Vice President," CNN, December 19, 2011.

8. Joel Rayburn, *Iraq After America* (Washington, D.C.: Hoover Institution Press, 2015), 222.

9. Robert Brigham, "The Lessons and Legacies of the War in Iraq," in *Understanding the U.S. Wars in Iraq and Afghanistan* (New York: New York University Press, 2015), 301.

10. "Arrest Order for Sunni Leader in Iraq Opens New Rift," *New York Times*, December 19, 2011.

11. Ibid.

12. "Iraq Vice President Denies Charges of Running Death Squads," Fox News, December 21, 2011.

13. Dexter Filkins, "What We Left Behind," *New Yorker*, April 28, 2014.

14. Rayburn, *Iraq After America*, 220.

15. Filkins, "What We Left Behind," *New Yorker*, April 28, 2014.

16. Michael Weiss and Hassan Hassan, *ISIS: Inside the Army of Terror* (New York: Reagan Arts, 2015), 89–90.

17. Emma Sky, *The Unraveling: High Hopes and Missed Opportunities in Iraq* (New York: Public Affairs, 2015), 185, 233, and 284.

18. Ibid., 95.

19. See the groundbreaking article by Filkins, "What We Left Behind."

20. "Arrest of Sunni Minister's Bodyguards Prompt Protests in Iraq," *New York Times*, December 21, 2012.

21. Ibid.

22. "Protest in Iraq Continue Amidst New Killing," Al Jazeera, December 28, 2012.

23. Filkins, "What We Left Behind."

24. Ibid.

25. Rayburn, *Iraq After America*, 241.

26. "Ramadi Protestors Reach Deal to End Standoff," Gulf News.com, December 30, 2013.

27. "How a Talented Football Player Became the World's Most Wanted Man," *Telegraph*, November 11, 2014.

28. Joby Warrick, *Black Flags: The Rise of ISIS* (New York: Doubleday, 2015), 253.

29. "Al Qaeda in Iraq Leaders Neutralized U.S. Says," *New York Times*, January 4, 2010.

30. "Al Qaida: We're Returning to Old Strongholds," Associated Press, July 22, 2012.

31. Jessica D. Lewis, "Al Qaeda Resurgent," Institute for War Reporting, 2013.

32. "Obama Sees Russia Failing in Syria Effort," *New York Times*, October 3, 2015.

33. Warrick, *Black Flags*, 293.

34. "Syria Exposes Split Between Obama and Clinton," *New York Times*, October 4, 2015.

35. Warrick, *Black Flags*, 278.

36. Ibid., 293.

37. "Al Qaeda Affiliate Playing Larger Role in Syrian Rebellion," *Washington Post*, November 30, 2012.

38. Warrick, *Black Flags*, 284.

39. "Qaeda Chief Annuls Syrian-Iraqi Merger," Al Jazeera, June 9, 2013.

40. "Al Qaeda Disavows Militants in Syria," BBC, February 3, 2014.

41. "Syria, ISIS Have Been Ignoring Each Other on the Battlefield Data Suggests," NBCnews.com, December 11, 2014.

42. "Al Qaeda Iraqi Chief Rejects Zawahiri's Orders," Al Jazeera, June 15, 2013.

43. "Zawahiri Bans Main Al Qaeda Faction in Syria," *Daily Star*, November 8, 2013.

44. "Al Qaeda Disavows Militants in Syria."

45. "Foreign Jihadists Flock to Iraq and Syria on Unprecedented Scale, UN," *Guardian*, October 30, 2014.

46. "Thousands Enter Syria to Assist Militants in ISIS," *New York Times*, September 27, 2015.

47. "Thousands of Fighters Join ISIS Despite Global Effort," *New York Times*, September 27, 2015.

48. "ISIS: Everything You Wanted to Know About the Rise of the Militant Group," CNN, September 25, 2014; "Thousands of Fighters Join ISIS Despite Global Efforts."

49. "Al Qaeda in Syria Denies Plans to Attack the West," CBS News, May 28, 2015.

50. Weiss and Hassan, *ISIS*, 150.

51. "Two Arab Countries Fall Apart," *Economist*, June 14, 2014.

52. "British Fighters Carries Out Deadly Suicide Attack," *Daily Mail*, October 19, 2015.

53. Jessica Stern and J. M. Berger, *ISIS: The State of Terror* (New York: HarperCollins, 2015), 96.

54. "ISIS Issues a Recording It Says Was Made by Its Leader," *New York Times*, May 15, 2015.

55. "Attacks on 3 Continents Expose Hurdles in Fight Against Terrorism," *New York Times*, June 27, 2015.

56. "Belgium Terror Cells Had Links to ISIS," CNN, January 17, 2015.

57. Robert Spencer, "Video of Paris Jihad Mastermind: 'It Is Nice to See the Blood of Infidels,'" JihadWatch.org, November 18, 2015.

58. "Brussels Attack: President Erdogan Says Bomber Was Caught in Turkey Last Year and Deported to the Netherlands," *Independent,* March 23, 2016.

59. "Brussels Attack: Police Hunt Bombing Suspect," *Guardian,* March 23, 2016.

60. "ISIS Claims Responsibility for Brussels Attack," *Independent,* March 23, 2016.

61. "Ted Cruz: Police Need to Patrol and Secure Muslim Neighborhoods," *CNN,* March 22, 2016.

62. "Inside the July 4th Terror Busts," *Daily Beast*, July 3, 2015.

63. Ibid.

64. "Thousands Enter Syria to Assist Militants in ISIS."

65. "Hacker's Kill List Shows ISIS 'Crowdsourcing Terrorism,'" NBCNews.com, October 16, 2015.

66. "California Attack Has U.S. Rethinking Strategy on Homegrown Terror," *New York Times*, December 5, 2015.

67. "Thousands Enter Syria to Assist Militants in ISIS."

68. "128 Jordanians Slain in Syria—Report," *Jordan Times*, November 30, 2013.

69. Brian Glyn Williams, *Inferno in Chechnya: The Russian Chechen Wars, the Al Qaeda Myth, and the Boston Marathon Bombing* (Lebanon, N.H.: University Press New England, 2015).

70. "Qaeda-Linked Militants in Iraq Claim Fallujah as Independent State," *New York Times*, January 3, 2014.

71. "ISIS Announces Conquest of Mosul," *MEMRI*, June 11, 2014; Warrick, *Black Flags*, 259.

72. "Qaeda Linked Militants Threaten Key Iraqi Cities," *New York Times*, January 2, 2014.

73. "Special Report: How Baghdad Fell—A General Disputes Baghdad's Claim," Reuters, October 14, 2014.

74. Ibid.

75. Ibid.

76. "How Can Militants Take Over Iraqi Cities?" BBC, June 11, 2014.

77. "Churchbells Fall Silent in Mosul," *Daily Beast*, June 29, 2014.

78. "Is This the End of Christianity in the Middle East?" *New York Times*, July 22, 2015.

79. "Only Days After Fall of Mosul, Iraqis Return to Find Lower Prices, Restored Services and More," Fox News, June 15, 2014.

80. "ISIS Seen as Liberators by Some Sunnis in Mosul," *Al Monitor*, June 10, 2014.

81. "Militants Seize Iraq's Second City of Mosul," BBC, June 10, 2014.

82. "UN Accuses Islamic State of Mass Killings," Reuters, August 25, 2014.

83. "Sharing a Border with ISIL, the World's Most Dangerous State," *Telegraph*, September 26, 2014.

84. "ISIS Leave Roads Lined with Decapitated Police and Soldiers," *Daily Mail*, June 12, 2015.

85. "In Iraq Residents of Amerli Celebrate End of Militant Siege," *Los Angeles Times*, September 3, 2014.

86. "Al Baghdadi Following in bin Laden's Footsteps," Al Akhbar.com, July 2, 2014.

87. "Islamic Leader Abu Bakr Al Baghdadi Addresses Muslims in Mosul," *Telegraph*, July 5, 2014.

88. "Differences Between Al Qaeda and ISIS," *Ibtimes*, December 8, 2014.

89. "AQIM Rejects Islamic State's Caliphate," *Long War Journal*, July 14, 2014.

90. "TTP Rejects 'Caliphate' of Islamic State, Abu Bakr al-Baghdadi as 'Caliph,'" SITE Intelligence Group, May 28, 2015.

91. "ISIS Threatens Al Qaeda as Flagship Movement of Extremists," *New York Times*, June 30, 2014.

92. "Coalition Debates Expanding ISIS Fight," *New York Times*, April 30, 2015.

93. "Islamic State Video Appears to Show Executions of Christians in Libya," *New York Times*, April 20, 2015.

94. "Coalition Debates Expanding ISIS Fight."

95. "After Sousse Tunisia Struggles to Contain Jihadists," CNN, July 6, 2015.

96. "Afghan Forces Defend Kunduz from Taliban," BBC, May 7, 2015.

97. "In Islamic State, Taliban Face Insurgent Threat of Their Own," *New York Times*, June 5, 2015.

98. "The Ankara Bomber Owned One of Turkey's Well Known ISIS Hang Outs," *Bloomberg*, October 15, 2015.

99. "Oil and Erbil," *New Yorker*, August 10, 2014.

100. "ISIS Beheads Captured American James Wright Foley," *SITE*, September 3, 2014.

101. "The Extremist Threat to Iraq Grows," *New York Times*, August 6, 2014.

102. "Haidar al Abadi: A New Era for Iraq?" BBC, September 9, 2014.

103. Muhammad al Maliky, "Mending Iraq," *Foreign Affairs*, January 19, 2015.

104. "Apparent ISIS Executioner: 'I'm Back, Obama,' " CNN.com, September 3, 2014.

105. "NATO Hatches Coalition to Take on Islamic State," *Foreign Policy*, September 5, 2013.

106. "Transcript: President Obama's Speech Outlining Strategy to Defeat Islamic State," *Washington Post*, September 10, 2014.

107. "After Beheading of Steven Sotloff, Obama Pledges to Punish ISIS," *New York Times*, September 3, 2014.

108. "President Obama's Speech on Combating ISIS and Terrorism," CNN, September 11, 2014.

109. "Remarks by the President at MacDill Airbase," Whitehouse.gov, September 17, 2014.

110. "The Turk Is Dead: Al Qaeda-Linked Terror Group Says Leader Died in Syria," CNN, September 24, 2014.

111. "Kurdish Female Fighters of Rojava," June 15, 2015. http://www.yourmiddleeast.com.

112. "Too Soon to Say Mission Accomplished in Kobane: U.S. Official," Reuters, January 27, 2015.

113. Ibid.

114. "U.S. Military Airdrops 50 Tons of Ammo for Syrian Fighters, After Training Mission Ends," Fox News, October 12, 2015.

115. "U.S. Aims to Put More Pressure on ISIS in Syria," *New York Times*, October 5, 2015.

116. "U.S. Says 6,000 ISIS Fighters Killed in Battles," CNN, January 22, 2015.

117. "U.S. Official: 10,000 ISIS Fighters Killed in 9 Month Campaign," CNN, June 3, 2015.

118. "Untangling the Overlapping Conflicts in the Syrian War," *New York Times*, October 18, 2015.

119. "Stalemated: 20,000 ISIS Fighters Killed by U.S.-Led Bombings Haven't Turned the War," *Newsweek*, October 13, 2015.

120. "Jordan Carries Out Airstrikes in Iraq," I24newstv, February 4, 2015.

121. "Pentagon: ISIS Finance Minister Killed," CNN, March 25, 2016.

122. "Thousands Enter Syria to Join ISIS Despite Global Efforts," *New York Times*, September 26, 2015.

123. "Islamic State Loses Around 14 Percent of its Territory in 2015," *Telegraph*, December 21, 2015.

124. "ISIS Lost 40 Percent of Territory in Iraq, 20 Percent in Syria: Coalition Spokesman," Reuters, January 5, 2016. "U.S. Scrambles to Beat Back ISIS in Libya," *New York Times*, February 22, 2016.

125. "ISIS Burns Fighters Alive After Letting Ramadi Fall," Fox News, January 12, 2016.

126. "ISIS by 2015's End: Battered but by no Means Beaten," *Vocativ*, January 1, 2016.

127. "A Frontline Report: The Ground War Against the Islamic State," *Combatting Terrorism Center Sentinel*, December 15, 2015.

128. "Stalemate, Size of ISIL Force Unchanged Despite Year Long Campaign," Fox News, August 4, 2015.

129. "U.S. General Strongly Defends Air Campaign Against ISIS," Fox News, June 7, 2015.

130. "Strikes in Iraq and Syria." http://www.defense.gov/News/Special-Reports/0814_Inherent-Resolve.

131. "ISIS Can Muster Between 20,000 and 31,000 Fighters CIA Says," CNN, September 12, 2014; "Abu Bakr al Baghdadi: The World's Most Wanted Man," *Telegraph*, July 1, 2014.

132. Alexandre Mello and Michael Knights, "The Cult of the Offensive: The Islamic State on Defense," *CTC Sentinel*, April 30, 2015.

133. "The Hidden Hand Behind the Islamic State Militants? Saddam Hussein," *Washington Post*, April 4, 2015.

134. "Former MI 6 Terror Chief Sawers: Terror Has Become Tougher to Stop," CNN, September 13, 2015.

135. "McCain Blasts U.S. Iraq, Syria Policy," *Arizona Independent*, May 22, 2015.

136. "President Obama's ISIS Strategy Falling Short?" Fox News, February 8, 2015.

137. "GOP to Obama: Airstrikes Not Enough to Stop ISIS," CBS, August 10, 2014; "Lindsey Graham: 10,000 U.S. Troops to Defeat ISIS," Bloomberg News, February 1, 2015. "Lindsey Graham Worries Islamic State Will Destroy Americans, Wipe Out Mankind," *Huffington Post,* September 14, 2014.

138. "Should the Phrase 'Islamic Extremists' Be Used? It's Debatable," NPR, November 25, 2015.

139. "Remarks by the President at the Islamic Society of Baltimore." https://www.whitehouse .gov/the-press-office/2016/02/03/remarks-president-islamic-society-baltimore.

140. "Obama Sees Russia Failing in Syria Effort," *New York Times*, October 3, 2015.

141. "The End of Pax Americana," *Foreign Affairs*, November/December 2015.

142. "U.S. Jets and Drones Attack Militants in Iraq, Hoping to Stop Advance," *New York Times*, August 8, 2014.

143. "U.S. Support for Action in Syria Is Low vs. Past Conflicts," Gallup.com, September 6, 2013; "Americans Are Wary of Iraq Involvement, but Many Support Airstrikes: Poll," *Huffington Post*, June 17, 2014.

144. "Do Americans Want to Send Ground Troops to Fight ISIS?" CBS, February 19, 2015.

145. "ISIS, Terrorism Seen as Graver Threats Than Russia, Ukraine," Gallup.com, February 13, 2015.

146. "Rand Paul on ISIS: 'Boots on the Ground Should Belong to Arabs,'" *Newsmax*, May 22, 2015.

147. "Biden Says ISIS Progress Halted in Iraq," *Wall Street Journal,* April 9, 2015. "ISIS has lost 25% of the Territory It Once Held in Iraq," CBS, March 13, 2015.

148. "Fall of Ramadi Reflects Failure of Iraq's Strategy Against ISIS, Analysts Say," *Washington Post*, May 19, 2015.

149. "Battling ISIS: A Long Campaign Ahead," *Financial Times*, June 8, 2015.

150. "Iraqi Forces Are Blamed in ISIS Rout," *New York Times*, May 25, 2015.

151. "A Round up of Ancient Sites ISIS Has Destroyed," CNN, March 9, 2015.

152. Jeffrey Goldberg, "The Obama Doctrine," *Atlantic,* April 2016. "Trainers Intended as Lift, but Quick Iraq Turnaround Is Unlikely," *New York Times*, June 11, 2015.

153. "Department of Defense Briefing by Ashton Carter," October 23, 2015. http://www.defense .gov/News/News-Transcripts/Transcript-View/Article/625812/department-of-defense-press -briefing-by-secretary-carter-in-the-pentagon-briefi.

154. "More U.S. Troops in Iraq May Be Needed for Conventional Warfare Ops Targeting ISIS," *Military Times,* February 1, 2016.

155. Brian Glyn Williams, "Op-Ed: What to Beat the Islamic State? Try the Afghan Model, Circa 2001," *Los Angeles Times*, October 4, 2014.

156. "Obama Sends Special Operations Forces to Help Fight ISIS in Syria," *New York Times*, October 30, 2015.

157. "Syrian Rebels Say Russia Is Targeting Them Rather Than ISIS," *New York Times,* October 1, 2015.

158. "Syrian Rebels Decry Airstrikes," *Guardian*, October 11, 2015.

159. "Obama's Call to UN to Fight ISIS with Ideas Is Largely Seen as Futile," *New York Times*, September 30, 2015. "Clash of Words in Speeches to General Assembly," *New York Times*, September 29, 2015.

160. "Islamic State Fighters Make Significant Gains in Syrian Areas Bombed by Russia," *New York Times*, October 10, 2015.

161. "By Focusing on Syria, Putin Is Catering to an Audience at Home," *New York Times*, September 27, 2015.

162. Charles Lister, *The Syrian Jihad* (Oxford: Oxford University Press, 2016), 30.

163. "U.S. to Putin: Welcome to ISIS Quagmire," *Daily Beast,* September 29, 2015.

164. Warrick, *Black Flags*, 234.

165. "Full Transcript of President Obama's Commencement Address at West Point," *Washington Post*, May 28, 2014.

166. "National Security Strategy," February 2015. https://www.whitehouse.gov/sites/default/files/docs/2015_national_security_strategy.pdf.

167. "Full Text of Obama ISIS Speech," *Ibtimes*, February 11, 2015.

168. "In Battle to Defang ISIS, U.S. Targets Its Psychology," *New York Times*, December 28, 2014.

169. "ISIS: The Inside Story," *Guardian*, December 11, 2014.

INDEX

ACKNOWLEDGMENTS

After the remarkable events of 9/11, I began to systematically record America's unfolding war in the distant Islamic lands that I had dedicated my life to studying. It was my goal to master this history on what I called "moving sand" and record it for posterity. This was an ambitious objective and one that required considerable help from many wonderful people from Afghanistan/Pakistan to Iraq and America. I owe them all a huge debt of gratitude.

First and foremost I would like to thank my parents, Gareth and Donna Williams, for taking me on my first to trip to the Islamic world as a nineteen-year-old in 1986 when we visited Bosnia. Seeing the graceful Ottoman minarets, bazaars, palaces, bridges, and castles in that beautiful Balkan country inspired me to dedicate my life to the study of the Islamic world as a young man. I was incredibly fortunate to have parents who fully supported me on my life journey and taught me not to be afraid of the world. They not only supported me, they assisted and encouraged me every step of the way. While they often worried about my safety, they never held me back. Most recently, they proofreed this book and it is all the better for their wonderful corrections and suggestions. For that and everything else I owe them a hearty *diolch yn fawr*.

Second, I would like to thank my wife and best friend Feyza. When we met in a pub in Hampstead, London, our soon-to-be best man, Anton, warned her "don't marry this guy, you'll end up in Iraq or some Godforsaken place like that." Thankfully, Feyza ignored him and married me. Since then, she has been a firm supporter of my work and has on occasion accompanied me on my journeys across the battle zones of Islamic Eurasia, from the Himalayas of Kashmir to the deserts of Afghan Turkistan to the hills of the Turkish-Syrian borderlands. *Teşekkürler canim.*

Third, I would like to thank my wonderful chairman Mark Santow, my friend and former chairman Len Travers, my indispensible secretary Sue Foley, and all my colleagues in the most talented and congenial History Department in the world, at University of Massachusetts-Dartmouth. I would also like to thank my colleagues Dana Fine, Michelle Cheyne, and Al Hirshfeld for the wonderful conversations and friendship on our carpool to work.

Fourth, I would like to thank the many people in the Islamic realms I have visited who welcomed me into their homes, guided me across their lands, and protected me when it was necessary. These include Vice President Abdul Rashid Dostum in Afghanistan, who hosted me in his compounds in Mazar-i Sharif, Kabul and Sheberghan during my visits and shared his remarkable stories of riding on horseback into combat against the Taliban alongside U.S. Special Forces in 2001.

I would also like to say thanks to the Afghan Turkmen's leader, Seracettin Mahdum, who guided me across the mountains and deserts of Afghanistan. Also *zor spas* (thanks so much) to Abdulkarim Karim and Diyar Jamil, my intrepid Kurdish friends who drove me the length and breadth of Iraqi Kurdistan, from the memorial to Hussein's genocidal gassing of the Kurds at Halabja to the Yazidi pagans' temple at Lailish.

While in Kurdistan, it was also an honor to be hosted by the Kurdish Peshmerga generals Sirwan Barzani and Bandal Bande in their frontline bases. I have tremendous respect for these gentlemen-warriors who are fighting the good fight against the ISIS fanatics and defending their people. I also owe a huge debt of gratitude to Kurdistan Regional Government Foreign Minister Falah Mustafa Bakir for his generous interview and the Kurdistan Regional Government's Chancellor of Intelligence, Masrour Barzani for his overview of his counterterrorism fight. I would also like to thank my Yazidi guide to the temple of Lalish, Thamer Ilyas.

I would also like to thank Mr. Ziyad Raoof, Representative of the Kurdistan government in Poland; President Ahmed Dezaye of Salahadin University; President Mosleh Duhoky of University of Duhok; and President Salah Saeed of Charmo University; and in no particular order thanks also to: Governor Farhad Atrushi, Dr. Saman Baban, Badal Bande, Dr. Asmat Khalid, Mayor Kaka Min, Vager Rabban the Bishop of Duhok, Ranj Sangawi, General Colonel Harry Schute, and Salim Saeed Taher.

I would like to give a huge thanks to Allan Pilch, who did a fantastic job of proofing and editing this book as well as indexing. I am also in debt to Tim Nelson, Jeff Nelson, and Ryan Mercer for their help in indexing this book. I would be remiss if I did not to thank Christopher Natola and Brian McArdle for their wonderful assistance in proofreading the manuscript. As always I would like to thank my former advisors who taught me Central Eurasian Islamic History in graduate school, Uli Schamiloglu and Kemal Karpat, and my friend and travel companion to Uzbekistan, the great Central Asian historian Scott Levi. Also *spasibo bolshoi* to my friend Glen Howard, president of the Jamestown Foundation, for his support over the years going back to the days when we met in 1988 while studying Russian. Last, I would like to thank Captain Mark Nutsch of the legendary Green Beret A Team "Tiger 02" for taking the time to share with my students his stories of his horse-mounted campaign alongside General Dostum to overthrow the Taliban.